JUSTICE 4 PETER

The true, most fascinating story of the orphan boy from
Hornchurch, Essex

Peter L B Ross
ISBN: 978-1-8383868-9-4

*Justice does not have a price! I have paid so much in my most
extraordinary life searching for it.*

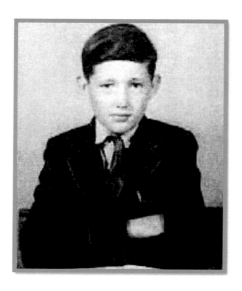

Peter as a young orphan boy in Hornchurch

Disclaimer & Copyright page

This haunting autobiography will open your eyes. It is my personal, unforgettable and extraordinary, untold until now, book of memoirs. Every reasonable attempt has been made to verify the facts against my retained full documentary evidence. The incredible contents are truthful and most sincere. This true but unbelievably heart-wrenching account of events from an extraordinary man's self-scrutiny and survival, tells all in this his autobiography.

All the events described in this book are true but names of many of the characters have been changed for legal reasons.

Published By: -

i2i

PUBLISHING

i2i Publishing. Manchester.
www.i2ipublishing.co.uk

Dedication

This is the story that will outlive me when I am gone. To keep the memory of my survival alive, I dedicate this autobiography to all the children like me and to those who have become immune to these events. PLB Ross

JUSTICE 4 PETER
The true, most fascinating story of the orphan boy from
Hornchurch, Essex.
Peter L B Ross
His autobiography.

*His survival after gunshot wounds to his head and shoulder after his
attempted murder, leaving him partially deaf and much more.*

'In this life the most incredible stories are true.'

This is one of those such stories.

PREFACE - INTRODUCTION

To those taking their time to read this book, they will be reading it through the tearful eyes of a boy incarcerated in an orphanage. Un-loved, no hugs or kisses just like the song, 'Nobody's Child' by Karen Young. You will learn the ups and the downs, the happiness and sadness of my childhood, growing up in an old Victorian orphanage called *London County Council, Hornchurch Children's Home*. Thirteen cottages set amid approximately ninety acres of playing fields and orchards. It should have been a safe and secure place for me and so many others. It was not!

Leaving behind my experiences of many very dark years of incarceration, I progressed up the ladder of success to become a successful businessman and a millionaire with a million-pound investment in the sterling money market.

While writing the words and adding the pictures to this book, I could hear the sounds and the shrieks of all the children's happiness and pain. A song played in my mind from the church hymn book, *My Forever Friend.*

To those reading this unbelievable story, I hope you will become my friend too.

All chapters in this book are true and written without any risk of a legal challenge of defamation, from those whom I refer to as the legal profession, or otherwise in this book. Some will ask why it has taken me until now to write this story. My simple answer is that I tried to forget and pushed the hurt to the darkest recesses of my mind. Maybe, I thought wrongly no-one would listen or care, but this story must be told! So, I do so before it's too late. My nine lives are running out, but I am a survivor, like those abused by the professionals, politicians and entertainers who deserve their long and outstanding justice.

I must also expose the caregivers, the people who should have been protecting and respecting the individuals in their care and not forgetting the failures of the various government bodies and the legal profession.

Although this book is suitably named, *Justice for Peter*, I seek justice for the hundreds of children who, like me, were abused physically, mentally, and sexually by the monsters who were supposed to be nurturing and protecting all of us. I want to tell the world my story in the hope that people will know a little of what I felt, living in the hell hole that was renamed, very respectfully, *St. Leonards Children's Home*. After many years of incarceration, this change of name was to shift the legal responsibility from the L.C.C. They were the legal owners responsible for maintaining the orphanage with payment of their employees' salaries, to care for its many children passing through, just as I did. So, justice would mean just that! The legal system had failed me and so many others in countless ways throughout the years. I have always been a fighter, and this will be my last fight for justice.

My mother was dearly loved by many London people, although she, Alice, did not even have a gravestone. This was because, when she sadly took her own life, that was considered a criminal act. Therefore, she was buried in non-consecrated ground in a church cemetery in Streatham, South London. Here, no gravestone or other marker other than a plot number was allowed for suicides. I have visited just as my sister and husband did. I always left flowers with my teardrops.

My mother Alice, sadly had to live through the war in poverty. She sadly died in 1950, in the reign of King George VI.

The home I refer to above was established during the reign of Queen Victoria on the 1st of September 1887. She could never have envisaged the monsters who would be allowed and well-paid to abuse the children that would pass through the orphanage. Here I am putting pen to paper on my autobiography and telling of my childhood spent in the orphanage that Queen Victoria had established for the purpose of giving safe sanctuary to children like me. The authorities L.C.C. after the Queen's reign failed so miserably to give this safe sanctuary as you will see within chapter 34, 'The Mapperton' case at the Old Bailey.

Below is a picture of the commemorative stone to celebrate the opening of this home.

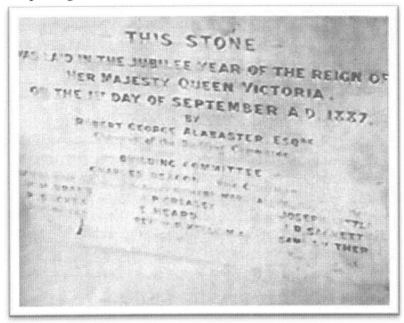

I cannot help looking and reflecting upon the fact that the building is still there now, protected with a preservation order, along with the remaining cottages converted into luxury apartments.
And this is the place I had spent all of my unhappy childhood.

Acknowledgements

I would like to thank my lovely partner **Anita**, for her love, help and sheer dedication in helping me through all my difficult years with this book. We laughed together and cried together, sharing my memories both good and bad. I would be lost without her; she is my rock.

To my son **Darren**, who has saved me from myself on more than one occasion. I must tell him that I love him very much and I hope that by reading this book, he will understand his father's life and forgive me for not telling him the story, until now.

To my most beautiful mother, **Alice**, for her writing of me and my birth in her letters to her sister Adeline, and a thank you to **Auntie Adeline,** who helped me to understand my mother.

A special thank you to **Uncle Bernard**, who I never met, but he told me so much through his letters to his sister about my mother's funeral.

The very extraordinary and brave **Mr Murgatroyd** and his family for helping me understand tragedy.

Dr Ivan Blumenthal M.R.C.P D.C.H. Consultant paediatrician for his kindness and friendship.

Dr Edward Tierney LLMRCPRCS (I) MRCGP, for his kindness and friendship.

My sister **Eileen,** her husband **Steve and Anita**, in the events at Alder Hey Children's Hospital and for just being there as part of my family.

Paul Alison and his lovely wife **Melanie** for putting up with me and 'travelling with me at 200 mph' in all my past work.

Patrick Thomas Fallon, who, without his and his wife's love and help, I would not have made it. His words were: *"A little help is worth far more than a few tons of pity."*

Derek Wood and his wife **Susan's** continued love and friendship and visits to my hospital bedside when I was in intensive care and during my stay in Rochdale Hospital for the mentally disturbed.

Dr Ann and **John McNown**, my very good neighbours and forever friends.

My very affectionate love to my deceased forever friends, **Eric** and his wife **Kath Kershaw**, and her recently deceased brother **Bernard Joseph Cribbens** (famous for *Hole in the Ground, Right Said Fred,* his other songs and his parts in *Railway Children* and *Carry On films*) for all of their love and kindness in wanting this book to be published.

To all the children that have grown up to call me 'Ga Ga' to learn the true story of Peter and Harris, the two little mice that they have all grown up with.

And finally, from my most humble beginnings, **Miss Surrage** from **Forbs Cottage, Miss Ann Jackson** from **Milton Cottage** and finally **Miss Dorothy**.

With my love to all those reading, having spent their childhood as I, at the **Hornchurch Children's Home**.

The i2i team for their kind help throughout the Covid 19 pandemic years of 2020-23 in putting together with **Anita** this autobiography.

Without any of you, giving me the love and strength and *a good talking to* at times, this book would not have been possible.

Contents

Chapter 1: My place of birth Ackerman Road, Brixton, London   17

Chapter 2: Hornchurch Children's Home – 'Forbs'   33

Chapter 3: London County Council and Hornchurch Children's Home – 'Milton'   51

Chapter 4: The cottage homers big, green, army type, Dennis school bus   71

Chapter 5: 1958, when I reached twelve years of age.   83

Chapter 6: L.L.C. Welfare officers' reports   105

Chapter 7: Religious foster parents   109

Chapter 8: My first job as an apprentice at Gatwick airport   117

Chapter 9: Meeting Sophia Lauren and Gregory Peck   123

Chapter 10: Working weekends.   135

Chapter 11: Entering my five-year apprenticeship with Gratts Brothers   141

Chapter 12: In January 1969 I am registered as an approved electrician   147

Chapter 13: Working at Macclesfield/Bury/E.L.S   155

Chapter 14: Asbestos, Turner Newall and Cyril Smith   161

Chapter 15: Today at Bury Market   169

Chapter 16: The owner of Carpet Warehouse   173

Chapter 17: Then and now, working for myself   183

Chapter 18: 1978. Building a luxurious bungalow on Bury Road and my warehouse.   191

Chapter 19: Relationship with Louie, owner of E.L.S.   199

Chapter 20: The Tree   203

Chapter 21: Success to multi-millionaire   211

Chapter 22: Caroline at Arndale Escalators'   215

Chapter 23: I first meet up with Derek.   221

Chapter 24: E.L.S   227

Chapter 25: Colindale, North London   233

Chapter 26: My solicitors involved in private, and company matters. Meeting John Trafford   245

Chapter 27: Journey for my uncle and my mother's sister   257

Chapter 28: Journey for my father   273

Chapter 29: Re-visit to the orphanage   279

Chapter 30: our home Woodlands 285

Chapter 31: Our home Redlumb, 16th circa barn 289

Chapter 32: Finding some of the wife's deception and brand-new house purchase. 305

Chapter 33: Meeting Anita and her children 315

Chapter 34: Old Bailey Mapperton Case 329

Chapter 35: C.S.A. and cheating solicitor 343

Chapter 36: My three daughters and doctor from hell 349

Chapter 37: Court order in sale of matrimonial assets, Hindclough Farm & Neighbour from Hell 363

Chapter 38: The round table charity 379

Chapter 39: Dog attack and having a sandwich 383

Chapter 40: Barnardo charity 391

Chapter 41: My bankruptcy by the Inland Revenue/Tax man 393

Chapter 42: My great meeting with George Carman QC and Imran Khan 401

Chapter 43: My attempted murder and lifelong injuries 403

Chapter 44: Now living next to the 2nd neighbour from hell 407

Chapter 45: My very nice Dr Schroeder& sad demise 425

Chapter 46: Helping Hand 429

Chapter 47: The very lucky escape on the train and the silver lining to this rainbow 433

Chapter 48: Visit to Psychic 447

Chapter 49: Sad Farewell to Reg 451

Chapter 50: My loss, but my gain of friendship with travelling people 453

Chapter 51: The last chapters and such a difficult search for justice for Peter 463

Chapter 52: My justice 465

Chapter 53: Now 74 plus years & the injustice of Stefan Iw'an Kiszko and his loving mother 471

Chapter 54: Did I receive my justice against NatWest Bank? (No, being the answer) 479

Chapter 55: My best memory: going to Brighton with my son. 485

Chapter 56: The Greater Manchester and Cheshire Police 491

Chapter 57: Public funding fraud 499

Chapter 58: Final chapter. Send in the clowns The 2001 independent review of legal aid. The women and men who stole from the world
503

CHAPTER 1: Ackerman Road, Brixton, London

1945. The war was over, and celebrations had commenced. However, my mother and her four children were still living with the aftermath. As she made her way along the bombed-out streets and awkwardly navigated her pram containing my youngest sister Sally through the rubble, with my older sister Eileen walking alongside, she found little to celebrate in the ruins of what once had been her neighbours' houses. Looking around at the devastation before her must have been shattering.

Arriving at a London Underground station reminded her of all the terrifying days and nights she had spent there when using it as their designated air raid shelter. Frightened and alone, she had no husband by her side to protect her modest family. Blackouts happened with such regularity that it had been normal to frequent the underground almost every day and night. Looking around the platform my mother would have seen a mixture of characters, both young and old. Some had mattresses set up, others had blankets, and some, with only the clothes on their back. They were all trying to make the best of a bad situation. Men were telling jokes, women telling stories, people were trying to sell paraphernalia and food and drink were being distributed between families. Sometimes actors and actresses from the theatre would sing, entertain, and perform tricks for the children. This would have been a welcome distraction. All of this was happening in such a small space whilst sirens sounded, and the constant noise of relentless bombing thundered from above. They all existed in extremely cramped conditions and the stench was dreadful as the public toilets could not cope with the infinite number of humans. But, in true British tradition, they *'Kept Calm and Carried On'*.

A ticket system was put in place to keep everything more civilised, unfortunately though, this system was open to abuse and some people paid unscrupulous individuals to acquire the best areas for them to occupy. Quite often fights would break out and blood spilled onto the platform. It must have seemed like forever, waiting for the 'all clear' and wondering if her home would still be standing when she returned.

Picture courtesy of the London Transport Museum

The past four years had indeed been tough for a woman on her own, living 'hand to mouth' on the food the ration books provided, bringing up her children the best way she could, with as much love as she could muster, trying to keep them safe from harm.

She would have most definitely frequented the clothing exchange, set up by the Women's Voluntary Service in 1942, handing over her coupons for the second-hand clothing offered to keep clothes on her children's backs and shoes on their feet.

London, being the capital, suffered the most aerial bombardment throughout the war years, from the blitz to the doodlebugs (V1 Flying Bomb). The devastation of not only residential areas but also industrial and commercial properties, spreading as far as the docks, was immense. 30,000 Londoners died and more than 50,000 were injured.

The clean-up had soon begun; the conflict had brought considerable destruction, and so began a long period of austerity. Crime was becoming a problem, the ration books remained, and my mother struggled to keep a roof over her head and her children clothed and fed. The younger siblings remained blissfully unaware, seeing everything as an adventure and the older brothers tried to help the best they could.

If you had the money to pay, the spivs were always on hand and could get their hands on almost anything. I am sure that my mother, along with many others, used their services when they could afford to do so.

© *Peter Ross – My Father*

My father was serving in the Royal Navy, stationed mainly in the Far East, during and just after the war, on his ship 'The HMS Marazion.' A China Station 'Hunt' class minesweeper did not come home permanently. He explained there was too much work left for him to do and was awarded the 1939-45 'Star Defence medal Atlantic Star', among others. He did come home on leave; I do not know how long his sabbatical was but what I do know is that when he returned to ship, my mother was pregnant with her fifth child ... Me!

I was born in July of 1946 in Ackerman Road, Brixton. I was baptised on Easter Sunday at St John's the Divine in Kennington by Priest Cyril Eastaugn, within the London borough of Lambeth, SW9 6SW. The road boasts that the music hall legend, Dan Leno, lived there from 1898 to 1901 and a plaque to commemorate this still remains there to this day.

Yes, I am a true Cockney boy, born within the sounds of the 'Bow Bells' (referring to the church of St. Mary-Le-Bow Cheapside, London. A baby being born within earshot is said to be a true Cockney). My home was a typical London terraced house with two steps leading up to the front door and the Hamilton Public House on the corner. Once inside a long hallway guided you to the staircase, the right leading to the bedrooms and the parlour on the left. At the end of the hallway, three steps lead down to the kitchen with a back door taking you into the rear yard. The house was a reasonable size for my mother's growing family.

I was a post-war baby, a rather large baby who resulted in a very difficult labour. My mother gave birth to me crouching over a bucket and from the letters I had in my possession, given to me by my mother's sister, Auntie Adeline, she was alone. I can only imagine the trauma she must have gone through. Giving birth is demanding for any female, but most have a doctor or midwife to hand. Likewise, in those days, everyone knew of a woman not qualified, but with plenty of experience in delivering babies who lived in the neighbourhood. Pregnant women would call upon these ladies to be with them when their time came. It's shocking to think that my mother went through all the pain and anguish of giving birth alone.

I was a happy, healthy baby, despite the circumstances which surrounded my birth, although, my mother later wrote to Auntie Adeline saying that she would have preferred to have a smaller baby to fatten up, rather than have a baby weighing 11lbs 2oz.

I was welcomed into the family by my brothers, George, who was eighteen, William, who was sixteen, and my sister Eileen, three, and Sally, who was one, along with various other family members and friends who lived nearby.

1947. My brother George was away completing his 'National Service'. This was brought into effect in 1939 and was known as 'War Service'. A Bill in 1947 was approved to extend this because of the 'Cold War' (tensions between the Soviet Union and the USA and their allies) and the 'Malayan Emergency' (A guerrilla war fought from 1948-1960.) Great Britain also had other commitments abroad.

National Service included all men aged eighteen to thirty and lasted eighteen months. Subsequently, it was extended to two years. Conscripts remained on the forces reserve list for four years and could be recalled to the expected units at any time within this period for up to twenty days, on no more than three occasions.

A letter of conscription would have to be sent to our home when George was seventeen and a half so that the family had time to prepare. That would have been an immeasurable hardship for my mother because George had been the man of the house, in the absence of my father, for the last seven years.

In 1949, my brother William would be in the same position.

For four years, my mother soldiered on amid the chaos, having just enough money to survive in those uncertain times.

She struggled to make the food go around, although the free milk and vitamins for the younger children helped a little. Like most mothers, she never thought of herself, trying her best to be a good parent in the absence of my father. I have no recollection of him ever being there.

1950. London was looking better. New prefab houses had been built, larger buildings had been restored, and although there were still some reminders of the war, they were shrinking. Furthermore, what was left, provided an adventure playground for children. The shops and markets were bustling. The newspaper sellers were doing good business; the underground was as hectic as ever, although, London, in those uncertain times, was far from how it should be and would remain that way for some time to come.

The war had taken approximately 450,900 British lives and there was not enough manpower to keep up with the rebuilding of the United Kingdom.

Two years earlier, the first Afro-Caribbean immigrants arrived on the Empire Windrush at Tilbury Docks, but unfortunately, the men who had come for a better life and to help rebuild, did not receive a kind welcome. Awful though this was, it did not really impact my family. Life was fine. We all felt very safe and loved. George had a sweetheart, Margaret, who my mother was very fond of and who helped her around the house when she could and William also had a new sweetheart, an Indian girl named Maisy. My sisters and I kept busy with our toys and childhood games. Life seemed normal, but sadly, all was not what it seemed with regard to my mother.

She had suffered ill health before and after my birth and had recently undergone a hysterectomy, but we little ones were innocents, too young to understand. She soldiered on, going about her daily chores, making sure that we were all cared for and writing positive letters to Adeline, keeping her secrets, but all of that was about to change.

On the 13th of April 1950 it all became too much for her. After tucking us little ones into bed and making sure that we were asleep my mother waited for my brothers to come home and go to bed. Everything seemed routine and no one had any idea what she was about to do.

© *Peter Ross – My beautiful mother*

That evening, Alice Marie Ross walked slowly down the three, cold, concrete steps and continued into the kitchen. She placed a cushion on the bottom shelf of the gas oven, turned on the gas, and my beautiful mother went to sleep forever.

Her mind must have been in turmoil, I can't even begin to presume what she was thinking, but whatever it was, in her mind, it was dreadful. I could speculate and say that it was money related, but my brother George was working, and what about my father?

My father had left both the Navy and my mother. He was working for 'Fram Filters', an engineering company in London, earning a respectable wage of £10.00 per week, plus a 10-shilling family allowance, but he needed that money for other matters.

Inexplicably, he had been concealing an affair with another woman. Perhaps that is why we never saw him. He eventually told my mother, and she could not see a future. She was forty-two, a middle-aged woman, with three young children. Who would want her? No man in his right mind would want that responsibility.

She was a beautiful woman, and I am sure she would have found someone to share the rest of her life with, but she was suffering from low self-esteem. Being cast aside by the man she loved, along with extreme exhaustion due to looking after three very young children, together with the recent trauma of undergoing her hysterectomy operation and still recovering, must have been a considerable pain.

Alongside feelings of despair and melancholy taking over her very being, in her mind, it was for the best. Discovering that my mother was a former patient in a mental hospital helped me to make some sense of her actions. Depression had taken over her very soul. We know the signs of depression nowadays, but back then there were no psychiatrists or doctors with a prescription for anti-depressants. People were told to 'keep their chin up' or 'pull themselves together'.

I don't know why, but on that night, I awoke and began to cry. My cries became more distressed and grew louder and louder, eventually waking up my brothers and sisters. My eldest brother, George, on smelling the gas, quickly opened every window and door that he could. The thought of him finding my mother's body during her swift actions is horrifying, but to find her he did, and he tried everything he could to revive her lifeless body.

George carried my mother outside the house, into the cold night air and tried artificial respiration (CPR), without success. The authorities were contacted; how this happened so quickly without the use of telephones, or any of the other technology we rely on today, I do not know, but the house quickly filled with people. All this activity was quite overwhelming for a four-year-old boy, who just wanted his mother. Eileen, Sally and I were immediately taken into a house across the road and then we were looked after by one of our brother's girlfriend's family for a short time until it was obvious our father didn't want or care for us. We were then sent into care by the London County Council, with their legal status standing in loco parentis.

My two brothers went to live with my mother's family and then with their sweethearts' families. I do know from the discovery of my mother's letters that my brothers had sweethearts then. I also know that they went into the Army and Navy to do their call-up services.

During the earliest years that my memory would take me back to, I can only recall when I was with my two sisters growing up in the orphanage. I can remember being there, but not my thoughts and feelings when it came to family life. My memory of my mother had gone. I had no memory whatsoever of my mother or father at that time. I know that I didn't get to be near my sisters very often to be able to hold their hands or have a cuddle. All I knew of my family is that they were in the orphanage at the same time as me. I do remember becoming more and more empty when they left the orphanage before me in later years.

George, who was now twenty-two and William, twenty, most certainly would have been questioned by the police as suicide was a crime until 'The Suicide Act 1961'. This must have been hard on them both. I remember in the later years, asking my brother William about my mother's death, but he refused to talk about our mother being wheeled through the hallway, on route to the ambulance outside waiting to take her to Kings College Hospital, Denmark Hill, London.

This newspaper report of the tragedy mistakenly assumed the suicide was the wife not the mother of my brother George Ross. *She was 42 and not as stated in the article.*

branch refuting "the monstrous attacks on health service expenditure" demands fundamental changes to enable hospital boards to spend more than five per cent. of their total finances on capital expenditure.

The branch also calls for chiropodist treatment under the health service to old age pensioners.

Found wife gassed

A former patient at a mental hospital, Mrs. Alice Ross (40), gassed herself at her home, 67 Akerman-rd., Brixton, the Southwark coroner was told on Friday.

Mr. G. Ross said he was wakened during the night and smelt escaping gas. Going downstairs, he found his wife with her head on a cushion in the gas oven. He carried her into the open air and tried artificial respiration without success.

He added that his wife had undergone a recent operation and was depressed.

What must my brother have gone through or been thinking? The sadness, the grief, the fear, vulnerability and the powerlessness of knowing life would never be the same again. For any of us.

If I had not cried out, none of my family would have survived. There was also the threat that the gas could have spread quickly to the adjoining houses in the terraced row. One little spark could have blown the whole side of the street to smithereens. The death certificate stated that my mother had died from carbon monoxide poisoning. The local newspaper elaborated on the events.

The funeral took place the following Monday at 9:00 am. The cortege consisted of a single Rolls Royce which had seating for eight people and the hearse which was bursting with wreaths from family and the many friends that my mother had made in London.

My Uncle Bernard, who had travelled from Doncaster to attend this very sad day, brought a large wreath in the shape of a cross. My brothers, George and William took it from him and gave it to the undertaker who placed it on top of my mother's coffin. Just that little gesture from my brothers gave my uncle so much comfort. In one of my Uncle Bernard's letters to my auntie Adeline, now in my possession, he says that my mother's funeral was majestic and although he knew my mother Alice was in the coffin, it was to him, as though it was a divine princess. I am so happy that my mother had the send-off that she deserved.

My mother was buried in un-consecrated grounds outside Mary-le-Bow church, Cheapside, in London's East End. This was normal practice in 1950 for anyone who committed suicide. No stone was laid; there was nothing to mark her spot, nowhere to leave flowers of remembrance, nowhere for descendants to visit. It was as though she had not existed.

After a brief stay with my father's family, my father himself signed the papers to hand Eileen, Sally, and I over to the authorities, who then stepped in and stood in 'loco parentis'. My Uncle Bernard also wrote in the same letter to my Auntie Adeline, who had not been able to attend the funeral, warning her about my father and his family. (See below) It also gives clues that my mother may have fallen out with her siblings, or they with her. Could this be due to my father? I leave you, reader, to make up your own mind.

Sally, Eileen and the author Peter

The letter that was referred to above was received seven days after the death of my mother. Below is the reply (the original is in Chapter 27).

Dear Adeline,

I am in receipt of your letter on the 20th of April 1950. Well, Adeline, all that has happened is now a complete mystery to me. Alice had everything to live for; I know it must have been so hard for her to bring up five children on her husband's pay. His job was fairly good, but the circumstances I found them in financially were awful. I could only give them what I could spare out of my wallet at the time, which was £10.00 as you see I had my railway fee to London, £2.20.

I bought a magnificent wreath in the form of a cross and took it on the train to London from Doncaster, anyway in London I took the tube to the oval, then I walked to Brixton.

Arriving at Ackerman Road, I found George at home with his sweetheart Margaret. George senior and Bill had taken the children to Sunderland to see people.

Alice was lying in the chapel of rest until Monday morning at 9:00am when we all arrived there. A simple Rolls Royce car, capable of taking 8 persons was waiting along with the hearse. The two boys carried my cross and handed it to the undertaker who asked who it was from and when he knew, he said it was to go on top. Then we all went to the hearse and drove slowly away. It was majestic. Although we knew that Alice was in the coffin, it was to me as though it was a divine princess, she was smothered in wreaths given by all the London people who dearly loved her.

I think I could discuss this matter better with you personally, as it doesn't do to say one's view of other people on paper, but a warning, be careful of what you do with the Ross people. If you wish to help Ross financially, only do it as though you are giving it to the children and Alice of course, dear. Use your own discretion, but be careful, as in this world you will find people who would fleece you right and left and never give it a thought. I am afraid that Ross would play on our sympathy. As I have said before, it is difficult to put one's thoughts on paper.

I am a strong spiritualist in my own mind and believe me, I will get the answers to the causes of Alice's death. I personally believe it had nothing to do with our family. However, from my observation following my stay in London, there is no answer.

Now Adeline, cheer up old girl, Alice is happier now. Alice has been with me all the time and she says hold your chin up Bernard, I am ok, I am with Ma and Pa and they are laughing at you sobbing.

Well Adeline, I must snap out of it. All the time I have been writing, Alice has been at my side and says all is forgiven. I am happy it wasn't our fault our family parted. After all, we think a lot of each other and always will.

Alice's last letter to me was looking forward to the marriage of her boys to the young ladies they are courting. I must say, they are sweet girls. One is Margaret who was Alice's right hand. I am to have her up to Doncaster for a long weekend shortly. The other is Maisy, an Indian girl and she is beautiful.

Well Adeline, it is midnight so I will get to bed very soon.

Bernard.

Sadly, Bernard took his own life (see chapter 27 – Journey to my uncle).

Subsequently, my sisters Eileen, Sally and I, were taken into care. My father had to pay something towards our incarceration. He managed to find thirty-five shillings per week out of the ten pounds a week he earned. To put this in context, today that would be just over fifty pence for the upkeep of my sisters and me.

Many years later I had so many very nice and special visits with my oldest sister Eileen. She gradually told me some of her painful memories. She told me how she remembered being seven years old when our mother took her own life. When the ambulance came to our home, she told me she sat on the stairs which positioned her to look into the kitchen. Looking through the bannisters she watched our mother being laid out in a box. She remembered wanting to climb in it and go with her. I can't imagine how she must have felt seeing that at such a young age. It must have been terribly heart breaking for her. She vividly remembers it to this very day. I was nearly four years old, and I can't recall any of that terrible and deeply disturbing time.

We both had more tears together, but at this late stage in our lives, as painful as it is, just being back together again and sharing our deeply troubled lives with one another is quite a lovely feeling. At long last, just having the feeling of that brother and sister relationship we had been denied through childhood was a very special time.

My sister Sally was five at the time of our mother's death, only two years older than me. We were protected from the turmoil. I am sure that we will have been kept distracted until it was decided what was to be done with us. It was obvious that we could not stay in the house, consequently, Eileen, Sally and I were immediately taken to Margaret's parents' house across the street for a short period of time. We were then taken to Sunderland to stay with our father's relatives.

CHAPTER 2: Hornchurch Children's Home – 'Forbs'

Hornchurch Cottage Homes.

The home had thirteen named cottages, and I would stay in two of them for the next eleven years of my life. I don't remember how I got there; I have no recollection of how my older sisters felt, as we approached this self-contained modest community. I was too young to understand the enormity of the situation that we all found ourselves in.

Built in 1870, the complex boasted a nursery, a swimming pool, infirmary, chapel, laundry, stores, workshop, and an assembly hall. Designed by FJ Smith, it was a long way from the workhouses that came earlier. It appeared to be a virtual paradise, but appearances can be deceptive. I am here to testify that for me, it was not!

High walls encased the whole of the complex; the entrance displayed seven-foot double gates, wide enough for a vehicle to utilize, and a single gate to the side of this for individuals to enter. The lodge was alongside this formation and inside, the main telephone switchboard was situated. A telephone operator would put through all the calls between the cottages, stores, hospital etc.

The porter and some of the staff also resided in the lodge and the porter kept an eye on everything and everyone entering or leaving the complex. The large gates were only opened for vehicles to enter when delivering goods, for example, food and supplies to the stores. It would have been impossible for a small child to even contemplate absconding.

The porter's lodge was where all the new children were brought when they first arrived; I have no recollection of this, but from what I have been told, the children were weighed, had their hair checked for lice, and then it would be sprayed with a fine white powder, which I believe was called D.D.T, as a preventative measure. The new arrivals also had their bodies washed, their clothes swapped for the home's uniform and finally, their details would be entered into the admissions register. Children would sometimes stay at the lodge for a few days until a place was found for them in one of the homes.

Surrounded by beautiful countryside, the complex comprised thirteen cottages. The girls' cottages were named after plants and flowers, Hawthorn, Laurel, Woodbine, Rose, Ivy and Myrtle. The boys' cottages were named after prominent men in history, Wellington, Forbs, Nelson, Milton, Landseer, Napier and Wallace.

51 The Cottage Homes, Hornchurch Road.

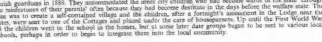

Thousands of children came through these gates in quest of a better life. The homes were set up by the Shoreditch parish guardians in 1889. They accommodated the inner city children who had become wards of the state 'through the misfortunes of their parents' often because they had become destitute in the days before the welfare state. The idea was to create a self-contained village and the children, after a fortnight's assessment in the Lodge near the gates, were sent to one of the Cottages and placed under the care of houseparents. Up until the First World War all the children went to the school in the homes, but at some later date groups began to be sent to various local schools, perhaps in order to begin to integrate them into the local community.

52 Ivy Cottage. Mr. and Mrs. H.E. Steed were Superintendent and Matron around 1913.

The dwellings were large Victorian buildings, not our idea of a rose-covered cottage. They boasted lawned gardens to the front and an asphalt yard to the rear. The yard had the only toilets for the children. The house parents had their own inside toilet and washing facilities; the children knew that this room, located within the house parents' quarters, was out of bounds and dared not enter.

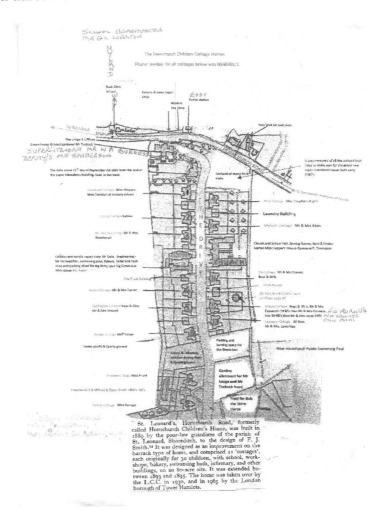

The cottages, along with the interior design, house parents etc., were put in place to mimic the authority's vision of what a typical family's way of life should be. In the midst of the thirteen cottages was a house set aside for the superintendent and his family. This house included gardens to the front and rear and incorporated a pleasant orchard.

I was placed in Forbs cottage with Harris and his sisters. The ground floor consisted of a large day room/dining room, with a kitchen on one side and the staircase on the other leading to a pantry and a scullery. Upstairs the bedrooms/dormitories were situated; the windows were sash windows, single glazed which rattled in the wind. There were no carpets on the floors, the beds were basic and set out in rows of ten, and each had a stand with a place to put our clothes. There was also a bathroom which consisted of two baths and two sinks.

Each individual cottage had been built to accommodate up to thirty children, who all had their 'chores' to carry out, such as laying the table, chopping wood, peeling potatoes and vegetables, blacking boots etc. The live-in house parents, whose titles were *house mother* and *house father*, usually a married couple, cared for the children and could be approached when the necessity arose. Everyone residing in the cottage answered to them. Others who helped in the home we called Miss or Auntie, and they would cook the meals and help with the care of the children.

Cleaners were also employed to clean and make the beds. There were many wet beds for them to change. I still remember that smell. In the dormitories, it was hard to get to sleep as children would often scream because of mice running the length of the room, under and around the beds. It was always freezing cold in winter, so cold that the condensation from our breath would turn to ice on the windows.

Before bedtime, we were made to line up and each of us would have to sit, half naked, on a line of potties, then after a short while, 'Miss' would check to see if we had done anything.

We had to lift ourselves off the potty, placing our hands down in front of us, standing on the cold solid wood floor and if we had, 'Miss' would wipe our backsides; we would then put on our pyjama bottoms and before getting into bed, we would get up to mischief, as children do, running and jumping around.

Sometimes we had pillow fights, which resulted in the punishment of a slipper raining down on our backside and only then would we get into bed. One of my few memories is of the intense feeling of sadness, crying quietly while trying to get to sleep. Whispers, along with the crying of others, frequently kept everyone awake. There was no bedtime story, no tucking in, or a kiss goodnight. None of us felt the cuddles, comfort, or contentment that children who have parents take for granted.

1951. My first recollection of growing up in cottage homes was around the age of five with my two sisters. We were not together very often, but I knew they were there. Smudge the cat was the best part of Forbs; I received the only love that I had ever known from that little feline. The cuddles and reassurance that a small child needed were lacking, to say the least, but Smudge helped fill that gap for me. The only family I had were eventually separated from me and it didn't take long to begin to feel unwanted, unloved, and alone in the world.

Whilst incarcerated, my only contact with the outside world was when my brothers George and William (Bill) visited with their young wives, Margaret and Maisy. I recall some weekends standing at the window looking up the driveway in the hope of seeing my brothers coming down to visit, but so many times this was in vain. It gave me the loneliest feeling in the world, and it was totally overwhelming. When this realisation sets in it changes you, I became very shy and introverted. We all saw it in one another, we were all in the same boat.

When my brother and his wife did come to visit to take my sisters and me out on a weekend, we were extremely happy and incredibly excited when the bell rang, but I always felt so incredibly sad and terribly unhappy when he would take us back. I would cry my eyes out. I lived and breathed for him to come and see me and take me away, but he would always take me back. I think they had an idea but didn't seem to know just how unhappy I actually was. They would buy sweets for the three of us, maybe hoping it would make us feel a bit happier clutching a bag of sweets whilst walking back into the orphanage. There was always a fight with the other children over the sweets once we got back in. I have to own up, that I was one of those other children when their families would visit and take them out and leave them with sweets. So, it was in those times 'dog eat dog', and we all got on with it. In some ways now they are happy and sad memories, but I was never ever a bully. I was always a softy and easily pushed around.

My brother Bill, his wife, Peter, Sally and Janet, his daughter.

Bill told the three of us that if it was raining, they wouldn't be able to visit or take us anywhere. On rainy days, I remember looking out of the window in anticipation, singing, "Rain, rain, go away, come again another day", repeatedly. I sang it to myself with so much intensity, willing the rain to stop. That little song has never meant as much as it did to me all those years ago. Hope and confidence become shattered when you feel unloved.

Always in my memory is the song I would hear in the latter years of my incarceration; Nat King Cole's "Smile Though Your Heart is Aching, Smile even though it's Breaking". Now in my twilight years, I reflect upon the meaning of that song in my life.

(Turn to the final page to see a photo of us two grown up, remaining old orphans with the photo showing us three children at the time when we were orphaned in 1950) with the smile on my face covering up. All that you will read inside the chapters in this book are shared with the greatest difficulties. I put pen to paper so that before I pass away, I will have told this unbelievable true story.

The Cottage home was situated next to the Hornchurch aerodrome (a mirror reflection of the place I am most reluctantly living at today). I often watched men jumping out of a basket, which looked like a box with cut-outs on two sides for the parachutists to enter, the roof equivalent to a tent which was secured underneath a huge barrage balloon. It held about six men. They would enter this contraption, clip on their harnesses, and wait for the balloon to get to the right height, before jumping out. An officer on the ground spoke through a megaphone, relaying instructions. Their parachutes would then deploy as they descended to the ground. The whole spectacle fascinated me.

There were never Birthday times, but I do remember Christmas. I can still see in my mind the older children sitting on the floor and sticking together paper chains and putting them up on the ceilings. We never had a Christmas tree ever, presents that we were lucky enough to receive were donated, some having been broken ones which were repaired in the church hall with the priest Mr Thompson overseeing these work before Christmas Eve.

Each toy was wrapped in Christmas paper and was given to us when entering the dining room for breakfast. There were never Christmas dinners or the pulling of Christmas crackers and feeling the joys that I know children feel having mums and dads sharing the magic on a Christmas morning and singing Christmas carols. There were always fights over toys and upsets through snatching from others. Toys were either taken or broken, we had nowhere to put them safely so when we went to bed the toys were up for grabs for anybody. In the morning your toy would be broken or gone (or as the song goes 'Dream on little broomstick cowboy, your toys will all be gone').

The best times at Christmas were at Lyons Corner House where they would sometimes arrange for all us orphans to have a party. I remember being fortunate enough to visit there only twice. Their staff helped to greet us, feed us, and send us away with a bag of treats.

To get us to Lyons Corner House in central London, a long line of black taxi cabs would collect us all from Hornchurch then in a continuous line, drive up to London and back. The black taxi cabs were everywhere and took priority. On this occasion they would park up in a long line in central London until we were ready, having been fed and feeling very happy, we were then to be taken back to the Hornchurch orphanage. We obviously didn't want to go back to the orphanage because we had experienced the nice kind ladies who had sat us down, fed us all and brought each of us a bag of treats. Their kindness and smiles have never left my memory. This same sort of event was also organised by the owners of Bertram Mill Circus and Haringey Circus. Staff would put us in the front rows to watch all the animals and the clowns and give us orphans special treatment compared to the other children, as they were fortunate enough to attend with their lovely parents and family. I was happy to watch the circus but felt sad watching kids with their parents, whom some of us never had or remembered having.

At Bertram Mills' Circus, I discovered that Coco the Clown was born in 1900 in Latvia. He ran away from his home in 1908 to find a circus that would give him a job. His name was Nikola Poliakoff, and he became an apprentice to Rudolfo Truzzi, a member of a Russian circus dynasty where he learned trapeze acrobatics and horse riding. By 1919 he was married with six children, joining Bertram Mills' Circus in 1929, staying with that circus for over 35 years when in 1949 he and his wife Valentina became British citizens. Coco had become the main attraction. In 1964 whilst at Bertram Mills' Circus he was awarded the OBE by Queen Elizabeth 2nd, for all his work, specifically with children.

He was the most famous clown in the world, boosted by many television appearances. I would only see Coco at the circus during the fifties. I would be six, seven and eight, when I would climb on board the big green bus, referred to in chapter 4.

As soon as we orphans saw Coco, we would clap and shout and scream whilst he would clown around for a while and we would be roaring with laughter, it was pure magic. He would have us all in the palm of his hand and would give us a sweet and colourful badge with his face in the centre. We orphans would wear the badge with such pride until they went missing after returning to the orphanage. The bigger boys or girls would have taken them, but they could never take the memories of Coco tumbling in his big red and white clown shoes with his bucket of water 'routine' when he would purposefully throw the water, making sure to splash it all over us orphans on the front row. This is a testament to his power, as this memory has lasted with me. In 1962 Eamonn Andrews surprised Coco in London on the show 'This is your life'.

In 1974 at 74 years old, Coco sadly died and is buried alongside his wife at 'Saint Marie's Church', in

Northamptonshire. His gravestone reads 'Coco the Clown, loved and remembered always'.

Many years later, my brother Bill remembered that I had visited the circus when I was only six, seven and eight years old. I would remind him of when he visited me in the orphanage and years later, visiting my home and my successful business (see chapters 18 & 24).

Bill brought me a magical gift, a painting he had done especially as a reminder of my visits to see Coco the clown. The painting has forever been hanging, proudly in my various homes since 1979 and even hanging on my wall in my latest home.

The loveliest thing for me after all these years is being able to bring Coco back to life in this autobiography, sharing all the love and fun that he gave to us orphans, myself included.

At Easter time in the Orphanage, Cadburys would donate a large Easter egg to each and every cottage. It took a hammer to break it into small pieces. We would all get a chunk of this thick chocolate and so did all the staff. We didn't get as much as we would have hoped for. The large egg was hollow so, no nice chocolates inside but what we were given was still very nice.

Another good time each year was with my brother Bill. He was the brother I saw the most and would take us to the band contest. This took place on the Hornchurch playing fields and the bands came from all over England in buses, masses of them. They all parked up and we would see all the band members climbing out with their musical instruments and then they would put on their outfits. These included the Queen's Guards and the Grenadiers and in turn, they would each march up and down, playing their instruments and drums which filled the air with ear-busting music. It was fantastic seeing the masses of people that would come and visit to see this sight and hear the music. We could hear it wherever we were in the orphanage, as it was right next door. We could see all the visitors, mums and dads, loving couples enjoying their time lazing in the sun on the fields full of dandelions, buttercups, and daisies. Later on, when they had all finished and everyone had packed up and gone, we orphans would climb over the fence and go looking for any money that may have fallen on the ground out of their pockets whilst lying and rolling in the tall grass. Those days were our best for our little earnings. The coins then were heavy, and we felt like we were rich with half a crown and two bob bits (never quite a pound note though). I did not understand how many shillings would even make one pound! A five pound note I didn't know existed, but I knew the true value of a farthing with the little Robin on the coin, four farthings to a penny and twelve pennies to a shilling. So, a few times yearly we would get some pleasure and something to look forward to.

Each year all the cottages would empty of the children for two weeks so maintenance work could take place; painting and decorating etc. The coaches were all parked on the drive outside every cottage. All the large wicker hampers were filled with clothes and food, and they were loaded inside the storage spaces. Then all the kids would climb on board, with the big boys and girls getting the best seats up in the back. The coaches all left going in various directions. When our coach reached its destination all we could see was a great big field full of tents with other children camping from different orphanages. The field was full of children, all from the same, sad background.

Some days we would go on daily hiking trips even though our shoes crippled us, even better sometimes we went to the seaside. One day I remember being so dehydrated I ran into the sea and drank the salt water. I soon wished I hadn't. I remember on one occasion after walking for miles, our feet throbbing with pain and full of blisters, we came to an orchard full of pears and apples. As usual we would be over the fence getting as many apples and pears as we could carry, even though we were in pain after hiking so long. The apples tasted lovely and crunchy, and they helped quench our thirst.

all stood out like sore thumbs.

Me during the course of the hike being told to smile for the camera, but we were not happy. At mealtimes we sat around a campfire singing and eating baked potatoes.

My best friend Harris. We were often subjected to denigration and derogatory remarks with little or no kindness shown as we

We all had a bit of a change of scenery but that was about it. We didn't get to mix with the other kids from the other orphanages, we were all just made to go on hikes, the seaside we were able to go to just the once. Then the time came to go back to Hornchurch.

When you are in an institution there are many children coming and going. Some boys were rescued from the terrible streets of London, bringing with them diseases and viruses and they spread fast. If one child caught something it was guaranteed to spread like wildfire through the whole of the complex. It was the same with parasites. I regularly had head lice and the 'nit comb' would come out. This was very painful and with each sweep a clump of hair would be left on the comb. The house parents would come round and spray us with a flit gun. The boys would simply have their heads shaved, but it was a different story for the girls, and it was awful to hear their screams when it was their turn for the nit comb.

Back at the orphanage I never really got to see much of my sisters; they played with the other girls, and we would pass one another and see each other at mealtimes. I always felt sad not being able to be with them but all the time I would look out for them. They got on with girls and I got on with the boys so that is how it went. There was one boy called Michael Massey who had a crush on my sister Eileen. He became more friendly towards me; he thought it would bring him closer to my sister. He obviously had the same problem as me in not being able to get close to her although I did get some comfort knowing my sisters were in Forbs cottage with me.

There were only three boys in Forbs cottage: Harris Ali, Anthony Grimmer and me. We were always together and became like brothers. Harris was an Indian boy and I a cockney, no two friends could be closer than us. We could be in the same boat with only one paddle but would always manage together.

There was one time I remember, late one summer evening, David, Harris and I crept out in the dark and ran up to the orchards behind the superintendent's building. We all knew that if we were to be caught, we would be in serious trouble, but we also knew there were beautiful apples and pears and juicy gooseberries that we could sneak back to the dormitory. So, as we were all carefully, quietly collecting the fruit, we heard a noise. Someone else had the same idea as us. We all froze and crouched down into the long grass, scared stiff. Then, we could see who it was, and it was only 'Miss Spooner' who was up to no good. So, she knew we were there and did nothing and she left the orchard leaving us boys behind. We snuck back to the dormitory, carefully carrying the fruits in our shirts and pockets, and wondered if we would get punished, but we never did. We also never spoke a word about seeing Miss Spooner. It had to be our secret. So, everyone was happy, and, on this occasion, you can bet your life we were.

Following the war and the breakup of the British Empire, Indian migration to the UK increased and in 1951 there were 43,000 Indians and Pakistanis in Britain. Most Indians came from the Punjab and Gujarat, the majority arriving with three pounds in their pocket, which was the limit set by Indian authorities. This money would just about pay a week's rent, so getting work was a priority. Thinking that Britain was full of palaces and a dream place to live, the immigrants were not prepared for the poverty and the appalling housing conditions they were faced with. I am not sure what the circumstances were with Harris; maybe it was simply that his parents could not afford to keep him. Immigrants were welcomed at first and treated kindly by some, but as the numbers grew, so did the racism. I knew nothing about any of that, I was just happy to have my friend.

On the twenty-second of June 1953 I was seven years old. Harris, Anthony and I were sent to the hospital within the grounds to be circumcised or to have 'the chop' as it was known. We had no idea what was happening, but we were taken to our allocated beds and given a gown to wear. I remember that it was a scary feeling and I wanted to cry, but most of all I wanted my sisters. In what seemed to me to be a lifetime I was eventually wheeled into the theatre and put to sleep. I then remembered waking up, all bandaged and in a lot of pain. It was extremely difficult to go to the toilet. We didn't understand why we had to go through this ordeal.

When Harris and I reached eight years old we had already gone through the terrible ordeal of being taken away from our families to be placed in Milton Cottage, which was obviously a difficult time for us being so young and having to leave our brothers and sisters. Harris had to leave his three sisters Jasmine, Maureen and Marilyn and I had to leave Sally and Eileen. Also, we were leaving all the other boys and girls we had become close to and whom we called our family. We were all in the same boat but some of us did have parents who called to visit sometimes.

There was a family called the Grimmers. There were two girls and one boy. On a really sad day, one of the Grimmer sisters died. Word went round like wildfire that Rosemary Grimmer had died in Hornchurch orphanage hospital. The mood changed quickly for all of us, especially for those who had been closer to them. It was a real shock and a very sad time. We didn't know how or why this had happened to her. There was a bit of a panic, and her parents could not be contacted.

One day we were sitting in the day room all still in a down mood, 'Two-way family favourites' was playing on the radio. It was the station that we usually played. A news bulletin S.O.S came on asking anyone who knew the Grimmer family to make contact with them. It became the sad hope that someone would soon make contact with the orphanage, to pass on the sad news of their loss.

Fantastically, all the way in Malta, the mother and father had heard the sad news and immediately contacted the authorities. They were flown in straight away from Malta to the orphanage to be near and learn more of their deceased daughter, Rosemary. The orphanage was in such silence and sadness, no vehicles were going up and down the drive, and children were looking out of their windows. It was said her mother requested a last look at her lovely daughter and her request was granted. If Anthony or his sister Elizabeth manage to read this, I want you to know that you and your two sisters have stayed in my thoughts to this very day and my love goes out to you and your families.

Death was never talked about, so we didn't have much understanding of how, or why, Rosemary was no longer with us. One minute she was playing around like the rest of us, the next she was gone forever. I remember the day she was laid to rest. I cried when I saw the hearse driving slowly by with a man walking in front wearing a smart suit and a bowler hat and carrying a stick, as they passed Milton cottage. Everyone stared as it passed and stopped at the church. I remember we were all given a penny piece, then we went to the church to hear the priest, Mr Thompson, give blessings and we all said prayers and sang selected hymns. It was a really sad and empty time. Then there was a silence, and the church collection bags were passed up and down and across for us all to put our pennies in the bag. When it reached me, it was very heavy, and this was one of the only times my penny dropped into the church collection bag along with my tears. Other times my hand would go in, but more would quickly and quietly come out and then into my pocket.

We then all stood outside to watch the hearse taking the little coffin up the drive and out onto Hornchurch Road. For most of us, it was the first experience of an orphan's demise, made worse by her being such a young child and one of our extended family.

The following page is of all the children in Forbes as I remember them and Miss Surridge our house mother

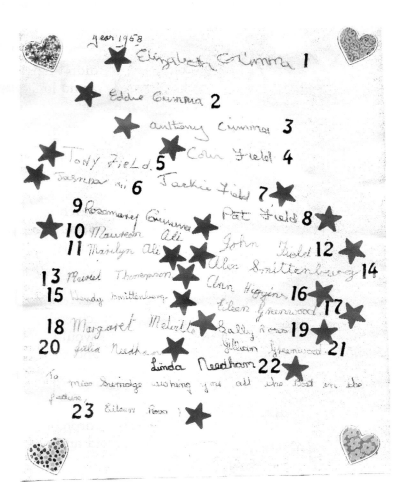

year 1958

Elizabeth Grimma 1

Eddie Grimma 2

anthony Grimma 3

Tony Field 5   Colin Field 4

Jasmina ali 6   Jackie Field 7

9 Rosemary Grimma   Pat Field 8

10 Maureen Ali   John Field 12

11 Marilyn Ali   Alex Smittenberg 14

13 Muriel Thompson   Ann Higgins 16

15 Wendy Smittenburg   Eileen Greenwood 17

18 Margaret Melville   Sally Ross 19

20 Julia Needham   Gillian Greenwood 21

Linda Needham 22

To miss Surridge wishing you all the best in the future,

23 Eileen Ross

CHAPTER 3: London County Council and Hornchurch Children's Home - 'Milton'

1954. Sweet rationing had ended the year before, and children were overjoyed. Chocolates and sweets had been rationed for ten years because of the war, but now the 12oz a month seemed like a distant memory to the children of Britain. Well, most children. At Hornchurch sweets were very scarce; the only time my sisters and I got sweets or chocolate was if my brothers came to take us out, or we took someone else's. That's how it worked. Nothing was sacred or exclusive to anyone. I learned that from a very early age. When we were lucky enough to have a boiled sweet, I would suck it for a little bit then put it back in its wrapper, get it out again and again then, when it was finished, I made sure I took the last bit of sweetness by licking the wrapper.

I was eight years old and now too old to live with the younger children, so Harris and I had to move to Milton cottage; overall it was a ghastly experience. We were forcefully taken away from what had been our family for the last four years and more importantly, our sisters, our own flesh and blood. Once in Milton, feeling empty, broken-hearted and very frightened, it was painfully clear that we had to fight with everything we had to fit in with the much older boys we had the misfortune to share a dormitory with. There was lots of bullying that us younger boys were subjected to, especially from the big boys in 'Nelson' next door. It seemed to be where all the tougher boys were. We tried to stay away from them. The Nelson boys always won everything because if they didn't then there were beatings. Milton wasn't as bad as Nelson next door because it had boys and girls in. The girls were nastier than the boys at times. They would get their fun out of tripping us up, forcing us to fetch and carry and humiliating us from time to time. It was, dodge it if you can, especially from the housemaster Mr. Percival. That was the first warning I got; "Stay away from Percival, if you can".

I have clear, vivid memories of seeing children arriving at the orphanage, and being brought to Milton into the day room. The day room was the place everyone would congregate, playing and listening to the radio, until we were forced out. The new children, we called them newbies, were brought in by the house Misses and they were left with us. I remember thinking I was glad I wasn't thrown into Milton straight away. We tried to support one another but there were some you just couldn't help.

They would stand there, obviously scared, and timid and just stay looking around. Some would just stare at the floor. A lot of us would just look over and carry on playing. Eventually one of us would go over. If it was a girl the older girls would go over and try to make them feel at ease, and if it was a boy, one of us would go over and take them under our wing. We were strangers to the newbie and didn't know their circumstances. Nor why they were left in the orphanage. Every child had different traumas and backgrounds, leaving only the scars that they knew about.

We dealt with things day by day. Everyone became one big family so we would try to make them feel better as they were standing there. As a child of eight the only thing that I thought about was a new friend coming to live with us.

Eventually, the newbies realised that crying was a waste of time. It didn't get them anywhere other than getting told to shut up or belted by the other boys. It wasn't a good idea to get on the older boys' nerves. It was tough, there were no real comforts or mummy kisses and cuddles. We were all unwanted for some reason or another and that's why we were there. The world treated us orphans differently, we were rejects.

We were not properly cared for; it didn't pay to show much weakness and you had to be fast on your feet. One thing us kids were good at was adjusting and acclimatising quickly, if you didn't your life would be more difficult. Those that didn't often became bed-wetters because they were too frightened or scared. Then there would be hell in the morning. Every bed had a pee pot under it, so bed wetting was not accepted. You'd get dragged out by the ear and made to stand outside for a while in wet pyjamas in the cold or depending on which staff was on that morning there may be a different punishment. You could get thrown in a bath of cold water with your wet sheet put in with you and bleach poured over, then you would get the worst scrubbing down in your life, nearly drawing blood. I only wet the bed once, I am glad it never happened again.

But it was the house masters we had to contend with. Mr Percival would always be smoking and was really nasty. If you were doing anything wrong, he would have you. His best weapon was his cigarettes, he would burn you with them on the arms mostly, sometimes he would make us line up in a row on the corridor and kick us, verbally abuse us, and burn us where our flesh was bare. If he saw you with your elbows on the dinner table, he would sneak up behind you and stick the cigarette in your arm or forearm. My arms are still full of scars. I look at them often and they are a sad reminder. Even if he was just in a bad mood, he would burn us or take the slipper to us. There was a small bunch he took a dislike to and would often pick on; unfortunately, I was one of them.

Some nights when he was drunk, he used to make us stand in front of a wall for what seemed like hours. We'd stand just looking at the wall. Sometimes we were made to stand in the corridor with only our pyjama tops on. If we weren't made to face the wall he would come with his stick and flick it at our willies and prod and poke it wherever it took his fancy. If you were made to face the wall our noses had to be very close to it, and then the smack on the head came. We used to nearly drop down because our legs began to tire, and the cold would get to us. We would think 'why am I here? I haven't done anything'. One time we were made to stand in a room facing the wall and found a cupboard. We were there for so long I eventually opened it and it had sheets and pillowcases inside. I also found a box of Cadbury's chocolate penny bars. So, it got to a point where Harris and I thought 'if we were going to get done anyway for not doing anything, we may as well have a small bar'. We had more than one of them because we were so hungry, and they were so nice. The house master, or his wife, would keep coming to check on us and the bigger boys were told to keep watch and give out punishments if they felt we needed it, which they often did and took great pleasure from. Then they would get their treats and rewards. We would get kicked or slapped in the head, making our noses and foreheads hit the wall at the same time, which wasn't pleasant. After the superintendent had finished with us, we could only just walk. Sometimes the creases on the backs of our legs would bleed. We got absolutely battered for eating the chocolate and were red all over after he whipped us with the slipper franticly and continuously. We also had the bigger boys to contend with and suffered at their hands. We would try and stay out of their way, but it wasn't always possible, and they used to get their fun making us suffer when the mood fitted. Everyone ducked and dived when Mr Percival was on duty. He certainly made our lives miserable. He often got drunk and went on a rampage, picking out different boys for different reasons. He was a carpenter and taught at another school before coming home and making our lives hell, sometimes forcing us to do woodwork and make pelmets for the windows that never had curtains. We were forced to do duties that were completely inappropriate for our age. There were no checks carried out on house parents and they seemed to have no experience in caring for children.

When Miss Anne was on duty, everybody loved it. Mr Percival would keep out of the way when Miss Anne and Miss Dorothy were with us, they were kind and caring.

Miss Anne was a lovely lady; Miss Anne Jackson was her full name, and she was in her early twenties. She was beautiful to me, inside and out. She loved listening to music and one song has remained in my memory: Emile Ford and the Checkmates singing: "What do you want to make those eyes at me for?"

Miss Dorothy

There were three dormitories each with ten beds which were not at all comfy, the frames were made of iron, painted in blue lead paint and the mattresses were filled with straw so whenever anyone wet the bed it gave out an unpleasant smell. On the inside of the windows, the condensation used to turn to ice, and we used to have a bit of fun carving pictures or messages on them with our little fingers. Then we'd put them under our armpits to try and get a little warmth in them again. We never had the luxury of central heating, and it got bitterly cold. The only heating was in the house's parents' quarters. When we had to go out to play, I used to sit and put my coat over my head to try and keep warm from my breath.

One of the tricks the older boys played on us was, that one boy would quickly and quietly get down on his hands and knees behind us then one of the older boys would walk up to us and push us over, causing us to fall backwards over the boy on all fours and hit our heads and bodies hard on the solid floor. There were many other tricks the older boys would play on us; we had to have our wits about us at all times. There was physical, mental, and sexual abuse in the orphanage.

There was a window out of our dormitory to the fire escape; at night we were able to lift the window, but it had heavy weights attached to a cord either side which made it noisy and hard to open. Harris and I would climb out of the window and to reopen it we used a spoon from the outside and would climb back in. We were able to go down and climb through the larder window where the food was kept; this window was always open for air circulation, which made it easier for us to get in and out. We would take whatever we could carry back to the dorm and share it with all the others, that way no one would snitch or 'grass' us up. There was always a house parents' 'little pet' who was likely to tell or give up our secrets. I was never a house parents' pet; I was glad really because the pets used to be taken out of the dorm all hours through the night. I never really understood why they had to go out when ordered. My only wish was to be in the good books with the house parent Miss Anne Jackson. I had a childhood crush on Miss Anne, she would always read a chapter from a story book at night when most young children would fall asleep. After reading a chapter, she would go to all the beds and give the boys a kiss goodnight. I was a shy boy and would hide under the covers hoping she would pull the sheet from my face and give me a kiss, but sadly she never did, and I went to sleep feeling left out.

We were given daily jobs, one of mine was the worst of them, cleaning the coal! This was dreadful. I had to separate the coal from the coke and the anthracite, bag up all the dust then fill the coal scuttles, which became very heavy with anthracite. Then I'd take it to the kitchen to keep the Aga going. When this was all done, I was covered from top to toe in coal dust. It was up my nose and lined the back of my throat; the only water I had to clean myself was cold water from a water tank in the yard. In the winter this would be frozen over. It wasn't a very nice feeling, after working a hard-dirty job to try and clean myself outside in dirty, stagnant, cold water. After I had finished cleaning the coal, I had to sweep the yard and after that, sort out the potatoes, which was another horrible job. The bad potatoes had to be separated from the good; they were really smelly and slimy.

Another one of my jobs was getting the potatoes ready for cooking. There was a very large, electrically operated, metal, spinning bowl, which had very sharp, cutting edges all over the inside. I would fill the bowl with potatoes and then plug in the electric large three-pin plugs into the wall. In doing this I experienced my very first massive electric shock. In the 50s the large pins on the plug allowed my wet small fingers to touch the pins as I pushed the plug into the electric on the wall. I fell thankfully, then my fingers came away from the plug. My hand and arm were paralysed for a short time, but my fingers and brain have never forgotten the incident. After being nearly electrocuted I was told by the not-so-nice Mrs Spooner to go into the day room as, clearly, I was in no state to continue doing the spuds. In a way, I was glad it got me off the spud job and after that I never put my hand on the electric plugs again. I was scared stiff of getting another shock with such force and pain. To this day I can say it was the worst feeling I had experienced in my life outside of the abuse from the house parents etc.

Now I am qualified in the full understanding of electricity thanks to my foster father. I learnt the reason why it was so bad to receive an electric shock back then. Electricity at that time was (DC), not as we know it today in the modern lives we live, our electricity is (AC) which is much safer and a massive difference in how all our electrical appliances operate. The DC electric in those days was deadly when coming in contact with anyone, as it grips hold of you and kills (just like they kill the pigs in the abattoir with high voltage stunners). Today all our plugs have fuses, unlike in my younger days, all the pins on the plugs are insulated part way to stop contact with little fingers, should children be plugging them in or pulling them out. This was a great idea that was invented around the fifties when all electricity changed over from DC to AC, with manufacturers making all the plugs safer with the appropriate fuses to protect the various appliances. There had been many factory workers that had been electrocuted for the reasons I experienced.

Another one of our jobs was sewing and darning holes in our socks; they always needed doing because our shoes were so badly fitted, we would have many holes to darn. We also had to learn how to knit. We would all be given as many balls of wool as we wanted and knitting needles. So, at this time in my life I can still hold knitting needles any length in my big hands and do some knitting, one purl one then back stitch when you reach the end. We all did this in the day room or dormitory at night. When the dark nights came earlier, lots of us would sit on our beds knitting long scarves which helped us get some real warmth in winter. We'd sew or darn any holes in our pants or jumpers especially in the elbows and any buttons to be sewed back on. Those that didn't mend their jumpers would stand out even more than us posh boys and girls being able to perfectly darn up the holes with nicely darned patches. There were always plenty of wooden mushroom needles and cotton to go around. I think they were donations for us all to darn up our clothes and socks. The best thing was it kept us all quiet and busy. I made a scarf for my brother, and it was his and my pride and joy. He was able to see my skills in the long and thick scarf I had made for him. He would always let me see him with it on when I was allowed out to be with him.

Our clothes were sent to the laundry only once each week, on a Monday. This was another reason why I hated the jobs I was tasked with. Each week our dirty clothes were taken from us after lining up to collect our clean clothes, we had to stand in our dressing gowns with our arms stretched out. A clean bundle of clothing would be placed onto our open arms, which usually included a vest, underpants, socks, shirts, and a handkerchief once a week. We had to try to keep our trousers as clean as we possibly could because they were not changed for some months later, I was never sure why. You can imagine what state they were in when they were eventually given in to be washed, especially mine after cleaning the coal.

On school days we would get up at 7 am and quickly wash in limited cold water, get dressed, have breakfast, and be sent out to school. We were always humiliated at school because we lacked any enthusiasm. I was always looking out of the window and was absent from school many times.

After assembly when our names had been called out, I would then escape just so I could not be with the children that were dressed well, happy and loved. Us Cottage Homers could never receive this. I felt like a fish out of water. Harris was at another school but not too far from mine. We would meet up and go off together. Sometimes we would wander past Mr Thompson's church, which had a wishing well just inside the gate for passers-by to deposit their money. We never received any religious instruction so, yes, shamefully we would help ourselves to a small share and call it a loan, saying one day I would pay it back.

From there we would walk to Roneo corner and then jump on the bus to Romford. We were looked at and seen as low lifes and we felt it and we were treated accordingly. We would see other boys and girls walking happily and looking very smart. We could only dream. I knew I couldn't be like them, but I do remember wishing I was a Barnardos orphan. The Barnardos kids were better dressed and seemed happier. We were obvious targets for the police, many times we were returned to Cottage Homes in the Black Maria van and each time we would be given the usual three of the best, or six of the best, depending on the hits on each hand. On departure, we would always get an extra one on the backside. We always left as fast as we could arching our backs so that the cane would miss or land a little less firmly. It stung like heck and the following day the marks were fully visible. But if Percival handed out the punishment it would last longer and hurt far more, and we would be made to stand half naked for all to see. The girls coming and passing by us. If we were seen trying to cover our bits, we would get our knuckles rapped with canes which was so painful.

On one occasion during our mission to escape over the fence around the orphanage, my foot got caught between the metal rails. Each of these rails had metal spikes on the top and I fell onto the spikes. One went quite deep into the centre of my chest and the other went into my arm. Blood was pouring all over the place. I was crying with the pain and scared stiff because I thought I was going to die. I gathered myself together and with much help from Harris and my determination we managed to free myself from the spikes. I was able to slide down to safety.

Harris went for help, and I was taken to hospital where they treated me, and my wounds were stitched up. Then they asked where the fence was that I fell onto. So, it was clear I was trying to escape the orphanage.

I had certainly paid the price on this occasion and surprisingly there was no punishment to be had. I did take the superintendent to see, and he saw all my blood all over the fencing and grounds. After the war it was uncommon to see large iron fencing and gates around many of the buildings and churches, the government had made an order for all steel to be removed from around all buildings and melted down to make guns, tanks, and aircraft and the likes. However, none of the iron railings gates and spiked fencing had been removed from around the orphanage so we were still in our prison. The scars are still visible to this day. The other scars are internal and will stay in my thoughts to the end of my days, but I am thankful that I now have my own son, and his son, and my other grandchildren, to tell many of my stories, the ones that they are old enough to hear that is, of my time in the orphanage.

Harris and I found a way of earning a little extra pocket money as cash was very scarce. We did get pocket money, a sixpenny piece (two and a half new pence) each week and we spent that at the tuck shop. Harris and I started to escape regularly; our only transport was running or walking. We were never missed because of the many other children and Percival and the other house masters being distracted with their daily jobs. We got great comfort and strength from one another; we were unstoppable, but we found happiness together on our travels.

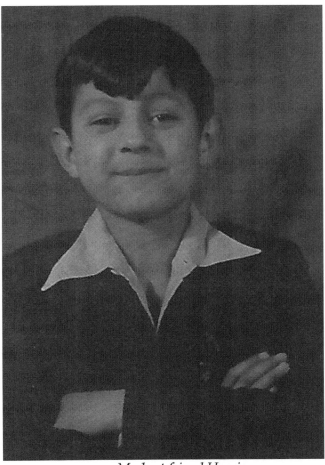

My best friend Harris.

When escaping we found a new spot where a cluster of trees grew, situated alongside the fencing, knowing this would conceal us where we each struggled to climb over. The first time we found it hard, but the more we did it, the easier it became.

Once out, we were on Hornchurch Road. After making our escape we went wherever our legs would take us. Later we would sneak back. Incredibly, no one had missed us and our speculation that we would be punished was unfounded. More often than not, we got back over the fence and mixed in again with all the other children as if nothing had happened. We were on a high but kept it our secret.

We soon got into a regular pattern of absconding without being caught, it was a fantastic feeling, but we knew that once outside of Cottage Homes we both stood out like a sore thumb. We were wearing our khaki shirts and shorts, long grey socks with holes we had darned ourselves and obligatory sandals. Everything that all the children wore had been clearly marked; *Mine. Peter Ross, Milton.* If we were ever found, individuals would be able to identify us and link us to the cottage and ultimately to Cottage Homes, but we carried on regardless. People passing by us clearly saw us but just went on with their daily routine; they didn't bother us at all, which was good for me and Harris. These were the times we didn't mind being looked down upon. We would get some pennies from our stash, with one digging and the other watching out for spies, and then off we went. We would buy ourselves bits to eat and carry on our adventures.

The next time, we decided to escape and go to Hornchurch Underground Station, with our confidence taking us further afield. We joined the flow of passing people and now we were in the middle of the day-to-day hustle and bustle. It was quite scary at first and we stayed close to one another and went with the flow. We watched and learnt how to obtain a platform ticket.

We got one each with no one asking us anything or pushing us aside. We had just spent our first two penny bit on our first ever platform ticket. We felt safe with a platform ticket each, we felt untouchable, and we walked on ahead with our little heads held high and fearless. This was our first experience of going up and down steps through tunnels and then seeing big wooden moving staircases which we found out to be escalators. We had great fun running up and down them whilst they were moving.

We soon learnt how to follow the routes. Standing on the platform was cool and looking down at the tracks many times saw mice running in and out and up and down. The first time was weird, it was like being in the devil's tunnel to us, feeling a cold rush and then a warm breeze which made me shiver from head to toe. Then hearing the rumbling after, it became super fun. Our stomachs rumbled and turned with fear and excitement, especially seeing the underground train approach with speed. The doors opened, the guard would shout, "mind the gap" and in we got, it was fantastic, the feel of the speed we would travel at was frightening at first, but it was better than being in any classroom. It was the best feeling one could have had but we never gave a thought to anything at that time other than our new adventure under the ground of London town. Until the day came, we got caught by one of the underground staff and we were made to stand whilst he blew his whistle and a police officer appeared and took us back to Cottage Homes in the big Black Maria police van. Sitting on the way back we knew what the night was going to bring. We looked at one another, smiled and stayed silent all the way back. They could punish us, but they would never take away from us what we had seen, and experienced.

Almost immediately after our caning for our escape, we came to realise that the empty bottles the staff had been collecting were taken back to the off-licence for a refund. This gave Harris and I an idea to get more money in our pockets, making this our new plan. On our next outing, we would get rid of the empties. We travelled along the road as usual but this time we were tuned into our mission and on looking around we saw an old shed next to the 'Harrow Lodge' off-license and realised they kept all the empty bottles in there. We just looked at one another in amazement, there was no need for words because we knew what one another was thinking. As I was the best at climbing, I offered to go over. Harris gave me a leg up on the gate and I climbed over, searched out and passed the bottles under the gap between the bottom of the gate which was just wide enough to pass through to Harris, and he grouped them together. When we had as many as we could carry, I climbed back over the fence and we made our way to the front of the off-license, walked inside and exchanged these bottles for the value of the returns.

When we were making our way back, with pockets full of big, heavy, old pennies, sixpences and threepenny bits, we realised that we had nowhere safe to keep our stash. There was no way that we could take it back to the cottage and risk it being found by our house parents who would ask questions, or even worse, have it stolen from us. I came up with the idea of hiding it in the air raid shelter, which was positioned behind Milton Cottage, and it was a place no one seemed to go. We agreed that this was what we would do. We went straight to the back of the shelter and dug a large hole and placed our money in it. We then buried it, putting a piece of slate over the top and a stone on top of the slate. It was better than a bank vault, our money was safe.

One night whilst we were in our beds, we were having a little chat, whispering, and being careful not to be overheard. Harris was in the bed next to me, and David Braithwaite was in the bed on the other side of me. David came up with the idea of making a den behind the shelter. It was a great idea, and this is what we did.

One summer night, making use of the light nights we started our den. We used the old empty coal sacks I knew were there after cleaning the coal. I just helped myself and we found timber so after building the timber frame and leaning it against the air raid shelter walls, we covered it over with sacks. This was fantastic for us, and we had many visitors. We used to have a stash of fags even though I didn't smoke and a stash of chocolate, apples and even toast that we would take around. It was dark inside, but we managed later to borrow candles from Woolworths in Romford, and this gave us some light and heat; we felt safe and happy. Our own secret little hideaway. We felt as if we'd escaped and when we had to come out again it was a feeling of misery walking back to the cottage, our knees and hands would always be dirty, but it was happy dirty.

One day whilst at the back of the old air raid shelter, we came across two old Silver Cross black prams. We managed to convert one of the old prams into a Go-Cart with a plank between the front and back wheels plus string holding it all together. One person would push from the back, and we would take turns to sit, using our feet to guide it. Many times, we fell off and acquired many wounds, mostly scrapes and bruises. We later found that this old cart had a dual purpose. We decided to take the Go-Cart out on our mission, so then we could carry more bottles. We found empty Corona bottles in some bins, they paid out two shillings and six pence for the soda syphons; big money to two children who were not used to more than six pence. The cart could hold more than we could carry; we filled it to the limit and returned everything we could get our hands on back to The Harrow Lodge off-licence on Hornchurch Road. This was one of our greatest achievements.

However, sadly, one night while out doing our bottle returns, Harris and I were met by the police, and we were taken back to the Cottage Homes. The police then marched us both up to the superintendent's office. The go-cart and bottles were left in the Black Maria police van. We were more upset about losing our go-cart than the fate that awaited us. This was as bad as losing a 'license to drive', our only vehicle. The money in our pockets was taken from us by the police. I sometimes wonder what happened to that. I like to think that they gave the money to charity rather than using it to buy a drink or two down the pub. Losing our cart took away our best source of income.

We were told to stand facing the wall as the police informed the superintendent of our crime, not knowing what our punishment would be. We stood trembling and our hearts were beating out of our chests, after the police left, our names were called at the same time. The cane came out and without asking for an explanation, or a word of warning, apart from "put your hands out" and then the cane rained down. We both got six of the best over the hands and backs of our legs, trying not to cry and play at being brave then marched down the drive and back to Milton, feeling humiliated. All the other children were watching us through the windows and knowing that we had been caught and caned. All the children residing in Milton wanted to know what had happened and how we got caught; we felt quite important as we told our story and revealed our injuries with red marks across our hands and the backs of our legs. When it was bath time, we would get another smacking off the Misses because they could see we had red marks from the cane, so they gave us more for the hell of it. Our luck had run out, but it was good for as long as it lasted.

One day we noticed a few of the bigger boys going across Hornchurch Road. There was an Esso petrol station with a sign saying 3/6d per gallon. Next to it was a toy shop called Watlins and next to that, was a paper shop and cigarette machine. We quickly followed and watched with great interest how this machine worked. They were obtaining fags for the house master. We found out there was change in the packets. We saw them manage to get another packet out without paying by pushing the drawer halfway back in and using a metal fork. By pushing the fork in they could pull another packet out. We couldn't believe our eyes, then we were told to clear off. We went off and quickly decided that when it got dark, we would have a go at getting some packets. Darkness came and we climbed over the fence with one of our two-shilling pieces and a fork we had smuggled out at tea. We got to the newspaper shop and stood at the fag machine. There were different compartments of different cigarettes, each packet came in packs of 10. We had to be quick, Harris kept watch and I attempted to do the trick. Nervously I managed to do the same thing I had seen the bigger boys doing. I only got one packet and then quickly another with the fork and then another. It became another good little money maker; we didn't do this very often, not having a two-shilling piece at hand. There was a 6d and threepenny bit in each packet, so later after emptying the compartment of whatever was left in the machine, we would get so many sixpences and so many thrupenny bits for two shillings. We would run off and bury the money but gave some of the cigs away to those who came to our den and sold a few for a penny each.

It wasn't long after that when we decided to spend our ill-gotten gains that we had hidden. We had another platform ticket each that we managed to purchase from our stash. We could regularly jump on a train and get off wherever we felt safe. Some days we had to run and dodge the busy ticket inspector, it was a doddle. We never got caught and were able to travel all over the underground this way. London at a very early age in our life became a magnet and we did whatever we wanted, seeing life outside of the enclosures of the Cottage Homes. It was like children today going to Disney Land with their family.

Harris and I were stuck together like glue; we never went hungry like we did in the Cottage homes, the big boys got the best on the table first. We would always manage to grab some food left for the picking. We had become skilled at the workings of the underground system and knew it like the back of our hands. Just for fun, we would sit on the circle line watching all the rush hour people jumping on and off the trains, to the circle-district-northern lines and others. Our new adventure on the underground amongst the hustle and bustle was a fantastic learning experience.

One day we noticed chocolate machines on the wall; of course, there were no cameras in those days. On these machines, 6d went in and one bar of chocolate came out in the drawer, the same procedure as the cigarettes. We were both again thinking the same thing. So, another day came, and we did the same job we had done with the cigarettes. Harris and I used to enjoy it whilst on our outings and we did take some back to our den and share it with some of the kids in the dormitory so no one would dob us in whilst we were missing.

During our excursion, on many occasions we would need to use the toilet, and these were found next to the underground stations. The toilets would have a sign 'Ladies' or 'Gentlemen', there were steps going underground and at the bottom was a shoeshine man and a gent's barbers. They'd be shaving gentlemen using a cutthroat shaver and a leather belt to sharpen the blade on, this was located next to the person in the chair.

The toilet keeper would arrive, opening the gate ready for business. The toilets were a hive of 'activities' and they were kept immaculately clean. The city gents would be greeted, giving up their umbrellas and bowler hats, they would be passed a white hand towel and after its use individuals would sit in the barber's chair for either their hair cut or a shave and shampoo. After giving his payment for the services and a handsome tip to the keeper, each individual would then take his umbrella and bowler hat on exiting.

Each man would have his shoes polished and then go about his business. One of the toilet attendants was once killed, falling off his horse on the way to work; it was discovered that he had left £7,000 (in today's value this would be well in excess of £7 million pounds) and this was long, long before the statutory instrument process to impose tax on his savings or inheritance tax.

The toilets would go to the left, or to the right and we would always wait for someone to come out and catch the door before it closed to avoid having to put a penny in the slot of a very large brass machine fixed onto the very heavy toilet door. Whilst in the toilet we would look up at the ceiling which had big square glass cobbles letting light in with pedestrians walking over the top. Some of those old public toilets today have been converted into luxury living accommodation on the Oxford Street underground. The Victorian Lavatory was built in 1890 and closed in the sixties, at the time of my visits. It is now a coffee and brunch café with the original porcelain urinals incorporated into the décor with decorative ceramic tiles.

Cigarette ends littered the underground and cigarettes could be purchased from machines everywhere. Thankfully I never took to smoking, but I handled many cigarettes in their packets, and they always had the change slipped inside. Back then Anchor cigarettes were sold separately, one for a penny or three in a box of matches for a penny, or a box of swan vestas for three pence. Smoking was everywhere. It came as no surprise to me when I heard many years later of the Kings Cross fire on the 18th of November 1987 and the thirty-one deaths resulting from that fire as I knew the same wooden escalators with wide gaps in between allowed rubbish to fall below and become a serious fire hazard. The fact it didn't happen sooner was simply luck.

I recall, in those days, city gents would always wear bowler hats, with shiny shoes and umbrellas. When their shoes would be splashed by another standing at the urinal, they would stop at the shoe-shine boy and have their shoes polished. I used to look in wonder and hoped I could be like these gentlemen wearing smart clothes and shoes one day. Thankfully today, the underground stations are mainly spotlessly clean, with smoking absolutely forbidden and cameras keep a constant watch over the safety of all the passengers. Thankfully there are no longer cigarette machines, but unfortunately there are no chocolate machines, underground toilets, barbers or shoeshine boys either, an experience I had learnt so much from. As far as we knew, no other kids from the Cottage Homes got up to this and I believe we were unique in our regular escapes. This is a far cry from my visits to London now and if I need the loo when in London with my son, he simply downloads 'lavatory finder' on his phone to track down the last surviving public loos or as they are sometimes referred to: 'Monkey Closets'.

Harris and I lived our lives in a fantasy land and kept away from Cottage Homes for as long as we could. We were classed as outcasts, unwanted; taunted that our mothers and fathers had not wanted us and that is why we were in an institution. Our hearts would sink when we had to make our way back, our moods changed into a serious mode on all our journeys back to what we called home, unless we found something we both found interesting and funny. We were glad on the other hand that we were making our own way back on the underground rather than being caught and escorted back by the police in the black van leading to getting a good beating. Milton was the worst house to be in, especially now we were getting older, and the abuse started to change in many different ways for us boys and girls. That's why we loved escaping, it kept us from being chosen for whichever kind of abuse the older boys and staff were intending.

CHAPTER 4: The cottage homers big, green, army type, Dennis school bus

One experience I still think of, more so than others, was the time the 'Carry-On' films were showing, and I had never wanted to watch any of that stuff. At the time, the Carry-On films were the source of talk and fun for many, but not for me. My memory of the big green Dennis bus has haunted me ever since leaving the orphanage and the face of the driver Mr Berry.

I would notice when looking to the right out of the window from Milton's day room the big green bus coming from the stores yard and passing Milton heading down to the end of the drive, past Forbes where my sisters were staying, then turning around and coming back. It passed the hospital and infirmary on the left and went back up again passing Milton. It would be empty except for the driver, Mr Berry, who I would watch whilst he passed and went up to the top of the drive to the superintendents on the left, turning round at Ivy cottage then coming back down and turning right into the stores yard and parking up.

I went over to have a look at the bus. The engine was still hot. I noticed the chrome grill with a large chrome radiator cap on the front. The bus door was closed, and Mr Berry was talking to Mr O'Connor. He was the handyman and would do any jobs required, electrical or otherwise. Where the bus was parked up in the yard, I could smell the petrol engine and I noticed the crank handle for turning the engine over was laying on the floor.

I can still, to this time, smell the cobbler's hot resin glue in his shoe mending shop which was opposite the parked-up bus. Then there were the clothing stores overlooking the yard and the food stores opposite. At this time, I was eleven years old. Mr Berry came to the bus and would open the door asking me if I wanted to have a look around; I wanted to do just that. I had never been on this big green bus before on my own and seeing the bus traveling up and down made me more inquisitive. Mr

Berry helped me up the steps on to the bus and I would hold and pull on to the handrail and he would push with his hand on my backside which I never thought anything of at the time.

On the bus it felt like being in Aladdin's cave because it was so empty. I can remember the smell from all the green leather seats and seeing all the shiny chrome rails going up and over the seats with handrails that went up to the ceiling. I went all the way up to the back of the bus, not having had the opportunity to sit on these seats before. I remember kneeling on the seats and looking out of the back windows then walking back down to the front where Mr Berry sat at the wheel. I passed him and the large gear stick and climbed on to the seat which was for the staff to sit on whenever the bus went out on journeys full of noisy children. I felt so happy, looking out of the front window. Behind my seat were the steps leading down from the bus and looking up to the back of the bus; at the age I was, it looked so very big. Then Mr Berry let me sit in his driver's seat and I am now in my thoughts driving this great big green bus. I manage to hold onto the very large steering wheel and remember looking over the engine to the left of me and all the shiny chrome work. I obviously could not reach the foot pedals; I noticed the key was still in the ignition. I was thinking about driving this bus in my dreams. I was driving up and down the drive with all the children watching me in dismay. But then it was time for me to go. Mr Berry got off the bus, taking the key and I climbed out of the driver's seat stepping down with Mr Berry.

He caught me and held me, patting me on the bum saying, "Off you go now".

I ran off back to Milton, so happy. I had now been on the bus and Mr Berry was my friend, so I thought. Most days I'd see him driving the big green bus past Milton. I noticed him glaring at me whilst driving past. I always made a point of waving at him because I thought he was my friend.

Then a few days later, I stood quietly looking out of the window as I often did, and I noticed the big green bus coming down and going past Milton. It was heading into the empty yard. It was getting dark; the lights were on. I was bored and had nothing to do so I thought I would go over. It was cold and raining and the bus was just parked up with the lights still on.

I got to the open door of the bus and Mr Berry said from his drivers' seat, "Do you want to get on for a drive?"

I was eager to get on, so I said, "Yes". I was so happy and thrilled being on the big empty bus, it was special for me. I sat in the seat next to him and he told me he would take me for a little drive, knowing I felt special being able to sit right up at the front of the bus. He closed the big doors and drove the bus out then went down the drive to Forbes cottage. He then turned the bus around and went back up the drive to the yard. It was just me sitting tall and feeling really, very special on the front seat of the bus looking out at the few big boys playing out. Then he returned to the place where I got on and he turned off the engine. I jumped up to go to the back of the bus to look out for anyone that was out there so they could see me on the back seats where us smaller kids never got to sit. I remember being disappointed because there was no one there to see me. I was looking around when the lights went off and Mr Berry came down towards me. I immediately felt scared watching him walking towards me in the darkened bus. I wanted to get off the bus. I could just see past him that the door of the bus was closed. I was trapped. I tried to squeeze past him but then I felt Mr Berry's hands on me. There was a scuffle, and I was trying to get away, but he overpowered me, and I was petrified. The more I struggled the more I felt trapped. He got hold of me so tightly and he was so strong. The next thing I knew my shorts were pulled down and with a struggle eventually I felt him painfully pushing inside my bum. I was in so much pain, holding on to the chrome on the seat and trying to pull away. I was crying with pain and such hurt and then he yanked me and lifted me onto him, pulling me until he was finished. It seemed like forever. Then he walked away, opened the door, and got off.

I was in pain and so confused. I could just about manage to see, and I noticed a mess all over the green leather seat. My foot slipped on the floor; the slippery white stuff was on the floor as well and it smelt like the hair cream the big boys used. I will never forget that smell for as long as I live. I pulled my shorts and underpants up feeling warm, sticky, and messy in between the tops of my legs and bum. I walked and limped slowly down the bus to the steps. I was terrified and tried to stop crying. I began looking around for Mr Berry but thankfully he was nowhere to be seen. In fact, there was no one to see the state I was in. I walked with difficulty the short distance in the dark over to Milton. My thoughts were all over the place. I felt ashamed and dirty and embarrassed. I went into the outside toilet feeling glad no one was there.

Sanitary conditions were poor to say the least, but this was all we had. The only other was in or around the back of the air raid bomb shelter.

I sat on the toilet looking at the mess, there was blood in my underpants, and I panicked because I didn't have any others. I didn't want a caning so I took them off and tried the best I could in the toilet to clean up the mess on me. There was never the luxury of toilet tissue, something we all take for granted these days. There was only hard sheet toilet paper on rolls or newspaper. Then there was a banging on the toilet door because someone wanted me out. I jumped with the shock, already scared stiff and confused, I wanted to just fall down and scream out loudly. I knew there was no point. Nothing would happen other than a clobbering. There were only two toilets for fifteen or so boys who would all want to use them. You can never take much time when you're on the toilet because there was always someone wanting to go next. In panic, I took off my underpants and rolled them up. I wiped myself as best as I could with the hard toilet paper then I put my shorts back on and finished quickly. I then left the toilet trying to put on a brave face. I limped straight into the washroom which thankfully was not far from the toilet and there was no one in there. With cold water only to wash, I put my soiled under pants under the cold running tap and washed them, then rinsed them out, all the time sobbing and still in pain and bleeding. Luckily, I found a flannel in the sink and rinsed it in cold water and wrung it out with my little hands. I rolled it up and I placed it between the cheeks of my bum. I cleaned myself, noticing the blood on the flannel. I rinsed the flannel out again then I kept it in between the cheeks of my bum and pulled my shorts up. I pulled my belt so tightly around me to make sure they didn't fall down and to also hold the flannel into my bum until I got upstairs to my dormitory, hoping not to get noticed by anyone.

There may be many readers saying, "Why did you not go and report this incident?" The answer was simple; I was far too scared to go to anyone, why would I feel safe reporting to the ones that were beating the hell out of me?

I had been eleven years old when they sent me to hospital just before Christmas 1957. They said I had fallen and injured my left elbow; it was the superintendent Mr W. Burgess, who had reported this so-called injury to the hospital. When the truth was, I had been beaten by Mr Percival. If I had gone to report my terrible ordeal he would have just simply hit or kicked or punched the hell out of me and called me a liar saying, "I had simply messed myself".

I could have said, "Go and look at the mess on the bus", but I was lost and frightened, I didn't know what to do.

I got to my dormitory, lifted the bed mattress at the top end and put my wet underpants as flat as I could on to the springs. Then I let the mattress quickly back down on them, thinking and hoping that in the morning they would be dry and clean. I stayed in the dorm, sitting in my chair, and feeling the comfort of the flannel still between my cheeks with the pressure of my little body sitting on them. At first it brought more pain and stinging, then the pain started to calm down.

With it being dark outside I left the dorm and went out on to the fire escape, sitting on the cold floor with my dressing gown wrapped around me and putting my knees up under my chin with all my weight on my bum. I tried to keep warm, staying for as long as I could, safe but cold out on the fire escape. I knew nobody could see me, but I could see from that position all those coming and going from below. At the time when all the others were in the dorm getting ready and into bed, I could go in limping without being noticed.

I got in bed keeping my shorts under my pyjamas with the flannel still between the cheeks of my bum and I remember pushing it up as far as I could, hoping nothing would show on my bed sheets. I was petrified of being given a caning on top of what I had already gone through. I laid there quietly, trying not to think, and trying to get some sleep, feeling a bit safer with Harris in the next bed to me and David Braithwaite on the other side. The way me and Harris and David Brathwaite were, they knew something was wrong as I was staying silent, also, they could see I had been crying and something was not right. It was like if you got chicken pox, everyone would notice. I quietly wept and I kept reliving the horrible, terrible experience until I eventually fell asleep.

The following morning, I woke up feeling very different within myself, still frightened, tense and still in pain. I quickly and discreetly got my underpants back on which were still damp, and the flannel was still in place. My bed, thank goodness, only had a small damp mark on it. I had my porridge with a sprinkle of sugar and milk. Then panicking deep inside myself, I quickly, whilst everyone was in the breakfast room having their toast and marmalade, went to the washroom. I secretly pulled out the flannel, hoping to avoid being seen by any of the staff. They were all still in the breakfast room. I washed the flannel again with cold water and noticed a lot of blood coming out of it. I cleaned the flannel as best I could, and I went back outside to the toilet. No one was in there as they were all in the breakfast room, meaning that I had more time to sit on the toilet and feel a bit more relaxed. I wiped myself with the flannel which was very painful. I then folded it and put the clean side of the flannel back in place. I pulled up my underpants and shorts and then went to the day room and sat looking out of the window. I wondered if I would see the big green bus passing, thankfully I did not. I obviously did later, but I never ever went near Mr Berry again. I would only see him when I had no choice in the matter. I also had to still get on and off his bus. I noticed the way he looked at me and I sat feeling scared. I noticed him kissing and putting his hands on the children, there was nothing I could do other than keep away from him. Thankfully, two days passed, and I kept the flannel between the cheeks of my bum and washed it. Then, thank the lord, Monday came.

Monday was washing day and all those reading this story that have gone through the orphanage system, as I have done, will know very well and will never forget the song we all used to sing, *"Today's Monday, Monday's washing day"*. There were six verses all ending with *"Is everybody happy, you bet your life we are"*. We weren't, but because it was Monday, I received my issue, all with 'Milton Peter' clearly marked on; a nicely washed clean vest, pants, socks, shirt and handkerchief. The first little bit of comfort I got to feel after that dreadful night.

Now I could get changed, dumping all my dirty washing in the big wicker basket upstairs in the hall ready to go to the wash house. I kept the flannel in place, washing it to keep me clean until I was all healed up. There was no more sliding down the stairs handrail as I always enjoyed doing. I was still in a lot of pain, and I was suffering terribly with embarrassment about what had happened. Harris was still wondering what was wrong with me; I was no longer joining in with the fun on the bannisters. I was feeling so bad I wanted to tell my sisters, but I knew I couldn't even begin to explain to them about my terrible experience. We were all very young; how could I tell them of such a thing that had happened to their little brother? I knew what had happened to me, but I couldn't bring myself to tell anyone. I didn't understand why it had happened to me. I just asked, "Why did Mr Berry do such a thing to me". I was simply too scared to tell anyone. I felt no one would believe me. I would then get ridiculed and made fun of, never mind the beating and the upset that would follow.

Whilst at Milton cottage I had been given an old wind-up record player that my brother had given me with some 78 speed Columbia. RCA & Decca and many other records and a little tin of H.M.V. needles. I would hide it under my bed in the dormitory. I treasured it, but like everything else it did not last long before it was broken along with all the records. Sadly, nothing was sacred. Whilst I had it, I played as many records as I could when I was on my own.

One weekend waiting and hoping my brother would come to visit it started raining. I had playing Nat King Cole singing "Smile though your heart is aching, smile even though its breaking" I took the record off the turn table with tears running down my cheeks and smashed it over my knee again and again until I saw blood coming from my knee. I was in such an emotional mess and desperate to see my brother.

I began gathering up the pieces and I took them to bury them behind the air raid shelter. That memory has haunted me and will for the rest of my days.

Ever since to this time, where now I have at the home, I am now living in. I have a most prestigious Pathephone No 8 wind up player, which can be seen in one of my photos with "His Master Voice" and Pathe Sapphire special sound box instead of the short stumpy little needles that I used to play on the 78 speed records one of which is "Smile" Nat King Cole. I still shed many tears on thinking back and I miss my brother dearly.

Weeks came and went, and it was time for my brother to take me out. On leaving Hornchurch with my brother, I felt broken, I became more introvert, and my brother asked me on the journey to his home, "Are you feeling ok?"

I nodded. I couldn't tell him, I didn't want to put him through the misery and pain, same as I was suffering. Then years later whilst at my brother's house he was watching 'Carry On Camping' and it caused me to feel sickness in my stomach. I can immediately put names to the actors. Hattie Jacques was Miss Spooner, Sid James was Mr Berry and so on. I hated the orphanage abuse in every way. It affected the way I feel and my outlook on life.

I left with no hope and no education. If it wasn't for the friendship with Harris, I don't know what I'd have done. However, watching the TV the day they had 'Carry On Camping,' on, I noticed on the camp site in the film, in front of Barbara Windsor, a much nicer luxury type Dennis bus. It was similar and reminded me of the cottage home's orphan's big old green type army bus. This made me feel sick with horror whilst my brother and his wife found this Carry-On lark funny. It was blatantly obvious I did not.

I left the lounge and went to my room in his house and tinkered with his army stuff and tools as I always did, especially when I was much younger. I loved seeing all his work things, there were all sorts and lots of it. I used to happily lose myself in play.

However, the time when I saw the posh Dennis bus on TV started me thinking back to the pain I had gone through after my experience on the big green army bus with Mr Berry.

I also remember the other children that would get on and off the bus, the steps being difficult to get up or down for all the small children. So, Mr Berry would always assist. I could also vividly remember him lifting them in the air, touching and kissing them (it's no wonder many of us had cold sores, he was always full of them). We all wore Khaki shorts; this was our usual wear making it very easy for him to fondle as I sadly found out, (as well as kiss) but at the age I was, I never had any idea of what was going on. I had no idea of what sex or touching was at that age.

I remember Mr Berry whilst he was sitting in his driver's seat, his hands grabbing the legs of small children between the gear stick and him leaning right out to the left with his left arm and his hand snatching out at children as they went past. I just thought he was being playful, teasing them. I remember seeing many of the older children steering clear of him when they got on or off the bus; then sadly, I knew why. I would sit in a seat near to the middle of the bus, far enough away from the big boys and enough away from Mr. Berry, as the back of the bus would always be for the older boys and girls. We would not sit on or go near any of the back seats of the bus, knowing we would only get done by the elders and they'd give us a belt and tell us to get off their seats.

CHAPTER 5: 1958, when I reached twelve years of age

When I reached twelve years old it was said of me that, "I was of low intelligence, slow mentally, ponderous and not at all sociable". I could hardly read, write, or add up. The only socialising I did was of course with Harris and David Braithwaite. I used to stand looking out of the day room window waving at a young girl in Wellington Cottage directly opposite. The glass was old and unclean, but I was able to just see her and she me. We never got to talk to each other, but we began to wave most days. It gave us a little feeling of comfort, especially on days when I was wishing for my brother to come.

My birthday was on July 20th and he would never forget it because his daughter Janet's birthday was on the same day. He would visit with Maisy, his wife, and Janet, his daughter, and we celebrated together on the front lawn. It didn't happen every year though. One year my brother Bill bought me a crystal radio set. I got it working in our dormitory and I could hear Radio Luxembourg in the late hours on earphones. Harris and David wished they could listen as well. I was able to connect the other beds in my dormitory with a very thin wire so we could have extra earphone headsets. These headsets were easy to come by (nicked) in those days, from Romford Market. We walked from Hornchurch to Roneo Corner and then up to Romford Market, for us it was a long way, but it was well worth the long-time walking and running which, we had to do to get there.

The atmosphere in the dormitory was magical. In the early hours Harris, me and David could hear the same sounds; it was fantastic, we could go to sleep listening to the sounds of the fifties and sixties in our dormitory beds. We never had them taken away by the staff because only we with earphone headsets could hear the sound. It was not like today with the radio on and everyone within earshot being able to listen. The dormitory would be silent, and we'd be under our bed covers listening to such sweet music. As long as it kept us quiet it was all good. It felt good that I had pulled it off, something like that in those days for children was very unique. We were left alone most of the time in the early part of the evening because the bigger boys were out playing cricket and football with the house masters. In a way it helped with the staff keeping watch over us and it kept us in our dormitory and not absconding.

One Christmas, when I was lucky enough to go to my brother's, he came to pick me up and on the journey to his home he told me he had a present wrapped up for me under his tree with all his other presents. I was overjoyed and very much looking forward to Christmas day. On the day when everyone was opening their presents, I opened my gift with great excitement because I hadn't had much experience of opening presents at Christmas. When I took the wrapping off, I found a Kodak brownie camera and film. I knew back then that the cost of a brownie camera was ten shillings and sixpence, an expensive item and for me such a luxury. I was in my dream world of being a photographer just like Anthony Armstrong Jones, even though I did not know who he was at that time of my life. I knew I was going to be seen as someone famous when I got back to the orphanage with my brand-new camera.

We had a nice Christmas meal with a turkey and all the trimmings, and I found a sixpence in the pudding which I treasured. When it was time, sadly, to go back to the orphanage, sure enough, everyone was so excited when they saw my brand-new camera. They were all eager to have their photographs taken. Some went and put their Sunday best on and had their hair done so they would look their best. I would then be their photographer. I took many photos of all the kids and the nice Miss Anne; some I show in this autobiography. I quickly filled up rolls of film in my camera and then took the film out of the camera and put another roll of film in. Long after I was left with full rolls of film, but I didn't know how to get the film developed. I hid the rolls of film in my dormitory and then the next time my brother Bill came to visit me I gave him the films and asked him if he would be so kind as to have them developed for me.

After I had taken the photos and before they were developed, the subjects of my photos were just as eager as I was to see the final product. When I had given the films to my brother, I told the likes of Miss Anne and Miss Dorothy and others who were equally as excited to know that my brother had taken the films to be developed. So, over the passing weeks of waiting for my brother to visit again they were also looking forward to him visiting.

The weekend came for my brother to take me out and give me the pictures that I had been eagerly awaiting. I opened them up and saw the photos I had taken, and I was so pleased and proud to know that I was going back to the orphanage to show all the photos that had been developed. Strange as it seems, over the weeks and months of waiting for these photographs to be seen by everyone I had taken pictures of, I had quickly grown up and I had become more sociable and respected, more so after I had shared the photos with the people, I had taken such nice pictures of.

What I also discovered was that my brother had a brother-in-law who worked for Kodak. He was called Freddy. Freddy was someone I later got to know and one day I shared his cooked pigeon and rode on the back of his very powerful motorcycle. I realised that it was thanks to Freddy that I had received such a wonderful Christmas present, and it was he who had developed all the pictures, giving me three copies so that I could give copies out to all those I had taken photos of. It made me feel like a bit of a celebrity, being the only orphan boy, to my knowledge, that had a camera of his own of such quality and was able to share with all those I had photographed. Now I share that pride and joy with all those who are reading this true story of the twelve-year-old, little orphan boy Peter and his wonderful camera.

To all of those in the picture below, I send to you, my love. When my time is up you will be in my thoughts.

Pat Bacon on the lawn outside Milton cottage.

Pat with the only piano behind her that I was able to play after leaving Milton cottage, only radio above provided by L.C.C

Photograph of me and my bike
bought by my brother Bill,
taken by Harris.

Photo I had taken of Harris.

Photo Harris has taken of me.

Photo of my brother Bill and Muriel Thompson outside Forbes on mine and Janet's Birthday.

Some of the children out of Milton on a so-called holiday hiking in our most uncomfortable shoes, feet full of blisters

The Royce brother and sister with the air raid bomb shelter behind them

This picture above shows the layout of all the cottages, hospital, church and orchard

This is me at thirteen years of age.

This little boy I can't remember his name. The photo taken not long after he came into Milton cottage.

It was the daily routine each day, seven days each week, every month of the year, that the day staff would come on duty every morning. Each morning we were woken; we would go to the downstairs washroom, where the house Miss would be holding a large jug of hot water. She would tip the jug and walk in a line to empty the hot water into each sink for each of the boys to wash in. I think the ten sinks were situated all in a row. If we didn't get the plug in quick enough, we would miss our share of the hot water, so we'd have to wash in cold water. She didn't give us very much time to do this and I was never quick enough. Consequently, I would always be washing in cold water and to this very day, I still wash my face and hands in cold water even though there is plenty of hot water, always available at any time of the day.

Bath night was even worse, there was one toilet and two baths, one opposite the other; one was for the girls and the other was for the boys. They were only a quarter filled and we would all stand in a line with a towel around our waists, each one of us waiting our turn. When it was time for me to get in the bath, approximately four or five others would have gone before me. It depended on where you were in the pecking order. There would be two Misses washing us, one on the first bath and one on the other. The bath opposite for the girls had no curtain, meaning that none of us had any privacy. You had to get your towel off, stand in the bath and Miss would rub us down with a soapy flannel. The soap stank, it was green Carbolic soap. After your quick rub from head to toe, she would pour a jug of water over us then you'd have to quickly get out. It would have been in our best interest to exit quicker if we had cane marks on our bums and legs.

Things changed, thank goodness. As we got older the girls would have the bathroom first, then it was over to us boys. I remember a sign that decorated the bathroom wall, saying 'Please remember don't forget, never leave the bathroom wet, nor leave the soap still in the water, that's the thing we never oughter'. After the boys finished in the bathroom the floor was always slippery with soap and water covering the floor. We would frequently get into trouble for leaving the bathroom in such a mess, but boy, it was good fun. We never had a toothbrush and toothpaste but were given a pot with paste in that was shared. We had to stick a finger in the pot quickly and rub our teeth with our finger then go off to the dormitory.

On the stairs some of the big boys made up a new game. It was disgusting really. At the bottom of the stairs there was a sideboard and on top of it were all the trophies and medals that Milton had won for football, rounders and netball etc. A few thought it a good idea to spit from the top of the bannisters and see who can get their spit into the trophies.

One day Mr Cooper was told this was happening. He came thundering into the day room shouting, "Who has been spitting and gobbing in the trophies below the stairs?"

Everyone stayed quiet and no one owned up. I had no idea who it was, but I did have my suspicions. It certainly wasn't me. He stared around the room at each and every one of us with his wicked evil look. He was fuming, his face was red, he was like a bull, with steam coming out of the nostrils. We were all scared. The cups were his pride and joy, they were our 'Milton cups'. Milton won the cup and Milton's name was inscribed upon it for that year. He was the P.E teacher of Highlands School (if I remember correctly) so, for our cottage to win the trophy was his pride and joy, after all, he was the big tough man with a big ego, the strong P.E teacher. As far as he was concerned, they were his. Whoever did it got us all punished for it. During the course of that week, everyone got a punishment. We got thumped on the side of the head whilst walking past him. He would carry his slipper or cane and wait at the door and get us whilst we walked into the dining room. This would be the chance for him to get everyone he wanted to get. There was only one door in and out and everyone went into the dining room for meals. So, for that week, every day, we would all get it, until he felt he had paid us all back. Whoever did it, did it again. This time it was hell for us all. He took it as if someone was spitting on him. We were getting physically abused all the time.

If you turned around and asked, "What was that for?" he'd reply, "You know what it's for".

Most of us didn't like Mr Cooper or his wife.

One Sunday, Harris and I had been playing late in the day room while the older boys were out playing football with Mr Cooper, who was a very strong football supporter for all the school teams. We were having a good time messing about as boys do and as we ran around the snooker table, we decided to play with the snooker cues using them as swords. We were having a fantastic time until they snapped into three pieces. Frozen with fear and feeling sick to our stomachs at what had just happened, our thoughts turned to what would happen if we were found out. We put the cues back on the table placing them as if they were still in one piece; then left the room, went up to the dormitory and quickly got into bed, traumatised. That night we heard the older boys returning from football and about to play snooker. Finding the cues broken, they obviously couldn't play. We listened more intently, trying to hear what they were saying; did they have any idea who could have done it? It was terrifying for us. We knew there were no other cues, only the two that we had broken. We just lay as still as could be under the bed sheets and prayed. When all the upset calmed down, we knew we had escaped the big boys that night, but it wasn't over. I eventually managed to go to sleep, as did Harris, and the rest of the dorm slept.

The following morning, I felt tired and sick, and I was trembling. We had no choice but to go down to the washroom and then go for breakfast. When we made our way to the dining hall the housemaster Mr Cooper was waiting and watching everyone who came in. One by one he looked at everyone in the line and when we reached the dining hall he shouted, "Whoever has broken the snooker cues own up to it now". Of course, no one would snitch! Mr Cooper noticed Harris and I looking at each other in such a way that it was obvious we were the culprits. It was only me who was sent upstairs to stand with my face to the wall and wait for my punishment. To this day I cannot understand why it was only me. I was kept waiting until after everyone had their breakfast, I was getting into a right state. The usual practise would normally be the slipper on the backside, or the cane on hands and backside. This occasion was very different. Mr Cooper came upstairs with his wife behind him, grabbed my ear and pulled me into the corner, up against the laundry cupboard. His wife stood at the door to the stairs and held her foot to it so there was no escape for me, and no one could enter. Mr Cooper then grabbed hold of me by my shirt, pushed me hard against the wall, lifting me at the same time so I was at the same height as him and he began throwing punches at me like a boxer to my face and body giving me the worst beating a young lad could suffer. Suffering more, but in a different way than I did on the big green bus. He just seemed to get carried away and it felt like I was going to black out. I was seeing flashes and feeling great pain. My nose had been broken and there was blood everywhere. Mr Cooper was fit and tough and had knuckles made of steel and boy did I feel them. Eventually, his wife said something, and he seemed to come to his senses and stopped. Thank God. I couldn't see very well; my face had been battered; my nose had been broken. He let go of me and my shirt was full of blood, and it was torn. I fell to the floor and sobbed my heart out. They both left quickly, and I heard the door close. I was left all alone for ages in agony. I was left there in the dormitory all day and night. No one in the dorm dared do anything for me, not even Harris. If anyone had heard my shouts and cries, they would have been too frightened to do anything. The next day I was hungry, in pain and very cold. I approached the window and after I had scratched and scraped a section of the frost off the window, I could see outside. I scraped off quite a large section hoping someone may see me. I could hear all the children going on their way to school. No one could see me, or so it seemed. Harris had told my sister Sally, and I could see she was looking all over the place; I knew she was wondering where I was. I did not know Harris had in fact told her. I couldn't believe it when her eyes stopped at the window, I was looking out of. I felt so relieved, but I was scared for her, what if she went and rang the bell to Mr Sanderson, the deputy superintendent?

Sally was only a year older than me, what must she have thought seeing me black and blue, locked up in the dormitory looking out of the window, but she bravely went straight to the superintendent's office and rang the big brass bell situated on the stone wall at the side of the door. None of us would ever push that bell for fear of getting into trouble, not even if we wanted to report anything untoward.

We just put up with things as they were, but Sally did push the button and said, "My brother is stuck up in the dormitory with a black and bloody eye and nose; I have just seen him at the window". The door of the dormitory eventually opened and looking in at me was Mr Sanderson, deputy superintendent with Mr Burgess superintendent asking, "Peter what have you done".

I was shaking with the cold and in fear of more to come and I just said, "I had fallen over", this was far, far from the truth and they could see it.

Miss Anne and Miss Mavis were there, and they told me to tell the truth, saying, "We know what the truth is, come on you need to tell us". It obviously needed to come from my own mouth.

I was too young and scared of the superintendent. I was sent to carry on the day as usual. My shirt was torn, full of blood, and it was replaced. I was taken to the hospital and then went about my day with Harris.

We tried to run away together but eventually we were brought back by the police. Maybe it was reported by the staff that we had gone missing, and it was then that I told the truth to

Miss Anne. Miss Anne reported the situation. My brother had a letter sent to him about it. He came to the orphanage and wanted to give Mr Cooper a good hiding, what else went on I don't know.

In other past events, in 1957 I was taken to the Old Church hospital with other terrible injuries, the worst being my broken arm and when I was there, for once I was made to feel warm and cared for. There was violence most days at Hornchurch for us Cottage homers. If we did get through a day with none at all, that would be our lucky day. There was also another kind of abuse. I can't say that it was every day, but it was regular. It's strange because at the time we didn't complain, there seemed no point. I suppose we felt it was normal the way we were used to living every day. It was only when we grew up that we came to realise more and know that all we were seeing and experiencing was not normal at all.

I think if it wasn't for Harris and our friendship and eagerness to escape, we probably would have suffered more at the hands of those who were supposed to be protecting us, but instead, they were dishing out torture for their own pleasures. Hornchurch was not a good place to be except for the two nice Misses and the wonderful friendship I found with Harris. Thinking back, I never once cried for my mother, or anyone as a lot of children did. Those children; boys and girls; black and white; Jewish or Asian, like Harris, cried and at times screamed hysterically for their mothers or fathers. I just cried empty and to myself, not having any memory of a parent's love and touch. Just knowing all of us children were going through Hornchurch Children's Cottage Homes, with very little love and no affection, just a name and Milton, was hard enough. All the others had their name and cottage that they belong to on all their clothes, shoes, and sandals.

The superintendent had to deal with what had happened with Mr Cooper, after piecing the obvious together. It was after this punishment on the 28th of July 1959 that the L.C.C official's investigation took place and my brother had certainly made his feelings known. Mr and Mrs Cooper along with their daughter were removed from Milton Cottage. There were a lot of us more than happy the day they left. We still knew we had to keep our happiness hidden, we were not out of the reach of other abusers by any means. In this regard just one example, my so-called welfare officer wrote lies as to what really did happen in her report. The exhibit in chapter 6 is just one extract of complete lies, as clearly on the 28/8/1959 I was only 13 and I could not read or write. This small example just shows how they gave a false account to the authorities who would write anything just to justify their actions.

Another example is on the 14/11/1957 when aged 11. I was in Oldchurch Hospital in Romford. The report falsely claims I had fallen and injured my left elbow! The x-ray showed a fracture separation of the medial epicondyle. This injury was in fact inflicted on me in a beating but would never have been referred to in the child welfare officer's report because as I had learnt, the so-called Welfare Officer would simply write up their reports in tandem with the house parents. Many, many years went by until on the 14th of September 1998, I was unable to communicate with the Metropolitan police in the Mapperton Case to reveal what really went on.

There were two, long overdue, separate hearings at the Old Bailey in 2001 with the civil action that should have been criminal against the London borough of Tower Hamlets council (the same should apply to Rochdale council in the Cyril Smith fiasco) after the Mapperton Case. Long after the 'caregivers' had gone and after Alan Prescott had left in 1968, street names had been named after those that had abused all us children. Havering Council later had to remove those signs immediately and re-name those streets, one street was called 'Prescott Close' but paedophile Alan Prescott was sent to prison. Alan Prescott was a JP, Labour Councillor, Assistant Director of Social Services, and Chief Executive of East End Charity Toynbee Hall.

All this was a startling mirror reflection of the endemic abuse by Sir Cyril Smith MP and all those looking away where all the cracks were blatantly clear for all the authorities to see. But instead, they did everything possible to cover it up, and this continues to this very day in 2022. Historic matters are being investigated by the police, along with the authorities mishandling of these most serious and horrendous cases. Life at the orphanage may have been bad, but it made me stronger, and I fought to become the person that I now am.

To get some understanding of the so-called 'well-paid for care' given to all the children at the Cottage homes under the strict control of the London Borough Council, see the 'Mapperton Case' at the old Bailey in Chapter 34.

Then in March of 1961, Mrs Cooper went on sick leave and the lovely Miss Anne was now in charge of us. Then Mr & Mrs Cooper and their daughter disappeared to another place or to their new 'playing fields'. Mr Cooper was a P.E teacher and was very strong and fit with his fists as I discussed earlier in this autobiography when I took a beating from him, with his fists of steel. I had sure been on the receiving end of them and so I was glad that the Cooper were gone, leaving Miss Anne in charge, but not for long. Replacing the Cooper, in 1961 were the incoming Uncle and Auntie: Mr & Mrs Jones. We were all told we had to call them Uncle & Auntie Jones. They brought with them their pet German Shepherd. I have absolutely no doubt that Mr & Mrs Jones were aware that the Cooper house master had left because of what he had done to me. I found the Jones's very strange and to make things worse I couldn't understand what they were saying half the time, they were both German. She had long blonde hair and some would call her a blonde beauty. She called him what sounded like Chitsu, strange as this was the name of the owner of the German shepherd dog that had attacked me (as I recount in chapter 39). The German shepherd, I think was called Sholts. Mr Jones had the dog always by his side when he had any of us into discipline. We sometimes wondered if he was going to set the dog on us and it became another thing we had to worry about. One day he called a few boys to see him, we had no idea why. One by one we went into his office. Whilst standing in front of him he pointed to the window. He had a 'dunkie', which I later found out was a condom, stuck but hanging from his windowsill. He was furious shouting and spitting as he constantly interrogated me.

I very nervously stood my ground and told the truth: "I didn't do it". I didn't even know what it was or what was inside it. He threatened to set his dog on me if I didn't own up. I kept giving the same answer and seeing the dog starting to become restless, I was shaking in my shoes. He eventually let me go. I later heard the older boys talking about having their way with his wife and bragging to one another. I didn't know at the time what they meant but we kept our mouths shut. I was so naïve. I got a real good belting one day for putting a pad with loops on each end of it across my mouth looping it on each ear and running around whilst playing cowboys and Indians with Harris. Miss Spooner saw me, and all hell let loose. She sent me to Jones' office and afterwards my backside was so sore I couldn't sit down for a few days. I was beginning to feel as though I couldn't stand the orphanage anymore, and I desperately wanted to leave to the point of feeling ill each day.

Both she and Uncle and Auntie Jones drank plenty of Dubonnet and he liked to be seen as a good house father. It was a betrayal. He brought with him his old, black, four-door car so all of us big boys and girls could have a go in it. We got to go up and down the drive, then he would let us take it to bits and put it back together. I got as far as taking the spark plugs out to clean them and then put them back, then I took the distributor cap off and noticed the four-cylinders and pistons petrol engine. Eventually, the car was impossible to drive so he told us to dig a big hole in the ground at the air raid shelter and push the car into the hole and cover it with soil and turf. We kept it as our new underground den, it was cool to go into in summer but got very wet on bad days. Whatever happened to this car after I left, I don't know. Some of the readers of this book from Milton will remember this old car and will remember Uncle and Auntie Jones. I got to leave Milton at fifteen and a half and didn't want to ever return as I could not take to Mr & Mrs Jones or their dog which was his pride and joy, far more than us orphans or his so-called blonde, beautiful wife. We got to know a few of the first names of our house parents, like Uncle Jack Percival, but we were forced to call them Auntie and Uncle. Even from them talking to each other as husband and wife, we never got to know their first names, except Uncle Jack Percival who would burn us with his cigarettes etc. Harris and I used to go and hide or escape for as long as we could, then climb up the fire escape to get back in. It helped to keep us out of arm's-length of the abusers and escape another night of abuse.

I am, at this time of writing with my pen, still too ashamed to pass the papers over for Anita to type out this ugly information into our computer. I know only too well how people think at my age. To write this true story is a very difficult area for me to talk about. I hope by the time this book is published I will be gone. I am not in good health whilst writing this true story, I know my family members will talk and will no doubt have sorrow in their thoughts for me. Should I still be alive I will undoubtedly feel shame and aching sadness. All those who get to read this should know how painfully difficult it has been for me and so many others who have kept their past horrors to themselves coming from Hornchurch, some far worse than mine. I just hope I can manage the final years or months of my life and after this story is told to be with my family and my friends without any words of this passing between us. As some of this has never ever left my thoughts or lips for the seventy-eight long years save for only one person. I have only ever told my very good friend Tommy and then when I was in my mid-seventies and he mid-eighties.

The years roll on and I receive my letter from the Metropolitan police in 1998. I am in an impossible position at this point of my life as I was being forced to go through yet another unbelievable experience with police involvement and most horrendous and false allegations against me, which are told later in the book, and I apologize to any of those that became victims of Mr Berry on his green bus etc. of which I am sure there were many. I believe the evidence that I could not give at this time would have assisted at the old Bailey trial, until that is, I later discover that the police lost the most important, damning evidence. Their records and all the tape recordings of the interviews of those who escaped their punishments were lost by the police and if I had assisted my evidence would have been lost. So, I now provide this evidence in this true autobiography. Had my evidence been provided, those found guilty like Mr Berry would argue that they are frail or too sick to receive time in prison and ought to be let free just like those that were found guilty in the Mapperton case.

Regardless of this 'many years too late' trial with all the evidence heard and lost, in October 2001 none of this put a stop to the abuse in Hornchurch. Outsiders were eventually allowed to enter after gathering in pubs. Making their way to the fire escape then entering up into Milton, they took their pick and abused many. When I was at Hornchurch there was a limit to who could come in and who could go out. It's strange for me to think of going out on the fire escape to sit in all weathers in silence, feeling it was my safe place to be. Then to learn later it was used as a stairway for an open house for abuse.

There seems to be no escape from this dreadful act in life and there never will be. I was in horror whilst living in Rochdale to learn about Cyril Smith and Sir Jimmy Saville, with all those at Rochdale council who simply looked the other way, even after Sir Cyril's death. They placed in Cyril Smith's honour a blue plaque above the town hall entrance! The book 'Smile for the Camera' which was exactly what we Cottage Homes orphans were told to do each time we were photographed. Falsely giving the impression that we were happy. Just look at the front cover of this book and find any trace of a smile on my face! This photo was taken after the incident of the driver on the green bus and Mr Berry still in the pay of the L.C.C., driving it.

I also very fondly remember the most beautiful, sweet voice of one of the cottage homer girls singing the song, 'The Shoemaker's Shop'. I later found out it was a song sung by Petula Clarke and I play it now at my home, telling all who listen the story behind the song. I recall, sadly, that of this poor little beautiful girl who was snatched in the dark one evening after her singing lessons near the church. She had been pulled into the bushes where she was then molested and raped. This is all I can remember of what was said of the incident. At that time, I would have been eleven or twelve around about 1957-8. I had kept my own experiences hidden and I could just imagine a small piece of what she must have gone through, except her ordeal was well known. Who did it, if he was caught, I do not know but I remember every time we would pass any bushes thinking, 'Could there be anyone hiding in them' and 'What she must have gone through?' So, in the dark we would always keep a watch out for any movement in the bushes when we were going up and down the drive, me being more paranoid than ever. I often wanted to tell my sister Sally as Eileen had gone, being older, Eileen had found foster parents, Mr & Mrs Driver. I could only hope she was finding life happier wherever she had been taken. I would look at my brother and long to tell him but having to go back to the orphanage after seeing him gave me a sense of shame, disgust and terrible fear. I felt it was better to not say anything at all.

I had a few fond memories of people around Hornchurch. I can recall there was Ron in the stores. Ron would deal with all the food and groceries, and he also helped Mr O'Connor do the fire drill, pulling the truck up and down the drive and connecting the hoses up to the red fire hydrants outside every other cottage. I am sure that the fire truck will be kept now in a museum somewhere with the white statue situated above the church entrance.

The fire truck was kept in a small purpose-built brick building at the entrance into the yard where the big green bus was kept safe. I vividly remember the nice smell that came from the cobbler's hot glue and the sound: tap, tap, tap of him putting studs into the shoes. Then there was the swimming pool behind Ron's store filled with cold water. I don't remember it ever being warm or clean. But I did learn to swim after being deliberately thrown in at the deep end many times, leaving me with no choice but to learn to swim and learn fast, just to get out of the cold water.

Of all the workers coming and going, Mr O'Connor was the nice and friendly one. Ron, I had no problem with, he was just a bit stricter. On two of my re-visits, I would meet up with Mr O'Connor and he took me and my daughter, showing us around, but the best of my visits was when I drove off Hornchurch Road into the drive and drove down and parked my brand-new car near to Milton, seen in a photo in this book. I went over and talked with Mr O'Connor. We were both happy to see one another. It was great to see him standing there after all those years. He certainly remembered me and was standing where the fire truck building is behind us. Then seeing children coming over quizzing us to find out who we were. I told them that I had also been one of them and Mr O'Connor remembered me and my two sisters well. It did not take much to convince them that I had been one of them. They were all looking at my nice new car parked up on the other side of the drive. I walked over and brought out sweets that I had purposely bought for this visit, but far more than was ever brought by any leavers re-visiting whilst I was there. The congregation of children followed us everywhere and I felt so proud, but I was so sad when I drove away waving to them with only my daughter in the car with me. So, to those reading this book who were also abused in the orphanage and on that big green bus, I am so sorry.

On the 14th of September 1998 the police contacted me. Certain things that were going on in my life at that time made it impossible for me to come forward with evidence. I knew this would bring visits to my home by the Met police in their Mapperton case and I could not go along with this. For that I am so truly, truly sorry and most importantly to Harris and his two sisters Jasmine and Maureen. I may not have recalled their names correctly, but should they read this, my sincere love goes out to you both and your families.

So, turning again back to the Carry-On films. So much of what I had seen of these various films is in my mind, the actors representing all those well-paid L.C.C. abusers who 'cared' for us through our most painful years of abuse. The work on the campsite with Barbara Windsor and the similar big bus in front of her will never leave my memories bringing nothing but sadness that she could never be anything like Miss Anne Jackson. Miss Anne did not need to act her part in looking after us Cottage Homer children. Miss Anne was beautiful throughout our journey, in every way possible.

Many years later whilst working at the Cunard building with the telephonist taking interest in why I wanted the telephone book, I went through all the names ending with Jackson and telephoned all the names I could, asking "If miss Anne Jackson was known to them, who had worked at the Hornchurch orphanage." Then unbelievably came an answer "Yes" I am Miss Anne's father, after telling him I was one of the children she had looked after. He most sadly told me she had been in a road accident and had been killed. I told him I was very sorry to hear about this, but he told me it was so very nice to be hearing from one of the children she had looked after. I told him how we all loved her, and we talked for a while.

CHAPTER 6: L.C.C Welfare Officers' Reports

Having now seen these reports for my two sisters and me, I see just how the L.C.C. has employed the services of so-called welfare officers who were basically anyone. They had no training in the field of the work they were doing, nor had they any qualifications. They would visit us after they had spoken to our house parents so that the reports would reflect what they said not the children. Their written, fabricated lies were from those who were dishing out their daily punishments. For example: on the 20th of June 1960 the welfare officer says 'It is extremely difficult to find out any of Peter's feelings when talking to him. Peter was spending most of his time in the kitchen and as a result was getting fat'.

The truth is, it was a job I was forced into doing which was to work in the kitchen, keeping the aga topped up and peeling the spuds, going outside and bringing in the anthracite coal for the aga. I was only 12-14 years old and working in the kitchen, so I was able to sneak out food.

On the same day the welfare officer visited my sister Sally. Sally said she wanted to leave Hornchurch at once but had no idea where she could go or what she would do. She said Hornchurch was a prison and she hated the place and did not join in any activities.

Then on the 1st of November 1960, the officer said Mr and Mrs Cooper were away on leave and Peter opened out a little more and was more communicative after Mrs Cooper had not had the opportunity to discuss him with me first. She continued to say, "When the Cooper returns Peter was very defiant, he had done nothing wrong". Mr Cooper was infuriated and was going to beat Peter, but he stood up suddenly and got one in the eye. The result was a nasty black eye for Peter.

This did not come to light until Sally reported to the superintendent that Peter was locked up in the dormitory. Mr Burgess, superintendent, was on holiday at the time so, in his absence an official enquiry was held, the result was that Mr Cooper was reprimanded, but no more. 'He is a school master and finds it very hard to change his attitude in the cottage.' (I said it was very interesting because it clearly showed that for all the abuse, we were suffering at the hands of those so-called child-care professionals, they did nothing!)

Throughout the years Mr Cooper, similar to Percival, was on full pay as a school master with his wife and they were on full pay from the L.C.C., as the heads in charge of Milton, where they both lived and ate free along with their daughter Clare. Within their well-kept and heated living accommodation situated in the middle of Milton, they had their own toilet which was out of bounds to all of us orphans. So, whilst they lived and slept in the warmth and comfort in their own accommodation, provided free by the L.C.C., we orphans shivered in our freezing cold dormitories. In my latter years there were some electric storage radiators under the very large windows, but they were useless. We huddled round them to get some warmth, but only in the day room.

On the 28th August 1959, Cooper said that I broke into their bedroom and after I had opened all their drawers, managed to get full details of their salaries and personal affairs. This was obviously untrue as I was illiterate in 1959. He went on to say I had broken a billiard cue recently and the house parents stopped my pocket money to pay for this and I maintained that this was unfair (it was completely untrue).

In 1959, I was thirteen years old. Mr Cooper had beaten the hell out of me over two billiard cues, it was never possible for me to have broken into his room or they would have had to repair the damage I was alleged to have caused. At that time, I could not read, write, or add up to even understand their salaries and personal affairs. It was utterly ridiculous for this so-called welfare officer to put her pen on paper in her report, without taking this matter up with her seniors, about the obvious child abuse that was taking place, involving the deputy superintendent.

Then I read her words, she wrote: 'So, the whole situation in Milton cottage is not very happy. At present Peter and another boy were found in the same bed one night. Mr Sanderson, deputy superintendent was called in and he gave them a thorough ticking off and this has been dealt with for the moment by putting Peter's bed near the dormitory door.' (I say, this again is also very interesting because these are the words that have come from those that have abused us, but there is no mention of the name of the other boy found supposedly in my bed, supposedly with me because it simply didn't happen).

Throughout my time at Milton there were ten boys in each dormitory with only a chair between the gaps of our beds and a small wooden cabinet for our clothes to be put in. There were never any times that boys shared a bed, or the other eight boys would see and tell all and ridicule us for being queer. This L.C.C children's department officers' report is 99% untruthful, fabricated and has been very costly for the untrustworthy officers, untrained in detecting the brutality and sexual torture of those in the pay of the L.C.C.

I also notice in the reports that this welfare officer refers to taking me out for lunch to have our meetings, but I never did go out to any free lunch. How would I have got there and how would I have got back? To my knowledge, she didn't drive to Milton because there was no car outside. I have no doubt whatsoever, with this being in her reports, she would have received in her pay the costs of such lunch! I have no doubt whatsoever she would have in fact gone to lunch with a friend obtaining a receipt and be re-paid, free of tax for this lunch on top of her pay, whilst carrying out her report, I presume, at her home. These reports are not worth the paper they are written upon, other than to have allowed the abusers to continue in their child sexual abuse, failing to protect us orphans until, thank

God, some many, many years later the evidence was proven at the Old Bailey in the Mapperton Case in Chapter 34.

Clearly, I had suffered intellectual disabilities in conditions regimented and institutionalised with physical abuse. We did during the time we spent at school suffer discrimination, so whenever anything ever went wrong or missing, we Cottage Homers were always blamed and caned.

There were no qualified social workers or welfare officers to turn to; we had to fend for ourselves as best we could and it was painful, especially in the playground. Now, when reading the written and typed reports held within the L.C.C. Archives during the time of our living in the Hornchurch Cottage Homes, I can understand why they seem to have conveniently changed the name to St. Leonard's. I believe this was to shift the legal responsibilities for all our abuse only partly referred to in the Mapperton case in Chapter 34. Clearly, the L.C.C were the legal owners, responsible for all the liabilities, maintaining and improving, with salaried paid staff, referred to in the report; where I supposedly had broken into the staff bedroom, finding the house parents' salary and private details. This was scurrilously and most shamefully untruthful and has never been challenged until now, as I am noting the true account in this autobiography.

CHAPTER 7: Religious foster parents

In the summer of 1961, Mr and Mrs Jones took over from the Coopers at Milton cottage. I became one of the many survivors of the most appalling abuse. I was discharged from the orphanage's care at Hornchurch in 1962, to my then foster parents, provided by London County Council. In my first home with foster parents, they were very religious, so much so that they kept their bibles close at hand and went to church regularly; on Sundays, it was 3-4 times per day. They often used to force me to go to worship. I remember one day I got a pair of my foster brother's pants and stapled his lining together inside each of the trouser legs. That's the only bit of fun I had. I knew I would never fit in there, yet on the report from the welfare officer dated 23rd March 1962 she falsely said, 'Peter appears to be happy; Peter appears to have made a sound relationship with his foster parents. Peter goes to church every Sunday with the Hendersons. Peter appears to be very well placed in this home'. This was far from the truth. I hated every minute of it. I also had the most serious disabilities in religious education at this age. I wanted to escape. I particularly dreaded Sundays.

The typed report by the welfare officer and her handwriting are how she wished to refer to the matters in her words, not mine. In fact, the final line saying: 'Before leaving I arranged to take Peter out for a meal' is untrue. It has never happened, and it says this on many of the documents. To suggest she would take me for a meal was ridiculous.

[illegible]
his door, as a result Peter fell off his vehicle. He was taken to St. Stephens hospital, found to have several superficial abrasions on his hands & a broken R/ wrist. I arranged to visit.

ABW.

10.10.63 Visited this evening on receiving information from St Stephens Hosp. that Peter was discharged. Peter described what happened, feels sure he is in the right. When asked for details of other vehicle he confessed he hadn't the name or number nor could he say what street the accident occurred in. I then asked if he had made a statement to the Police & he said he was doing this tomorrow. He also said his brother Bill was dealing with the Insurance Company about damage to the "bike". Bill is apparently familiar with procedure and wants to handle the business. Mrs Penhearow is looking after Pete, he has his hand in plaster and says it is 'not very painful'. Arranged Peter should see the doctor tomorrow & that later he should send a medical certificate. I told Mrs Penhearow if Peter was not to receive wages she was to send the certificates during the period of Peter's incapacity & we would pay full subsistence.

[illegible]eter ROSS

OFFICERS' REPORTS | Page No.

3.11.63 Visited foster home today, Sunday, and was very surprised to see the condition of the motor cycle. There was obviously an oil leak and many parts of the cycle was rusty, the v.p.c. on the seat was torn and altogether it looked a wreck to me and I did not hesitate to tell Peter what I thought about it. Peter said that it was a bargain at £40 and that he had paid £5 as an initial payment, that the previous owner made an arrangement to accept a £1 a week until it was cleared. I told him that I thought he should hand it back and save his money, and even if he could not get his original deposit back, he should regard it as good experience, with even the loss of the £5. Peter did not like this at all and still maintained that he wanted to keep it. I then reminded him that he would have to be responsible for the payments himself and that he was to ensure that he did not use the motor-cycle as he is not yet entitled to ride it. I said that by law, in view of the H.P. of the motor-cycle, that he could not even take it out on the road until after his 18th birthday. I later saw Mr. Penhearow and told him what we had discussed. He was absolutely in agreement and was very grateful that Peter was spoken to on these lines. I left it that as the deposit was Peter's own money, and he is earning, that it would be up to Peter to decide whether to return the cycle or keep it and waste his money. I felt at that point that Peter was not in any mood to be persuaded.

Before leaving I arranged to take Peter out for a meal at the end of the week.

AC/ACO
116

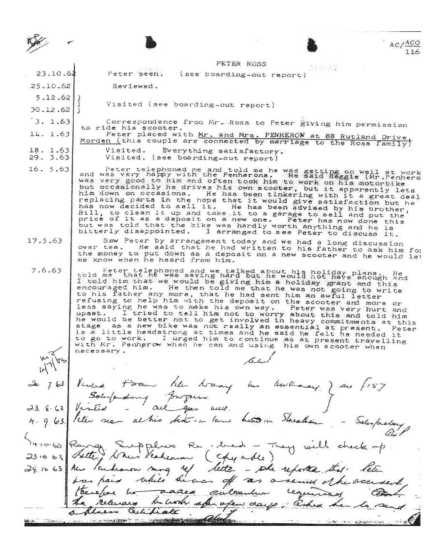

PETER ROSS

23.10.62	Peter seen. (see boarding-out report)
25.10.62	Reviewed.
5.12.62) 30.12.62)	Visited (see boarding-out report)
3. 1.63	Correspondence from Mr. Ross to Peter giving him permission to ride his scooter.
14. 1.63	Peter placed with Mr. and Mrs. PENHERON at 88 Rutland Drive, Morden (this couple are connected by marriage to the Ross family)
18. 1.63	Visited. Everything satisfactory.
29. 3.63	Visited. (see boarding-out report)
16. 5.63	Peter telephoned me and told me he was getting on well at work and was very happy with the Penherons. He said Reggie (Mr. Penhero was very good to him and often took him to work on his motorbike but occasionally he drives his own scooter, but it apparently lets him down on occasions. He has been tinkering with it a great deal replacing parts in the hope that it would give satisfaction but he has now decided to sell it. He has been advised by his brother, Bill, to clean it up and take it to a garage to sell and put the price of it as a deposit on a new one. Peter has now done this but was told that the bike was hardly worth anything and he is bitterly disappointed. I arranged to see Peter to discuss it.
17.5.63	Saw Peter by arrangement today and we had a long discussion over tea. He said that he had written to his father to ask him for the money to put down as a deposit on a new scooter and he would let me know when he heard from him.
7.6.63	Peter telephoned and we talked about his holiday plans. He told me that he was saving hard but he would not have enough and I told him that we would be giving him a holiday grant and this encouraged him. He then told me that he was not going to write to his father any more, that he had sent him an awful letter refusing to help him with the deposit on the scooter and more or less saying he was to make his own way. Peter was very hurt and upset. I tried to tell him not to worry about this and told him he would be better not to get involved in heavy commitments at this stage as a new bike was not really an essential at present. Peter is a little headstrong at times and he said he felt he needed it to go to work. I urged him to continue as at present travelling with Mr. Penherow when he can and using his own scooter when necessary.

After a short time with the Hendersons, I was so unhappy I ran away to live for a short stay with my eldest brother, who was in my eyes, my only lifeline.

He let me stay at his home and it felt fantastic for me to have a proper feeling of a loving home life with the comforts of a comfy bed and carpet under my feet and he found me my first job. With no education and unable to read or write or understand anything other than to escape abuse, I was doing any jobs I was told to do. I was more than happy doing them even though I was behind with my grammar. At the end of each week for my work I received a pay packet, seeing for the first time a one-pound note with a ten-shilling note and some coins being the extent of my pay. What a wonderful feeling that was. Then my brother, shortly after, took me to see his wife's brother to do some work for him.

His name was Reg Penhearow, and he was married with two young children, Sally and Steven. He suggested getting me a job as his apprentice where he worked which was Gratt Brothers, and he did. Whilst working with Reg and still living at my brother's, I travelled on the back of his motorcycle back to his home and I helped him to work on his house.

One night whilst we had been busy working away it had got to 9:00 pm and Betty said to Reg, "Why don't you let him stay over? There is a camp bed in the small back room if he doesn't mind sleeping in there".

I obviously did not refuse so I stayed and was up bright and early Sunday morning to finish off the job with Reg. The only problem was I didn't want the job to finish. I was feeling quite sad at the thought of leaving and later in the day I stood outside having a drink and I really didn't want to leave. I noticed the garden needed doing and I went to Betty and asked her if she would like me to stay and do all her garden for her. She was very happy with the idea; I worked hard for her and made the garden neat and tidy, and I even painted the fence.

I played some games with Sally, and she liked having me around. I made her giggle a lot and Steven the baby was contented when he was with me.

Whilst I was having dinner with Betty, she told me she and Reg had been talking and wondered if I would like to stay with them permanently and become a proper part of the family. She also explained to me that they would have to make arrangements with the orphanage and have me legally removed from their so-called 'care'. I panicked for a moment because I thought I would have to go back in there until it was all sorted.

Betty wondered why I looked so shocked and sad, so I asked her if I would have to go back there and, to my greatest relief, I was made happy and content with the single word "No".

She also told me, "We won't let them take you back. We will fight to keep you if we have to".

What a wonderful moment that was. I will never forget it! I could see the warmth in her smile as she spoke and looked at me.

I just sat looking at this beautiful, blonde, kind and loving lady sitting in front of me speaking the words "We will keep you safe here with us".

I believed every word she said to me. I knew I could trust her, and Reg and I were ecstatic. I walked around the house and I felt like I was in heaven with the feeling of knowing this was going to be my little family and my first new home with lush carpets, curtains, an indoor bathroom, hot water, and central heating, all the home comforts which at one point in my life I didn't even know existed and it was full of love.

I was there and stayed there. I had no worries about packing anything because I had nothing to pack. The only things I had were the clothes I was standing in. Betty and Reg soon made all the necessary legal arrangements to take over legal guardianship and I didn't need to take one step back into the orphanage. Fantastic!

My brother said he was happy for me, knowing that I had been heartbroken thinking I was soon going to have to go back to the orphanage, possibly until I reached 18 years old.

Bill was thrilled for me to live with Reg and Betty. I couldn't stay with my brother and his family; they couldn't really accommodate me. It was soon time for Reg and Betty to sign all the papers and I became a new member of the Penhearow family. Some weekends I would go and see my brother Bill and help him as well. I didn't mind doing anything for all of them, nothing was too much trouble.

This lovely family Penhearows had to take over parental responsibility for me, so they signed on the second of April 1962 after I had been living with my foster parents for some time. I saw their name at the top of a document with their signature at the bottom and was told that the council was loaning my foster parents: one single bed, one mattress, one pillow, 2 pillowcases, one blanket and 2 sheets. This was only provided because I had been sleeping on their camp bed. I was a proud and happy young fellow. Little did I know my real lessons in life were just beginning. Lessons with many great memories that no school can ever give.

Shortly after, Reg came and took me to where he worked, 'Gratt Brothers Electricians', and he had arranged for me to see his boss, a man called Mr Bill Etherington, and one of the Gratt brothers. They were aware I was illiterate, but they gave me a trial and took me on, starting on a probation period of two weeks which I did and sailed through, and I enjoyed it. I was feeling happy and eager and soon learnt from those who were kind enough to give me extra attention. I picked up things fairly quickly as a result of their patience and I was gaining confidence.

115

PETER ROSS

23.10.62	Peter seen. (see boarding-out report)
25.10.62	Reviewed.
5.12.62) 30.12.62)	Visited (see boarding-out report)
3. 1.63	Correspondence from Mr. Ross to Peter giving him permission to ride his scooter.
14. 1.63	Peter placed with Mr. and Mrs. PENHERON at 86 Rutland Drive, Morden (this couple are connected by marriage to the Ross family)
18. 1.63	Visited. Everything satisfactory.
29. 3.63	Visited. (see boarding-out report)
16. 5.63	Peter telephoned me and told me he was getting on well at work and was very happy with the Penherons. He said Reggie (Mr.Penheron was very good to him and often took him to work on his motorbike but occasionally he drives his own scooter, but it apparently lets him down on occasions. He has been tinkering with it a great deal, replacing parts in the hope that it would give satisfaction but he has now decided to sell it. He has been advised by his brother, Bill, to clean it up and take it to a garage to sell and put the price of it as a deposit on a new one. Peter has now done this but was told that the bike was hardly worth anything and he is bitterly disappointed. I arranged to see Peter to discuss it.

The nine entries above in the L.C.C. report appear to show great work and concerns in relation to my welfare and my foster parents. I know nothing whatsoever of the two visits or phone calls and neither do my foster parents. In 1963 the report shows how dedicated this officer was that she does not even spell the name of my foster family correctly. The report says I telephoned her. This is blatantly untrue as at that age I would not know how to phone anyone, let alone have her phone number. I leave you readers to work this lie out.

CHAPTER 8: My first job as an apprentice at Gatwick airport

Each morning I am now taken by my foster father, proudly sitting on the back of his motorbike, to Gatwick airport serving my apprenticeship with him as a foreman. He would take me to every job he was working on then back home to his wife, my now foster mother. Gatwick airport was on the A27, long before the fast motorway that is there today. At the time the Gatwick train station was and is the only train station connected to the airport terminal. So, from leaving the Hornchurch orphanage I was experiencing the fast-moving traffic around me and aeroplanes flying off all over the world and I'm finding it all awe-inspiring to take in but staying close and doing all I was told and taught by my foster father and foremen.

Whilst travelling each day to Gatwick, sometimes on my scooter, I noticed the A27 sign to Brighton. I wasn't aware it was a seaside resort until in the summer I noticed loads and loads of motorcycles racing past, then loads and loads of scooters. I discovered they were called 'Mods and Rockers' from my other co-apprentices working at Gatwick. They said it was a meeting-up place where all the Mods & Rockers showed off their bikes and scooters. I decided out of curiosity to join and follow them to Brighton. This was my first-time passing Gatwick, where I had felt safe riding the bike from my foster parents to Gatwick to work and back. Now I am going on my own and well out of my comfort zone, (again I feel an odd ball amongst the pack of Mods & Rockers) I am not dressed in full leathers I don't even have a motorcycle helmet on.

When I arrive at Brighton, I see all around me those on posh bikes with crash helmets and leathers with 'Hells Angels' all over and scooters with masses of lights and mirrors, bristling in the sun and reflecting off the mass of chromium plated exhaust pipes and handlebars and here I am with a basic motorbike, a Panther 250. It was all the world to me after my old

Vesper GL2 that hardly ever went above 40mph. At least my Panther would do 100mph, but the best I ever did reach was 80mph. I was scared of going any faster and this was only when

the roads were clear and on sunny days. Having a crash helmet on wasn't compulsory in those days. I did come off a few times and to this day I still wear the scars with very fond memories that I have passed on to my son.

A photo I have cherished and kept safe all these difficult 59 years since I was 16 with the Mods and Rockers in Brighton. The photo is unique in that it is from the time photos from a machine on the Palace Pier took 15-30 minutes to develop, long before the instant photo booths people use today for passport/licence proof. Sadly, in 1975 the pier was deemed unsafe for public use and shut down. In 2003 the pier was set on fire, and I believe it was sold for £1.

Today the remains are as seen in the photo with me lying on the beach with the red bucket containing a gift I specially made and took down to Brighton for my sister Eileen, which can be seen on the very last page.

On the job at Gatwick, I was close up to all the aeroplanes flying in and out at all times, magical it was. We worked on the runway lighting, and I took great interest in all the rabbits running all over the place with the loud noises of the aeroplanes landing and taking off with dust and grit flying all over, it was fantastic. Then whilst working on the overhead lighting inside the airport terminal up high on the scaffolding, I would listen to my brand new transistor radio that was given to me by Betty's brother. He was called Siddy and I was happily working away. There were a lot of activities going on around me and to my surprise there was some filming taking place which I found myself working quite near to. There were also, passing by me, all the pretty airhostesses and pilots each pulling their bags in their immaculate uniforms. This was the first time I had ever come close to so many pretty young girl stewardesses and pilots.

Gratt brothers had a large shed. It was an electrical store for all our requirements, and it was situated away from the main airport terminal in a field going towards the area of East Grinsted. There were many Dakota aeroplanes and aircraft hangers with old DC3 Dakotas and C47s with Douglas Airways on them and C47 Dakotas. I noticed lots of workmen coming and going in army jeeps, pulling trailers with aero engines and much other, I just did not understand why there was a lot of hustle and bustle. My curiosity set in, and I went to have a look around. I was eventually met by one of the workers. He asked what I wanted, and I explained I was working with Gratts electrical in the airport terminal. He obviously noticed I was young and innocent and of no risk to him. He could see Gratts electrical sign was clearly on the outside of the store shed, which I loved going over to because of the man who worked in the stores. He went by the name of Lardy. Every time I visited the store, he would always have his record player playing Jim Reeves songs. I got to know the Jim Reeves songs and I would sing them to myself thanks to him. As the years passed, I purchased these records and I still play them to remember this time on my Revox system with such sound quality and every time I listen to them, I am back at Gatwick with Lardy.

The workman who had approached me then showed me around. He was working on a BAC 111 airplane. I followed him up the ladder into this massive plane, never did I ever expect this. My memory took me back to the Hornchurch Orphanage where I saw planes coming and going and barrage balloons with men jumping out and parachuting down to the ground. Now here I am, 16 going on 17, in this massive aeroplane, being left to look in at the pilot's seat. I am sitting in it looking out at the sky and I am in total disbelief of where I was sitting. I then went all the way to the back of the plane which was massive to me at that time. Then my mind goes on to the experience I had gone through on the Big Green Dennis school bus except I am older and wiser and would fight back like hell. The man was simply having a cigarette and I could smell in the air the sweet smell of aviation fuel and hearing engines roaring and it didn't seem to matter.

This nice man who let me look around the plane was stood enjoying his cigarette. I then climbed back down the ladder thanking the man with a big smile for allowing me to spend my ill-gotten time looking around all these wonderful sights around me. I had to get back to the job I was working on, and I immediately went to Gratts stores to get the items booked out that I needed. I got back to the job I was doing, working on the cabling up above in the false ceiling.

I would spend many hours working unsupervised, so I wasn't missed on my escapade looking at all the aeroplanes. Then Reg or another of the electricians would see me at dinner break and see that all was well, and they would continue as normal. From time to time, my work would be inspected by Reg or another electrician then Reg would take me on to another part of the job.

Throughout all the time I worked there, I never had any safety hat on as it was not a requirement in those days. So, I was young with longish hair and had good looks and I could sing all the songs that were in the hit parade and many of Jim Reeves's songs. A lot would hear me, and they would listen intently to my lovely voice. Then when I went home with Reg, I noticed that the BAC 111 that I had been looking around had been taxied round to the position near where I was working, which continues in Chapter 9. My days working at Gatwick were much better than ever going to Disneyland but on top of this I was also getting paid travelling expenses without any tax. So, all in all I was getting paid for having the best fun ever with rides on the back of Reg's motorbike or me riding my scooter, having the time of my life.

One of my jobs whilst working as an apprentice was to make tea, coffee, and anything else the electricians wanted, even going out to get cakes and lunch. Each week us apprentice lads would take turns to get the morning tea, dinner, and afternoon tea. Everyone made a payment to the tea boy, and he made the money meet the requirements being careful to make a small profit.

However, my food was always with Reg because all the others were unaware I was his foster son and that I lived with him. Some of them were not happy with my relationship with the foreman, especially when they saw me arriving and leaving work on the back of his motorbike. Then, whilst others were on the tea boy job, I would like 3 spoons of sugar in my tea, meaning that I would eat into their sugar supply. The simple need for sweet tea was what eventually led to my fist fight.

I was working away and happily singing when the tea boy came over and hit me. I could not understand why he did this and said nothing. He told me to come and fight him, referring to me as foreman's good boy and hit me again until I could take no more. I grabbed hold of him and pulled him down to the floor, holding him by the neck and putting my weight on his body, pleading him to stop. He continued to punch me, mainly in my ribs. I held him, squeezing his neck until he was frothing at the mouth and gasping and when he stopped thumping me, I got up and walked away from him. He then got up and walked away from me and we got on with our work. I said nothing to Reg.

At dinner time, we all met up and nothing was said. It was as if nothing had happened. From then on, we appeared to get on together. I did my turns like the rest of us and made a profit, not counting how many spoons of sugar everyone put in their tea. Tea boy week was a good way to earn money and enabled us to go to the cakeshop instead of working.

CHAPTER 9: Meeting Sophia Lauren & Gregory Peck

Whilst working away at Gatwick I loved singing my head off to all the Beatles songs, that I still sing to this day, playing on the radio from the pirate radio station, which in those days was stationed out at sea. The DJ, Tony Blackburn, played for the first time the song '*As tears go by*' by Marianne Faithful. I fell in love with the song and would sing my heart out to it when I was busy working away. I still sing these songs to this day. One day I heard a voice calling up to me and on looking down I noticed this most beautiful lady and a very tall man stood by her side. They both had big smiles on their faces.

In disbelief I stopped what I was doing to say, very shyly, "Yes" to this beautiful lady with such lovely eyes, hair and face and a bright smile. My heart was melting, and my hands started shaking, my feelings were indescribable.

She shouts up to me saying "Can we please borrow your radio?" At this point I am feeling like being lifted into heaven, looking, and hearing the voice of an angel asking me for the loan of my radio. What an experience (Sophia Loren & Gregory Peck).

I very clumsily climbed down from the scaffold, not taking my eyes off her smiley eyes on me or Gregory Peck, though I had no idea who they were at the time. I reached for my radio and handed it over to Gregory Peck and he immediately turned the dial from the radio station to find the horse racing that I had been totally unaware of with no idea that it was the Derby horse racing day. I could hear they had got the horse racing channel on with my radio balanced on the shoulder and very close to Gregory Peck's ear with Sophia listening intently on the other side.

I then discovered they had both placed bets on the horses, and had it not been for my transistor radio they could not have listened to the race taking place.

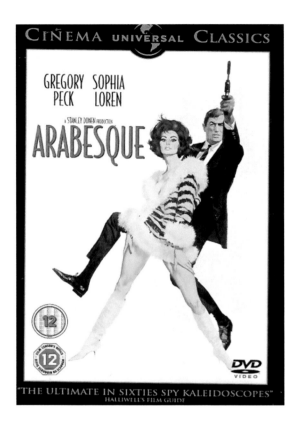

I had, for the first time in my life, awoken to the beauty of such a person calling me for my radio and had fallen madly head-over-heels in love with her in my mind. I left my radio with them and continued with my work. Sophia and Gregory had not long since arrived and I noticed all the vehicles parking up in the car park and taking over the airport section that I was working in. I also noticed that Sophia was with her family and makeup artist etc. staying overnight in a mobile home with all her family and some children, all speaking in Italian. I could watch them all through the windows of the airport terminal as I was above them.

This picture is how I remember Sophia in our meeting in 1962

When Sophia wasn't filming in the airport, Gregory was elsewhere. It was summertime and nice and hot and Sophia would be with her mother, lazing out in the sun or (lazing on a sunny afternoon as the song went). I would be working above, opposite, hearing all the loud talking and screaming in Italian. I hardly ever heard Sophia talking in English except when they would be filming. I was fortunate to be there at those times of filming.

My Foster Mother couldn't believe it when I went home and told her all about my experience of meeting Sophia Loren and she could see how smitten I was with her. She was smiling and happy for me, enjoying such exciting days, whilst I was working away. I had found out who Sophia and Gregory were. I don't know how I managed as a young man to keep my concentration on the work that I had just started to do. Working with electrics can be dangerous as I had experienced in the orphanage whilst preparing the potatoes, especially being up on a high level as I was.

Each day I would race to be up and back on the motorbike or on my scooter to get to work and be amongst all the activities with the full crew, but mostly Sophia, who had by this time accepted I was just a young working boy, smitten by her looks and when glancing over at me she would give me a smile. My transistor radio had been returned to me and I never knew if they had won or lost their bets. I couldn't and wouldn't dare approach them, I just was simply transfixed and mesmerised by the presence of such beauty. Thankfully the foreman was my foster father, so I was able to assist the Dan-Air staff and film crew by the sorting out of their cables and lighting. I was responsible for keeping things going until their departure.

One morning when I arrived at work, still riding on the back of Reggie's motorbike, we passed fire engines parked up just at the side of where Sophia was staying. I thought something had happened. All the firemen were there with their hosepipes and in full uniform and it was quite warm, and Sophia was still in her mobile home. Next, I see Sophia with Gregory and all the film crew. I was completely clueless about how important all this filming was until I saw how much time Gregory spent talking to them all.

They were all set up for filming with a mass of film extras having arrived. They were all dressed in raincoats and hats, and they even had umbrellas and it wasn't raining, in fact, it was summer and lovely. Then, when the filming started there were two lorries parked up. Sophia goes in the back of one hidden from view, Gregory stood with the film crew at this point and all the extras were pushed up in a bunch against the wall by the lorry parked up and they all had their umbrellas up. At that point, the fire crew, with their hoses pointing up into the air turned their hoses on. There was a complete sudden change in the weather and a complete downpour of rain. Gregory got into the back of the lorry finds Sophia and takes her out, covering her up in the pouring rain and rushing across and past all the extras who all had their umbrellas up. At this point I climbed down, and I squeezed in amongst them to watch Sophia being dragged by Gregory to an awaiting Dan-Air aeroplane that was ready to take off (but it didn't really take off) and this would be repeated on re-takes by the film crew. It was 1962/3 and I was 16 going on 20 in my mind, serving my apprenticeship and having the time of my life.

The following day the film crew were all packing up. Sophia and Gregory had gone; the mobile home was driving out of the car park, and everything had been cleaned up and was back to normal. I was disappointed to see them go, and I didn't get that one last smile or wave. But getting back on with my daily work routine, I knew I was lucky to have seen so much of a film crew with such a beautiful lady.

Many, many years have passed since this filming, and never did I know that these activities had led to a film I know now which is called Arabesque. The time with Sophia and Gregory at Gatwick had never left my thoughts and I am now over 74 years old. So now I tell the story to my family and in 2016, my son for my birthday investigated this film, found it, purchased it, and wrapped it up and gave it to me. See picture on previous page.

So, after 55 years I have the film that I had never known was out there to see and for the first time in 2020 I sat in my final home/resting place and put on the film to watch with my family after they have listened and learnt of all the tales I have told from my hard-working past. Of the boy with no hope, love, or kindness, until he met his foster parents who had lived all their lives in Morden in Surrey, not too far from Gatwick. I was very lucky and very thankful that my foster father was a foreman throughout his time in Gratt Brothers. He started off my apprenticeship with Gratts, paying my travelling expenses and travelling to work every day from Wicklow Street in Central

London. Tax was never deducted from my travelling expenses from my small apprenticeship wage. But then it never cost me anything to get to Gatwick and back because most times I was on the back of the foreman's motorbike having the experience of a lifetime. I loved my apprenticeship at Gatwick; I would have walked, ran, done anything to get there if it was only just to see Sophia.

One day word came around that Mick Jagger and the Rolling Stones were coming through. I rushed and ran to see them and so sadly when I got back to carry on working my radio had been taken and was never returned. However, I got to see them taking their flights in and out of Gatwick. There were many other famous people coming and going, too many to put in this story, but I knew it was the start of my journey in gaining all the experience that I have carried and used all my life. The airport today is nothing like it was in my days in the 60's when going on an aeroplane for a holiday was so expensive and not an experience for most. The first time on an aeroplane for many was with Dan-Air, it had the cheapest flights at that time. The air stewardesses were like watching a fashion parade between British Airways, Caledonian Airways and others. Then came the arrival of Laker Airways. Freddie Laker pushing everyone aside making the competition between them, pushing the prices down with holiday makers then pouring in, filling up the airport concourse that became so overcrowded and bringing about the many expansions to what it is today.

I enjoyed managing to learn and finish a job well done. When I was not working weekends and holidays, I would spend my time working with my foster father either in his home or on his motorbike or doing repairs on my own Vespa GL2 scooter, just to get around on it. It would only do about 40-60 mph, but it was my little bit of heaven and freedom. Betty used to sometimes climb on the back with me and I would take her down the road to the shops and back, great memories.

When my foster father went to work at Gratt Brothers HQ on Wicklow Street, London, he got a company car leaving me to get to the jobs he gave me on my own. After all, I was learning really well and Reg had confidence in me riding on my little Vespa GL2, but it wasn't anything like being on the back with Reg riding his motorbike. I missed the thrills of being on the back with him, he knew all the short cuts and was a skilled rider. Then one night he came home to talk to me about the Vespa not being safe or good enough for racing around London. Sometimes I rode Reg's motorbike, a 250cc Panther Twin which had a very fast 250cc Villiers engine. Unknown to Reg I had already been riding it all over the place whilst he was driving to the office in his car. Obviously, my foster mother would know I was taking his motorbike out on the road as you couldn't help but hear it and I was riding it without a licence or insurance. Thankfully it was taxed so I was never stopped by the Police! Reg said to me, "Peter I am aware that whilst I am working away at head office, you have been taking my motorbike out on the road". With my head bowed in shame having been sussed, he said with a smile on his face, and Betty's, "The bike is now yours!" Wow! A feeling I will never forget.

In those days it was not uncommon to not have a crash helmet on, so with my skills, I learnt from Reg I would enjoy riding fast with the air rushing through my face and hair, in the sun. This was a fantastic thrill except when hit by a lit discarded cigarette or a wasp or fly. Otherwise, my freedom of speed on the road was fantastic.

Each time I took his Panther 250cc bike it always had fuel in the tank otherwise I would not have taken it. The key Reg always left in the ignition in the locked garage at the bottom of the garden. So, I built up my skills and confidence and in doing so it led me to become the proud owner, thanks to Reg and Betty's love and kindness.

At the weekends when doing repairs with Reg on his motorbike, I was always watching and helping wherever I could. Reg would smoke Old Holborn tobacco, and when the tins were empty, he used them to hold all his screws and things. Each tin lid would have a label showing their contents all stacked in neat rows on his work bench. I watched him stripping the engine down and removing the clutch, which required a new one because of the speed he used to change gears with me on the back, loving every moment, I'd even enjoy the times we would come off in the winter snow. With oil all over his hands and fingers he couldn't roll up a cigarette, so I became an expert at it for him. I would open the tin lid, pull out a rizzler, put it in the palm of my hand then pinch and pull just the right amount of tobacco to go across the rizzler. Then very carefully I would roll it up, lick the sticky bit, turning the cigarette with my fingers, then pinch off each of the bits that were sticking out at each end and all times putting the bits back into the tin. Then I would put the cigarette in between my lips, strike a Swan Vesta match, put it to the cigarette, take one drag but never ever inhaled, then hand it over to Reg. I did try once but coughed my guts up. Whilst he was working, I'd roll up some spares and place them on top of the tobacco with the rizzler papers and close the lid.

In between all this, and me being Reg's basic oil rag/helper, there were times when he needed some parts in order to fix his bike or he wouldn't have been able to get us to work. He would give me a list of what he wanted, and some money then send me on my scooter to Pride and Clarks on Streatham High Street or sometimes Godfreys on Croydon High Street, to collect the parts. I knew where they were, having been there with Reg previously. I also had some reasonable idea of what he wanted. I would get the parts and return to see my smiley-faced foster father who, in those days, had no phone to check if I'd got there safely or got the right parts until my return. Despite having no real understanding of the motorbike parts, I did manage to get the right ones and he would take them and fit them. Then he'd let me kick over the engine on the kick start, which had quite some kick back, and it would start up. To me this was a great feeling. He was able to just do anything and make it work; he was unbelievably talented and made things I did not understand look easy.

So, working with him each day and watching him with great care accelerated my interest in all he was doing. It has made me what I am to this very day. One year whilst travelling to work on my own motorbike, Christmas was coming, and I was working for a short spell on electrics at a wine distillery. It was called Bluementhals near Battersea power station. I can still remember the smell of the wine and oak barrels and the dray horses and carts coming and going. It was a one-of-a-kind smell; it was a sweet and sour mixture that I loved working in, but never did I ever drink any. Somehow, I was scared of alcohol and still am to this very day, having seen in my childhood in the orphanage what dreadful effect it had on those 'caring' for us! Their fags and booze were far more important than us orphans.

At Christmas time, my foster mum and father would have family calling and Betty, my foster mother, liked the occasional drink of Drambuie. I managed to sneakily get a large, expensive bottle of Drambuie, after all I was doing a big job for little money. I was so thrilled carrying it back home for Betty. At Christmas I wrapped it up for her and put it under the Christmas tree along with a tin of Old Holborn tobacco for Reg, my foster father. The two purchases would have easily outstripped my two- or three-weeks, meagre apprentice wage.

I was now putting my own 2 stroke petrol into my motorbike to get to work and back. So, by the time I would pay Betty for my keep I had very little left! I watched Betty and Reg's faces intently when they opened their Christmas gifts, and we all had a good laugh and hugged each other. I shook Reg's hand, and I could feel such strength along with the gentleness and kindness he was giving me.

Throughout my time working with my foster father, I discovered that everything we worked on was copper. Copper was very valuable. We all called it 'Bluie' and each day working at my apprenticeship everything that I handled related to copper: copper wire, buzz bar, pyro and of course brass and lead, sometimes mercury which was difficult to tip into a bottle. At the end of each day the copper, brass, and lead would be collected and stored safely under the Foreman's lock and key, but I discovered that all the electricians would take some copper scrap ends, lead, and brass back home with them. My curiosity led to noticing the Gratts van calling and taking away all the scrap copper, brass, and lead. This of course was long before aluminium became a cheaper substitute and copper prices were so high, with the obvious scrap value being below silver and gold. The lead was too heavy but copper cable was plentiful. I did take advantage of as much as I could carry on Reg's motor bike whilst holding on to him as his pillion and when we came off in the snow and ice, I would quickly pick up the scrap then get back on. At Reg's garage I collected the lead, copper, and brass, then Reg would weigh this in at Christmas and this helped to pay for the Christmas party and drinks.

My much-loved foster parents

Betty and her son Steven

The photos above are some 48 years later. Notice the 1962 report, then please look into the eyes of my foster parents' faces and notice all their love and devotion. They have shared all their years together, bringing into this world their son and daughter and sharing so much of their lives with me and so much more as I have told in this story. Later you will read the letter that Steven wrote to me in 2021 which takes us to the time of this book and no doubt to the end of my days. See letter on final page of this book.

CHAPTER 10: Working weekends.

I aimed to keep some of my weekends free to be with my favourite brother. I was around 18 now and able to work at my brother's car repair business on Acacia Rd, Norbury. Just up the London Road, towards Thornton Heath, was Wates Building Services HQ. My brother would collect their executives' damaged cars and I would go with him. I am now a passenger with him, driving in the best made cars of those days and he was proud to show me how fast they would go from his garage up Green Lane.

My brother Bill in top of   picture working at his garage

Green Lane was close to my brother's home on St Oswald's Road. I learned a lot whilst working by his side. My brother knew all the police very well as his garage was just opposite the Norbury police station. In later years, during the 70s and 80s, on the other side of the road facing the police station, was a sex shop called Mary Millington's. The sex shop obviously brought a lot of custom, coming and going at all hours with cars and motor bikes blocking up the small access from

Norbury High Street into Acacia Road to his garage. See map of the whole area below.

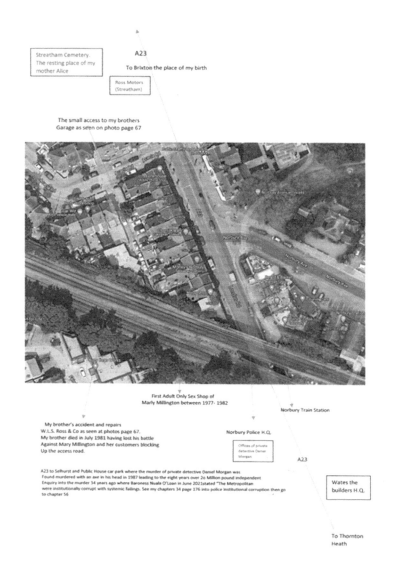

Streatham Cemetery.
The resting place of my
mother Alice

A23

To Brixton the place of my birth

Ross Motors
(Streatham)

The small access to my brothers
Garage as seen on photo page 67

First Adult Only Sex Shop of
Marly Millington between 1977- 1982

Norbury Train Station

My brother's accident and repairs
W.L.S. Ross & Co as seen at photos page 67.
My brother died in July 1981 having lost his battle
Against Mary Millington and her customers blocking
Up the access road.

Norbury Police H.Q.

Offices of private
detective Daniel
Morgan

A23

A23 to Selhurst and Public House car park where the murder of private detective Daniel Morgan was
Found murdered with an axe in his head in 1987 leading to the eight years over 2o Million pound independent
Enquiry into the murder 34 years ago where Baroness Nuala O'Loan in June 2021stated "The Metropolitan
were institutionally corrupt with systemic failings. See my chapters 34 page 176 into police institutional corruption then go
to chapter 56

Wates the
builders H.Q.

To Thornton
Heath

This caused much stress and aggravation for my brother because when Wates the builders executives would bring their cars for repairs, they could not get to his garage, highlighted in the photo attached, up the small access road because it was blocked with the cars that were accessing the front and back of the sex shop. My brother was obviously furious with Mary Millington and her partner's sex shop. He went to the police opposite to complain many times. The police noticed cars were parking up on the London Road, under the railway bridge at the front entrance and the back. So, there were many sad times for my brother to battle. The sex shop had taken over the area, making my brothers legitimate car business impossible. All this was my first experience with the adult sex trade along with the misery that it brought upon my brother and his workmen in his business which was called W.L.S Ross & Co Accident Repair specialists. The police were constantly visiting the sex shop as it was affecting the public who were going into the front entrance of their Norbury police headquarters. Little did I know my life was going to be full of problems much larger than this.

Years later came the murder of private detective, Daniel Morgan, who was found in a car park with an axe in his head in 1987, 34 years ago. This led to the longest ever police investigation taking over eight years. From my own experiences and personal investigation, I can entirely understand the feelings of those left of the Morgan family who have sought justice and the many millions of public funding into police corruption. This matter is still ongoing into police corruption in 2021, at further costs to public funds.

I had become so happy with my foster parents, and I felt loved and content, but I started to think about my mother, which surprised me because when I was in the orphanage for all those years I never did. I suppose it was because I never had a mother, as far as I knew, and therefore never thought of it. Living with Betty and Reg and seeing how wonderful a mother, Betty, was to Sally and Steven, made me think, and I asked Betty when I was sent to the orphanage. I knew that she would know because Betty and Reg would have seen all the documentation from the orphanage. She told me that I was four years old and surprisingly the same age her little boy was. On looking at Steven I started thinking of me being his age and going into the orphanage which made me wonder why. It was a strange and very sad feeling.

I started to think all sorts of things like 'I have a mother, everyone has a mother', yet I never thought of a mother being mine, ever! I think Betty must have felt the need to sit me down and have a heart-to-heart talk with me. I wanted to learn everything I could about my mother at this point. So, Betty told me with great difficulty that my mother had taken her own life and that was all she could tell me. She did say she was surprised my brother Bill hadn't told me because she believed he would know more. Maybe Betty knew but she wasn't saying it and I felt it best not to ask her. She had done enough and was being a brilliant foster mother to me and it must have been awkward enough for her. The next time I saw my brother Bill I chose what I felt was the right time and asked him. He wouldn't tell me any more than what Betty had told me so I didn't feel I could push it further. I was very confused and still didn't know what had happened. I was becoming more inquisitive. Then one day whilst I was at my brother's garage, he told me to jump in his car because he wanted to take me somewhere. He took me to Streatham and then slowing the car down, he drove past Streatham cemetery and just said to me, "Son, this is where your mother is, she is in there somewhere", and then took me back to the garage.

On our journey back, my brother Bill told me I have an uncle, my mother's brother, who lives up north. and the fact that his name was my middle name. Also, my grandson's name being my middle name and that of my mother's bother. (See my fascinating discoveries at Chapter 27.) He rode an RAC motorbike and sidecar and worked for the RAC up north somewhere, but no other details. I put that in the back of my mind and felt a bit more content. But I knew I was going to have to one day find this uncle of mine, especially with him being my mother's brother and the fact his name was my middle name. See my fascinating discoveries in chapter 27.

CHAPTER 11: Entering my five-year apprenticeship with Gratts.

So, it was on the 3rd of December 1962 when I entered a full, five-year apprenticeship with Gratt Brothers. I felt so happy and proud, and, for the first time, I felt a proper feeling of being a part of something good. I was also holding a certificate for my apprenticeship.

My first wage packet came. It was £3, 11 shillings and 6 pence.

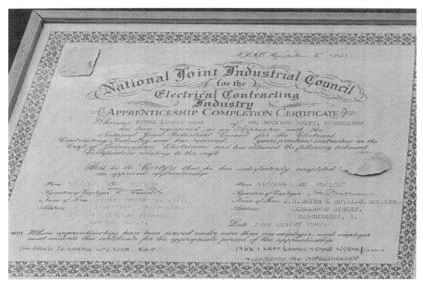

My apprenticeship eventually took me up north where I was told my uncle was, but I had to concentrate on getting to the end of my apprenticeship. I kept focused and determined.

I left the big job at Gatwick Airport to work for a time at London's Heathrow Airport. Again, I would travel on the back of my foster father's motor bike, but this experience was nothing like Gatwick, in fact I did not like it at all. It was more or less the same kind of work and learning but I suppose no airport would be the same after the experience I had with Sophia.

I was eventually glad my foster father moved on to another contract and I with him. This would be at Woolworths on Kensington High Street next to Kensington Palace. Whilst working at Woolworths there was a girl who I had never seen. It was my singing that brought her attention to me, all the time I was working, I was singing. The timber wall separating those that were working for Woolworths and me eventually came down and I carried on singing whilst working, so this girl came over to me and we arranged to meet up. A date was made, and I walked to where she was staying.

She told me she was staying in a bedsit in Earl's Court with a boyfriend, but she was originally from Manchester. I did not have a clue where Manchester was. Having got to know her briefly we started a relationship, she became my very first girlfriend. I had no experience of girls before, even though there were girls in the orphanage, but there were never any intimate moments; we were like brothers and sisters, one big family. What was even worse was that we were never taught about birds and bees, and I was clueless. I remember getting a hard smack around the head for putting a pad with looped strings at both ends on over my face and looping it onto each ear and using it as a mask, playing cowboys and Indians, that's how naive I was. I hadn't a clue about anything. So, this relationship was the beginning of a totally new experience for me.

Then, low and behold I was told I had to go and work in Manchester and then back to London. I would go up north to work, being paid a travel allowance between London and Manchester. For a while I stayed in bed and breakfast places rather than travelling back south. I soon found my way around the area in Manchester where I had to work and was busy working at the Bradford Road gas work. My days were about working hard doing my electrical work and going back to the B & B, sleeping then working again. I was saving as much as I could as often as I could.

Soon, however, in 1962, my girlfriend told me she was pregnant. I was only 16 years old then and was scared stiff. She was pregnant with my child and went back to live with her mother in Manchester. Nine months later she had a home birth, and I became a father to a daughter. I travelled back to London to see everyone and told them of my first experience with a daughter; and how I was being pressured into giving the child a name by the mother's four sisters and her mother and her father.

They all told me; I should get married to her and give the child a name and then go. This in itself wasn't a very nice experience; trust it to be me. My brother Bill had told me not to go back to Manchester or to get married but to support the child and that's it. I didn't take my brother's advice and I went back to Manchester. During all this time I would be working, and I took on two jobs, so I rarely got to see them both, but they never went without. I was still able to put money away in my account in The Halifax. I wasn't a big spender; I didn't drink or smoke like most did in those days. Smoking seemed to be a fashion, or for some a total addiction.

She stayed back in the north with her mother. It was arranged that I would send her money through the post. My brother etc. was not happy at all. I still have the receipts to this day, to be seen later in the book. I would obviously travel up north to see her, and then go back to Morden to carry on working with Reg from time to time. Years passed, and I was told that another child was on the way, so I had to make changes in my life, I had no choice in the matter.

I had no alternative but to leave London in 1963 and travel north where I would live with her parents in their council house. My brother advised me not to go because he had doubts about the whole situation. But I went anyway and managed to find another company which enabled the completion of my apprenticeship. This forced me to change my employment from Gratts in London to W.H Smith & Co in Manchester, which can be seen on the certificate later.

I had no choice then but to sell my motorcycle. I loved the relationship I had with my bike, but now I had to run and walk and use public transport to get to and from work. I was not happy at all with this decision. I reflected upon all I had gone through in my very sad childhood. I had no one to turn to. I had to go because I could not live with myself knowing I had become a father to two children. I did get married and gave the children my name as was expected of me. My daughter Julie had my mother's name Alice, but on her birth certificate it is Alison.

Betty and Reg would come up to see us, it was lovely seeing them again. In 1966 I was only 20 years old and still serving my apprenticeship as can be seen by the dates on my document. I show this as it proves the truth behind this story. Without finishing my apprenticeship despite all the difficulties, I had, I would never have received the only qualification of my life. This was all I knew to obtain my wages and pay my way in life and now for my children.

My Beautiful foster mother, Betty with Sally and Steven on a visit, holding Julie Alison Ross

My daughter can be seen in the photo above.

I completed my apprenticeship after five years on the 20th of July 1967 with W.H. Smith & Co Electrical Engineering Ltd. in Manchester. I was living just for my work as an electrician and my children. Then one day I walked into a Ford dealership garage in Northenden. The garage was called Barrow & Son. I told the owner's son Peter Barrow that I understood cars and had worked with my brother in London on the weekends. After a trial they accepted me whenever I wanted to work on an hourly basis. I got to working at weekends, using all the skills I had learnt from my brother and Reg. I would prepare cars after their repairs in the body shop. I was rubbing down cars after they had been resprayed, and I would put them all back together again to go on sale in the car sales area fronting the main road. I would work on the cars so late in the night on Saturdays that I would sleep over in there and continue working first thing Sunday morning. The owner's father and son, Walter and Peter

Barrow would lock up on Saturday night leaving me and trusting me to continue working unsupervised. The proof of my work was clearly seen from the cars I had prepared ready for display on the sales forecourt. Then on Monday first thing when the garage was opening up, I would jump up, sort myself out and then get on the bus to Manchester and run to the gas work up Bradford Road where my first job was. At Barrows I would leave with my pay in cash, no questions asked. The number of cars I got through would impact my pay. I would work really very hard and, if it wasn't for all the work I learnt from my brother Bill, I wouldn't have found it as easy as I did. So I was thankful for my brother's wisdom and for him passing it down to me. I used my money to pay for food and lodging and other essentials, then I had to continue my electrical work. I had to become a workaholic or there would not be as much money as there was.

I really missed everyone, especially my brother, Reg, Betty, Sally, and Steven. One thing the orphanage did for me was to put me in good stead for being able to roam around the country alone, like in the Peter and Harris days, and now, knowing what hard work was. Being in Manchester wasn't as hectic as London for me, so between the wages from my two jobs, travelling allowance, and scrap money for lead, copper and brass five days a week (sometimes seven and with my out-of-town allowance), I was able to save up for my first house.

Reg & Betty. Such an unbelievable, loving, couple. I miss them so very much.

CHAPTER 12: In January 1969 I am registered as an approved electrician.

I left W.H Smith on 11th July 1968 and then I went to work for another company called Robert Springer Electrical Company Ltd. On 2nd August 1969, I became a registered, approved electrician with the Joint Industrial Board for the Electrical Contracting Industry, working my way up my ladder of success whilst still working on weekends.

Whilst working my way up to foreman electrician I was responsible for many electricians and their apprentices on many contracts, one of these being Manchester City Football Club at Maine Road doing all the new lighting on the four very high lighting towers. After climbing up to the top using a rope and a pulley wheel, we would pull the brand-new, specially made Thorn high-lux lighting back up, ready to re-fix. This then required me to go outside of the tower, leaning out with just a leather belt to give safe working. If the belt did not hold tight, it would have been a very long fall to the ground; I would certainly never survive.

We would be paid a good amount extra for this work. It was called 'danger money', free of tax. I would always volunteer my services for this work because of the danger and there were very few volunteers; heights did not bother me. I was always available to do this work when it was not raining. In between, I would do work inside the football club where they had a large function room with a bar and all the catering staff dealing with the events that took place.

Springers Electricals had the same contract at Salford Rugby Club, so I was asked to do the same work there. There were two additional lighting towers that required a much greater risk as we had to attach our own scaffolding from the ground up to the full height of the lighting towers. They were very high so not many wanted to go to the top of them; it seemed as high as Blackpool Tower. Then the same process was carried out with the same leather belt supporting my weight, leaning out to unbolt then refit the new much brighter high-lux lighting. I was only one of very few volunteers having gained the experience of this work at a young age, with the bonus of the extra money on top of my wage.

Whilst I was doing all this work there were many who were stopping and watching. At Maine Road the manager would watch me. He was Malcolm Allison who I got to know very well along with many of the players such as Mike Summerbee and Francis Lee. Throughout this time, I was 19-20 years old doing the electrics for a brand-new sauna near the changing rooms. When it was time to test the sauna, Malcolm had sent the full squad on a coach to practice as usual on the playing fields next to Southern Cemetery which was down Princess Parkway, near Chorlton-cum-Hardy. This gave a two-hour gap for Malcolm to have an undisturbed test of the sauna.

I got to test it out alongside Malcolm. He was a Londoner and we got on really well together. He knew immediately from my accent that I was from his neck of the woods. We got on so well he invited me to have a kick about on the pitch with him and the players. The football squad arrived back from practice to have their showers and then go into the sauna themselves. Some were going in the sauna for the very first time. It was big enough for the full squad and I stayed there with them, and we had great fun jumping into the plunge pool, water going everywhere as we were all stark naked.

I took him up on that invite a few days later and we had a kick about, which was a fantastic experience. There I noticed loads of footballs in the changing rooms and on thinking back, I wish I had got one and got him and the players to sign it for me. Being sat naked in the sauna with Malcolm was a better experience than playing football.

From all this working hard and 'danger money', never going out drinking or smoking enabled me to save here and there. It wasn't long and I was then able to purchase my first house. It needed a lot of work, but with all the things I had managed to pick up on along the way from Reg and my brother Bill, I was confident I could do it all on my own. It was a semi-detached house, Number 7 Horncastle Road, Moston, near Manchester. I was then only nearly 20 years old, and I had great difficulty in obtaining a mortgage at that time because of my age but the house was £2,000-11-6d (two thousand pounds eleven and six) back then. I had saved a very large deposit, and this was enough for The Halifax to advance on the back of my small wage whilst I was working at Bradford Road gas work. The Halifax took into account my untaxed travelling allowance which was more than I paid on my mortgage.

I had so long been looking forward to having a place of my own and my wife stayed with her mother whilst I did most of the work on the house. I was still working my first job on top of everything else and at nights I re-wired the whole house and decorated it. I replaced all the ground floor joists as they had dry rot. This I did whilst pulling up the floorboards to do the electrics and putting back new joists with new T&G flooring. I had many more jobs awaiting me. All these working experiences I had watched and taken careful note of whilst serving my apprenticeship along with other trades. In order to collect all my materials, I had to go on the bus. This became very difficult, but the bus drivers would let me on and off with kindness in those days, thank goodness. During my busy day-to-day routine, I started to learn to drive, and I got through my driving-test first time. Through all my graft and slogging my guts out I managed to obtain a car, what a wonderful feeling this was. I was so proud of myself. When I had finished the house, it was obviously worth more, so the building society lent me the retention money after the work had been inspected by the surveyor.

By this time, we had a little boy which I couldn't believe but it was what it was. I worked and worked to keep up with everything. I used to store all my copper under the stairs and then I would weigh it in a scrap yard called W Lumb on Kenyon Lane in Moston.

They got to know me quite well and one week when I had got my copper to take to the scrap yard, they told me that my wife had already been in with the pram full of copper. This came as a real surprise to me as I hadn't noticed any had gone. I often brought it home and I was very busy. I was very disappointed she had kept it quiet. There were other problems within our marriage. She was turned against me by her family who were always interfering. She began to get angry at me for always working and not being around much and got aggressive at times. One day she slammed a glass door on me. I was cut badly on my face arms, legs, and my right foot. I still had to go out to work, blood all over me. This was the last straw. Before I left, I had to tell her to go back to her mother before I came home that night. I took a detour to the hospital to get stitched up. I was in a bad way. It was sad for the children but her leaving meant they would not have to see or hear any more abuse. My life seemed to be falling apart but I had to keep working. I am full of scars to this day. We decided to stay separate, so I had to make arrangements to find a divorce settlement which would be half the value of the house and payments for the children.

My work still came first but helped me to get through all the pain and misery. If I didn't work, the children would suffer, and I didn't want that. I stayed at the house on my own and carried on doing it up when I was able to, in between working. I also had regular visits with my children, Julie and Peter, and they would come to stay over with me (Chapter 17). Julie saw and remembered her mother's outbursts. I was very busy and still in charge of many men. The company Springers had got a contract for doing all the electrical work on Bury Market indoor and outdoor and in all the shops around. I was put in charge of all of this work, and it was hard, but I succeeded. I had good relationships with the men that worked alongside me. In between all this I would make payments towards my daughter's and son's needs. There was no C.S.A in those days and I had a moral responsibility, with my thoughts of not wishing a child of mine to suffer any hardship like I had, but my work had to *always* come first, so I did not get to see my children very often.

This is a very small example of how at 23 I could not spell or calculate feet and inches with any confidence: only thanks to Reg, I could work out 3 feet was from my nose to my fully stretched out arm to my thumb. I noticed back then many others used this method of measuring cable lengths. So, it became normal for me to do this throughout all my years, and it proved to be very accurate in all my work, as seen in the following chapters. My difficulties in spelling would be seen by those that I worked for. This would be much the same as my brother from another mother of the same age, the cockney Harry Redknapp, the manager of Spurs Football Club. Harry thankfully had a mother and father to watch his achievements in life and I was able to watch him in I'm a Celebrity. So, in some ways, I was able to connect with Harry and his lovely wife when she went into the jungle to meet him.

This is a sample of how payments were made; see above my improper literacy.

Then I received through my post this letter wanting to know all my income and outgoings. They wanted as much as they could get from me, as quickly as possible.

SEDGWICK, PARKINSON, PHELAN & ROWLEY
SOLICITORS
COMMISSIONER FOR OATHS

Telephone: 061-432.7281-2-3, 061-434 4448 & 4126

CANADA CHAMBERS,
36 SPRING GARDENS,
MANCHESTER, M2 1EL

CRR/GB/R:85

Our Ref.   Your Ref.

23rd February, 1972.

Dear Mr.Ross,

I received your letter and I regret that the information you have given me though full is not clear enough for the purposes of your affidavit.

I should be grateful if you will confirm to me that your hire purchase repayments on your motor vehicle are exactly £25.00 per month and if not, how much exactly. I need also to know the registration and make of the vehicle and the amount outstanding and to whom the payments are made.

Please confirm to me that your mortgage repayments are exactly £24.00 per month and if not exactly how much. Could you please advise me as to how much is outstanding on the mortgage.

I should be grateful if you will give me the same information with regard to the rates. Are they exactly £94 per annum. The same with regard to the car insurance and the television. Are they exactly £66 and £25 respectively each year?

You mention "telephone for my work" but you do not say how much per week that runs out at. You mention a Transit van running costs but again do not say how much this does cost. Please confirm the registration number to me of this van and that it is free of hire purchase.

Can you please let me know the exact amount of the electricity bill.

Continued...

- 2 -

Will you please advise me of the full name
and address of the cleaner you employ.

I shall also be grateful if you will advise
me of the other work you do same time and also the
amount you earn when you work.

Please let me know how much on average you
spend each week on food and particularly let me know
what expenses over and above the usual you have when
you are working away. Please confirm to me that these
monies are re-imbursed to you by your firm.

Have you really no further expenses other than
those that you list?

Please let me have this information as soon
as possible.

Yours truly,

Mr.F.L.E.Ross,
7 Newcastle Road,
Moston,
Manchester.

CHAPTER 13: Working at Macclesfield/Bury/E.L.S.

So, after a time and finishing at the gas work, I was now working in 1969 for Springers Electrical in Withington, Manchester, sub-contractors to I.C.I in Macclesfield.

My basic rate of pay was 76p per hour with my country travel allowance of 25 shillings per day. See letter below.

HP/MB   GG/EE

Hargreaves & Co
341 Palatine Road
Northenden
Manchester   M22 4FY

Hargreaves solicitors

25th July 1972

Dear Sirs

Re :   Mr Peter Leslie Bernard Ross
7 Horncastle Road, Moston

We acknowledge receipt of your letter of 21st July 1972 and give the following information concerning the above-named employee, which you have requested.

Mr Ross : Earnings

His basic rate of pay per week is £0.76 p. per hour for a 40 hour week, plus overtime is available.

When working away from home he is entitled to a lodging allowance of £2.00 per night over 15 miles away from the shop. He can, if he wishes, take a "Country Allowance" of 25/- per day in lieu of travel time and fares, but as Mr Ross usually works in such areas as Carlisle, Huddersfield, Leeds, etc. he therefore takes the lodging allowance.

In the last 17 week period he has been paid £60.00 for lodging allowance.

The total amount earned by him over a 17 week period this year amounts to the sum of £766.17.

His total amount earned by him over the period of last year amounts to £1,766.13.

We trust the above information will meet with your requirements and also that of the Registrar of the Manchester County Court.

Yours faithfully
Robert Springer Limited

    H Price

H Price
Managing Director

So, the amount that I earned over a 17-week period was £766.17p and the total over the year was £1,766.13p, with my home having cost me £2,000 11 shillings and 6D. I was able to drive to work and back each and every day and I was obtaining untaxed, out of town travelling allowance to work and back as referred to above. The other electricians that had to travel by train from Manchester to Macclesfield from the railway station, had about a two- mile journey to run or walk to the I.C.I work. I did this journey occasionally and the timing was tight to be ready to clock in for 8am. Before long some of them wanted to come in my car. We all received the same amount of travel expense and therefore agreed to travel together to work and back. They paid me half of their allowance and between the three or sometimes four of them, this came in very nicely and I was going there anyway (one of them was called John Moyes seen in Chapter 14). I kept my car in good working order, serviced it on time and kept it clean, taxed and insured. So, we never broke down. There was one strict rule. That anyone not on time would be left behind, or we would have all been late and this would have cost us greatly because on arrival at I.C.I we had to clock in and out each day. Amazingly life ran like clockwork.

There was another strict rule: no smoking, and no making bad smells in the car as for some reason some thought it was funny; I didn't think it was funny at all. Each day we would be working alongside each other's trades, and we would get to know each other well and rely on each other. It was great fun as well as hard work. At dinnertime we played football, and we had many great, serious games. On one occasion one player received a head injury when he went head on into a metal box on the wall. We kept this quiet until we were all back at work with each other covering up for him then, when he was working, we pretended he had had an accident and took him to the sick bay. This was accepted and the injury did not stop him from continuing with his work. He just had the rest of the day off, staying in the sick room and came back in my car at the end of the day.

Keeping discipline and friendship with many men (never girls) was not an easy task. In those days you would never see a female electrician or plasterer or plumber. I was always a leader of men. Reg had taught me well; he got me to understand the value of copper and lead, and this was always one of the perks of the trade. Everything we handled at I.C.I up to this time was copper and lead. At I.C.I there were some very heavy cables, and these belonged to them. However, when as a team we had pulled the cable off the very heavy drum, any off-cut measure should go back to I.C.I, but this did not always happen.

We would very quickly cut lengths that we could handle and hide them in the long uncut grass, then take the rest back to I.C.I management who were always happy to receive this and they would put it into their locked shed with other cables we had given in. We would then pass our cable over the perimeter fence, not seen by I.C.I security as they did not have security cameras in those days. If we had been caught with the copper cable this would have been instant dismissal (it was known by the bosses of I.C.I that this practice was taking place). But as long as they were receiving the lion's share of what we took, they either turned a blind eye or they were happy with what we had given in. It was very much duck and dive to safely get the copper cable out this way. On one occasion the cable was wrapped in the overalls of one of the electricians and on each of our overalls were our name tags. On driving away past security we would stop, then collect the cable from the other side obviously out of sight of security, then we would take it home.

One late evening, I received a telephone call from one of the apprentices telling me that he had not retrieved his copper hidden inside his overalls. This was an absolute emergency as his name was in them, so I went to collect him in Stockport, and I drove all the way back in the dark. He knew the exact place he had left it and went to get it and got back in the car. I drove him back home and had I not taken this action, the following day it would most likely have been found and it would have been obvious who had left it there. It was a great relief to me on my part as no doubt we would have all been affected, but instead we just continued as normal.

We made money through our hourly pay but more in travel expenses and the retrieval of copper, lead, and brass. Back in the 70's, plumbers would be in the scrap yard weighing in for cash with their copper pipe and very heavy lead, but this was never as profitable as what us electricians would come away with.

Still at Robert Springers I was sent to take charge of the new Bury Market place after the fire. In some ways I was not happy with this as I was no longer receiving my out-of-town travel expenses. At this time, I was only receiving local travel allowance to Bury which was not far from my home. I no longer had to get up in the very early hours of the morning, which was better for me, and being foreman made me feel proud as I was now with the site agent for the whole development. The contractors were Lowton Construction Co Ltd, the site agent Tony Urn and the Clark of the work Mr Fred Eagles. Fred would inspect everything for the Bury Council. He would be responsible for signing off any day work sheets that were not part of the contract or any out-of-hours work. He was a stickler, and his name was very fitting of him. So, now I am respected by those in positions I used to always look up to, and here I am now in meetings with them. See Chapter 15 at Bury market graveyard!

One of my best memories was of my skills when the site agent was in an absolute panic. A crane operator working in an area with a lot of water and mud was receiving serious electric shocks and he would not get back into his crane and carry-on work. On taking my test equipment to the crane, sure enough it was all *live*. I had access to the electricity substation and immediately shut down the site electricity and I went back to the crane and did the same test, proving it was now safe. I climbed on the crane to make sure the driver was ok to continue doing work but only to move the crane a short distance so I could find where the cable was that had gone through his metal tracks. I couldn't find the cable so the site foremen, Tony, got his labourers to dig out the area of the tracks from the crane and sure enough they dug up the damaged cable. I went into the trench to look at the damage and got my hacksaw and tools and cut right through the cable with the labourers holding each side. They then lifted each section up into the air and out of the way so that I could make the section safe, going to the electric substation.

I was able to cut this back and tape it up, making it temporarily safe by removing the fuses, allowing for the electric to be switched back on. Later in the day a replacement section of the heavy, electric, copper cable with the jointing packs arrived on site when I cut out the section of damaged cable re-joining it with the new section. Obviously, I kept hold of the damaged section of the copper cable. After this the new cable was protected and covered over and all was sorted in the same day, meaning that the full site work could continue. This job was all done in a day, so Springers Electrical Company was very, very happy as they were receiving the top rate of pay for this work. Lawtons Construction was also very happy and my friendship with Mr Eagles improved immensely, and I was happy cutting up and stripping the damaged cable ready to take to the scrap yard, with much other scrap copper pyro cable, and the money was shared out between the others under my control.

CHAPTER 14:   Asbestos, Turner Newall and Cyril Smith

In March 2014 I received, in my post, a letter from the solicitors Pannone asking if I was the Mr Ross who worked for an electrical company with a man called John Moyes. They said if I was, could I contact them. The name instantly came back into my memory. I contacted the solicitors and asked how they had my name and address and the solicitors explained they had asked John's wife if she could remember any of her husband's workmates. She remembered my name very well, just as I can remember many names from my past, working with many electricians. I asked how they obtained my details and to my surprise, I was told they did a simple search of my name at Companies House and my electrical company name with all my details came up. This rang all their bells of enquiry, and they wrote to me.

At first, I was a bit suspicious, until they told me that John had passed away with an asbestos-related death and it would be most helpful if I could help in any way by explaining what work John Moyes carried out. Pannones did not give me any other details but they asked if I would be prepared to make a full written statement of fact to the best of my memory on paper so they could transcribe it in their proposed action on behalf of John's wife and family. Because of my inability to spell correctly I was embarrassed, so I said I would be happy to receive another phone call and give a telephone interview to be recorded using my memory of the facts and for them to transcribe it. They agreed to do this, and my phone rang on the agreed date and time, and I was ready to part with as much as I could remember. After I had finished giving my statement, the solicitor said it was fascinating to listen to all I could remember with so much detail.

Later Pantones sent me a draft of my statement to read, this took the best part of an hour of my telephone recorded account explaining my time working with John Moyers. After reading it I noticed Pannones solicitors had made my statement just as I had spoken it over the phone without changing and it gave a truthful account of what I had said. I agreed to call at their offices in Manchester to sign the original, having it witnessed on 29thApril 2014 and they provided me with a copy. Sometime after I had signed the statement, I had remembered I hadn't mentioned that John had also worked with me on the new Bury market where all the electrical cabling and lighting were all fixed above and below the asbestos tiles around the whole shopping precinct and walkways. In 2019 I decided to go to Bury to have a look around and see if I could see the work we had done, only to discover that all the asbestos tiles and lighting had been removed. I did not go back to Pannones to explain this omission as I had been told I had provided enough information to enable the maximum award of compensation for John Moyes and his family. What a wonderful feeling that was for me to read this in a letter one morning at my home whilst I am going through a nightmare with my former solicitor and former wife etc.

IN THE PROPOSED ACTION

B E T W E E N:-

JOANNE MOYES
(AS EXECUTRIX OF THE ESTATE OF JOHN MOYES DECEASED)

Claimant

- and -

ROBERT SPRINGER LIMITED

Defendant

WITNESS STATEMENT
ON BEHALF OF THE CLAIMANT

INTRODUCTION

1   My full name is Peter Leslie Bernard Ross and I reside at Hindclough Barn, Over Town Lane, Redlumb, Norden, Rochdale OL12 7TU.

2   I make this statement at the request of the claimant further to the late John Moyes' exposure to asbestos during his employment. The following paragraphs are from my own knowledge, information and belief.

3   I worked for Robert Springer Limited between approximately 1969 to 1973, as a qualified electrician. National Joint Industrial Council Registration number 10563. At that time, I think the address for the company was 2 Cotton Lane, Withington, Manchester.

4   I worked on different jobs for Springers and I worked my way up to Charge Hand and then Foreman. I remember working with John Moyes and I remember being charge hand over John. I specifically remember working with John at the Turner & Newall factory in Trafford Park. Springers had a contract to Turners and I remember that we worked there on contract for around 12 months. I remember John Moyes working with me at Turners. John was quite a character and a laugh. I remember that we all worked well as part of a team, doing the same work and mucking in together and we all got on well. We would all help each other out. If John was working on a motor that had to be dismantled on the top of a vessel, I would sometimes go up and help him and work together and we would talk.

5   I remember when you went to the factory at Turners you went through the front doors where the offices were and as you walked through there were samples of rocks that had been imported that were there to demonstrate what Turners did. There were offices on the ground floor and upstairs. I can recall quite clearly that when you walked through into the factory there was a fog of dust that was flying everywhere. You could see men with white suits on through the fog. I did not know about the dangers of the fog, and I walked through without thinking about it. I remember there was asbestos flying about everywhere. The factory

was not very nice. I did not really have any idea of what I was going into, I do not think any of us did.

6. We did electrical work on contract to Turners. I remember one of the jobs was doing electrical refurbishment of the offices, which involved putting new lighting in and new power points. The majority of the work I did at Turners was in the factory itself. There were men that Turners employed who had white overalls on with masks, but as electrical contractors we were not given any advice on the dangers of asbestos. We were not given any masks or any other protection, and we all breathed it in.

7. I remember in the factory there were big vessels where the asbestos was churned into a powder and each of the vessels had a big electric motor on which was on the top which was like an agitator with a shaft that went through it and that was moving all of the asbestos into particles. These vessels gave off a lot of dust. I had to go in and work on the motors that were on top of the vessels and so I was working literally stood on these vessels with the asbestos in. John also did this same work.

8. the motors on the vessels broke down fairly often. I remember the motors themselves were air cooled which would move the particles all over the place. They got the asbestos dust into the electric motor, which often made them brake down. As part of mine and John's job as electricians, we would have to go and disconnect the electrics to the machinery, turning it off at the mains, putting a padlock on it so no one else could turn it back on and then we would use a brush to brush the asbestos off the motor to get to the screws and nuts to undo the terminals to disconnect the wires. A mechanical fitter would then come and take over and take the motor out and replace it and then we would come back again to reconnect the motor. There would always be a stand by motor for when they broke down so the machinery was not off for too long. I would say that this motor replacements was necessary once or twice every year or so.

9. The vessels were massive. You had to go up steps onto a gantry to get to the top of the vessel where the powder goes in, with the eclectic motor at the top driving the agitator. If one broke down, we would get out tools and then climb to the top and start work.

10. I think there were at least 10 of these vessels in the factory and they were approximately 20 to 30 foot high off the floor and 10 to 15 foot wide.

11. I remember seeing men working at the top level where the motor were and I remember them having wellington boots on and an overall and a mask, but none of the contractors that worked there had anything like that. I just had an overall. I was never told to wear a mask or given a mask or anything.

12. Whilst we were at the factory, they might also decide to close down a vessel so that it could be descaled or if the agitator had damaged the coating. People would do this work whilst we worked around them and that also created dust.

13. We also tended to any other electrical equipment in the factory, including the lighting which was above on the factory ceiling. The lighting would get covered in the asbestos dust and so therefore produce less and less light over time. As part

of mine and John's job, we had to get a cloth to clean the light and put new lamps in.

14 Also, any machinery that broke down, we would have to go in and diagnose what the problem was. We would have to go through the drawings and work out from the drawings what was inside, and diagnose the problem and then correct it and fix it.

15 I remember that the asbestos powder would be packed into bags and then stacked and stored and taken away on lorries or on a truck on a railway line. This asbestos packing would all be done in the factory around us as well which was also very dusty.

16 My overalls would get full of dust and I then had to go home with this dust all over me and wash the overalls myself. I did not know at the time of the dangers of asbestos and never really thought about it.

17 One of the other things I remember about Turners was when I went to use the facilities in the gents' toilet. To one side of the toilet, I remember there was a bucket with a piece of paper pinned to the wall asking people to put a sample of urine in the bucket. I never knew what this was for and no one ever said. I think I recall the note on the paper just said "Please pee a sample in the bucket" and I think people obviously did because the bucket often had a lot in there, and I often did as well, but I never knew what that was for.

18 The environment was very dusty indeed. We never really knew about the dangers of asbestos at the time. No protection was given to any of us working for Springers.

19 We worked from 8.00am until 5.00pm or 6.00pm or later every week day and we often worked weekends of 8.00am till about 4.00pm, 5.00pm or even 6.00pm on Saturdays and Sundays. I remember that myself and John wanted to do overtime in the evenings as well as weekends and so we often worked late. John and I wanted to do this overtime because you would be paid either double time or time and a half, or also be given a day in lieu when it was a bank holiday. This was known as "double bubble". John and I did overtime whenever we could.

20 I remember at 10.00am we had a 20 minute break. Dinner time was 12.00 till 1.00pm. We had an afternoon break at 3.00pm for 20 minutes. We took our breaks near the offices where there was a little place that we could go and sit down, and there was also a hut outside which was like a works cabin for the Springer workers, where we congregated and had kept our own stuff.

21 I also remember working on contract from Springers to JCI in Macclesfield. I remember near to the laggers mixing asbestos material with water and by hand putting it onto the pipes and smoothing it so that the asbestos cement would set around the pipes which would protect the pipes. I think the name of the laggers' firm was William Press Limited or John William Press Limited, who were pipe fitters. I recall that this was a massive plant and there was a mass scale of pipework. I remember being in the area when the laggers were doing that. The electricians and laggers often worked close to each other. We were pretty much working on top of each other. I would be there doing the electrics for the motors and lights and things like that. I remember John Moyes being at JCI for a short

What I find fascinating in the Pannone statement above and their success in relation to the rightful compensation for the deceased wife and family, is that there are many others out there who will have suffered the criminal negligence of Turner Newall when they chose to make Cyril Smith a substantial shareholder. This enabled the cover up of the deaths relating to those working at their asbestos factory when it was so obvious Cyril Smith resided in Rochdale. He was a Rochdale Liberal party MP between 1972-1992, then he was awarded the Queen's Sword on his shoulder to become Sir Cyril Smith. He would regularly visit the Turner Newall Rochdale work off Rooley Moore Road, which was called Forest View, Spodden Valley and leads to the most beautiful, protected Healy Dell. The asbestos work closed many years ago, with vandals setting fire to it and stripping out the valuable copper. Rochdale Council did not police the contaminated site properly, which left behind further contamination of the whole area due to asbestos. Some buildings partly remained and the whole site was completely unsafe and not possible for re-development, leaving all the surrounding properties and families badly affected financially and otherwise. But not so for Sir Cyril, his mother, family, and friends like David Steel MP and Jeremy Thorpe MP to mention only those few who have supported and taken part in his most disgusting behaviour. This was very much like that which took place within the orphanage that I grew up in, when the local authorities turned their heads away, allowing it to happen and wanting to preserve their comfortable lifestyles. All those young boys were simply trying to find scrap metal to take to the scrap yard to make a few shillings, and they would find themselves taken away by Cyril Smith for his sexual gratification and the most despicable and unforgivable crimes whenever it pleased him.

Whilst this activity was different from my own, the pain and the memories are all the same. So painful that we never tell anyone due to the shame we felt. The Mapperton Case (chapter 34) was a disgrace. Again, the police lost vital evidence, making it impossible for all the cases against the abusers to get a fair trial. This was the explanation from the abuser's barristers in the High Court, making it impossible for the judge. The judge allowed the abusers to walk away free without any blemish upon their character and all this was paid for by public funds without anyone being prosecuted for their crimes, not allowing the jury the opportunity to find them guilty or not. They walked away with their heads held high to continue their lives with full pensions paid for from state funds. The redeveloped, remaining cottages and up market housing estates are on the roads, named after those abusers.

'I believe there is a place for corporal punishment....there is a place in law for a good hiding.' Smith in the Rochdale Observer, 21 April 1979.

'We earnestly hope that we have found for boys a home in which they can find the right moral and character building influence.' Smith at the 1964 AGM of the hostel.

All the new houses were built on the surrounding lands of the orphanage where we orphans would play, hide, and do sports on sports day, climb the trees, and have fun. It was never fun and some of the Victorian cottages that I was brought up in had approximately 30 children in each. Of the 13 cottages some have been converted into luxury appartements which I visited, unaware at the time that the place was being converted into housing. I took many photos which I will show later, but whilst I took the photos, I was back revisiting my childhood memories, hearing all the sounds of the many girls and boys. Only now, I have my 11-year-old daughter Angela with me and my brand-new, top of the range Mercedes Benz parked outside with over £3 million turnover within my business and just under £1 million invested on the sterling money market and a most luxurious home to drive back to in Rochdale. Sir Cyril is very much on my radar with my hands tied behind my back and gagged from talking, but no longer do I walk with pain and hurt from the past. I can now talk, with help, for all that may read this story. This obese, honoured by the queen, sadistic paedophile and prolific offender would refer to all his co-directors by their first names. The use of asbestos material became banned in 1999. In 2001 Turners and Newall/Turners Asbestos was listed in the stock exchange market where Cyril Smith had investments of 1,300 T & N shares, making him a multi-millionaire MP Director, and also a predator. In 2001 T & N went into voluntary administration. The asbestos mines in Johannesburg Swasey Land stopped mining, leaving all the surrounding areas of the mines covered in asbestos fibres and dust. Whilst Sir Cyril lavished himself with the proceeds from his time as a director of T.&. N. Thankfully all those abused by him found that on the third of September 2010, Sir Cyril Smith died.

I noticed one of those who suffered so much was also called Alice, the name of my mother. There is a TV documentary called *Alice: A Fight for Life*. She explains how asbestos workers were dying from cancer which I had not known before *Alice's Fight for Life*, but what I describe in this chapter is precisely how T & N were secretly making tests on urine in the ladies' and gents' toilets because they were aware that the urine testing would prove positive for cancer in all of their workers, including those in the Johannesburg Swasey Land asbestos mines.

CHAPTER 15: Today at Bury Market

Much of the land that was being developed belonged to Bury Council and the Central Methodist Church off Crompton Street. However, it was said in my investigation that some belonged to St John's church. There was a very large cemetery, and the graves were all being dug up. All the gravestones were stacked and recorded by the church authorities (presumably for any living relatives to be able to trace their remains). Some of the gravestones are still in the gardens near Marks & Spencer's at a site called Saint John's square. All the bones being unearthed were placed in a large box whilst a priest was present, overlooking the removal of the bodies and bones and collecting any trinkets, being passed up and handed over to the person in charge. This was an unbelievable sight. I was seeing lead sarcophagus; the lead was very heavy and worth a lot of money and the contractors were putting it to one side for themselves. These had to be opened to access the bodies/bones.

This memory is etched in my thoughts and in some ways has left me with very ugly reflections. The contractors were finding burials that were not known to the church and each had to be carefully dismantled and some had stone sides and a stone lid with bones inside. They went down five compartments deep, possibly a family tragedy, where each were buried at the same time, one on top of the other. Whilst I find this very unusual to see, I had never understood graves or whole bodies in skeleton form. When I now visit Bury market, I cannot help but think of those that were left and are still underground, as not all the bodies were uncovered.

Indeed, some were found when the drainage was being dug deep into the ground and each time that bones were coming out of the ground the job had to stop until the priest was present to arrange their transfer; bless them all. I believe all that was uncovered required the Queen's consent, then they were taken to another burial place and this, I was told, was the Bury

Cemetery place. I haven't done a forensic trail of the past to elaborate any further other than to say, "I was there" and I am still having difficulty understanding how there were so many graves that seemed not to be known at the time by the church authorities.

On my recent visit I noticed that nearly all the asbestos ceiling tiles have been removed in the newly constructed town centre development. All the ceilings above the public walkways and offices had 2ft by 2ft asbestos tiles, where holes were drilled, two on each side, then fixed with self-tapping screws into the suspended ceiling. Then cut into the asbestos tiles were holes to allow the copper pyro cables to come through for the lighting for all the pedestrian areas and offices above. I believe the asbestos tiles were to give fire protection for the residents living above. So, this is why I have showed the asbestos use at Bury and other places I have worked at, which is referred to in more detail in the statement where none of us working at the various sites with asbestos were aware of the most serious dangers we had been exposed to. But now seeing it nearly all removed at Bury town

centre tells its own story.

I had done electrical work for Granelli's ice cream shop in the 70s, and I knew the family owners. I decided to stop and talk to the man selling ice cream at Granelli's and discovered his name was Vincent, one of the sons of those who started the Granelli's shops in Bury right from the beginning in the early 70s. Whilst in conversation with Vincent, I told him how his parents had approached me to carry out their electrical work in their two shops.

I am now talking to the son about his mother and father and how I remembered him being a young teenager when I knew his parents. I told him that his family were one of the first to open up ice cream shops in the Bury town centre, and I was able to explain to him all about his uncle and dad living next door to each other in a big, Victorian, semi-detached property. It was his mother and his uncle's wife that ran the two shops, and they did a splendid job at it. I continued with a very close relationship with the Granelli family, Mary, Liz, John and Trish on my birthday with Darren.

His dad and uncle had an ice cream factory here in Heywood. He was certainly enjoying me giving him new memories of his father, his uncle, and his nephew Peter. He was quite shocked to hear all I had told him. I went on to tell him how I knew his uncle had a boy called Peter who is now an accountant and how I had done work in both their homes whilst they were growing up in their teens and that I could remember them when they were young boys. Vincent enjoyed my taking him back all those years in his childhood, and how I could talk to him about his mother, who is now old and frail, and how she was brought into her Bury shop to be there whilst all the staff were working. Her grandson, Vincent, is now selling Granelli's ice cream and driving around in an ice cream van just as she did when she was younger, as seen above. I would tell them of Louie, Vincent's father and his father's brother, wife, and son who all spent their married lives next door to each other at 63 and 65 Hind Hill Street, Heywood. It was a lovely visit, and knowing I had left Vincent and his mother touched with memories in a very lovely way, with such wonderful memories, makes me sure I will go back to see him again. I have taken the time to wander around and reminisce and go and see and discover that some of my work is still there, to think how much hard work I had done in my past life and how much energy I used. I had to oversee all work. I had taken on all the responsibility and the men in bringing Bury shopping centre to what it is today.

I asked the people who were working in and around Bury Market, but no one knew that they were walking over a former cemetery, no one knew anyone who saw what I saw and experienced. I was beginning to wonder if I had dreamt it. I carried on walking around and still remembered carrying out my work on the new development, as it is today. When handing over the completed shops on which I had worked hard with other workmates in different trades, some of the tenants would approach me asking if I could do some work for them, (in my own time) on the weekend and after work or at night, all to be paid in cash. This seemed to be a great idea as we were already on the site, and I knew every detail of it. So those that were working under my control, only on five days a week, were given the offer to continue working after 4 pm and at weekends for cash doing the fitting out and electrical work for the new tenants. I gave a price for the job and the tenants agreed. They made an upfront payment then a further payment in between with the remaining on completion, all in cash. This went on without any problems and was kept completely separate from the contract work that was overseen by the Clerk of Work and Mr Eagles. Between all this, work on my house was less of a priority as my cash paid work was what was driving me on. Most sadly this September 2022, I am at the funeral of Vincent. His family invited us to the service and the 'after service' with his family and friends.

CHAPTER 16: The owner of Carpet Warehouse

One day I was walking around with a drum of cable under my arm and saw a carpet warehouse in Manchester. I spotted a carpet that I liked; a salesman came over to me and I asked him how much the carpet was. We started talking and he asked if I was an electrician. I told him I was, and he explained he was looking for someone to carry out some electrical work. I asked him what the job was, and he showed me, asking me how much it would cost. So, after looking at the value of the work against the cost of the carpet I took a chance and said, "How about I do the electrical work in exchange for the carpet?" This was immediately accepted. The carpet roll was removed and put into storage ready for after I had done the work.

On the following Monday after work, the warehouse was open until 8 pm so I went and started the job and did the same on Tuesday and Wednesday. The nights were light because it was summer, so I had no problem doing some of the work later on. When the job was finished, I was taken home with the carpet, so they knew where I lived and after this my phone never stopped ringing. I discovered it was the owner of Carpet Warehouse, wanting my services. This continued and nearly every weekend, in between working for Springers, I would be working at his warehouse in Manchester, being paid each time in cash, from the weekend's sales after they had been calculated up.

So, I would go away on Sunday paid up and eager to get back the following Saturday. I then learnt that some of the other staff that were working there were made up of his family, so the amount of cash that was being taken in the business was under the family's control. Then, in turn, many of the family started asking for my services at their homes. So now I am juggling keeping up with working five days each week for Springers, weekends at the warehouse and now their family homes, then the home of the boss which was very luxurious. I was burning the candle at both ends and it was becoming impossible. When all was done, I was happy and so was he. We kept in touch and our relationship blossomed into a fantastic relationship for many years. That will come later in the many chapters following. I laid the carpets, working very hard to finish all the jobs in my home.

My home was improving very slowly, and the demands were coming fast and furious from the owner of the Carpet Warehouse. I had an opportunity knocking on my door because he trusted me and wanted me to do all his work all over the place. I had to make a decision which was very difficult as I was wanted by two good paymasters. But as seen in Chapter 13, my pay was under a pound an hour, plus travelling expenses, then double time for weekends and bank holidays, with tax deducted on top of that! So, my decision was to go with the boss of the warehouse with his luxurious home. It wasn't long before I decided to start working full time for myself, acquiring my own business and being my own boss, but I missed being with the men I worked with at Springers Electrical Company very much.

I was now working for myself in a warehouse in Wolverhampton with my first large purchase of a van and caravan. I loaded up all the materials and necessary items, staying and sleeping in my caravan inside the warehouse I was working on. On arrival, there was no electricity to connect to and the building was empty and dark with only my van lights to see around on the first night. Just outside on the pavement I noticed a telephone box which had an electric light inside. It was just within reach of my cable, so I connected the junction box in the corner, at floor level inside the phone box.

Now I have electricity to operate during the day and night enabling the use of my electric tools with the caravan using gas to make my food and tea. I am making fantastic progress, I borrow scaffolding, working all the hours I can work doing as much as possible then getting my head down in the caravan. Other shop fitting contractors arrive on completion of my work and the electrical supply authorities put an electric cable into the building with meters connecting to my electrical work. The building then has full lighting and power ready for the public to make their purchases. Obviously, the cable was removed from the telephone box whilst a generator was hired for the last week before the electric authorities connected the cables and the meters were installed. I owe a great deal of gratitude for the forbidden use of that telephone box along with many other similar reasons to borrow electricity from street lampposts to make my work possible in the many other warehouses throughout the UK which made me a success.

1972. I re-mortgaged half the value of my home 7 Horncastle Road, Moston, Manchester, at its market value and paid this half over to my wife in a divorce settlement as referred to in the solicitors' letter in chapters 12 & 13.

Whilst doing work at Louie's, the E.L.S owner's home, Louie had a visitor who was an architect and he introduced him to me. He was called Keith Davidson. He had called to see all the work I was doing. It was in accordance with his drawings, and he was clearly impressed with all my work, so he asked me if I would like to do some electrical work for him. I was thinking he meant for his home. I told him I would if it did not affect my work with E.L.S. Then Louie said to me in his Yiddish fun talk, "Now you can bite off two of the hands that feed you". So, I happily said "Do you have my details?" His reply being "Of course".

They left me to continue my work with Keith, later returning telling me I would be hearing from him soon. That soon came in my post, and I received a bundle of drawings with the name 'Keith Davidson & Partners Architects' on Old Hall Street, Liverpool. Back then I hadn't a clue how to work out imperial to metric, or scale measurements to calculate the price of the work, but I had the help of Terry (seen in chapter 17). Terry had brains that I did not possess, so whilst Terry was pricing up the work, I left to do a site visit. I contacted the architect to let him know I had his drawings and for him to contact the main contractors, 'Tysons', to advise them I was making my visit to the Cunard Building in Liverpool. The main contractor, Tyson's, were to receive from the cost of all my work a two and a half percent main contractor's discount. I had not got a clue what this meant but thankfully Terry did know.

On my arrival at the site and looking at all the drawings I noticed the Cunard Building is right next door to the Liver Building with the ferry terminal across the river Mersey opposite. To me all this was like a dream. I had heard of these places and now I am living in this dream and cannot believe I am in a position of so much trust and to be entering such prestigious offices within the Cunard Building. In my hands are all the architects' drawings allowing me full access over the entire building. I went to the 3rd floor and met a representative from the company Edward Billington & Sons. The person I met I later discovered was a relative of the family of Edward Billington. He showed me around, then I met with a man called Mr Parkman of the company Ward Ashcroft & Parkman, who I found out later, was Brigadier Parkman. He showed an interest in me. Looking into the unfolded architects' drawings, I told him I was pricing up for all the electrical work. He wished me good luck in my work, and he went back to his offices on the same third floor. Later, with the help of Terry, I submitted my price. To my utter disbelief I then discovered the estimate for my work, with the two and a half percent added in, had been agreed with stage payments on the progress of my work paid by the architects Keith Davidson & Partners.

The work progressed to a satisfactory completion, with five percent retention held back until six months after the completion of all my work. This was so that any problems I was responsible for would be resolved. Simply, I did not receive those retention monies or any future work if I had not attended to any problems of which thankfully there were none. So, I received all the retention monies back from the architects. At the time I was then working on a home belonging to one of the directors of Edward Billington & Sons. This would take me for the first time in my life to travel under the River Mersey through the Mersey tunnel to his lovely home in Heswall. With no such luxury of satnavs in those days, I went through the wrong tunnel, but with my A-Z I was able to correct myself and then arrive at the correct destination.

During this time, when I was working at the Cunard building and the Liver building, I noticed all around Liverpool building work were taking place and there were very large cranes on all the building sites. Each crane had the sign 'Tyson's Builders' at the top. This would be at the time of the Toxteth riots and the re-development of all the rundown terraced properties and derelict mills and warehouses facing the river Mersey. Most of these are now leisure areas, museums to the Titanic and Starline shipping along with the Cunard shipping.

The celebrations of all Tyson's builders' work, along with my work that had taken place in the Cunard building, promoted my company name for all the electrical work I had been involved in. Shortly, I show a photograph below of myself holding the architects' drawings with my sandwiches and a plastic cup inside the Cunard building with another photograph with me now at 74 years old sat at the same window with the Liver Building seen through the glass window.

So, here I am looking at my company name upon the promotion brochure for all my work with the architects Keith Davidson & Partners, work for Edward Billington & Sons, along with the main contractors Tyson the Builders, Liverpool. To me this was like receiving my cap and gown after having studied at university, when in fact I still could not read or write or add up with any level of accuracy.

As time passed, I received a quotation from the same architects for another large contract for a company called Cabot Carbon LTD, in Ellesmere Port. They had noticed my details from the architect's documentation. Through all this work my main advantage over others competing for these jobs would be that their pricing involved much greater amounts. But I would work late into the night and sometimes 3 am and 4 am in the morning, and also weekends, which gave me a free run to do all my work without any of the building contractors in my way, just as I had done in the Cunard building. I had never needed to rush my work to go to the pub as I had never been a drinker or had many interactions with those who were. I would simply have a cup of tea and eat my own homemade sandwiches which can be seen in the photo in 1982 when I am 29 years old, inside the Cunard building. Doing these work during ordinary working hours would take at least twice as long, so this gave me my advantage and success in carrying out all my work whilst there was no one around except the cleaners and the caretaker and security staff to the buildings I worked on.

The only problem I encountered during all my work at the Cunard building was, with all the workers coming and going, all the Edward Billington & Sons' staff were experiencing sharp electric shocks. Sparks could be seen when walking around the offices, touching the computers, door handles, or light switches and so on. It was thought it was a problem with my electrics. However, thankfully I was able to prove it had nothing to do with my work. It was in fact static electricity build up whilst walking around and over the newly fitted carpets, in particular from the female staff that were wearing nylon clothing and stockings. So, whilst I was there (until the carpet was removed later) a large watering can was used to wet all the walking areas on the carpet, which resolved a lot of the static electricity problems.

On my many visits to Louie, I would tell him of my work, and he would say he already knew about the problems with the static electricity from the carpets because this was one of the main items that was sold in his carpet and furniture warehouses I worked on throughout the UK. Louie and his wife Barbara were obviously aware of all my jobs, which also took me to Liverpool, and I got to know the Liverpool area like the back of my hand. I received another large E.L.S contract on Hanover Street where across the road is the famous boys private school called Blue Coat. Up the road from the new E.L.S store was the Beatles Museum, long before it was moved to its present location on Mathew Street. I visited both of these in order to go down memory lane to my singing of all the Beatles songs whilst working with Reg throughout my apprenticeship years, especially at Gatwick airport where I met Sophia Loren. On my dinner breaks whilst working at the Cunard, I would cross backward and forward over the river Mersey many times hearing Gerry Marsden singing the wonderful song *Ferry across the Mersey,* by Gerry and his Pacemakers. So, when I got to meet Gerry with Anita and her children (in chapter 47), I told him how in my younger days I worked in Liverpool and would go across on the ferry from the Cunard building and sit many times listening to him singing, but this was a most wonderful experience for me to be hearing Gerry singing in his concert and shaking his hand.

Years after meeting Gerry with Anita, one bank holiday I took Anita to Liverpool in 2017 to go across the Mersey on the ferry and I showed her a lot of my past work. I took her to the Cunard Building and the Liver Building. At the Cunard, the security man approached us as it was closed on this day. I got to tell him how I had worked on the building some 40 years ago and that I knew the building inside out. He enjoyed listening to some of my stories, whilst watching Anita some of the time, and he seemed quite overwhelmed with me being able to share my knowledge on the security system and where the fire alarm control box was, which was out of sight of all those who visited the Cunard. He had completely dropped his guard and enjoyed the time we were together. So, he ushered us inside and I was able to show Anita a lot of the work I had done. It was a great feeling but sad for me at the same time, and after a while we said our goodbyes and I took Anita back to the Ferry for a last crossing listening to Gerry singing *Ferry Across the Mersey*. It was a lovely day, but very cold. Looking down the river was a lovely experience and being with Anita. I later took her to watch a film show in the Red Star Museum. We looked at all the exhibits of the Titanic and its sister ship, hearing all the sound effects throughout the building.

So, whilst Covid had struck the world in such death and destruction during 2020/2021, I asked Anita if she would go back to Liverpool with me to re-visit for the purpose of this autobiography. On our arrival at the Cunard, I spoke with the security who contacted Edward Billington & Sons. They took great interest in my autobiography and read some of it with me sitting at the head of their board room table. I was again privileged to be escorting Anita around all the work I had done, and she took photographs, some that I have attached. These include one with me standing holding my autobiography, standing in front of the yellow painted Rolls Royce with psychedelic Beatles painting all over it, which we then got to sit in with the chauffeur driving the car. Then we spent time browsing through my autobiography, bringing an end to our lovely visit into my very difficult past.

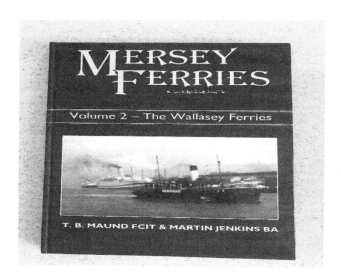

15

16

Here I am in 1982 29 years old working in the Cunard building.

Here I am June 2021 invited back into the Cunard building regardless of Covid 19 looking over the works I had previously done in 1982

I am outside the board room of Edward B 'lington's & Sons who have kindly invited me in to look around having shown the proof within my autobiography.

Never ever in my wildest dreams would I have thought I could be sitting at the head of this massive board room table of Edward Bollington's & Sons were so many transactions have been made since my workings in 1982

Me at the entrance of the Cunard building with the Liver building next door in June 2021

The lovely ending to my re-visit to Liverpool with Anita taking all these photographs.

CHAPTER 17: Then and now, working for myself.

I was now self-employed and very successful, having a working relationship with the carpet and warehouse company and family, saving as much money, as often as I could. I purchased a small piece of freehold land in Rochdale, and I built my first detached house on its grounds in a small cul-de-sac called 11 Hastings Street, Deeplish, Rochdale. This was in between working at Bury Market. In the precinct there was a cake and sandwich shop where I'd go for my dinners. There was a pretty young girl who would often serve me. She was attracted to me, and I to her. Sometimes I would eat my dinner in my new car, a Cortina 2000E and she saw me a few times.

Me working on Hasting Street new house with my van below. The solid copper was over a ton in weight and my workman is stripping it next to my van.

The value of the copper paid for much of the house. It's me on its roof. There were four others hidden away as they were so valuable back then and more so today.

One day she was with her girlfriend, and she was wearing a short skirt. They looked very nice, and she plucked up the courage to come and talk to me. I was always so very busy; I hadn't got time to go out socialising nor did I drink or visit pubs etc. I was living alone in my house in Moston, and my time was taken up at weekends with E.L.S and when I wasn't working, I'd be with Peter and Julie. I didn't have the time to find or think about relationships or friends. We agreed shortly after to meet up. She was younger than me, which made me feel more relaxed about the whole thing after my first bad experience with my older wife. One night after work I met her outside the shop. I took her for a drive, and we talked. I dropped her off at home and drove away. I saw her again the following day and then eventually it became every day during the week. I told her I had two children, and a home of my own and she asked if she could meet them.

When I had a weekend free, I picked her up and we went to get Julie and Peter. I took everyone back to my home. We all seemed to get along and the day flew by, then I dropped her back home. This became a regular pattern until one day I came home from working with E.L.S and she was outside my home with an overnight bag in her hand. Now, thinking about it, she probably thought I was a good catch, and she was keen to break free from her parents. She lived with her parents on a council estate called Dickie Bird in Bury, along with her brother, Brian. I obviously let her stay the weekend and took her home on Sunday afternoon. I was as usual working a lot of the time for E.L.S. at weekends, then in Bury doing work for Granelli's and trying to fit everyone in was difficult. One day I felt I wanted to end things with Elaine, so I told her this. After not seeing her for a short time the phone rang and it was her mother, pleading with me to go and see her, this I did. What a mistake that was. Looking back, I should have followed my gut instinct. This story unravels in the following, very difficult chapters.

Now at this time, I regularly look at the Deeplish house, which takes me back to all the risks I took in building my detached house myself, back in the early 70's, with various work men and friends I had gathered along the way, and it all came together. I paid for all of this in cash with no cheques or promises to pay later. On completion of what was a substantial house, I was able to go back to the building society where I had taken out my first ever loan and re-mortgage the Moston home. I took out another loan on my brand-new detached house which

Elaine in Lytham with Peter and Julie Alison Ross at Peter's Birthday party

I had built and paid for and then sold my Moston home, having built this new detached home at 11 Hasting Street, Deeplish in Rochdale, using the proceeds of the sale to fund and build up my electrical business. I was happy to move to Rochdale. I was then able to start up my own electrical business in Rochdale, a very short walking distance from my home. I had no problem in keeping the mortgage payments up as I was able to utilise the mortgage in my company business. I never, in all this time, had any holidays. Work would never permit this; work was my life and it had cost me dearly in more ways than one. So, with the mortgage on my brand-new detached home I purchased a D.I.Y. shop on Oldham Road and Durham Street, turning it into an electrical shop with eventually my girlfriend, Elaine, working at the shop counter selling all electrical items. We had by this time our first child, Angela. She was able to bring the baby to work in her pram. She also brought her father in to help her and work in the shop. He was an electrician also, so I was happy with that. The shop was doing extremely well, which enabled me to take on another employee to work alongside her in my shop. I knew him well, he used to also work for Springers Electrical with me, small world.

My electrical shop behind the counter.   *Me above the shop in 1976.*

Terry in my office above the shop. Terry working behind the counter.

With things going well for me, I purchased another shop on the other side of Oldham Road and I easily turned it into a two-story cafeteria. I named it 'The Jubilee Café' as it was brought to life during the year of the late Queen's Jubilee, with me employing various other staff to open and close and serve breakfast and dinner six days each week. Everything in the cafeteria, i.e., the stainless-steel ovens, hobs, a Bain-Marie, chairs, and tables etc., all came from a contract I had with E.L.S at Nuneaton. It was a closed-down factory which had provided all the staff with their dinners and so on.

In the conversion that I carried out for them, I was able to make a deal with E.L.S for all the canteen equipment to be offset against the value of all the costs of my contract work with them. It was a brilliant deal, and my café was set and ready to open in 1977 in celebration of the Queens Jubilee. I went to the effort of putting up a union jack flag and pole on top of the electrical shop.

I now had the cash flow from both of my businesses, the café and the electrical shop and also from my very successful contracting work with E.L.S.

CLOSING DOWN SALE
PRIOR TO MOVING ON JULY 4th, 1981
HUNDREDS OF ELECTRICAL ITEMS MUST GO

We are clearing out our stock at well below trade prices.

Cables	per 100 metres
1.0 mm	£9.14
1.5 mm	£11.48
2.5 mm	£16.40
4.0 mm	£32.78
6.0 mm	£46.85

All Cables and Flexibles at Well Below Trade Prices
Cable prices subject to 15% VAT

SHOWERS . . .
Rodring 7kw .... £39.00 incl. VAT
Heatrae Sadia 7kw .... £49.00 incl. VAT
7kw Stabiliser Shower complete with curtain rail ...... £52.00 incl. VAT
6in Ventilating Fans, Xpelair and Vent Axis ...... £28.00 incl. VAT

ACCESSORIES . . .
Lamps, Tubes, Tungsten and Fluorescent Fittings
Well below trade prices.
MK Switches, Sockets, Plugs, etc. Immersion Heaters, Bulk Head
Fittings, Kettle Elements, Unalites, Striplites, Belling Tango Pan
Heaters, Outdoor Floodlighting, Selection of Track Lighting.
Friedlands Bells and Chimes.
Hundreds of other heavily discounted bargains.

P.L.B. ROSS ELECTRICAL CO. LTD.
(Members of NICEIC, ECA, JIB)
52 OLDHAM ROAD and 133-137 DURHAM STREET
ROCHDALE

Telephone 48755
24-hour answering service

Hours of business:
8.00 am to 6.00 pm
Monday to Saturday

My electrical sales were broadcasted on Radio One regularly. It was a great feeling to hear my name regularly advertised over the radio whilst I was travelling around the country for E.L.S. Every week I would advertise in the Rochdale Observer, just one small sample seen on the previous page, and I would always make sure my prices were cheaper than my competitors'. All this made me, and my shop well known in the area, especially with my company's name and N.I.C.E.I.C. qualification logo printed on my vans. But, in my inner thoughts I realised I still couldn't properly read, write, spell, or add up!

One day whilst I was in the electrical shop, the girls in the café sent a delivery man from Wall's Fresh Foods. He brought in with him a large number of sausages and bacon and other items that were in his van. He told me they were returns from Tesco and asked if I would like to purchase any at a much-reduced price. I made a deal with him, taking everything, he had and when he was in the area, I would always be happy to purchase all of his goods as they were in perfect condition. Each week he would call, and I would agree a cash deal on everything. This was fantastic because it could all be cooked straight away and I didn't have to go to the wholesale trade supplies, where I had an account, to purchase these items. This would have cost me far more, plus tax and time to transport and collect, and it was never as good a quality as what I was getting from the Wall's man.

A sad occasion that goes through my memory was in 1977. The Jubilee Café was advertised, I was working away and my two children, Julie and Peter, decided to visit the café hoping to find me. I hadn't seen them for quite a while, but I always kept my maintenance payments on time. When Angela was born and Elaine started working in the electrical shop, I made her father a director of my company and I looked after him very well, providing him with a car and an ex-gratia payment when he retired, referred to in chapter 18. Elaine decided she didn't want Julie and Peter in our lives, and she made my life hell over it. She was happy with me taking care of her parents and her having all she wanted but she didn't want to share our good fortune with my two children. I wasn't in a position to go against Elaine regarding her feeling on the matter. It became very sad and an uncomfortable time for me, plus, I was always very busy and went working all over the country for E.L.S. so then I had no choice but to keep my distance from them. The day arrived when they came looking for me with pride, seeing my electrical shop with my name on the front, happy and hoping to see me. Sadly, Elaine saw them and made them feel unwelcome and told them to go away and not return, so they made their way back home to their mother. I can understand how they must have felt, and it broke my heart, which has never been mended. My only comfort was that I was able to meet payments to their mother. She had happily remarried.

Whilst I was away on various contracts, I was able to use my electrical shop to hold all my very expensive stock for my contract work, as well as selling some of it in the shop in between. There was a lot of cash circulating in my purchasing power from trade wholesalers, then Walton's Electrical, now Newey & Eyre. My electrical company was now with 90 days credit so my orders were always in large amounts so I knew I would have cash in the bank, gaining interest until I had to pay their invoices. At the same time, all the contract work used stage payments which were continuously paid. Most of them were paid within 30-60 days. To get an extra two and a half percent early payment discount, I still had another month's interest left in the bank. In those times it was 11 percent in the pound. I eventually reached the million-pound investment, putting it on the sterling money market with interest to cover paying my men their wages and in case there was very little work, which never happened.

I decided to sell the café as a going concern, one being that the police were always parked up at the back enjoying free breakfasts and much more was going on when I was away. The proceeds I banked, then if I had no contract work for my workmen the interest, I was receiving from the bank would cover their wages. Work I had locally for various jobs I did myself. I then purchased more land and built a large warehouse with a large car park for my electrical business on Norwich Street, Rochdale.

I was building an industrial unit at the back of my shop on Oldham Road, on Norwich Street. As the shop was on the main road there was no easy parking. Lorries would become a problem whilst delivering heavy, copper cables etc. causing obstruction on one side of the road. Seen in the photo above.

I had my electrical shop up for sale after I had finished all my work on building my new warehouse and was moving in. I was able to move my electrical goods into my brand-new warehouse at the back, making it a safer, happier place of work for all to obtain my electrical goods before the shop was sold. It made things easier for all my contract work in the contracting business all over the UK as seen in part in chapter 21.

Not long after selling the café and whilst I was still working on the industrial unit, I read in the newspaper about a piece of land for sale on Bury Road, Bamford. I bought it and I decided to build a large bungalow on it. I started all the necessary arrangements and started on the groundwork. It was said by a surveyor friend, "I was always travelling at 200 mph" in business and he couldn't keep up with me. I was then introduced to a very nice Irishman called Tommy, he specialised in foundation work and drains. On meeting Tommy and finalising his contract in a deal, he shook my hand and whilst shaking hands, I knew we were going to work well together, and we did. So, I was now able to start building and funding my luxurious bungalow in chapter 18, with Tommy by my side.

CHAPTER 18: 1978. Building a luxurious bungalow on Bury Road and my warehouse.

In 1978 I purchased a substantial piece of land in Rochdale on Bury Road. I decided to build a bungalow with a swimming pool at the back with a sauna and steam room inside, making it my second house build whilst still contracting for E.L.S. all over the UK. It became a luxurious property known as 640 Bury Road, Bamford, Rochdale. This was alongside my other successful ventures. I was a workaholic, which is one thing I am proud to say. I wasn't a drinker or a smoker and if I socialised it would be organised at my home with selected friends. I was happy being a very good provider for my family. Never did they go without nor did those working for me. Whenever I left home for work, I would always be just another person working alongside my men all over the UK.

COOPER & JACKSON   ARCHITECTS · SURVEYORS
PLANNING CONSULTANTS
June 1979.

To whom it may concern,

Re: Detached Bungalow & garage at 640 Bury Road,
Bamford, Rochdale.

We place on record our knowledge and periodic supervision of this property (designed by Mr. F.L.B. Ross in association with his own Design Consultant) during its construction dating from Spring 1978 to Spring 1979.

One of my luxurious properties that I built, whilst at the same time building the warehouse.

My warehouse being built on Norwich Street.
Inside completed warehouse Rochdale, second floor

It was during the course of building the bungalow that I met Tommy. His very skilled profession was drainage and concrete work. He shook my hand on a deal to do all my foundations and drains on the bungalow. As soon as he placed his large hand in mine to shake hands, I felt that a most sincere friendship was to follow. Over the years we built up this very strong friendship and he told me how he came over to England with a ten-shilling note in his pocket and a suitcase with all his worldly belongings in it. We had a lot in common, we both had started off with more

or less nothing with no help from anyone. We both had self-motivation in us to survive. He had three daughters who over the years I watched growing up along with his lovely wife, Nancy. Tommy would always say to me over the years "Oh, I'd love to be a shilling behind you". We have had many moments of sadness and much happiness together over the years and he worked by my side often. I later discovered that he also had a difficult childhood.

I sold the electrical shop on Oldham Road, Durham Street, whilst keeping up all my other contracts. During this period, I had accountants K.P.M.G doing my company accounts where all the various purchasing and sales were taking place along with VAT, plus my own P.A.Y.E. and private company pension were all paid to the various authorities along with the payments coming in from the electrical sales. With things moving at such a fast pace, I purchased another piece of industrial land and built another warehouse with three separate units on Lily Street, Rochdale. This became another success and by this time I was married again with two daughters. I decided to give my father-in-law a job as he was out of work. He was a qualified electrical engineer, so father and daughter were working alongside one another. My wife decided to take on a nanny who was the daughter of a friend of hers and she took on her friend as a bookkeeper later. A few years went by, and her father retired, we gave him a good send off and he took a generous payoff with a nice car. See next page to show my generosity in an ex-gratia payment to my wife's father.

This certificate above made it possible for me to trade between so many and for my accountant at K.P.M.G to carry out the necessary tax returns for all those that I had employed. With many working away from home, receiving untaxed travelling expenses and lodging i.e., sleeping on the job, there was a tremendous incentive to stay away from home.

PART LETTER OF 3RD SEPTEMBER 1987

KPMG Peat Marwick McLintock

- 2 -

2   Ex gratia payment

The company could make an ex gratia payment to Mr Whittaker. The first £25,000 of such a payment would be exempt from tax in his hands, provided it can be demonstrated that there is no contractual obligation or expectation of payment, and the payment cannot be deemed to relate to services or duties performed by the departing employee. To avoid the Revenue raising this contention, any payment should be made after the employee had left. You may wish to consider giving Mrs Ross's father his company car, by including it in the £25,000 at market value. On the other hand, if the company continues to own the car and Mr Whittaker continues to drive it, it may be assessed as a second car benefit on Mrs Ross.

The drawback to this alternative is that it is unlikely that the company would be able to claim such a payment as a deduction from its profits for tax purposes. In order to qualify as a deduction the payment has to be wholly and exclusively for the purposes of the trade. We consider that in this case the company would be unable to demonstrate that it was. However, you may be content to bear the tax cost in the company as long as Mr Whittaker does not have to pay tax on the payment.

In the case of a large payment, the first £25,000 is exempt and then on the next two bands of £25,000 the employee pays half the tax and three quarters of the tax respectively calculated at his highest rates of tax. So that he will only pay the full amount of tax on the excess over £75,000, but this is probably outside the scope of the present situation.

3   Disability

If the employee is no longer able to perform the duties of his employment due to debilitating illness, any payment received on termination of employment is exempt altogether. We understand that Mr Whittaker has been in ill health recently, but we are not certain as to the nature of his condition. If it can genuinely be shown that he is unable to perform his duties, we recommend that a ruling from the Revenue should be sought <u>before</u> Mrs Ross's father retires as recent experience with the Revenue suggests that it is difficult to convince them after the event in this type of case and matters may drag on for some time. We feel that on balance you may not wish to subject Mrs Ross's father to this kind of inconvenience.

It would again be difficult to show that the payment had been made wholly and exclusively for the purposes of the company's trade.

4   Contribution to a Pension Fund

Although this is not quite what you asked for, it is perhaps worth thinking about setting up some kind of pension scheme for Mr Whittaker. Using this method, the company would make a lump sum payment now and Mr Whittaker would receive a pension for the rest of his life, which would be taxed together with his income from any other sources. However, such a scheme would need to be approved by the Inland Revenue SFO, and would be subject to certain maximum limits based on length of service and the level of final remuneration. The available pension is therefore likely to be small. We consider that there may be some difficulty in obtaining approval due to the amount involved. Even if SFO approval were obtained there is no guarantee that the lump sum would be an allowable deduction in computing the company's taxable profits.

A very small sample of my generosity in the retirement of my Father-in-law, including a car he used until he ceased driving.

The two new detached houses being built in front of Linkside Bungalow. Linkside – front lawn with two houses.

A lot of the payments were made possible over the many years by taking scrap cable and copper to be weighed in for cash. This was used in payments for food and many other necessary essentials like the toilet rolls (in chapter 25) whilst working away from home for many weeks and months over the years.

After a year living in the house, I built on Bury Road, I put it up for sale as I discovered a very large bungalow. It was called Linkside on Sunny Brow Road in Middleton. I saw the opportunity to build houses on the front piece of land leaving the bungalow far more secure and private. The property overlooked North Manchester Golf Course at the back. I purchased it and sold Bury Road. After moving in I decided to build another, substantial, indoor swimming pool. I straight away asked my friend Tommy to come with his workmen and his JCB. I brought some of my own workmen in as well. I did most of the electrical work in between going off to various sites for E.L.S. Then we started an extension on one side of the house for a kitchen and a playroom for the children, and then we did another extension on the other side for a large bedroom.

Throughout all this work Tommy would be supervising all these projects whilst I was away. Never did I question the value of Tommy's work. I would always pay for his work immediately after he asked for payment. He was my most trusted and wonderful friend. After every concrete job Tommy completed, he would always inscribe his initials and the year in the cement before it set. He did this every time he did work for me on numerous jobs. His initials are still visible to this day.

About a year after obtaining planning permission for two houses to go on the front of my land, Tommy was the first on the job again with his men and JCB to start work on the two houses with the same architects I had used on every development over the years. After obtaining planning approval, they would always supervise those work to comply with the various regulations.

Whilst Tommy, or should I refer to him by his company name Everest Construction Ltd, was working on the two houses being built on the front of my bungalow, I had a very large contract for E.L.S at Great Clowes Street in Salford. A very large factory building, as seen on the next page, was to be converted into a furniture and carpet sales show room.

The roof required substantial repairs as a lot of the Welsh blue slates had been stolen but there were more than enough slates left for me to do the two new houses I was building at the same time. So, having removed all the remaining blue slates and taking them back to the bungalow, there was a sufficient amount to

cover the two new houses with plenty left over. These houses can be seen today with those roof slates which came from the warehouse. The warehouse roof was re-covered with large, sky-blue, plastic-coated roof sheets making the building look brand new and completely waterproof. Tommy would be working with his men and mine seven days each week, my lads would work night shifts on the factory below as well as during the day on the houses above.

I worked hard and supervised all the work for E.L.S throughout, to always ensure approval by the local authority up to the opening for the public to make their purchases. It was another fantastic success to the satisfaction of all the E.L.S. directors who came to the opening. Regardless of all the difficulties I still had from the lack of education as a young boy I never let it hold me back.

Blue tiles off the factory roof building in Salford and being taken back to Linkside for two new houses.

CHAPTER 19: Relationship with Louie, owner of E.L.S

I formed such a close relationship with Louie and his family and all his staff throughout the UK. Whilst I worked at Great Clowes Street, I passed a very large synagogue and shops catering for the Jewish customers.

On one occasion I called at the Manchester Great Orthodox Synagogue to ask where I could find caterers to cook a family a Kosher meal at my home in Middleton, not far from Cheetham Hill. The person I asked had long hair and white string rope hanging from his waist coat, he was so helpful. He knew I was not of his faith but after I told him what I wanted, he gave me the name and place to call and gave me a little card with the Star of David on. I took this with me to the address he sent me to.

On my arrival at the address the only word I can remember is 'Shalom'. The lady gave me a nice smile, and after explaining my plans she said that all I would need was the use of a clean kitchen and her staff would deliver the food and utensils required. I explained I had my own silverware, jugs, dishes, and bowls along with silver knives, forks, and spoons in a wooden box in the lounge. She told me that to create an orthodox Kosher meal her staff would use their own cutlery at the table for my guests to enjoy a beautiful Kosher meal. She said that they would arrive and put all the food into my kitchen oven, then set out the table with a special tablecloth for the special occasion.

On listening to this lady who appeared to be in her 60's it was clear she was Jewish and some of what she said to me I could not understand, but that did not matter. All that mattered to me was she was clearly trying to be as helpful as she could. The next point of concern was the price. She asked me how many people would be at the table and I told her it would be 4. She told me the price and I then asked if I could call back when I confirmed the date that my friends will be calling, knowing that Saturdays are the Jewish Sabbath day. I thanked her for her kind words and told her I would be back.

I then found an opportune moment to ask Louie and his wife if they would visit my home in Middleton, seen in the photographs in this book. Barbara showed delight at this idea, and it was formerly agreed, a date was then given to me later by Louie, which was a Friday. I thought this was perfect and I could now go back to the lady I had spoken to and as soon as she saw me, she remembered me well. I told her the date and brought with me, what was in the 80s, a substantial deposit with the remainder to be paid on arrival at my home. The Friday date arrives, and they arrive before Louie and Barbara and prepare the table with the Jewish tablecloth covering the full table. They put all the food into my kitchen and stayed there whilst I was eagerly waiting, nervously. My wife had taken my children to be looked after, then, like clockwork, Louie and Barbara arrived at precisely the time they were invited.

I found out later that they had visited the Great Clowes Street store for a surprise visit, without warning the store manager, my home being only a short distance from the store. On arriving they found I had planned the full Kosher meal in readiness for them. Before they reached my door, they could smell the food. I invited them in, noticing they were having a good look outside. They had never been to my home before, but I had shown off some photos on my visits to them and Louie said that I had a very nice place, asking if he had paid for it all. Barbara, with a big smile on her face said one word: "Louie" in a strict voice. We shook hands, no hugs but the handshake was very warm and meaningful. They had known of my daughter's injury at Arndale, having sent a beautiful and very large teddy bear, see chapter 22, to my home, which I had taken to the hospital.

When Louie and Barbara noticed the table clearly set out for their visit, they took off their coats and sat down. I had already told them to come hungry but did not explain further. I quickly went into my kitchen and said to the ladies waiting with their black uniform and white pinnies on, "it's all over to you now. Then I returned to the table. We talked about a lot of things, and this got the party started with the catering ladies coming to serve red wine although I did not have any. I did most of the talking and there was lots of laughter whilst the meal was being served. I have to say, not ever having had Kosher food, that it was fantastic. I noticed Louie and Barbara were both well enjoying the surprise.

The food and the red wine were going down well. Not once did they ask to be shown around our home. They could see coming in our lounge, the front and back with very large glass panels, and the swimming pool out the back and the swing and slide. They were very impressed and happy in our company. It was Louie who first asked me, when he noticed my coil of cable under my arm, if I was an electrician, and we made a deal for my work against the cost of his carpet. This was many years before sharing our meal together and now I had my own luxurious home and cars, entertaining him and his wife.

After the meal was over and throughout, the ladies would be bringing and clearing the table all in the full Jewish tradition, serving desserts then serving coffee with After Eight mints. At the appropriate time I got up and went into the kitchen and gave the nice, kind lady an envelope with the remainder of the money and a thank you. She said as soon as all was taken away and the dirty dishes were washed, they would leave the kitchen exactly as they found it. In fact, one would hardly know they had delivered such a wonderful feast in my kitchen and then gone.

Then it was time for Louie and Barbara to leave and they thanked us for an unexpected surprise. I said looking at Louie, "I am so proud to have met you". Louie with his usual grin put on his coat and they left, saying "Mazel Tov". I noticed their car was waiting with their chauffeur who got out and opened the door for Barbara, with Louie going round to the other side. As they drove away, I could not help but notice such pride in their waving goodbye.

That most fond memory has stayed with me and will stay with me for the rest of my life. In lots of ways Louie and Barbara became another Reg and Betty to me, except this was a most pure, and close working relationship that was so successful and without each other's trust we both would have failed.

CHAPTER 20: The Tree

During the early 80s, I was at home and received a phone call on behalf of the owner of E.L.S, Louie Rosenblatt, telling me he was looking at premises on Prescot Road in St Helens, which could become the new headquarters for E.L.S. This was opposite St Helens glass work, and he asked if I would meet him there.

We met up and looked around, with an agent selling the property with him answering any questions. I noticed on the gable wall a very large crack and subsidence, so I went outside on my own to find a very large tree with branches towering over the roof of the building with droppings and leaves all over the roof and moss growing from all the roof tiles. As a result, the property had been on the market for a long time previously. The property was a very large Victorian house and it belonged to the church and was used for their church business. The frontage was looking onto Pilkington glass work. It had a large tarmac area for car parking, allowing space for the E.L.S owner's Black Rolls Royce Corniche convertible with its E.L.S private registration plate and his son's brand-new Rover sports car, plus plenty of space for any visitors.

At the rear of the property was another large car parking area for all the office staff and at the side of the building were large newish Portakabin offices that were attached to the main building. Despite the main building having such subsidence, it was still perfect in my view for the E.L.S to move into. The E.L.S owner and his family cars would all travel from their homes in Liverpool.

During my private talks with Louis, out of ear shot of the selling agent, I said I had been all around the outside and I had seen where the subsidence has come from; I noticed that one tree in particular was so large and clearly the cause of the problem on the gable end of the building.

The agent confirmed that there was a preservation order on the trees, making the sale less attractive for prospective purchasers. But if the tree could be removed and under pinning of the wall was to be carried out, then patching up the brickwork and re-plastering work on the inside would be all that was required. I went on to say to Louie that if the price was reduced substantially due to these problems, and if he was in a position to make an outright purchase, I would make the transaction easier by simply removing the largest tree. Louie looked at me and asked how the hell I was going to do that without causing the building to collapse. I said to him that I had a very large, sharp, electric chainsaw and this brought a tremendous grin to his face. So, with great confidence, he bid farewell to the agent, and we left, and I said that this was a fantastic location to move to and I was up for the challenge. I was eager to do it.

A few weeks passed when I received a phone call from Louie asking me to call up to his luxurious and beautiful home named Rood House, off Allerton Road in Liverpool. I would pass his Rolls Royce outside, ring the doorbell noticing underneath the Jewish mezuzah fixed on an angle to the side of the door frame. I rang the bell, and his wife Barbara came to the door, welcoming me. The first thing I did was take my shoes off, then she took me to Louie in the lounge. He poured himself a large glass of whisky from his beautiful, crystal decanter, then poured one for me. We sat talking in his wonderful lounge, then he asked me to look at his swimming pool, which he was having converted into a music room and study for his and his son's work. Keith Davidson and partners were his architects in Liverpool and had done all the drawings for the planning authorities. On this occasion, the architect would use their own builders to do the work, but Louie wanted me to do all the electrical work; this I agreed to. This would not involve me doing any paperwork at this time. Louie knew I had difficulty with paperwork without help from others and he would simply pay me from his safe, which was hidden in his bathroom in the airing cupboard, adjoining his bedroom. When working for E.L.S, the payments I would receive were shown on the next two pages. So, this shows how much trust Louie had in me, even introducing me to his very friendly solicitor Lawy Daufman.

I would also meet Louie's children growing up, two girls and a boy. I would then carry out work on their homes when they left home and got married. I was at the wedding celebrations of one of his daughters and his son's when he got married, always wearing skull cap (kippah) on my head, as all should, when celebrating in the Jewish faith.

At Louie's home with a glass of whisky that I had not drunk, Louie asked how long it would take for me to deal with the tree problem, with a smirk on his face. The deal would soon be done, and he expected the exchange of contracts within the next week. I was getting nervous, but I did not show it, it was like dropping a bomb on me. I believe this is why he poured a large glass of whisky as soon as I arrived.

So, with my great acting skills and confidence I told him to leave it with me and that I would get back to him in the next few days. He explained he was leaving this with me and to let him know before I started the job. In other words, I took this to mean he was putting all his trust in me to remove the tree without any come-back on him or the E.L.S Company Ltd.

I went home and immediately contacted a good friend of mine called Peter Edwards. He was the owner of a company called Edwards Crane Hire. They had a crane that I knew could more than handle this particular job and lift the tree with my supervision. I took Peter up to have a look at the job one Sunday afternoon, the site was closed off, but I could park up and take him to show him the tree. I told him if he put one of his cranes on Prescot Road, it had to be on a Sunday when the Prescot Road was not too busy, I would bring my men, one of whom would be a banksman for the crane driver to direct the traffic after we've put the safety cones to the front and rear of the crane. Peter saw this as no problem for him, he was an ex-army man and he got all his training whilst in the army and got the picture of what we were up against, then we drove home. I thought

Peter was going to tell me I must be mad, with the risk of something going wrong and backfiring on him being so high, but he didn't, in fact Peter said it was a brilliant idea. I said I would tell him as soon as I cut the trunk and that it mustn't swing on to me and more importantly it mustn't swing on the house or the whole lot will crumble. So, I asked what his thoughts were. He asked, "When do you want the job doing?" I asked if I could arrange for three very large skips to be delivered into the rear car park during the next week. Come rain or shine would he have his crane driver on the road first thing the following Sunday morning and he said, "I have just the man for the job". I asked, "How much?" and he said, "Let me give this some thought on the way home". So, driving home I told Peter what I wanted after the tree had been cut and for it to be lifted over the top of the house without any damage to the roof. The crane would extend its boom and reach to the position where my men will then direct him to lower it, so that it rests on the three skips to enable me and my men to then cut it up and put all the branches and the logs into the skips.

Peter gave me a price before he got out of my car and, with my relationship with Louie, I had no problem in asking him if it would be paid in cash with no paperwork. He said yes, and with this I told him to go ahead and that I would be on site next Sunday morning good and early, ready for the crane to arrive at 8 am. On my estimation the crane driver would be on his way back home down the East Lancashire Road by dinner time or before and if so, it would have made a good profit. I talked with Peter over that week, and he told me that all was organised for the Sunday start. I arranged for the keys to be collected from Louie and the skips to be delivered from the Rochdale firm, where I also had a good relationship with the owner.

With my men, I drove up the East Lancs, noticing in front of us at 7.30 am the massive Edwards crane, so on passing we pipped and waved so that he knew we were now ahead of him. On our arrival, we opened up the building. The skips were in a line as asked for and the crane arrived at 7:50 am. He parked up in position, put his riggers in place and my men grabbed the heavy timbers and put them in position for the crane driver to put the legs down and the crane then lifted the wheels off the road. The crane driver jumped back into his cab and raised the telescopic boom. Meanwhile I had my men put the electric supply at the position of the tree trunk with my very special, sharpened chainsaw plugged in. At this point I would go and cut the tree with my men standing back, having lashed the chain from the crane attached to the hook on to the tree, then removing my extension ladders, which I still have whilst writing this book.

I am happy now to take the risk and cut the tree. At this time the crane operator had put strain onto the crane from the tree up to three tons. I then went into the tree and got the chainsaw and started to cut very carefully and things were going great. So, I kept going until I got halfway through the trunk, and all was still well. The crane operator is told we are halfway through, and he puts further strain from the tree onto the crane. I stood back watching and all was still ok to my amazement. I started up the chainsaw and continued to cut when I noticed the chainsaw was not getting stuck and the cut was getting easier and the gap in the cut was getting wider than the blade on the chainsaw. I continued and as I got nearly to the end of the cut, I noticed the tree gently lifting, it did not swing, and I could not believe it. I dropped the chainsaw and very quickly moved away, giving the crane driver the sign to lift the tree and I watched in amazement as the tree went up, up and up and it is now above the height of the house. I looked at the crane and I noticed cars had stopped and were all watching. To my dismay, so was Louie's son, who on seeing me and the tree moving over the roof of the building got back in his car and he and his girlfriend drove off at great speed.

The crane man takes the tree over the top of the house safely then lowers it on the other side with my men directing him to the skip, as where he was, he couldn't see them. My men pulled at the trunk to get it in line with the first skip. We told the crane driver to lower the large and very long branches slowly, as the tree is lowered, the thick branches start to crack with the weight of the tree on top of the skips, the chainsaw is brought over, and I cut away at the large branches with my men pulling them away. We told the crane driver to lower the jib to take the weight off the crane altogether and allow us to disconnect from the tree trunk. Then we told the crane driver to pack up, which didn't take him long, the outriggers went back in, and the timbers were all put back on the crane. The crane operator did not even look at the tree as he just wanted to drive away before the police arrive.

The Prescot Road traffic is moving now the crane has driven away. The security guard at Saint Helens glass had seen all there was to see and gone back inside. I contacted Peter to tell him the job had been done and his driver had left to go back to the yard. It was just gone 10 am so he would be back at his home for 12 noon. My men and I would work on until 8 pm. I was drilling very deep holes into the remaining trunk of the tree that was about five foot in diameter so I had many holes to drill with a heavy-duty drill which would get very hot and had to be left to cool down to continue drilling all the holes. Then on sweeping away all the wood, drilled out for the holes, I filled them with red diesel, then the trunk was covered over with a black plastic sheet with garden peat and soil on top. I then returned to my men still clearing and sweeping up. The three skips were full and overflowing, even though all the branches had been cut into small pieces, then the very heavy trunk pieces were put on top to push it all down. We filled my van with heavy logs, and I took them home with me. Then on Monday all the skips were removed and there was a final clearing up of the car park, making it much cleaner than when we had started. I then got a phone call from the delighted owner Louie, saying, "thank you" and "very well done".

No legal action was taken by the local council for the removal of the tree, no one even noticed it was gone. This made it possible to access the gable of the building to underpin the section requiring concrete and cut off the offending roots that were growing under the building. During the course of the following week, after all the work were completed, E.L.S started their move into their new headquarters.

I would say this job was the greatest risk I had ever taken on, for all my work and my men. We did not have any safety equipment or helmets. Had it gone wrong, my men would simply say, "That's life Jim but not as we know it, beam me up Scotty". No safety equipment would have prevented some 10-15 ton of tree falling on us. Instead, all that helped me with that Sunday work were paid very well, in cash with no deductions and most of those that helped me were electricians all working for me at E.L.S.

CHAPTER 21: Success to multi-millionaire

Throughout the years there was so much work Louie did not even ask me to give a price for, I would do the work and charge accordingly. Never enough for all I did, and I knew Louie had the same thoughts and this will be seen within the very small, two sample ledger pages below.

This is a small sample of my order book back in 1988 showing a cash flow in the multiple of millions GBP.

On reflection of these work and many others I will always remember hearing the words said to me on leaving the orphanage, being told I would never get anywhere whilst I had a hole in my f---ing arse. Well, the abusers were the experts in what holes in the arses were for. The ledger sheet shows six hundred and five thousand, five hundred and ninety-five pounds seventy-eight pence, still outstanding to me in September 1988. This just showed how wrong they were, but it made me more determined to be successful in my life. Not only did I do the value of work shown, but I also funded them as well.

THE ELS GROUP
THOMAS HOUSE, PRESCOT ROAD, ST. HELENS, MERSEYSIDE WA10 3XB
TEL: (0744) 612181   TELEX: 629043   FAX: (0744) 20566

Back
Use other side first

LINKES

Name	E.L.S.			A c No	
				Card No	12
				Credit Limit £	

Date	Ref		VAT	Goods Inc VAT	Payments Returns	Balance
April 1988	Balance B/Forward					1,622.31
1.4	Cheque				50,000.00	1,622.31
25.4	Cheque				50,000.00	1,572.31
4.5	Cheque				50,000.00	1,522.31
9.5	Cheque				50,000.00	1,472.31
16.5	Cheque				50,000.00	1,422.31
23.5	Cheque				50,000.00	1,372.31
30.5	Cheque				50,000.00	1,322.31
6.6	Cheque				60,000.00	1,262.31
10.6	Cheque				50,000.00	1,212.31
21.6	Cheque				50,000.00	1,162.31
1.7	441 Rotherham - Dining World			100,000.00		1,262.31
1.7	442 Rotherham			200,000.00		1,462.31
1.7	443 Dudley - Dining World			100,000.00		1,562.31
1.7	444 Enfield			100,000.00		1,762.31
1.7	445 Hartlepool			100,000.00		1,962.31
12.7	446 CR NOTE - MANCHESTER				B 267,725.00	1,685.14
12.7	447 CR NOTE - NEWPORT				B 248,250.00	1,446.65
12.7	448 CR NOTE - BRISTOL				C 266,090.00	1,180.505
27.6	Cheque		50,000.00			1,130.505
4.7	Cheque				50,000.00	1,080.505
11.7	Cheque				65,000.00	1,015.505
18.7	Cheque		50,000.00			965.505
25.7	Cheque				50,000.00	915.505
2.8	Cheque				60,000.00	855.505
05.08	Cheque				50,000.00	805.505
22.08	Cheque				50,000.00	755.505
27.08	Cheque				50,000.00	705.505
05.09	Cheque				50,000.00	655.505
10.09	Cheque				50,000.00	605.505

THE ELS GROUP
THOMAS HOUSE, PRESCOT ROAD, ST. HELENS, MERSEYSIDE WA10 3XB
TEL: (0744) 818181   TELEX: 628063   FAX: (0744) 20582

Name		E.L.S.					Front	
Address							A/c No	
							Card No	.13
Terms							Credit	£

Date	Ref		VAT	Goods/Net, VAT's	Payments	Balance
September 1988						605,3
16.09		Cheque			50,000.00	555,3
15.9		Cheque			50,000.00	505,3
23.09		Cheque			50,000.00	465,3
20.09		Cheque			100,000.00	365,3
28.09	451	Goods – MANCHESTER		247,220.00		622,5
07.10		Cheque			100,000.00	522,5
14.10		Cheque			100,000.00	422,5
22.10		Cheque			100,000.00	322,5
31.10		Cheque			50,000.00	272,5
05.11		Cheque			100,000.00	172,5
12.11		Cheque			50,000.00	122,5
22.11		CHEQUE (			50,000.00	72,5
25.11		CHEQUE			50,000.00	22,5
10.12		CHEQUE			50,000.00	(27,1
16.12		CHEQUE			50,000.00	(77,1
29.12		CHEQUE			50,000.00	(127,1
16.01		CHEQUE			50,000.00	(177,1
09.01		CHEQUE			50,000.00	(227,1
20.01		CHEQUE			50,000.00	(277,1
27.01		CHEQUE			50,000.00	(327,1
01.02		CHEQUE			50,000.00	(377,1
10.02		Cheque				
07.04	452	CR.NOTE – MANCHESTER			17,500.00	(394,6
10.04	453	INVOICE – POOLE		244,750.00		(157,9
10.04	454	INVOICE – PORTSMOUTH		247,750.00		89,82
12.07		Cheque			73,156.53	16,69

CHAPTER 22: Caroline at Arndale

Whilst carrying out all these works, my daughter Caroline had been in the Arndale with the nanny shopping. Whilst there, she became trapped in the escalator. Her leg had received a serious injury. The escalator caught her wellington boot on the side and the friction of it then pulled her leg in. It was a terrible ordeal for Caroline, and she was just five years of age at this time, horrifically injured on the 12/8/1985. The incident took place at the Middleton Manchester Arndale shopping centre. I was working away in London and saw the nanny taking Caroline and my younger daughter Jennifer out that morning as I left. I was told that Caroline had to stay trapped until the fire brigade got there, they had to use special hydraulic, jacking equipment to release her, whilst the paramedics obviously sedated her. What our little girl must have been going through, I cannot imagine. They didn't want to risk turning the escalator back on to reverse it because they had no idea which way it would go. Everyone could hear her screaming and they sent everyone out and closed the whole Arndale down.

The local press had followed the fire engine, they call them ambulance chasers, and they took pictures of Caroline when they had released her. She was taken to Booth Hall Children's Hospital. When I heard that my daughter was in hospital, I immediately jumped in my car and returned home so that I could be with her. All of us were obviously upset. We stayed with her as long as we could but couldn't stay overnight with her and we were told she would have to have skin grafts as all her muscles and tendons had been severed and she would have scars for life.

The next few days consisted of just being with Caroline and trying to keep in touch with everything and everyone at my jobs by telephone. Caroline was made comfortable and was not long after operated on and having skin grafts taken from her left thigh, to be placed onto her right leg. At this time, the hospital did not have a spare wheelchair and the one in use could cause cross contamination. As luck had it, right next door to the electrical shop on Oldham Road was a factory, called McGlocklin's Company Ltd., which manufactured brand-new, state-of-the-art wheelchairs. I knew the managing director and his son, so I drove straight to his factory. When he saw me, he said he was so sorry to hear of the tragic injuries that my daughter had received which he saw on the TV and heard on the radio. I told them I needed a new wheelchair and they had loads of brand-new ones, ready to deliver to various customers. They told me to pick whichever one I wanted, and they would immediately deliver it to Booth Hall Hospital. I thanked them and told them I would sort the costs out ASAP, but they told me not to worry. I distinctly asked if they would engrave a plaque to be fixed onto the wheelchair saying 'Donated to Booth Hall Children's Hospital, from Caroline Ross' and we left it there after she was discharged.

The day after, a very large hamper with sweets and many splendid things arrived for Caroline and the other children to share, along with a very large teddy bear which can be seen when Tommy is next to Caroline's bedside. Then, to my absolute shock there was a knock on my door, and it was a mother of another child who had also received an injury on the same escalator previously, and the Arndale centre simply sent the child away and the mother wanted to tell me her story which I listened to with great interest. Failing to understand how this injury to my daughter could be possible after another child was injured, I decided to make a visit to the Arndale shopping centre, noticing the escalators were still in operation. With my limited knowledge on health and safety in a public place I noticed there were no emergency stop buttons at the top or bottom of the escalators. I spoke to the management to make myself known to them and I requested, with immediate effect, that they closed the escalators to prevent any further serious incident. If this was not acted upon, I threatened that I would call back with a very heavy sledgehammer and damage the escalator to put it out of action. I left, then I discovered that they had shut the escalator down. I knew I had to take on a most difficult and painful job whilst my daughter was lying in bed in hospital in such pain, which was taking legal action against the owners of the escalator who refused to admit their negligence. This I could not accept. So, I contacted my Manchester family firm of solicitors to act on my behalf, and for the care of my daughter. After paying their costs they advised me to accept an offer that had been made by the insurers of the Arndale in settlement of her injuries. This I could not accept; it was a ridiculous offer. Instead, I discharged their services, making payment of all their costs and disbursements.

Then I heard of another accident with a 4-year-old in 1985, which was the same year. So, there were, very sadly, four children. I have all their names and details but for legal reasons I cannot refer to them in this book. Eventually Caroline was out of hospital and back at home. At this juncture whilst I was back in London working, I employed the services of a London firm of solicitors and barrister called Michael Beckman QC, and solicitor Barry Samuels. I travelled to meet them at my venue in the Holiday Inn, Swiss Cottage London. Also, Jim Callaghan MP became involved. I decided to contact BBC's Watch Dog programme. The BBC Watch Dog came to my home and did an interview on camera with me and my daughter, Caroline, and this went out live. The Arndale refused to be involved in the program, saying only that they would carry out the work to meet their legal requirements, when in fact they had decided to use their financial muscle against me and planned to appeal against their conviction. On the 14/1/1987, thankfully they lost their appeal. This led to a Writ in the High Court Queens Bench Division on the 17th of March 1987, Ref No 1987RNO1004 (an infant suing via her father and next friend) with the kind help of the most thoughtful, QC Michael Beckman and solicitor Barry Samuels, I won a most successful case against the Arndale Centre owners.

Thanks to the joint efforts I was successful with H.S.E, prosecuting the owners of the Arndale shopping centre, having received an expert's report proving that the escalator had eleven most serious defects, and in part thanks to contacting the BBC in the appeal against their fine. This was the reason for them not taking part in the BBC Watch Dog programme.

The award monies were put into an infant investment account, under my control as father and next friend for her injuries, until she reached the age of majority, making a substantial amount of interest with no tax deduction. This continued until the 16th of April, approximately 1997. I was wrongly, and in my opinion, unlawfully removed as my daughter's trustee by the joint actions of my former solicitor John P Trafford and my former wife. Therefore, I lost control and protection of my daughter's investment. In London I appealed this decision but lost. Her investment was soon gone, thanks to her mother who had earlier married John Trafford.

Approximately three years later they became divorced on grounds of his adultery, having made my daughter's friend

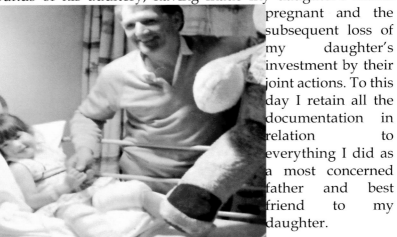

pregnant and the subsequent loss of my daughter's investment by their joint actions. To this day I retain all the documentation in relation to everything I did as a most concerned father and best friend to my daughter.

Tommy Visiting Caroline after the accident in the Arndale

Brecher & Co Solicitors

78 Brook Street London W1Y 2AD

D. J. Brecher	C. F. Stone	Jane M. H. Henry
H. A. Brecher	S. M. V. Lightman	P. M. Pepperell
A. A. D. Wiseman	D. H. Kustow	G. S. Simmons
L. H. Starling	S. A. Remington	Debra R. Shaw
H. Bart-Smith	Susan M. Freeman	Shelagh M. Taylor
G. D. Herman	B. R. Samuels	M. Broughton
T. H. W. Piper	M. Silverman	G. Sherriff
I. D. Green	Norma R. Simon	
A. E. Laycock	Tessa Rudnick	

Telephone 01-493 514

Telex 263486 Brelaw C

Cables Brecherlaw Lon

FAX 01-493 6255 (Gro

DX 13 London

Our Ref   BRS/EWD/97770

Your Ref

Peter Ross Esq.,
Woodlands,
Canterbury Close,
Broadhaigh,
Bamford
Rochdale

12th January 1988

Dear Peter,

RE :   CAROLINE'S ACCIDENT

May I extend every good wish to you and your family for
the New Year.

I have received a draft Statement of Claim as settled by
Sidney Ross and amended by Mr. Michael Beckman Q.C.   I
enclose this and should advise you that I must serve this
on the other side by the 20th January 1988.   Could I please
ask you to let me have any comments you wish to make by
Monday of next week at the latest, namely the 18th January.

Michael Beckman has approached the matter on the basis
that the whole system was dangerous and should have been
taken out a long time rather than any failure to give signs
or warnings.   This latter failure can be dealt with by
way of a Reply if it is raised substantively in the Defence
served on behalf of Charlwood Alliance Holdings Limited.

In relation to special damages I should be grateful if
you would let me know whether you have in fact paid any
hospital bills etc for Caroline and if so could I please
have a copy of any receipts you have receipts and would
ask you to ensure the originals are kept safe.

Yours sincerely,

BARRY SAMUELS

See this dreadful ordeal in chapter 26.

CHAPTER 23: I first meet up with Derek.

In 1977 I first met up with Derek. He would have been in his early 20s when he called into my electrical shop on Oldham Road for electric cable and many other items which, if they had all been brand-new, would have cost a lot. He explained why he wanted the items; he had started working for himself. He had a little VW camper van parked outside my shop, and his workplace was a little shed, he told me, on a farm near Buckley Hall Prison. I agreed to go up with him to look at how best I could help him, with some of my second-hand items, saving him not having to pay a hefty price if the items were new, and also to give him some help and advice on the best way to do all the electrical work as he was not best experienced. On looking at his workplace I knew I could provide him with all his needs and by him using the items I had taken out of buildings that I had worked on. I could sell them on as second hand or use them on other jobs for myself. They were all in perfect working order and I could see Derek was more than happy with this. So, I got all he required into my van to deliver them for him, passing the prison along the way and looking at all the prisoners behind the fencing.

On giving over to Derek what he needed, he asked how much he owed me. I said, nothing, you can have them, but at the same time I asked if he could make me a trailer to be pulled on the back of my van, capable of carrying over 1 ton. He told me he had no problem with that. The next time I saw him he told me he was getting on with building the trailer and would I go and have a look at it, so I did, expecting to see a small trailer but instead I saw it was big enough to put a car or a van on, capable of carrying 3 tons. I could not believe he had put so much time and effort into this for me. I asked how much I owed him, and he said, "just pay me for all the new parts I have purchased", which were the bits that connected to the tow ball on my van and the lights on the back of the trailer. All the rest he had either got from a car breakers yard and metal that he had left over from various jobs. We came to a gentleman's agreement on payment in cash no questions asked. I then asked Derek if he would like to do some work for me on different contracts, some being far away from home. He said, "leave it with me to think about and have a word with my wife," as this meant staying away from home over night and he had 2 young boys, Mathew, and Simeon, who I ended up getting to know very well. A few days passed and Derek arrived at my shop for some additional items of electrical for his work and he told me he was willing to try out doing some of the work for me because he could make up a lot of items in his Rochdale workplace. Then we could take them together in my van to places I was working, for him to put them together by welding them on site.

We met up and got on with the first job. This went so well we were stuck together like glue and went from job-to-job at different places like Huddersfield and Leeds. Always behind us on our journeys was the trailer that he had made, and it lasted over 15 years. It went through unbelievable journeys without any trouble. Then, one journey coming back from Liverpool on a dark night with eight forty-five-gallon metal drums with red diesel in them, the wheel came off on the motorway. Thankfully I was able to pull on the hard shoulder and was able to recover the wheel. I then contacted the RAC from the emergency phone on the motorway. They arrived and put another wheel nut and split pin into the stud holding the wheel and the RAC men told me to drive slowly. They asked how far I was going, and I said Middleton. They told me they would stay behind me all the way home, and they did with their lights flashing. What was amazing is they never complained that the load I was carrying was unlawful. I thought what nice blokes they were as they must have known. When we got to my home it was gone midnight. I asked them in and gave them a bowl of soup while we had a good chat. They commented on how lovely my home was, then when they got up to leave, I handed them a nice gift, placing it in one of their hands. They left with big smiles on their faces. I just thank God the police did not stop to find out what was on my trailer.

Derek and my relationship went from strength to strength, now over 42 years on and we are still close and friends to this day, along with Mathew and Simian his two sons, who both have their own children who will get to know their grandad and grandma when they get to read this story.

We worked in many places together, Derek and I, day and night, sleeping next to each other with other men of mine, sharing our thoughts and risks we have taken along the way. During our work we had such fun along the way. To name a few of the places we have travelled to together: Sheffield, Great Clowes Street, Salford, Manchester, Oldham, Gateshead, Hartlepool, Leeds, Preston, Birmingham, Derby, Colindale, Thurrock, Enfield, Leicester. Rotherham, Weston Super Mare, Liverpool, Newport, Oxford, and that is only a short list, there were many others. Never ever was there a time that for all Derek's good work would he be waiting for payment, and never ever did I ever question the amount he charged because never was it enough to cover the fun that we all had together. This chapter could go on and on and on, but I will just give this last one example: one of Derek's workmen, an expert welder and supposed airline pilot, would go out with all the men at night for a few pints. He would put on his pilot's uniform and cap which got the girls heads turning and he started talking in a posh accent and pretended he was an airline pilot; he wasn't, but by God he was good at pretending! Then on one night there was a police raid in the building where we were staying. One of the neighbouring properties had reported there had been a break in and they had seen men going into the building. The wing commander jumped out from behind, lifting himself off the shoulders of the police officers and into our room with his pilots cap on with a big smile all over his face and ten pints in his belly and said to the officers, "Do you not realize I out-rank you officers, I am a wing commander." The police at this point, whilst we are watching and laughing, simply didn't know how to deal with the situation, so they shone their bright torches into our faces, some keeping their heads down. I obviously got up bidding the police farewell and good night and went back to my camp bed next to Derek. The following day everyone was in hysterics. Derek and I, still laugh to this day. So, on this, it is very nice to share this story with all those taking their time in reading this unbelievable relationship between me and my good workmen, whilst staying away from home. Auf Wiedersehen Pet; I say this, as this was how the police referred to their experience in another chapter with a police visit. So, this is the only way I can describe how it was, but it was so much better.

Some of my workmen having the usual fun whilst working away from home

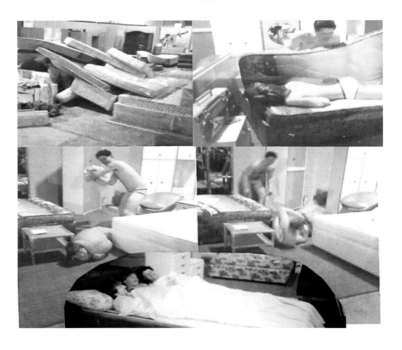

Me on top of forklift truck pouring water over my workman and him tied to the lamp post in Sheffield town centre.

Now, whenever we see each other, even 36 years later, we don't have to say a word, we each go into laughter, and we just cannot stop talking the night away with he and his wife Susan telling of all the experiences we have had together. Derek and I are so similar: we don't smoke we don't drink or do drugs etc. We were both simply family orientated.

Derek and his sons frequently worked on security fencing and gates around industrial units. Then in 1987-89 Derek fitted all the steel work within the renovated 1608 circa Tythe Barn in Redlumb, Norden, called Hindclough Farm & Barn seen at chapter 31. This would become our final family home and offices to work from, having approximately 3 acres of land. We re-established our registered company offices at that address; see a picture taken from the Lancashire Life magazine later.

Unbeknownst to me, whilst all this was taking place in 1987-1989, my wife and my solicitor had other hidden plans, of which I had absolutely no idea. They had diverted vast amounts of money. I did not know obviously, or miss these diversions of monies, as long as the accounts were showing good profit. Our pensions were worth one million, plus there was nearly nine hundred thousand invested on the sterling money market. When my wife asked me to sign off the accounts, I would be happy to sign them, having no idea of the vast amounts of movement of cash.

I later discovered she had managed to forge my signature upon vast amounts of documents and cheques whilst I was away from home and office. On my late discovery of this practice, I noticed that she had managed to forge my signature so well that I had thought that they were my genuine signatures, up until they were placed before a forensic writing expert. Then I was able to prove that they were indeed all forgeries. I then discovered who they were all paid to, and I took out proceedings against the bank. During one of my first visits to the bank, the manager who knew me well said to me "Mr Ross, surely you would have noticed over a hundred thousand pounds had gone missing?" My immediate response was, "When you trust those closest to you and there is such an investment on the money market, I simply did not miss a hundred thousand and more". On taking proceedings against the bank this required both directors to consent to any proceedings; my wife of course would not consent to this, and she was the only other director. The costs up to that point had been lost, with the case being discontinued/struck out by the court. This set case law Ross-v-Trafford. There is no mechanism to break the dead lock between two directors. So, effectively she had walked away from this crime until this writing about the truth of all these events and other incidents will be revealed in the coming chapters.

CHAPTER 24: E.L.S.

I have been asked what brought my success in business and the answer is quite simple – the people I got to know, such as the owners and family of E.L.S.; serving the electrical apprenticeship with my foster father Reg, who taught me to always think ahead; and the fact that I go to help anyone who needs it, for example when I first met the owner in my first visit to E.L.S with a coil of cable under my arm. Ever since that time, whenever I received a call for help, I was always there, rain or shine. Over the passing years this was never forgotten by E.L.S.

One small example is on Boxing Day in the 80s, I received a phone call to say a roller shutter door was stuck in the open position. They couldn't close up to leave at the end of trading. There had been thick snow also on that day. Nevertheless, I got in my van and drove from Rochdale to Saltley Trading Estate in Birmingham. It took me at least three hours. On my arrival I noticed snow had blown into the store and into the electrical connections at the top of the roller shutter, causing it not to operate. There was no chain to simply pull and bring down the shutter. I got a ladder from my van to reach the height of the motor which, if the electric had been operating, would have turned down the shutter. Instead, I got a spanner on the motor wheel to turn the shutter down by hand. All the time snow was blowing on me and I was freezing cold.

Once the door was closed the staff were able to sweep up the snow, leaving the heating on to melt away any ice and snow left after I had gone. I removed all the water to enable the electrical motor to operate the roller shutter for the following morning, as it did. To make sure it wouldn't happen again I placed plastic sheeting over the top and tested the up and down working of the shutter. I had a cup of tea and a chat with the manager then I left to drive the three-hour journey back home in thick snow, reducing the motorway down to two lanes. All of this work did not give rise to an invoice or charge for any of the time spent that day, doing the journey there and back and on Boxing Day. It was simply part of the service I gave. This was talked about between the owners of E.L.S and the staff about how I would always turn up no matter when or where the problem was, in any of their stores around the UK.

Another example was when frost overnight burst a copper water pipe above a false ceiling. It flooded the floor in the store at Derby. No one working at the store could find the stop tap to turn off the water. Water was gushing out constantly. The best I could do under those circumstances was to tell the manager to go and turn on all the water taps fully in the toilets to reduce the amount of water pressure coming from the burst pipe then to do the best he could until I arrived. I took with me all my plumbing tools and immediately on my arrival I took my ladder and went up it with a lump hammer to bang flat the burst copper water pipe until the water stopped to allow the mopping and the vacuuming of all the flooded carpets etc. In the meantime, I traced back the pipe to the stop tap and turned off the water. I cut out the damaged pipe and connected it with a new pipe, then wrapping the section above the ceiling with pipe insulation, turned the water back on. I spoke with the manager over a cup of tea, then left on my journey back home from Derby on icy roads. Back then there was no gritting of roads as there is today. On this job I was asked to submit an invoice as there was a substantial insurance claim for flood-damaged goods. My invoice supported descriptions of the cause I had given for the flooding. The cause was that on the night of the frost there had been a power cut, and with this the heating could not come on via the frost stat. Obviously, the insurance company verified this with the electrical authorities. In the same area there were other incidents much the same; I could see this as I was driving away.

The value of the insurance claim for damage to the items that were in perfect condition before the flood, created a flood damage sale. This brought about a far greater profit to the owners than had they all been sold in the normal process of business. What was spectacular was, after the insurance loss adjuster inspected all the damaged items, they were paid for in full under the insurance policy. All those items were then sold off at a massively reduced priced on a special one-day sale. The store was packed out. There were many other examples like I have described where my help turned tragedy into fantastic profit to E.L.S.

In these stores when there was a problem and I had travelled for long periods of time, I would sleep in them, and, if my men were with me, they would sleep in them also.

There was one occasion when I was called upon to help a film crew connect up all their apparatus, and it was not possible to just plug into an electric socket. I went up with my men, working through the night and the following morning. The security guard stood at the entrance doors, keeping order on a one-off event. Bernard Manning was due to arrive to be filmed in the very large Birmingham store. Outside parked up at the entrance was his white Cadillac '1 LAF' registration number and another 'BJM 1' on his white Rolls Royce. This brought so much interest that the place was full, a lot of them only wanting to get his autograph.

Whilst Bernard was being filmed with a roll of carpet on his shoulder, I said to him "Hi, Bernard, I live not far from you up the road just off Moston Lane". He looked at me with his big round face, with dimples on his smiling cheeks, and said, "What the F---ing hell are you doing up here"? I explained "I came up especially last night to do all the electrics for all of you lot", pointing to all the film crew. He turned around with the roll of carpet still on his shoulder and nearly knocked someone's head off with it.

Whilst I was looking at Bernard's fancy cars parked outside, it took me back to my visit from the orphanage in the black taxi cabs to Bertram Mill Circus. When Coco the clown, with his trademark face makeup and his big nose and white face, stayed in my memory, then and now, which is over 60 years or so. Coco was in his honking car with doors and wheels falling off in the rough and tumble fights with the buckets of water routine, involving a plank of wood that would turn and knock someone to the ground. So, when I watched Bernard in the filming that he did with a carpet on his shoulder, then knocking someone to the ground and all the film crew and others were full of laughter including me, Bernard was clearly copying from the slap stick routine of Coco the clown. May he rest in peace with his lasting memory in this autobiography for everyone to read. All this was great fun and I got to talk with Bernard in between his filming, and all he would do was tell jokes one after the other. We were in absolute stitches.

Bernard never contacted me to do any electrical work in his club, which is a pity because it wasn't long after that it caught fire and he blamed it on Des O'Connor, but that's Bernard. So, over the many years of my services to E.L.S group of companies, I would become the very first involved in fires, of which there were a number. The fire-damaged goods would be sold off after insurance had paid out their full value; advertising would regularly go on tv as either fire sales, closing down sales, massive clearance sales etc.; and the public would queue up and go wild for bargains. Then in 1988 it became law that all furniture must be made with fire retardant material, meaning all furniture prior to 1988 had to be sold off cheap at massive, reduced prices. I was always present, and I would be with the owner of the E.L.S group of companies like his right-hand man. Then his son Paul would step into his shoes.

CHAPTER 25: Colindale, North London

In 1986 I had a very large contract on Edgware Rd., Colindale, North London. It was an old Royal Air Force HQ converted to a very large B&Q, D.I.Y store and their London HQ. It had been empty for over a year. I was now taking to London all local tradesmen in a convoy of my vans filled with the different materials needed. All the men had to stay away from home so brought their change of clothes and camp beds, which we used regularly on different contracts with sleeping bags, food, tea and washing facilities so it made it possible that we could all stay day and night within the building that we were working on. Upstairs in the offices us electricians would sleep, and we'd have the best choice of rooms. Ceiling fixers, joiners or carpenters were in another room and so on.

I would always stay with my men 'the electricians' and on this contract my good friend the pipe fitter and welder and sheet metal worker came. He was called Derek (referred to above) and he brought his very young son for the experience, and what an experience that was! Derek, on leaving home was the only one whose wife had made him a flask of tea and coffee and sandwiches etc. So, he did not have tea with all the lads on arrival at London, which was after the fun convoy run between Rochdale and London. When I say fun, I mean fun. They would pull into the service station on the M1 and park up next to each other and go off to use the loos and come back to the vans. Then sit in the vans having a smoke and a drink. They had a stick with a hook on each end and they would put bags of crisps and other things in them. These would be passed between vans to save getting out and passing them to each other and would be repeated many times. If someone didn't have a fag and wanted one, they would light the fag put it on the stick and pass it through. They thought it was fun.

Once, there was an unbelievable smell coming from one of the vans and we had to evacuate it and investigate. It was found that one of the gas bottles that had been loaded in Rochdale had not been turned off properly and had been leaking all the time. So, the van was full of gas and had someone lit a cigarette, it could have gone off with one hell of a bang. Thank God this didn't happen. I know one would say this was just stupid and dangerous and daft, but when you get a group of men driving in a convoy for the first time in their lives such a long distance and full of boredom, it is amazing what goes on. The convoy then set off again to Colindale, here we come.

Arriving safely in Colindale, the first job was to find out where we would all sleep and where we would have our tea and food. Whilst unloading all our vans that we had driven inside the building, closing the large roller shutter door behind us, we went and filled the large kettle with water and put it on the gas stove to boil. All the cups were in their places on the table with sugar and biscuits. The tea was made, and the call went out for all to come and have their tea. Derek and his son, Mathew, did not participate but they sat around with us all drinking our lovely tea and coffee and Derek drank from the flask which his wife had prepared. So, after the usual banter, talking about the journey down and all the fun along the way, it was off to get our rooms ready for sleeping and putting up our camp beds. This left only a short gap in between each bed, just enough for boots and bags and clothes, reminding me of the L.C.C dormitory, but with all the same mission in mind, to get the job done. Then we all familiarised ourselves with the layout of the building from the plans, ready for an early start first thing in the morning.

THE VAN
WITH ASTLEY
SIGNS WAS
MY VAN, THE
PHOTO WAS
TAKEN BY ME
AFTER ASTLEY
FROM ROCHDALE
HAD FINISHED
FITTING ALL THE
ELS SIGNS ON
THE FACE OF
THE BUILDING ON
COLINDALE ROAD
LONDON

JUST 5
OF MY
MANY
WORKMEN.

THIS PHOTO
SHOWING HOW
MY MEN HA
FUN WASHING
DOWN THE
'VANS' IN

LONDON

Those that like a pint went off looking for pubs and later turned in for the night, so we thought. That night we all got hardly any sleep since everyone except Derek and his son came down with the trots and terrible stomach cramps. Making it worse, the one thing we had not thought of before we left Rochdale was bringing loads of loo rolls and we needed plenty of them, so it was a search to find whatever we could use. We all eventually managed to get uncomfortably through the night. The following morning, I had to find out what the hell it was that had caused the problem of us all being ill. Derek immediately explained it had to be the water, as he and his son were the only ones not affected. We went to the tap used to fill the kettle and we traced the pipe that went directly to the roof above the offices where we were sleeping. After looking at the roof, we noticed a large header tank, holding possibly 50 gallons of cold-water storage. We got ladders and went up through the ceiling to the very top of the roof and looked down into the tank where we found floating above and below the water the remains of dead pigeons, and many of them. So, having found the cause we emptied the tank and removed the old tank. I sent out a replacement tank that was plastic with a lid on, fitted it back in place and put the water back on so everyone recovered through the day.

The job continued and then the following day, with all the various tradesmen knowing what their jobs were, working together and moving the job on. At the end of the day, there was time for all to get washed and changed to go out and look around North London on foot, finding the best pubs. At this time there were lots of Irish men staying in various bed and breakfast places, they were working on the new motorway, the M25 ring road, so my men got to know other drinking pals and have a great night singing and drinking with the Irish lads. Our men returned back to sleep it off ready for the next day's work, but on their late return, obviously very jolly and in singing moods, they woke us all up. They fell into their beds without undressing and all went quiet. All of a sudden me and Derek were awoken by the sound of banging and shouting and there were flashlights blinding us coming from all over the place. We noticed a load of police officers looking in on us all. I couldn't work out what was going on or if something serious had happened. Worried and blinded by the flash lamps, Derek and I got up and talked to the senior police officer who told us there has been many complaints about a break into this building and a breach of the peace. I explained who I was and that there was no break in. By this time all those that had caused the problem were long gone, with their heads down, asleep.

The police told me that one of them causing the disturbance had dark skin. Thankfully he was well under his covers fast asleep, with their flash lamps shining all over the men, they didn't find the black man. But one man who was awoken turns over and looks up at the police officer shining the light in his eyes and he says to the officer, and I use his words, "Will you Fuck Off!!" At this the police officer turned to the other and they were clearly amused by what they had seen. I distinctly remember hearing one officer saying, "This is like Auf Wiedersehen, Pet". The officers left and I was able to get back to sleep. The following morning everyone was in hysterics because all those that were with their heads down with Tony Blackham were all under the sheets laughing their heads off that night.

I had, in between getting the job on course, organised in my head a journey that was pulling at me with us being in Colindale and me knowing Brixton wasn't that far away. I headed out for the underground and travelled to Brixton to see where I was born. I was off on my journey hoping to see the house where my mother gave birth to me. I got off at Brixton and walked to Ackerman Road but sadly it had all been knocked down and a new development was nearing completion. I stood glancing around. My thoughts went to thinking of my mother and visualising her there. Then my thoughts went to doing a search in a library to see if I could find anything that linked me to my mother and the year she lived there and when I was born. I knew from my mother's death certificate which I had obtained, that she had died from carbon monoxide poisoning from coal gas. Libraries normally have archives and newspaper clips. I saw a policeman and he told me to jump on the bus to Streatham library, this I did. I asked the lady in the library if I could look at records linked to Ackerman Road and the day my mother died. To my surprise and amazement, she told me to go to the newspaper archives in, low and behold, Colindale. I couldn't believe it. I made my journey back to Colindale and when I got there, I just called in to see how work was going on, and then I found the newspaper archives which turned out be a stone throw away from where I was working. To think I was so close to the history I have been searching for and wondering about since leaving the orphanage.

I got to sit down and scroll through various rolls of microfilm until I reached the date that my mother died and then to my horror, I saw the article, showing all the very sad events that took place in the house where I was born when my lovely mother took her own life. It was a very sad and difficult time for me. I requested newspaper copies seen in the first chapter and I walked back to my contract and men and got on with my work.

The contract that Derek had with me was to do the sprinkler system and make the large supports to support the roof over the new offices. They were made of heavy tubular steel with fixing supports welded on and when he finished them, he would send them off for sand blasting, then chromium plating. The offices were always the last job and time was running out for us as Christmas was coming fast upon us. I obtained the address from Derek so I could go and collect the tubes from the address in Derby to save some time. When I got there, I found that they were already closed for the Christmas break. I was in desperate need of this order of tubes so I could finish my contract on the offices before we all finished for Christmas. Thankfully I had a joiner with me, so in desperation, I told him to take the door off the building which he did. Thankfully the building wasn't alarmed, but there was a big dog there, but surprisingly where the dog was, it couldn't get to us, but we could hear it barking. We found my order of chromium tubes, done and all wrapped up ready for delivery. So, instead we collected them and carefully placed them in my van then Andrew re-fitted the door onto the building, leaving everything as it was when we arrived, and we carried on with our journey to London.

When we got to our job, I told Derek all about what we had done. Derek was a bit worried about it as he knew them well and I let Derek know it would be me who would have to suffer the consequences if there were to be any. I had already paid for the work they had done on these tubes plus they never told us they were shutting so early for Christmas, and they knew the order was needed before Christmas break. Without doing what we had done the store would not have been completed ready for opening on Boxing Day. I was worried about what we had done all through Christmas and into the new year. Gladly when the Christmas holidays were over and they opened again, and absolutely nothing was said, it was another mission accomplished, with everyone happy.

One evening I decided to take all my lads who had never been on the Underground before or seen London on a trip. The furthest any of them had ever been, was Blackpool, so I told them that there were strict rules, we all had to stick together no matter what. So, we walked from the store up the road to Colindale Northern Line Underground where I purchased the tickets for all of us and I kept hold of them. Everyone was aware that I had got the tickets, which was my way of keeping them all together. We all get on the train, getting off at Leicester Square, me showing the tickets to the ticket inspector who let us all through his gate without going through the barrier one by one. Now we were amongst the masses of people, me leading knowing where we were heading and we went to Carnaby Street then Covent Garden, Trafalgar Square then on to the Queens House. Then I made a cut through back to Oxford Circus and then we headed on up China Town for some Chinese takeaway. I decided to show them Soho (a big mistake) and going up we passed a few scantily dressed girls asking my lads if they wanted a good time. I kept a watch over them all from the back which was another mistake as they fell into the deadly trap. Me being at the back, the one in the front I noticed being dragged into one of the joints and being offered liquid refreshments. We were now sitting round drinks tables, the girls coming over asking what we would all like. There is a big guy on stand, making sure that drinks are ordered so we get our drinks and I say, "That's it lads drink up and we are off". Not being a drinker myself I am not bothered; except I couldn't help noticing that all the drinks being taken to the tables were by girls with nothing on except stiletto heels. So, I got up and got ready to leave. I had the tickets to get back, so I paid the ransom bill for the drinks, and we got the hell out of the place fast and got back on to the Underground at Leicester Square.

So upwards and onwards, the job was sorted, and the place looked fantastic and ready for the public to start coming in after E.L.S had put all their goods in for sale. But there was just one last job, the sprinkler system which had not been water pressure tested. The store staff were in the process of recruiting and interviewing in the new offices I had just finished. The nice new chrome tubes were holding up the roof and inside these tubes were the electric cables for the computers, telephone cables and pipes for the sprinklers and water pipes.

Derek opened up the very large water main operating the sprinkler system that would put out any fire within the building. The sprinkler pipes were above all the ceilings in every part of the building. I started to hear the rush of water pressure going through all the pipework and Derek was watching and listening to downstairs at the same time, looking for any possible leaks, when there was an almighty crash. It was so loud I thought that the weight of the water had forced the whole of the ceiling down somewhere and that would have crashed down on all the furnishings and displays all set up and ready for Christmas opening and Boxing Day sales. I was panicking inside and couldn't work out what had happened, but we had to work fast. Derek rushed to instantly turn off the water valve, then we went to investigate, only to find one of those being interviewed for the sales managing position at the store had, instead of walking out through the glass doors, walked through the full glass window next to the doors and that is what had caused the loud crash. One of the girls that was interviewing and myself ran to assist the man, who was cut to bits and bleeding. I ran and got some large kitchen roll to rap round his cuts and he looked like a Mummy by the time I had finished. An ambulance arrived and took him to hospital. Derek and I then get back on with what we had to do and re-tested the sprinkler system. Everything was perfect. The pressure was up and there were no leaks, and it was certified fit for the public opening. Emergency boarding up of the window was done, until later in the day when a local contractor fitted a new large plate glass window.

Then we heard from the hospital that the man had been discharged after having many stitches and that he had been high on drugs, and that's the reason he had walked through the glass window. So, he never got the job or damages for his injuries, and we simply got on with the job and I had to pay for the glass he walked through. There was another situation like this in Leicester town centre where late at night there was a drunk leaning against a large display window. He was singing and dancing to the passing traffic in between drinking from his bottle. One of my men filled a bucket up with water and went to the window on a floor above. In perfect timing with the traffic slowing down he poured the water all over him. This they thought was funny. The drunk left and returned with a brick and threw it into the window. When I discovered this window broken, I was told was an accident. But then I found out the truth

I had to pay the bill for the large window, so it wasn't so funny after all.

At the end of all this work I had promised to take all my lads on a Christmas do at a Schooner Inn restaurant. They had reserved seating for the night. We arrived and our tables were all set up upstairs with Christmas hats and crackers. Downstairs was fairly full of families with children, so we all sat upstairs at the table, pulling our Christmas crackers and putting our party hats on, having fun with the bits of toys within the crackers that were making noises of all sorts. There were other families upstairs with us with their children and they joined in with us, blowing the party flutes and pulling party poppers with all the other little things. All the staff were serving up the meals, throughout and there was Christmas stuff flying all over the place between our table and the others.

Then we noticed some people from downstairs were coming up to find out what all the noise was. After the main meal it was time for afters, and I ordered apple pie and custard. When it arrived on the table, my apple pie was picked up by one of my lot and put straight into my face. This takes off, and I am stood feeling a right one, now having a bunch of well lubricated workmen chucking stuff all over other tables and all start joining in. The downstairs lot were still coming up seeing what was going on and they cracked up with laughter, and some went back down with some of the kids left joining in.

Then it was time to play another game whilst the staff were clearing up the tables and the mess. The game was to each put a 10p coin in between their legs right at the top and then have to walk without dropping it and get it into a small glass on the floor. Whoever won got all the coins surrounding the area. We were all in fits of laughter, it was so funny to everyone. Now all the downstairs lot were coming and joining in, the laughter had everyone upstairs, even the staff coming to see what was funny. It was just watching the way everyone walked with the coin put right high between their legs especially the females with skirts and dresses on, and it was always the kids with short legs that won, taking home lots of winnings.

Me and my lads having a well-deserved tea break after completing our job getting ready for our journey home

Then it was time to go back to store for our last time and pack up for the next day to head back to Rochdale. However, when I went to sort out the bill downstairs, I said to those at the payment desk I was sorry for all the mess and the state we had made of the place, and I was in total shock when they asked if we could come back again tomorrow. I left them with a most generous tip, but most importantly a most memorable Christmas gathering of good, hard-working, Northern lads working in the South/North London then Essex. These contracts became the same pattern all over the UK, day in day out, different places and different fun to be had. We were fortunate to be able to have the fun we had along the way in between the hard work.

.

Below is a list of contracts showing only part of the 1.5 million of un-invoiced work taking place.

STATEMENT OF ACCOUNT F.L.S.

ROTHERHAM	300,000	00
DUDLEY	100,000	00
ENFIELD	200,000	00
HARTLEPOOL	200,000	00
OLDHAM	200,000	00
BARNSLEY	200,000	00
CHESTER	200,000	00
NUNEATON	200,000	00
WEST THURROCK	200,000	00
	1,800,000	00
Balance of 14/3/88	(1,573,309	22)
	226,690	78
CHARLTON approx to date	100,000	00
	326,690	78

Balance of 17/2/88
P.L.B. Ross Electrical Contracting Co Ltd..   152,596   03

By the 1980s I had contracts all over the UK. I had gone past the million pounds turnover and by 1987, with just under 1 million pounds invested in the sterling money market where interest payments were enough to cover the staff's wages when our work had slowed down.

By this time, I had formed other limited companies, all trading between each other e.g. My building company built domestic houses and industrial buildings. My electrical company carried out all the electrical installations, purchasing all the electrical requirements from my electrical retail warehouse supplying all the company's needs, enabling VAT and Corporation Tax to be used and paid under the careful accountancy firm K.M.P.G, carrying out the various company trading accounts, noting my ability to be generous.

CHAPTER 26: My solicitors involved in private, and company matters. Meeting John Trafford.

Between 1970 up until 1978 all my solicitor requirements were handled by a large Manchester firm of solicitors. In 1985 I instructed them to take proceedings against the Arndale Centre, or should I say the owners 'Town and City Properties Ltd'. I privately funded all the legal costs of these solicitors. I could have, if I'd wanted, obtained legal aid in the name of my daughter; she in her own right would have been entitled to legal aid in this matter, but rather than go through the exercise of obtaining legal aid I chose to fund all the costs myself.

However, after months of work they were doing on my behalf, for my daughter, my solicitor suggested that I should accept a financial settlement award of damages plus costs. When he told me the amount I should accept, I was very angry and terribly upset. I felt this was an absolute insult and injustice for my daughter, given all that they knew of her injuries and the good relationship I had with this solicitor over so many years, and I felt they had let Caroline down. It was even suggested I could have a claim through my household insurance policy, which may cover this type of negligence. However, there could be an exclusion clause for injuries sustained by members of my family. Counsel on the 19/5/1986 on quantum was suggested in the region of £15,000. My solicitors were forcing me to accept this advice, or I would end up having to pay all my costs. I was in an awful situation having to make such a decision relating to my daughter. I had seen how horrific her injuries were and had been at her bedside at every opportunity I could make to be with her at the same time that I had my work commitments in London. It made my situation worse. I decided to see if I could find another firm of solicitors in London. So, sadly my friendship with my solicitor friend came to an end.

At this time my daughter, Caroline, was 5 years old, with the most serious, life-long injury. With my own understanding of escalators, I had to make very difficult decisions. I knew that the escalator that had caused her so much injury had to conform with British Standards and on my visit to the Arndale to look at the escalators, I knew then that they simply did not conform to British Standards.

My solicitors would not force the owners to admit liability. I effectively dismissed them, but this was after I had instructed a London firm of solicitors called 'Breacher & Co' to obtain all the files from my existing solicitors. To do this I had to agree to pay all the costs, enabling them to take over the case. Whilst this was happening the Health & Safety through Rochdale Council would successfully prosecute, on my insistence, 'Town & City Properties Ltd', the owners, for their negligence This success boosted my confidence in dismissing my Manchester solicitors, with 'Breacher & Co' successfully retrieving all the files with payment on account. This also boosted my confidence in getting on with all my E.L.S contracts all over the South and North of England.

Whilst I am now in a position to stay overnight at the 'Holiday Inn Swiss Cottage', leaving my car safely in their underground car park, I would go by underground tube train into central London and visit the various places of interest. On one of those visits, I was simply in the right place at the right time. Whilst I was walking on the embankment, I noticed Richard Branson's Virgin Atlantic challenger 2 pulling up with Richard jumping off first. He ran up the stone steps leading from the Thames to the roadway where I met him. He immediately noticed me with a beaming smile on my face. We shook hands and had a photo taken. He says to me "I must go" and he runs off very quickly into the road stopping a black cab and he jumps in. Then I notice some activities around a new car parked up with security men standing around it. I noticed one had a hidden small arms' gun inside his jacket. This took my interest and I return back to the stone steps noticing Mrs. Thatcher and many, many others still left on the boat but following Mrs. Thatcher up the stone steps were her security in front and behind. There was only me at the top of the steps to greet her. Obviously, this had been kept quiet from the press or the place would have been full of on lookers. Denis her husband was not with her or from what I could tell nor was he on the boat.

So, as she reached the top of the steps holding on to her handbag fascinatingly. I was there to greet her. Her security was standing back as she was clearly happy to meet me and stopping to chat as seen below in one of the very many photos including Mrs. T with all surrounding her whilst she was climbing down from Richard Branson's boat. I was able to walk and talk with her until she reached her awaiting armoured security black car. We said our farewells and she shook my hand. Then she and her security team got in the car and they sped off. Mrs. T. giving me a very warm and friendly wave. There was another girl standing with me who was able to say "Hello" and shake Mrs. T's hand. So, at this point I was in absolute disbelief and happiness having met with Richard Branson completely on his own then running off to catch a black cab then Mrs. Thatcher with no one whatsoever pushing me aside, as seen in the photo. Never in my wildest dreams would I have expected this let alone 36 long years later on, I would be putting these truthful events into my autobiography.

Armed Guards

At this point I had a contract in West Thurrock in Essex, where I had some building regulation problems. I no longer had my Manchester solicitors, and I couldn't burden my London solicitors to become involved in my business matters. When I was back home in Rochdale, I made enquiries and I was told that a good solicitor for planning disputes and building regulation problems was a solicitor called John Peter Trafford LLB, at a Manchester firm. I made the necessary arrangements to meet up with this solicitor at his offices. He showed great interest and happiness in taking up instructions from me and even travelled alongside me in my car for a site visit to look at the problems I had. The planning issues were relating to half hour or one-hour fire protection within the structures of the building I was contracted to do. Effectively all the contracts I was doing around the country were the same and if one-hour fire protection was required on one building, then it followed it would be required on all of them, and this would increase the value of work considerably. Mr Trafford contacted the various authorities, which led to there being a court hearing to take place, which became discharged. Thankfully the various authorities accepted that the work I was doing was compliant and the actions of the councils went dormant. I would pay for the good work of Mr Trafford's firm. Whilst travelling between sites with Mr Trafford he got to know more about me and my family. We got into discussions relating to work, which led to talking about our families. I went on to tell him I had three daughters and he told me he had two children. I mentioned to him that one of my daughters had been seriously injured on an escalator and he took particular interest in this topic. I told him I previously had a Manchester firm of solicitors who I had dismissed as they wanted me to settle my daughter's damages and I had gone to London and obtained the services of Michael Beckman QC who received a much bigger settlement and that I had it safely invested, and I was receiving updates on the investment each month. This would give Caroline on her 18th birthday, a very substantial payment for her future use. This I was very happy with. I told him how we had a nanny looking after the children whilst my wife would be at the shop, when it suited her, or at the warehouse with her father selling electrical goods. He knew I was a hardworking, devoted father and a good provider for my family.

John Trafford became my solicitor in regard to all my planning and building regulations disputes for work and personal work. He knew by this time I had purchased a luxurious home in Bamford, Rochdale called Woodlands. To my knowledge he had 'never been' to my home. He had however, been to my site on Chichester Street where I was building my industrial units. On occasions, my wife would come to visit me at Chichester Street, and it was here that she met Mr Trafford.

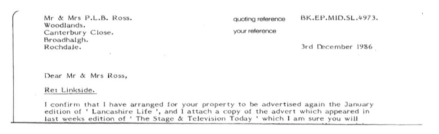

He was impressed with all of my achievements, and he knew my work took me all over the UK, taking me away for many days at a time, sometimes more. My motivation and enthusiasm had taken me from nothing, coming out of an orphanage to being a millionaire, fun-loving father, and a very good provider for my family. Eventually, my wife wanted dogs, German Shepherds, then it came she wanted horses and other animals.

I thought I should buy a farm, so, I looked for a farm. A farm I soon found; it was derelict, but I wasn't afraid of a challenge. The farm/ barn was on a best offer auction in the newspaper. I placed my offer, and I soon had a 16th century farm/barn in Redlumb, Norden that had witchcraft history with it, at the same time having my lovely home in Bamford. It was too posh really, especially for my vans to keep going in and out of. So, Woodlands went up for sale with some of the brochure pictures on these pages.

Woodlands
(Pictures on the interior follow on the next page)

Pictures from inside my home at Woodlands

Dining Room

Family Dining Area through to Kitchen

For those reading and taking time to understand what a wonderful achievement I had made in my life whilst living at this beautiful home, my wife had a beautiful gold jaguar parked outside the front entrance.

My wife had later changed her white jaguar for a brand-new gold jaguar.

The Mercedes was my car, very nice it was too. I travelled many a mile in that car, very comfortably on my long journeys all across the country.

My work was my life and it had to be if I was to keep providing my family with all the luxuries they were wanting. My children went to a private school in Rishworth. My wife had cleaners and nannies, working some days when it took her fancy, she had everything and more.

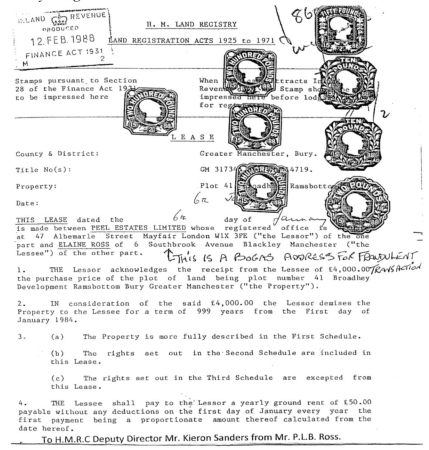

INLAND REVENUE PRODUCED

12. FEB. 1988

FINANCE ACT 1931
M   2

H. M. LAND REGISTRY

LAND REGISTRATION ACTS 1925 to 1971

Stamps pursuant to Section 28 of the Finance Act 1931 to be impressed here

When Contracts In Revenue Stamp should be impressed here before lodging for registration

L E A S E

County & District: Greater Manchester, Bury.

Title No(s):   GM 31734 and 4719.

Property: Plot 41 Broadhey Ramsbotto

Date:

THIS LEASE dated the 6th day of January is made between PEEL ESTATES LIMITED whose registered office is at 47 Albemarle Street Mayfair London W1X 3FE ("the Lessor") of the one part and ELAINE ROSS of 6 Southbrook Avenue Blackley Manchester ("the Lessee") of the other part. *This is a bogas address for fraudulent transaction*

1.   THE Lessor acknowledges the receipt from the Lessee of £4,000.00 the purchase price of the plot of land being plot number 41 Broadhey Development Ramsbottom Bury Greater Manchester ("the Property").

2.   IN consideration of the said £4,000.00 the Lessor demises the Property to the Lessee for a term of 999 years from the First day of January 1984.

3.   (a)   The Property is more fully described in the First Schedule.

       (b)   The rights set out in the Second Schedule are included in this Lease.

       (c)   The rights set out in the Third Schedule are excepted from this Lease.

4.   THE Lessee shall pay to the Lessor a yearly ground rent of £50.00 payable without any deductions on the first day of January every year the first payment being a proportionate amount thereof calculated from the date hereof.

To H.M.R.C Deputy Director Mr. Kieron Sanders from Mr. P.L.B. Ross.

Unbeknown to me, she had made another purchase of a brand-new house to live in. One will notice from the date on the registration document and the date on the document above to try and understand the deception that I was totally unaware of. The rest of her fraudulent actions are in the following chapters.

Things were still very busy and with such success I decided to purchase another, much larger, piece of development land which I called 'Heritage Park'. It is still under the same name today at Chichester St, Rochdale. This development was to be my last to give rental income forever and security for when I have gone to those Pearly Gates to leave behind for my wife and now three daughters. My first tenant was The Body Shop, Anita Roddick of the body shop organisation, on a 15-year lease with three yearly rent reviews. Another tenant was the Greater Manchester Bus company, storing all their antique buses, see photos below with my eldest daughter on one of them. The other tenant was Coats Brothers, ink manufacturers and the other unit was for my companies' own use. So, having completed the development and all units occupied I had a very substantial rental income for life (so I thought). Note the purchase of a brand-new house with stamp duty.

'Heritage Park' Industrial Units. My daughter Angela
My office and warehouse

Whilst all this development work was taking place, I was still with my contracts all over the UK, keeping my friendships with the directors of all the companies and visiting the luxurious home of the Carpet Warehouse owner in Liverpool. In December 1990 I discovered that my trust had been seriously damaged, both in those in whom I had placed my trust at home and in my work. This wrecked my life's work, (see the effects of these disastrous actions at chapters Solicitors, Doctor and Wife from hell). There can be very few comparisons, if any, of the journey I have travelled through my life. These give me the reasons to put these truthful events into words from the boy who never received an education and still to this day relies on others to put this appalling, incorrectly spelt, writing on paper, for you readers to read and hopefully understand.

CHAPTER 27: Journey for my uncle and my mother's sister

Many years had passed, my brother Bill with whom I was very close and loved and idolized, died of cancer; my heart was broken. His body was donated for research so there was no funeral. I went to ask my other brother George about the mystery of our mother's passing. I got nothing from him. My sisters weren't in attendance after my brother died. We didn't see much of one another with us all being separated at different stages in our lives. So, when I approached George, he just broke down in tears and wouldn't tell me anything. A few years later my brother George died. I was by his bedside when he took his final breath.

With both my brothers deceased now, I got to thinking about my sisters. I decided to go and see my sister Eileen. She was older than me and Sally, so she must have memories. She was 11 years old at the time of our mother's passing. I again asked the question. She started slowly to tell me some of what she could remember. She told me that she remembered when she was 11 years of age being taken out of the house and the smell was terrible. All the windows were being opened, and that had it not been for me crying in the cot awakening those in the house, we would have all been dead or the house would have blown up. Coal gas had gone from the basement kitchen and up the three floors above and there lived another family above us. I discovered it was a London County Council rented property, an end three story block of many a terraced row of council homes all with linking and open roof spaces, so the gas would have gone between our home and all the rest and could have blown up the full row. Across the road were shops, one called 'Guppies'; today the full row of Victorian properties with basements are all gone. The rest she told me on our later gatherings together.

So, I had learnt where my mother was laid in Streatham Park Cemetery grave number 48659 and that she had a brother. Years go by and I am older and wiser and in business. I made a trip back to Streatham and I went into the cemetery. The staff at the cemetery were able to trace my mother's burial place in an un-consecrated grave. This was because she had committed suicide (this was a criminal offence in those days), but having found her resting place, I went and got some flowers and placed them on her grave. I got to thinking if what had happened would have been made public in the newspapers, with it being a criminal offence. I knew the age I was going into the orphanage, so I placed it around that year. I then went to the newspaper archives in Colindale off the Edgware Road, North London. There I sat and searched and found on the microfilm the news item which said, 'Women 40 gassed herself at her home 67 Akerman Rd, Brixton'. I was mortified. I took a copy and when I got back home, I contacted my sister Sally; she told me she did not know but said there was something that had happened, but no one would say what it was. I had a feeling, this unknown force, that was pushing me to find out all about my mother.

My real journey then started; I remember my brother Bill telling me of my mother having a brother. I had been named after him, my middle name being Bernard. So now I had an uncle called Bernard Mason Smith. My brother had told me he was working for the RAC up North. With my living up North, I returned home and went about my business that had become a great success, employing many staff contractors and sub-contractors working all over the UK.

I was working at Gateshead and Hartlepool living in Middleton, Manchester. On leaving my home in Middleton, I called into the motorway service station for petrol at Hartshead service station passing an RAC customer membership mobile office. I decided to chance parking up my car and went in to see if I could obtain any information relating to a patrol man called

Bernard Mason Smith. On asking the very polite girl how I can find information on an RAC patrolman, I noticed sat behind me, an elderly RAC man having a drink of tea. He said to my question to the girl, "Why who wants to know?" so I turned to him and said, "He was a relative of mine, he was my uncle and I had been named after him". I showed him my license so that he knew a little more of who he was talking to. He put his cup of tea down and said, "Follow me". I was not sure of what this meant so I asked where we were going, he then said, "Your uncle was my best friend and if you follow me, I will explain".

I was taken aback and couldn't really believe my luck in meeting my uncle's friend by chance. He told me to get in my car and follow him. I got in my car and drove close behind his RAC van, arriving at a place called Ossett. We got to a very nice, large, house where he stopped, and a lady came out to greet him. I got out of my car and they both welcomed me into their home and over a cup of tea the R.A.C. man told me his name was patrolman, Len Hobbs. He was the commander over my uncle for all his memberships and paperwork and monies in my uncle's possession.

He then tells me sadly that whilst my uncle was on duty on the A1 going North, he had an accident with another vehicle, and he received a notice from the police and thought he had caused a serious injury to the occupants. The police notice did not tick the appropriate boxes on the notice properly. So, he drove his RAC motorcycle on the day he received the notice to the road passing over the river Don. He then jumped into the river and with his full RAC uniform on that was very heavy with the water it pulled him under and took him in the fast flowing freezing cold water down river. Miraculously a passing motorist saw him jump, pulled over and dived into the river to save him (it transpires that he was a trained expert life saver). He managed to get hold of my uncle and pull him to the side of the river, and he was still alive. By the time the ambulance arrived, however, my uncle was pronounced dead. So tragic and very sad it was for me to now learn of my uncle Bernard's suicide.

The man who rescued my uncle was put in an ambulance and taken to hospital with his injuries and hypothermia at this time. Len Hobbs' wife had made many cups of tea and biscuits and Mr. Hobbs asked if I would like him to take me to see the man who had saved my uncle. Immediately I said, "yes please", and leaving his wife we got into my car and Mr. Hobbs in full uniform directing me to his home which was not that far from where he lived. I just could not believe this journey I was now going on. I soon forgot about my journey for work.

On arrival, I parked my car and Mr. Hobbs went up to the door, leaving me in the driving seat. A little while later he returned to my car and said that I was welcome to meet this man, he and his wife had agreed to meet me. At this point my mind is running all over the place. I should be at Gateshead at my work, but now I am going up to this man and his wife, into their home and she looks at me with Mr. Hobbs and invites us in. We go into the front room, and all sit down and holding my hand he says, "This is the first time I have met anyone relating to the man I had saved", he had tears in his eyes and so did I, and we hugged each other. I would say he was in his 80s and he got a cigarette and lit it. Then he went to a drawer in the corner of his room, bringing to me a large folder and a box of newspaper cuttings. One document he showed me was a Bravery Award and there were many others for me to see. One of the newspaper clippings said when he dived in to save my uncle, in his pocket was his wage packet, but when he was undressed in the ambulance it was noticed his wage packet had gone therefore it had gone down the river Don. That saddened me even more and it stuck in the front of my mind.

So, from that day to the day of my visit with Mr. Hobbs he had never received any thanks for all he had done other than receiving his bravery award. At this time, it was late, and I clearly could not continue to Gateshead or Hartlepool, so I gave my thanks to him and said I would love to call and see him again, this was agreed. I drove the RAC man, Mr Hobbs back to his home and then I drove back home to Middleton. I couldn't settle my thoughts; I certainly couldn't believe the chances of me bumping into an old friend of my uncles so easily. It was fate, it was meant to happen. I thankfully arrived home safely with my concentration on the journey home being all over the place. I go home, and I tell this unbelievable story to my wife. Then the following day I drive to Gateshead and Hartlepool, (very early this time) to get on and catch up after my day of findings and a totally mystifying experience.

It was as if some sort of unknown power was guiding me and pushing me to find out more. I wanted to desperately get back to Mr. Murgatroyd and his wife again.

A couple of weeks went by since meeting the man that had pulled my uncle from the river Don. I had been thinking long and hard about what I could possibly take with me for Mr. Murgatroyd as a token of my thanks. Having seen him smoke I decided to go and find and purchase a beautiful, solid, silver cigarette box from Butterworth's jewellers in Rochdale and I took it to get an engraving on the side saying, 'To Mr. Murgatroyd in thanks for saving my uncle Bernard Mason Smith'. I made the arrangements to deliver the gift box and inside the box I filled it with cigarettes. It held 100 cigarettes but more importantly inside, on the top of the cigarettes was a wage packet with the money in that he had lost in the river Don, see letter, award and news article attached.

I contacted him and made the journey down. I drove back to Mr. Murgatroyd's house, and I was very excited and was looking forward to presenting him with my gift. He saw me arrive and welcomed me in and I placed my gift for him on a table. I asked him to open it after I had left. We had another lovely meeting and he told me how he was going on a trip to Doncaster on business and that he was a sales engineer. He was 63 years of age at that time. Whilst he was driving along, he saw this lady on the bridge, and she was waving franticly to flag him down. He stopped, and he saw my uncle struggling and drifting quickly in the fast-flowing river and being taken down river. He told me how he quickly ran to the right place along the riverbank, then he dived in.

Tom, 62, leaps in river to the rescue

COMMERCIAL traveller Tom Murgatroyd, 62, was once a swimming champion. Yesterday he became a hero.

Tom was driving across a bridge when a woman flagged him down.

And 25ft. below he saw a R.A.C. patrolman floating in the icy river Don at Doncaster, Yorks.

Tom scrambled down the bank, plunged in, and reached the patrolman, Bernard Smith, 58. But Mr. Smith, a widower, of Wheatley-Lane, Doncaster, died.

Tom was taken to hospital with cold.

As he left hospital last night, Tom of The Balk, Walton, near Wakefield, said: "I just had to help.

The river was terribly cold and the man was very heavy. I really had to struggle to get him to the bank."

Police said Mr. Smith's motor-cycle combination was parked on the bridge. They were investigating the incident.

Yorkshire Post
16 Feb. 1966

River hero, 62, loses rescue struggle

By Daily Mail Reporter

COMMERCIAL traveller Mr. Tom Murgatroyd, 62, dived into an ice-cold river yesterday in a vain bid to save a drowning man.

He swam 25yd. downstream to grab R.A.C. patrolman Mr. Bernard Smith, 58.

He hauled him to the bank of the River Don at Doncaster, but the patrolman died in the water.

Mr. Murgatroyd, of The Balk, Walton, near Wakefield, was treated in hospital for exhaustion.

He made his rescue attempt after clambering down the river bank at Doncaster's main bridge, where a woman had flagged down his car.

Brave

He said: "About 30 years ago I was swimming champion in a brass foundry, but it took all I had to get the man back to the bank.

"It was terribly cold and the man was very heavy because of his storm coat and boots.

"It seems that I was just too ...

A police officer said: "Mr. Murgatroyd was very brave. The river can be treacherous." Bernard Smith, a widower, ... his home in Wheatley-Lane, Doncaster.

... said last night: "His motor-cycle and sidecar was parked on the bridge. We are investigating."

MAN LOSES WAGE AFTER RESCUE ATTEMPT

Yorkshire Post Reporter

A SALES engineer who dived into the icy River Don yesterday in a vain attempt to save a drowning man said last night that he had lost a wage packet containing between £28 and £30.

Mr. Thomas Murgatroyd, 62, of The Balk, Walton, near Wakefield, told The Yorkshire Post: "The packet was in a trouser pocket. Ambulance men recovered my watch, keys and loose silver, but no wage packet.

I have told Doncaster police, and they are investigating."

Mr. Murgatroyd, once a swimming champion, was on Doncaster's river bridge when a woman stopped his car.

Swam 25 yards

Twenty-five feet below he saw a half submerged RAC patrolman floating downstream. He scrambled down the slippery river bank and plunged into the swift-flowing river.

Then he swam 25 yards in 12 feet of water to grab hold of the patrolman, Mr. Bernard Smith, 58, of Wheatley Lane, Doncaster. With Mr. Smith in his arms, he dog-paddled back to the bank and flopped down exhausted. But Mr. Smith died and Mr. Murgatroyd had to be rushed to a nearby hospital numb with cold.

MODEST HERO'S RIVER RESCUE BID FAILS

COMMERCIAL TRAVELLER Tom Murgatroyd, 62, was once a swimming champion. Yesterday he became a hero with a daring rescue bid.

He was crossing a bridge over the river in the centre of Doncaster, Yorks, when a woman flagged his car down.

Twenty-five feet below he saw a half-submerged man floating downstream in the icy River Don.

He scrambled down the slippery river bank and plunged into the swift-flowing river.

Then he swam 25 yards in 12 feet of water to grab hold of RAC patrolman Bernard Smith.

With Mr. Smith in his arms, he dog-paddled back to the bank. He flopped down exhausted. The 58-year-old widower, Mr. Bernard Smith, of Wheatley Lane, Doncaster, died. And Mr. Murgatroyd was taken to hospital numb with cold.

Last night a police spokesman said: "Mr. Murgatroyd was very brave. The river can be treacherous and it must have been terribly cold. He certainly was a hero."

Heavy

As he left hospital modest Mr. Murgatroyd of The Balk, Walton, near Wakefield, said: "I just had to help the patrolman. He seemed to be half-drowned. I slipped my watch into my pocket and went in.

"It was terribly cold and the man was heavy because of his storm coat and boots. I really had to struggle to get him to the bank, but it seems I was just too late.

"About 30 years ago I was swimming champion at a brass foundry, but today it took all I had to get the man back to the bank. But once I had gone in I just couldn't turn back."

The police spokesman added: "Mr. Smith's motor-cycle combination was parked on the bridge. We are investigating the incident."

VAIN BID TO RESCUE RAC MAN IN DON

A 62-year-old man today dived into the icy waters of the River Don at Doncaster in a bid to save an RAC patrolman who had apparently fallen from St. Mary's Bridge.

Both men were taken to Doncaster Infirmary, where the RAC man was found to be dead.

Only a few hours after his rescue attempt Mr. Thomas Murgatroyd, a sales engineer, of The Balk, Walton, near Wakefield, told his story to an Evening Post reporter.

He said: "I was driving over the bridge when I saw a lady waving. I stopped the car and ran to the bridge, where I could see that a man had fallen over.

JUMPED IN

"I climbed over the fence and ran down the river bank for about fifty yards, where he had drifted.

"I took my topcoat off and jumped in. I managed to get him to the bank but could not get him out. Some other men came and we got him out of the water.

"I gave him the kiss of life until the police arrived. It was damn cold," he added.

'NONE THE WORSE'

After a hospital lunch Mr. Murgatroyd waited for fresh clothes to be brought from home, then left none the worse for his ordeal.

An eye witness, Mr. Barry Smith, of Riverdale Road, Scawthorpe, told a reporter that he saw the patrolman stop his motor-cycle combination on the bridge, climb over the railings, and fall into the river.

WHITE

Wonderful linen bargains in ...
OPEN ALL DAY

Marshall & Sne...

He managed to get to my uncle and pulled him to the side and it was bitter cold. He was exhausted himself when he'd managed to get to the side of the river with my uncle. The riverbank was quite steep, and he couldn't manage to get him up as he was heavy because of his uniform being so wet. Some men came with a rope, and he tied the rope around my uncle's waist, and they pulled him up and then they helped to haul him out and up the bank. He told me he didn't think he was dead and whilst at the riverbank he tried to give him the kiss of life and ordinary artificial respiration. He told me he had to go to hospital as well as my uncle and he stayed overnight and was treated for exhaustion and exposure and was released the next day.

He said he had sadly learnt that Bernard had lost his life that day he was pulled out of the river. He told me that he had learnt Bernard lived for his work and he was unhappy because he had been involved in a motor accident and he thought he would lose his job, so he jumped into the river. He got up and handed me some copies of the newspaper cuttings and his award. We had a cup of tea and I stood up and gave him a hug and shook his hand and told him it was time for me to leave and I thanked them both for their kindness and bravery once again. We were both very emotional on my leaving and sadly I never saw him again, but I did receive the beautiful letter on the following pages from him:

61 The Bath
Walton
Wakefield
3-2-76

Dear Peter,

I feel I must write to thank you for the wonderful cigarette box you brought me yesterday. It is something I shall use every day, and will be treasured for the rest of my life. I have always felt that during my life I have been called on, more than my share, to deal with people in distress, and can only assume that some greater power has seen fit to mould the my purpose in life, and my reward has been that on these occasions, I have done my best. Among my my one regret is that on the occasion my best was not good enough. When you left me last night I switched on the television and the first thing I saw was service station on the M1 at which they were dedicating a plaque to the people killed in the bombed bus, when I think of all the circumstances which led to our meeting, I am led to conclude that some greater power than mere chance has controlled our destiny.

As it is only 2 weeks to the ninth anniversary of Bernard's death, do we know that it is not he who has sent you as a messenger to thank you for my efforts. We shall never know the answer to this query, at least not in this life. I can only say that meeting you has given me great pleasure, and I hope you have received some consolation from our meeting. I wish you every success in your investigation to find the truth of your own troubles. I am convinced you have been given this mission for a purpose, and I am sure that the solution will give you peace of mind, and retribution to the guilty, if any guilt exists.

Again all my thanks for your kindness and all good wishes for the future

Yours very sincerely,

Mr. Murgatroyd's bravery award.

COUNTY BOROUGH OF DONCASTER

The Guildhall
Doncaster

W. T. DAVIS

CG/AJK/66/1/1

4th May, 1966.

Dear Mr. Murgatroyd,

Attempted Saving of Life from Drowning

With reference to the occurrence on the 16th February, 1966, when you bravely attempted to rescue a Mr. Smith from drowning in the River Don at Doncaster, I have to inform you that the facts were reported to the Royal Humane Society.

I am delighted to inform you that the Society have been pleased to award you their Testimonial on Vellum, and that the award will be forwarded, in due course, to the Chief Constable of Wakefield City Police for arrangements to be made for presentation. I have no doubt you will be receiving a communication from him when he receives the award.

May I take this opportunity of adding my congratulations for your gallant efforts on this occasion?

Yours sincerely,

Chief Constable.

T. Murgatroyd, Esq.,
61 The Balk,
Walton,
WAKEFIELD.

On leaving Mr. Murgatroyd and his wife, my thoughts were thanking God I had travelled on this journey for my work and found him. I went to Mr. Hobbs's home, and I had a further meeting with him and his wife. Mr. Hobbs had obtained from his HQ all the documents relating to my uncle and he tells me that at the time of my uncle's death he had been assigned to go to my uncle's home to retrieve all the RAC belongings and look into his personal documents to find a possible relative. Mr. Hobbs, being my uncle's best friend, had been aware he had a sister, so going through his things he found her contact details and the address was in Scotland. He said an officer of the RAC in Scotland was sent to that address and found an elderly lady living there. After confirming she was indeed the sister of my uncle, I learnt that my mother had a sister, and he gave me her address. So, a few days later, after calling at my work in Gateshead, I drove to that address in Scotland (no satnav in those days or postcode).

It was approximately 9 pm when I arrived at the address and a light was on. The house looked old and unkept. I was concerned at who might open the door, and it was at such a late hour. I got to the door and was hesitant for a few moments because of the late hour but something told me to knock on the door, so I did. Nervously, I waited and heard the sound of a key turning in the lock, as the door opened, I saw the face of an old lady with long silver- grey hair looking at me. It was like looking at a ghost staring at me. I said not a word. She stared at me and said that I was Alice's son, Peter and asked me to come in. It was just so unreal, spooky, remarkably she just instantly took to me, and she had no mistake or fear about who I was.

It was cold in the house; she took me into the front room where a small coal fire was burning. She was quite a frail, old lady but she was happy I had made this visit and found her. This I found unbelievable. It was as if someone had warned her, I was on my way to her, which was impossible because she had no telephone, and no one even knew I was going. I still felt spooked, and I could hear a grandfather clock ticking. She told me to sit down, and she said to me, "I knew you were out there somewhere because your mother had told me of your birth in her letters she sent me, which I still have, they are under my bed upstairs along with some letters from my brother, your uncle Bernard." This was music to my ears, but I didn't ask at this point to see my mother's letters and handwriting. She then went and made me a cup of tea and then went upstairs and came back down with a box with all the letters in, and her brother's medals. She told me about a letter that he wrote to her whilst attending my mother's funeral which is attached in this story. She said she had wondered when or if she would ever see me. She didn't ask me very much, but we talked and talked, and she held my hand and was stroking it with the other and she just couldn't believe that I was there with her after all the years since my mother's last letter to her.

She told me things about my mother and how my mother gave birth to me, and I was eleven pounds two ounces. It was an awkward birth and a terrible experience, and she never wanted to give birth to another child again. She told me how my mother did so love me. She then told me that I would learn more once I had read the letters. I said I would have to leave as it was after midnight. She asked me to stay and so I did with it being so late and she showed me a room and told me I could sleep there. She gave me a hug and a kiss, said goodnight and left. I was feeling very strange and shivery. The room was freezing, and it was just as old as the house in its décor; it still had a gas lamp on the wall. It was cold and damp and the bed was full of soap. I moved the soap to get in and I got in with all my clothes on. I couldn't get to sleep. Each hour I would hear a big-ben-sounding clock which was at the bottom of the stairs. I simply laid looking around the room and the ceiling, falling asleep little by little between the hourly clock's chiming. The following morning going downstairs she was in the same room and with her was the cardboard box. She said, "Peter, all the letters in this box are from your mother to me. There are some from your uncle Bernard, my brother to me, now you must have them, they tell everything about you and your sisters and brothers. There are also some photographs of your uncle Bernard and your mother," and without any hesitation I took them and looked at my mother's writings and my uncles.

My mother's writing, I simply could not read but I felt this lovely content feeling, knowing I was holding paper that my mother's hand had been on. I thanked her and she said we should go for some breakfast. Just a few yards from her house was a shopping area with a café, and we went and had just a tea and toast and she insisted on paying. I could not interfere with this. We sat talking, she clearly knew the people in the café. Eventually we left the café and said our goodbyes. She wanted it this way and I never ever saw her again. But whilst with her she told me of my uncle Bernard and that she had a visit from the RAC and went to deal with his funeral arrangements. She told me she had a letter and his medals, so now I have my mother's letters and photos of me with my mother and her brother's letters and she gave me his medals. I took my mother's letters to have them professionally transcribed, (was all this coincidence or was it some cosmic force taking place) as these were inexplicable events. But more important was how all this influenced me, and I was drawn further into my searches.

I am convinced that this letter, along with many others including my uncle's medals, was meant to be given to me from beyond the grave by my uncle and my mother. See the full, transcribed letter in chapter one.

CHAPTER 28: Journey for my father

I never had any contact with my father. When I left the orphanage, I was able to send a letter to him with help from my foster mother, but his reply was repulsive, his letter stated I should remain in the orphanage. Thank goodness I met Reg and Betty, my saviours. It was only after I found my mother's sister in Scotland and after she gave me the box of letters and medals of my uncles, that I found out from the letters from my uncle Bernard to his sister, my mother, that my uncle had travelled to London on foot to be at my mother's funeral. In his letter I exhibit (in chapter one), you will see he wrote in meticulous detail all that took place, how he saw his sister for the last time, my mother. His letters prove conclusively that he had psychic contact with her. He wrote the letters on an RAC large note pad where you will see he refers to my father, not on very friendly terms, and explains that he should never ever be trusted. But he tells his sister to look after the children, meaning we were subsequently orphaned.

Never did I see my mother's sister until that night when I knocked on her door and she instantly knew who I was. Then I got to hear later on that she had passed away, and to me and my sister's complete dismay, we discovered she had left us a substantial sum of money (just as her brother had asked of her on behalf of their sister, my mother). I was in complete disbelief that this money would come to me as at the time I was not in any financial difficulty whatsoever.

Then came later another big surprise when I received a totally unexpected telephone call from my father's sister's daughter, a cousin I had never met, telling me that my father was seriously ill in hospital with heart problems and would I possibly go and take him home to his wife in Halstead in Essex, a place I had never been in my life.

I only had my A-Z to find my way, so I set off to Sunderland and then to Essex, a very long journey ahead of me, simply out of duty which I took upon myself to go. I took my middle daughter Caroline with me so she would be able to see her grandfather for the first time ever and most likely the last. So, from Middleton in Manchester I drove to Sunderland hospital. No motorways, only A-roads with approximately three hours of fast driving to find the hospital. Then, finding the ward my father was on and carrying my young daughter with me we saw he was on his own. None of his side of his family were there to see me or my young daughter and say their hellos or goodbyes.

He was clearly very frail; he did not know who I was or even who he was. The hospital had been told to release him and for me to sign, taking responsibility for him from their care. I did not give any thought to whether he would make it all the way to Essex approximately six hours away. He sat next to me in the front passenger seat, with my daughter in the back falling asleep, hardly a word was said. I did stop on the way back and we had some fish and chips at the seaside but still hardly any words.

Eventually in my A-Z I found Halstead and his home, by which time he was not looking well at all, obviously the journey had taken its toll. I went and knocked on his front door, it was long past midnight, and his wife was waiting for my arrival. When the door opened and she came out to my car noticing my daughter was now awake, she said nothing to her, not even hello. I assisted my father from the car to the house with her holding him on the other side. When she tells me she can take care of him now, she does not offer me or my daughter in or even for a cup of tea or the use of the loo and just says goodbye, closing the door on me. I could not believe it. Now we have to travel all the way back to Manchester, stopping at Birmingham for refreshments and the use of the loo for my daughter Caroline.

Continuing my journey back home, fortunately I had my car telephone to keep in touch with my wife. This I can say was the most unbelievable and worse journey in my whole life but as daft as it is, I am glad at least my daughter was with me all the way, meeting her granddad. Caroline then was only five years old; it was six months after her ordeal on the escalator and she would listen to our favourite music I constantly played on my tape player. Some she got to know, and her singing along helped make the journey happier for us both. This time I can date most clearly with her still being in recovery from her injuries in the Middleton Arndale Centre, so the year was August 1985, and I would say this brought father and daughter so much closer.

I took photos of her with her grandad, my father, along the way to his home when we had stopped at the seaside to get fish and chips. The photos clearly show my father looking out to sea, only now do I understand why. I now have his naval history provided to me by the MOD along with his medals. I am positive, psychically feeling, when he was looking out to sea, for his last time, he was seeing himself during his time serving in the war in some of the many ships he had sailed in. I wish I had known at my time with him on the beach that day that he was to die days after I had dropped him back home. He died not knowing who I was, our last journey together was distant and sad.

With all that I had discovered, my thoughts were that my father could never come to terms with his wife doing what she did. The acts of my mother were all over the newspapers. I do not believe to this day for one moment that she understood when she did what she did that it could have blown up the full row of houses with many asleep in their beds. So now perhaps I can forgive those that kept the truth to themselves. They wanted to protect me from knowing. More importantly, I am sure that the court, even in those days, under the children's act would have wanted to protect us three young children from any possible reprisals: in those days it was a serious criminal offence to commit suicide and, in this case, possible killing and injuring so many others at the same time. There is one wonderful blessing I have discovered. It was my crying that awoke my eldest brother who opened all the windows and doors, and the evacuation of the area took place until the properties were safe for those affected to return.

Now reflecting upon the information, I had obtained from the L.C.C archives I can understand how the L.C.C authorities have systematically accepted reports that have no reflection or truth of what we orphans were going through over the many years of our incarceration. Clearly the L.C.C had condoned this abuse by employing those with no qualifications in understanding children or indeed the children act as it was then in the 40s, 50s and 60s.

The report refers in a lot of detail to their contact with my father, who was clearly responsible for my mother's demise and then leaving us three orphans dependent upon the care of the local authority, whilst he could continue his good life having holidays abroad with another.

The L.C.C. took their time chasing him constantly for child support. To this he reluctantly paid from his £10 weekly wage packet ten shillings family allowance. He failed to make regular payments of 35 shillings each week for his three children.

My father clearly did not care about his parental shortcomings. He would very sternly tell the L.C.C not to send their post to his home address because his wife would not take kindly to receiving such a demanding post at his and her new home address, where she was looking after her own daughter. Obviously, this was unknown to me. I had a very distant half-sister who clearly never got to know us whilst she was growing up. She had a brother and two sisters growing up in an orphanage which was not very far from where she was living with her mother and my father. It is obvious my father would not want her to know anything about his previous wife, my mother, who had taken her life in the way which she did and could have killed everyone within the property; with the exception of him, because he was simply not there to help her with any of the difficulties each day and night that she would be on her own to cope with. Then he said to the L.C.C, when I was fifteen and a half and desperately wanting to leave, that I must stay for another two terms or until I reached the age of 18 years old; my age then giving consent to leave and stand on my own. He simply was not interested in me or my sisters as long as it did not interfere with his wife and daughters' holidays abroad, with us stuck in the L.C.C.'s care.

Do I regret going to collect him from the hospital, yes! Do I wish I had left him in Sunderland, leaving others and his wife to make the arrangement for his return home from Sunderland? I have no doubt had I not done this journey with my daughter he would clearly have died in the hospital. No, I cannot regret this on reflection, based on everything in this autobiography.

CHAPTER 29: Re-visit to the orphanage

Whilst continuing my searches into my long-lost mother and sharing these extraordinary discoveries that I feel are too unbelievable to be true, I had to keep up with all my contracts and men that I had working for me. I was travelling all over the country, but I still managed to keep everything on track. I now had a very nice, high-powered Mercedes motor car so my travelling became very comfortable whilst cruising along the motorways. I had three daughters, the eldest approx. 13 years old. She was a Madonna fan so when I was on my travels with work I called and purchased tickets for her and me so I could take her whilst she was on school holidays, a nice little treat for her. I used to tell her some of my little stories of being in an orphanage in Hornchurch in Essex and that it was a long way from our very nice home in Middleton, which had an outdoor swimming pool and indoor sauna with the obvious luxuries that went with them. I asked my daughter Angela would she like to go with me and visit the orphanage and she said she would.

I made the arrangements with the authorities to make this visit possible. Then, during her school break from private school in Rishworth, we drove down to London, staying at the Holiday Inn Swiss Cottage with tickets to the Madonna venue. Madonna was at Wembley Stadium. I purchased the best seats in the press area rather than be amongst the crowd in the stadium, so we were with the press, meeting Madonna at the end of her performance. Angela was just so overwhelmed with it all and she certainly had a wonderful time. The following day after breakfast we drove to Hornchurch orphanage.

We were met by a man who was still there since I had left the orphanage called Mr O'Connor. He remembered me and he was very impressed with the man I had become and more so with the car in which I had driven in. He showed us around and took us to my old family 'Milton Cottage', meeting some of the children. I had taken some sweets just as other parents did when

I was there. The kids that were outside all came over to see this tall man and young girl that had come in a very nice large car. They were very inquisitive.

They all congregated around us when they saw I had a big bag of sweets, standing in front of us with their hands out, happily taking the bundles of sweets that I was trying to give out in an orderly fashion. I started to tell them that I was once one of them living here in Milton Cottage and now I am visiting with my daughter. They all stared at me with smiles and wonder in their eyes.

Knowing I had to press on with Mr O'Connor, I decided to just throw the sweets all around for them to all run and pick up. I'd have loved it if this had happened for Harris and me when we were at this same age outside Milton Cottage. The orphanage all seemed quite the same but brighter and cleaner. It was certainly a strange and emotional feeling walking with my daughter by my side through the driveways and paths by the cottages. Then Mr O'Connor took us into the church. The bibles and song books were all over the place with the money bags I had referred to. They were all over the floor. I picked one of them up and placed my hand inside.

My daughter went looking all over the church whilst I was talking with Mr. O'Connor, and I asked the obvious questions about the staff who were there when I was living there. She then came back, pulling at my arm whilst I was in a conversation with Mr. O'Connor. I looked down at her and she held a song book up to me and told me to look at the first page. I took the book, opened the cover and on the first page it said in my sister's handwriting 'Eileen Ross' (See copy). The chances of walking into this church with my daughter, 13 years old, walking around and picking up this book, only to be a book on the church floor that belongs to my sister Eileen, were a million to one. I was mindful that my sister had left the orphanage almost 25 years earlier. Mr O Brian took one look at me in disbelief. I immediately dropped the money bag back on the floor and I felt a slight chill blow over me; there was something certainly following me and guiding me through all these strange and magical events in my life. Mr O'Connor told me I could keep the book. I held the book very tightly and thought of my sister, and we had a good look around. My daughter had no idea of all the misery I had gone through at this place, and it was nice, but painful, walking around the place. Harris kept going through my mind. Different rooms brought different feelings and emotions through me. I could still remember the abuse I suffered as if it was yesterday. It started to make me feel like I'd seen enough, so we said our thankyous and we left the orphanage. I had a feeling that the place was a lot easier and felt more relaxed. The bad masters and misses had left. As I looked at some of the children, I felt happy for them, but sorry because they were there. I drove off feeling so different and a little empty. I had to try hard to be the same happy father, coming on a special happy adventure, as we were before getting to the orphanage. Angela was feeling quite proud of herself having found my sister's song book. I think it was the song book that helped me feel jollier for our journey homeward bound, but always in the back of my mind, haunting me, was the abuse I had suffered at the hands of the abusers. On returning to our Middleton home with the book, Angela was quick to tell her magical story, and we put the book away and kept it safe.

Some years later we moved from our Middleton home. I did so love that home. I enjoyed the swimming pool and the fun we all had jumping and running around the pool with balls and water shooters and diving in. Even in winter months we had fun out there and then we would run to the sauna and hot tub, totally happy memories! We moved away from Middleton because of the terrible ordeal that took place in Middleton Arndale centre.

Below are pictures taken on our re-visit to the orphanage.

On one of my visits talking with Mr O'Connor I was told my best friend Harris had been sent to prison on the Isle of Wight, 'Parkhurst'. This really did upset me, as no matter how hard I tried, I could never find out why, or if, he was still in prison. I was told the priest Mr Thompson had been sent over to the prison to see him. So, in this story I live in hope that this will reach him somehow, and for him to discover that since leaving Hornchurch, he has always been in my thoughts. I have such sadness thinking he could still have been in prison at the time I was visiting the orphanage.

I did not find out what crime he may have committed. But I have no doubt it would have been as a result of his incarceration like me; but clearly, he was never able to deal with it like we did when we were both in Hornchurch Victorian orphanage. It is possible that Harris's sisters who were in Forbes, Jasmine, Maureen and Marilyn, may possibly get to hear or hopefully read this chapter and contact him for me. I have been very fortunate never to have spent any time in any prison, but I can imagine what this must have done to Harris after leaving our prison at Hornchurch.

Angela stood back of Forbes.

One of my brand-new mercs with private reg parked outside Milton.

the redevelopment was taking place.

Me ringing the bell at Milton.

Angela back of Forbes on swings

The refurbished Harrow Lodge off licence we took the empty bottles to

Seen in the pictures above are two different Mercedes the black car is where the orphanage was still in operation. The other car is on my visit when the orphanage is undergoing re- development.

CHAPTER 30: Woodlands

We moved to a very much grander home in Bamford but sadly it didn't have a swimming pool. But it had an outdoor sauna and shower and more, seen briefly in chapter 26.

Not too long after starting to live there I decided to arrange what turned out to be the most expensive and splendid party I had ever had in my entire life. I had the money and I wanted to share it with my friends and family. I arranged for private contractors to put up a very large marquee with a wooden dance floor and Ladies and Gents loos outside, security at the gates, music organised with a professional singer and dancing through the night. Flood lighting was provided inside and out with electrical insect killers to deal with the midges, all topped off with a professional film company to record the full event.

It took some organising, then when all the guests arrived each couple posed with me and my wife and had their photographs taken. Everyone obviously looked very splendid. Then they would congregate in the living room which lead out into a section of garden, and it was nice weather so they could sit with whatever drink they desired. There was everything at the bar they could wish for plus there were waitresses taking snacks around of little salmon and caviar nibbles etc.

Everyone eventually made their way into the very large marquee, see last page photos, and sat being waited on by all the catering staff, serving them with caviar, wine and drinks and food of all sorts. Then it was time to address all my guests with my speech to thank all those that had answered their invitation and turned up, some from far away, some staying overnight. One guest was a barrister called Michael Beckman QC along with Barry Samuels solicitor. Michael danced with my eldest daughter. There were quite a large number of people there, all from different professions, that we had met over our years of climbing to the top.

Whilst I was standing, addressing everyone and making them laugh with some of our humorous stories, I came to the bit I was looking forward to the most, where I turned my attention to my sister Eileen. I had beckoned my daughter Angela over to be at my side. Everyone now had their eyes on me, Angela and my sister. I told my sister of our visit to Hornchurch Orphanage and how Angela had found a book on the floor. On opening this book, she found your name written on the first page inside it (I had kept it quiet from Eileen for years). I lifted the book into the air and said to Eileen that I would now return this book to you, then walked over to her table and I could feel the suspense and disbelief in everyone, particularly my sister Eileen and also Sally. Of, course all this has been professionally recorded. I know Eileen, to this day, keeps this book close to her and has told this unbelievable story to her own children and her grandchildren. The full recording of the event after this book will be professionally transferred onto DVDs.

At the time of this party, I am at the top of my success, with contractors working all over the UK and unbelievably in Bexley and Beckton in Essex, so I decided to drive back to Hornchurch to visit the orphanage once again but now in another of my (luxury) cars whilst carrying out contracts in just two of those named places in Essex. I drove in, only to find most of the orphanage had been reduced to rubble with very up market posh apartment conversions in its place. Forbes was gone but Milton had been divided, like some of the other cottages, into some luxury apartments. Today they are worth up to, well in the millions, surrounded by an up-market housing estate accessed from Hornchurch Road.

When the streets within the housing development were given names, it had been decided to name after all those who had, so called 'looked after' us children, over the past decade. When this was done and word had travelled, many complaints started and were being made to the authorities into the inappropriate use of those names because of the terrible nature of the abusers bearing those names. They were soon replaced with the names present today. A happy ending for those fortunate people to be now living in the Old Victorian Orphanage, made into happy new homes, and where my memories from the old orphanage live on in the chapters in this book, particularly chapter 3.

The 1980's became the years for provisions of plenty for my family and future income from my private pension, tax planning and lifelong rental income with continuous work in service charges on all the commercial property portfolio I had built, seen in chapter 26 and chapter 50.

CHAPTER 31: Redlumb 16th circa farm/barn

Living at Woodlands was most pleasant, but it wasn't me. It was too elaborate, and it became strained because of my work vans and men coming and going. It was all totally out of place. The beautiful lawns were being ruined by the various dogs my wife had got. The gardener was constantly picking up dog droppings and it just seemed like we were fish out of water. I saw an advert for a Barn/Farm, and I made an arrangement to view and meet up with the agent Bridgewater Estates, owned by John Whittaker of Peel Holdings. When I spoke to a representative, they knew I was serious and was prepared to pay cash. She also saw my lovely new car with a private reg, and I told her that if I managed to obtain planning permission, I would pay an extra £10,000 and that clinched the deal.

She came to see me at my house in Bamford, Woodlands. It clearly took her breath away; she was mystified as to why I wanted to leave where I already was. The children had already started to talk of horses and even more animals on the list of wants. I knew my new purchase of a farm was the right move. The barn pictured below was situated 30 yards away from the farmhouse. It had no electricity or water, but it did have a very deep old water well at the side of it. The farmhouse had electricity and water from the old well but there was also a squatter.

The squatter was living in the farmhouse, and he was storing bits of wood that he could burn to keep him warm. He was using an old outside water closet where there was a plank of wood with a hole in it and a bucket underneath. Part of my deal was that I would deal with the squatter.

When becoming the owner of the property I approached him. I asked him to remove himself from my property. I placed a nice amount of money in his hand, and he was happy to go on his way. To my surprise he gave me a pair of his old iron clogs, which I placed later on the roof truss in the refurbished barn. My

Solicitor Trafford was involved with the Rochdale council in the change of use of the barn to a residential property.

The Old Tythe Barn

Farmhouse

This he enquired on, and the council would not be moved on granting change of use in the green belt, but I started work on the farmhouse. I had got my planning permission for this through my usual architects. Then, having got permission, and the council having inspected the work on the farmhouse for building regulation approval, at the same time as the council's visits, unknown to them, I was secretly getting on with the work on the barn. We got to know the neighbour on the top of the hill, he was called Tony. I more or less permanently employed him and others to work alongside my men when we weren't away with E.L.S. The farmhouse was renovated in around twelve months, and we moved everything out of Woodlands and then put it up for sale. Woodlands was instantly sold to the neighbour and a friend of ours, Bill Walsh, and obviously we did an instant sale. I stayed in contact with Bill and his wife long after, as they were also friends from a very good holiday and golf friends of mine, Eric and Kath. They had an apartment in Malaga in Spain.

The proceeds of the sale were incorporated mostly into the barn and my companies. There was a stream we discovered that ran all the way through and passed both properties which meant I then had to build bridges over the stream to access the two properties with vehicles. Previously the only access was by horse and cart. I had to get a driveway from the top of the lane down in and up to the farm first, so we had decent access with our nice cars. The only toilet I have referred to is in a date stone of 1601 recorded in the library in 1906 where it refers to a modern closet. It is still there at the time of writing this autobiography.

The farmhouse had two stables made for Angela and Caroline to each have a horse. Kennels were made for the dogs; the girls and Elaine were soon to make friends with Tony's wife Joan. Joan adored horses and had some of her own. She was also paid very well and regularly for teaching them to ride their horses; she taught them all they needed to know on how to care for horses and stabling, tack etc. She would come and work in the stables mucking out when we were away as a family, which wasn't very often. I obviously had to keep coming and going because of my projects with E.L.S.

When I was at home, I was constantly down at the barn to help with the renovation work doing the electrics. It was decided we would build a huge ménage for the horses to gallop around, and we had five more stables built in front of the barn, so when the children would be in their bedrooms, they could open their windows and speak to their horses and were able to see them through their windows. Another two stables were incorporated into the barn. This meant that the barn was no different to the old days, when a barn was used for man and beast to sleep in. I put good lighting through each one of the stables, as well as the barn. They were able to play music for their horses at night or whenever they wanted. I even had bunk beds made so they could sleep over the top of their horses within the stables if they chose to and have friends to stay.

A lot of work was being put into the barn for the purpose of the animals seen below and for my girls to be happy there. This was after all going to be our last move. I was wanting it to be perfect for them all. We had the stream made so water would collect to a certain depth, an area where it would be possible for them to walk their horses down to drink and bathe. The water would overflow running under and through a bigger bridge. I also had a water wheel fitted on the other side of the bridge behind the barn. There were many trees at the back of the barn, so I had a tree house built for them, and under the tree house I had swings made up. In one area a huge tyre swing was made, it would fly over a huge dip in the grounds. A lot went into the whole development. There was room for my vehicles and storage and offices for work. A horse lovers haven. We all got a horse at one point, we got to know the bridleways around the barn and had many a good horse trekking afternoon. We would go for walks up Knowl Hill and when we were at the top I could look down and feel so proud looking at my Farmhouse and Barn. The girls were so happy there, they loved the horses we managed to get, and I thought my wife was happy, outwardly yes inwardly no. She, my wife, was certainly a good actress, full of deceit hidden from me when I was home and whilst doing all the work to achieve such a beautiful home with all their wants provided. I was still working all over the UK to achieve such a level of success for us, I thought.

One afternoon after a tea break the lads were back on the barn and I decided to go for a walk to look around the village. I had looked into some of the history around Redlumb and there was a pre-war cotton mill at the back of the village. All the people who worked at the mill resided in the cottages. There was a small chapel in the middle of the village for all the children to go to school and pray on Sundays. There was a corner shop that had been converted into a home, which still to this day has the same post box built in the wall, which is still emptied every morning. The streetlamps were gas. They had a 'knocker upper' who would tap on the windows with a long stick, to wake everyone up to be at the mill on time. The surrounding area of Redlumb was stone extraction, coal mining and farming.

Everything in the mill worked off a water wheel which had a leather belt that went round the water wheel through the pullies to operate all the different machines in the factory, each having leather belts. There was a man employed to keep the belts in good condition and he would replace the leather straps in different sections. If he didn't keep it in good order, then the whole factory would come to a standstill until a replacement belt was fitted. He used to work on the belts whilst the wheel was turning, he had to because the continuous running of water kept the wheel turning. One day he was replacing the strap and got caught, because it wasn't possible for him to stop the wheel. Whilst the water was turning the wheel, he was pulled round and round and he was pulled up and hit the ceiling and was smashed against the wall, which sadly took his life. Because of him dying at the mill he obviously never went back to his cottage, 91 Redlumb and it fell into dereliction. Whilst on my walk I went to look at this 91 Redlumb cottage, still there and derelict. I had found out who owned it from the cottage next door Number 89; there lived a single man who also owned number 87. He had knocked them through into one large cottage. It was a nice village but needed some attention and bringing back to life a little. After looking around the place I went back home to the barn. The cottage I had to have. I didn't discuss it, I just decided to buy it and go and speak to the few people who were already living in the village. I learned that the man who had converted the two cottages was not a well-liked man in the village, especially with the owners of 91 and 83. They couldn't have any toilet facilities because he was refusing them access on to his land, where there was a septic tank built and paid for by R.M.B.C. The facilities were there but they couldn't go into it. Rochdale Council still had to send a vehicle to do what was called 'slopping out', for those without the septic tank facilities. He did everything he could to stop happiness in the village. He was hoping to obtain their properties on the cheap so he could do them up and rent them out.

The above picture of Redlumb village after the war showing the corner shop for all the villagers needs, including re ironing the clogs. The only post box on the corner.

That made me more determined. The old folk in the village were highly delighted when I came along. An old lady in no. 83 called Olive Maxwell asked me if I would buy her cottage; she hadn't been able to sell or move because she was in a desperate situation because of the old man, 'Mr Freedman'. She was over the moon when I offered good cash plus all her legal costs included in the deal. She readily accepted. She was not in good health and pleased to be able to move away and live the rest of her life in peace and have some quality in her life. No. 91 was owned by a good friend of hers, Mr Arnold Taylor. He sold to me at the same time, on the same day with him also receiving a good price including all his legal costs, all paid in cash to them at their joint solicitor's offices in Manchester. Thankfully I had known their solicitors for many, many years and I referred to them in chapter 12 as they were still my solicitors at that time. I took them in my car to Manchester and back. I became the owner of two cottages in Redlumb village; they needed drainage for the sewer and water and complete refurbishment. I managed to purchase the existing septic tank from the Mill owners. They no longer required it as they had built a brand new one for all the brand-new apartments within the mill. The old septic tank was too small for the refurbished mill occupants. They were also glad when I came along because of me buying the septic tank which is still in use today for 91 & 83, thanks to all my efforts.

Mr Freedman was now defeated. He knew I had got the means to put all the drainage from 91 & 83 across the land. At the front he was making a possessory claim to this land but failed to do so at all his costs and we successfully connected into the old mill's septic tank. I opened up the land at the front, taking down trees and clearing the area. I made the land flat and safe and placed swings and slides and benches for children to play on with seating for parents to sit at. The cottages were refurbished but kept as seen in the photo. I allowed two of my men who worked on the cottages to live in them with their families. They lived there rent free for a while until they moved on in their lives. The village was a happier village, I am pleased to say. Another proud moment I had achieved in my life, coming from the orphan boy with no hope.

The picture above is how the village, and the mill and cottages were during the first and second world war. The mill on the left, the cottages in the middle with the grassed area in front that I put swings on. Hindclough Farm on the right.

There was also witchcraft taking place at one time around the farm, barn and Knowl Hill. I found a witch's prayer in the cavity in one of the walls of the barn. I was told to place it back in as work progressed. There were witches' markings in the stones on some of the walls at the farm and barn especially on the water closet on the farmhouse and these markings are still visible to this day. A legal, restricted covenant was put in place on this modern, outside water closet by me so it could never be removed. See recorded 1609 date-stone, recorded in 1906. Everything was coming on nicely.

At the barn I built a very large, safe, horse-riding ménage. The whole arena cost over £30,000 with tarmac hard base and a sand layer over the top and then a soft and expensive surface covering called 'Plasada'. Drainage was underneath taking water down into the stream. The whole ménage was substantially fenced off with a large gate going in one side and a large gate going out the other side on to a bridleway and public footpath. The whole area was flood lit so that at night from both properties we could see everything clearly that was happening with the children and their horses. When snow fell and covered the whole area it was a fantastic safe area to go on ATVs, pulling sledges around the ménage. There was so much fun besides riding horses around.

I had a deep bore hole drilled by the side of the barn next to the well; we went to a depth of a hundred feet where it reached pure, crystal-clear, drinking water, which was then used for all the needs of the barn. The well had been made safe so that no one could drown in it, and I had a large septic tank built on the land of the barn which was for both farm and barn to go into. It only required cleansing every year or so.

I also went to the trouble of obtaining the old red telephone boxes. These old Red Her Majesties Telephone Boxes in the 1940's/50s/60s were the most vital means of communication, especially between the emergency services. One simply dialled 999 or 100 for the operator. The only phone number installed into my brain was the contact phone number of the Hornchurch Children's Home which was Hornchurch 48901. The operator would say, "Now put your money in, then press button A," then you would get through. When your time was up the operator would cut in and say, "Do you want to put any more money in?" At that point you were disconnected. This was a regular occurrence, in my case, when making phone calls to my brother Bill. The Red phone boxes in those days were very well kept, cleaned and painted. The G.P.O would empty them of the cash regularly to stop them overfilling with coins and getting stuck (this was bad luck for us orphans) if I hadn't got there first. Today, what's left of them around the country are mostly so badly unkept, vandalized and used for unhealthy activities. In London in particular, stickers stuck to the glass make a very ugly sight of what had been a most important feature and beautiful sight around London.

These were my memories of the past and now I'm in a fortunate position financially. I travelled to Nuneaton, where there was a sale taking place. Whilst there I was able to purchase three of these cast iron red telephone boxes and three old street gas lights as illustrated in the Christmas card I had made in the next pages.

Others being uplifted were sold like mine but most of them went to the scrap yard, sadly they would go for their scrap value. At great length and expense, I arranged for their transport and delivery to my farm and barn homes, each weighing over two tons in weight. I had them completely removed from the concrete base attached to the floor, and completely removed all the glazing then repainted them and reglazed them, then lifting them with great care and placing them into the concrete that they sit on to this time. One of these has a black slate floor which is situated in the grounds of the old 16th century Barn which each year is lit up via an electrical time clock. So, whenever I would pass these phone boxes, my memory always took me back to us orphans opening the door and pushing our little fingers up where the returned coins would come out after you had pressed button B if you hadn't got through on the call you were making. We were able to move them, making the coins fall out into our little hands.

The Barn was soon to be finished after all our hard work. Inside and out was done with great care and quality. Inside we even had a very large fishpond with koi carp in. After approximately a year we moved out of the Farmhouse into the barn.

Menage   *One & two stables. Stables three-seven Office*

Now we are living in the Barn, all seemed fine. Most animals you could think of we had, even dog breeding of various breeds. After about a year or so living there at the Barn with the farmhouse being used for offices for my companies and out-buildings being used for my wife's dog breeding. All was going well. I thought this was all my wife had ever wanted to do for herself and the children.

Christmas 1990.

It was the build up to Christmas and I went with my van to buy a large Christmas tree. On my return home each year, after all my efforts, they were never good enough, but I still went up and placed it at the top of the stairs in the barn, decorating it and I placed presents underneath. This year, things were not happy at all. Something was just not right but I couldn't put my finger on it, but I knew matters of money were not as they should have been. Then my wife received a phone call from my pension adviser Mr Booth. She came to me and told me that he wanted to speak to me because he was being blackmailed. I told her I was not going to talk with him as I was not happy with my pension valuation and things weren't right. She went to talk with him, about what, I do not know.

There became an even more uncomfortable atmosphere between us both. The children were preoccupied with the horses and the goats, dogs, rabbits and chickens etc. I was still driving them over to Rishworth School each morning and picking them up at school end. Then one evening when I came home, I found a lot of things had been removed from the barn. I went up to the farmhouse and I opened the door to find she had moved a very large amount of her belongings and the children into the farmhouse. She told me not to go for the children anymore and that she is now going to stay at the farmhouse. I asked her why and she didn't want to discuss anything with me and there was a cold as ice look on her face. Rather than have a war of words with her, as she was much better with words than I, I left. I went back down to the barn thinking it would all blow over.

The school break came for Christmas, and she was still at the farmhouse. I was coming and going not knowing what to do. I wasn't picking up any calls as I didn't want to discuss any of the matters with anyone, not even my friend Tommy. I was still unaware of the full reasons as to why my wife had decided to take the children and leave me, even though it was a very short distance away. Christmas came and went. The farmhouse was quiet, all the curtains were kept closed so I couldn't see my children and they couldn't see me. My friend Tommy called to see me, and we had a talk. He offered to go up to see them and I told him no. Something was very wrong, and I hadn't found out yet what it was.

One night it was pitch black outside and I decided to creep up to the farmhouse. The lights were on in the lounge, so I put my head carefully to the window and I listened. Then I heard a male voice along with my children's voices. I listened more intently, there were different sounds I was hearing; the television was going, and I was trying make out who this male voice belonged to. It was familiar to me. After being at the window, freezing cold and listening to everything I could hear, I was able to understand conclusively that it was my solicitor's voice, John Trafford.

I had thoughts of going into the house, I had a spare key; anger was building up inside me. I didn't want my children to be confronted with me, him and my wife in the house. For my children to be in a state, seeing and hearing whatever would have taken place. I decided to go back to the barn to gather my thoughts. I was in a dreadful state. I needed to calm myself down. I made myself a cup of tea and thought. I had got over most of the shock of them leaving me already. I guess it was comforting knowing they were only next door and things could change. I was still confused about the phone call she wanted me to take from Kevin Booth, but why was my solicitor there? I decided to wait and see what the next day brought.

The next day I carefully moved around the barn. I waited until the opportunity arose and I managed to take a photograph of him. My instinct was to attack him, but I could not let my children witness this and I went back to the Barn. I was trying to keep calm. I didn't want trouble with my children around.

Later, I decided to telephone his wife Christine whom I had never properly met before. I asked her if I could speak with John to test the waters. She told me he was not there, and he had gone to live with his father at the vicarage. His father was a vicar at the church in Little Lever, Greater Manchester. At this point I had to tell Christine that I was sorry, but he is at this present time living with my wife and children.

Immediately she was in complete shock, and she asked me if I would go to her home and talk to her. She gave me her address in Bury, Avallon Close.

I drove over and, on my arrival, I noticed she had a neighbour in to console her and they were having a glass of wine. When her four children were in bed, she decided to phone and speak with her vicar father-in-law. She spoke to him, and he told her that he didn't know of the whereabouts of his son.

Christine told him that he was living with a client's wife, Elaine, and that her husband was with her now. With this he put the phone down on her. She tried to ring again and again but it was engaged; he must have kept the phone off the hook. I had more discussions with her then I left to go back home.

Over the Christmas break with plenty of snow, outside it looked like the picture Christmas card I had printed below, with me seen pulling a horse on the other side of the fence, enjoying time with my children, but now my barn was my prison. I was without my children, the dogs, goats and the horses and the snowman.

Hindclough Barn & Farmhouse

Now I was imprisoned in my wonderful Barn that had become just a dark, lonely, empty, cold shell. It was emotionally, physically and mentally breaking me down, the whole situation was destroying me. My children, wife and solicitor lived only thirty yards away from me, next door in the farmhouse. I stayed in for days on end seeing no one, nor talking to anyone. There were wooden shutters closed on every window. Someone was banging on my door; it was my very good friend Tommy. He knew what was going on by this time and he wanted to know how I was. Talking to him made me feel a bit better. My phone had been ringing and I hadn't answered it, but next time round I promised Tommy I would, so we could keep in touch. I couldn't let them destroy me.

I had to go out to the shops. On leaving the barn I knew I had to drive past them. It was torture. I could see them looking out at me but with no friendly response. There were animals that had to be cared for. Angela would come down to the stables to look after the horses, but she made no effort or attempt to come and see me. I think Angela was taking the whole situation very well. I knew when I left, they would enter the barn, taking more of their belongings. I didn't want to force any situation or make my daughters more troubled than they already were. It was a terrible situation to be in, my solicitor was gaining full control of my family and my company matters, see below letter. I knew I had to play the whole situation very carefully, as previously he had been a passenger in my very nice new cars and he got to know me well and my companies' activities and was taking advantage of my, now, weakness. He was clever and very shifty. He had the legal know how. I knew he would be working to make it hard for me. He wanted all my hard-earned money, blood, sweat and tears. I had to quickly regain my emotions; my weaknesses I knew, would give them more power. I had been experiencing financial problems and much upset earlier in the year with E.L.S before all this had arisen. Sadly, it came to the point where I had to stop contracts for them as their money flow slowed down. My company wasn't getting money from each contract I had funded. I had no choice to stop working for them and lay off my men on everything to do with E.L.S. Plus I knew I had problems with my pension and Kevin Booth. No one was talking to me; when the questions were asked, I was stonewalled. I felt like a leper. This was most painful because I could not function properly or even drive my vehicle safely, as will be revealed in chapter 36.

CHAPTER 32: Finding some of my wife's deception and brand-new house purchase.

The Barn is a very large, old, circa 16th century building with our bedroom having his and hers walk-in wardrobes where all our clothes are kept. My wife had very expensive taste in clothes, shoes and jewellery. One can only imagine the number of things she collected over the years of our being together. Her clothes were kept on large racks on wheels, so she decided this needed a removal truck to take them all away. Because of her quick decision to leave me at Christmas, she obviously had to leave a lot of things behind after having taken all she had required plus she had the keys to get the rest at a later time. But whilst she was away living next door to me, I went in looking for photos of our children that she kept in a large box.

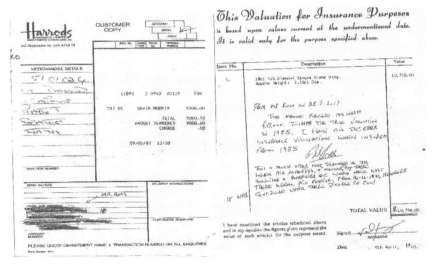

I never used to go through her belongings; I never had the time to even if I'd have wanted to and I never went in her handbag. I never felt I had to. On getting to the box, I noticed an envelope right at the very bottom underneath all the pictures. On opening up its contents I was staggered at what I discovered;

there were bank accounts and there were receipts for all sorts of purchases, even a brand-new house and investments and share bonds with all transactions to an address unknown to me. I started to become very anxious and distressed. No wonder my business began to suffer and run out of funds. One cash transaction was a deposit of £30,000 into one of her undeclared hidden Halifax accounts, even worse was that this was unknown to H.M.R.C who later made me bankrupt.

So now I am looking at what could only be described as the most unbelievable deception, thinking to myself where the hell had she got all this money from without me knowing, in particular these massive purchases with the house being the biggest over £100,000 plus all the luxuries that go in it. When I looked at the dates on the bank statements and the house purchase only then did things add up. The house was purchased in February 1988 and the income shares in 1987 (my solicitor's wife gives birth to her twins on the 26th of February 1989). So, I have found evidence that I have paid for a brand-new house in 1988 and now today I know it was obviously for my wife and solicitor to live in with my three daughters. Until she found out that his wife was pregnant with twins and that scuppered her ship, and she did everything possible to cover up her mess by selling it. I started to go through some of her coat pockets and bingo I found bank receipts showing monies going in different bank accounts, some with an accommodation address and later in time in the divorce court it was discovered that she had many secret different bank accounts. No wonder she had to find a bookkeeper that was her friend. It was the bookkeeper's address. I later discovered that she was using it as her accommodation address. The plot was certainly thickening.

Obviously, I now required yet another solicitor. I could not for financial reasons go to the wonderful London solicitor and barrister, seen in the photos on the final pages and, in any event, they would have been conflicted to have acted for me in these matters. I had no choice but to turn to the solicitors that were involved in the conveyancing in the purchase of my farm and barn, called 'Heyman & Co'. I made arrangements to go to a meeting with them in Haydock, taking with me as much information as they would require. Unfortunately, the most important documents were held at the Farmhouse. I knew John Trafford would obviously have gone through our documents to discover, for example, how much my company was worth, pension, investments, industrial properties, two cottages rented out in the village near to the farm and barn and much more. Solicitor Trafford was still legally on the court record as my company solicitor. At this point, I discovered that I could not remove him as this would require joint consent of both directors and she would obviously not consent to his removal, especially at this time. She needed him to cover all her tracks and destroy me and everything I had worked so hard and long for, with me putting my life at risk so many times to get where I had, for her and my children.

After talking with my new solicitor, I told him of John Trafford's not moving into my property, which was also my company offices, with my family driving around in one of my new company cars. I'm at this point needing proof of his presence there. Mr Heyman says to me I should place a chain round the front gate, (seen on the Christmas card, seen in chapter 31) at the entrance of the farm and barn, making it impossible for him to leave for work the next day. I needed to get the evidence that he was staying there. So, very late in the night, I went and locked the gate with the thickest chain and padlock I possessed; he would then not be able to get out to go to my workplace in the morning. This I did, I have to say, even though it was my property, and I was worried about my actions, especially with my children seeing what I had done. Eventually the following morning my doorbell rang and unsurprisingly, the police were standing at my front door. They had to park their police vehicles in front of the gate with one of my new vehicles parked on the inside. The one John Trafford was taking it upon himself to travel to work in, right under my nose. The police had spoken to Mr Trafford, and my wife, and they asked if I would remove the pad lock and open up the gate. I agreed but first I said to the police that I wanted to talk to my solicitor Heyman & Co, I would then come out as soon as I had done so.

After discussing the matter with my solicitor, he agreed I should remove the padlock and open the gate but only after taking the details from the police officer with the name and number of who had reported the matter of obstruction to the police. The police confirmed, to my surprise, it was indeed my solicitor, Mr Trafford. Having obtained this information and with the police present, I removed the padlock and chain, it was recorded. Mr Heyman then reported John Peter Trafford to the solicitor's complaint authority. They eventually came back with this response that they do not regulate the ethics/morals of a solicitor. The very unpleasant legal process/divorce started and became the worst experience any man could ever experience in divorce and live to tell all the most serious criminal events that took place.

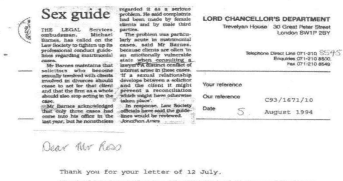

Sex guide

THE LEGAL Services ombudsman, Michael Barnes, has called on the Law Society to tighten up its professional conduct guidelines regarding matrimonial cases.

Mr Barnes maintains that solicitors who become sexually involved with clients involved in divorces should cease to act for that client and that the firm as a whole should also stop acting in the case.

Mr Barnes acknowledged that only three cases had come into his office in the last year, but he nonetheless regarded it as a serious problem. He said complaints had been made by female clients and by male third parties.

The problem was particularly acute in matrimonial cases, said Mr Barnes, because clients are often in an emotionally vulnerable state when consulting a lawyer. "A distinct conflict of interest arose in these cases. "If a sexual relationship develops between a solicitor and the client it might prevent a reconciliation which might have otherwise taken place".

In response, Law Society officials have said the guidelines would be reviewed. *Jonathan Ames*

LORD CHANCELLOR'S DEPARTMENT
Trevelyan House 30 Great Peter Street
London SW1P 2BY

Telephone Direct Line 071-210 8545
Enquiries 071-210 8500
Fax 071-210 8549

Your reference
Our reference   C93/1671/10
Date   5   August 1994

Dear Mr Ross

Thank you for your letter of 12 July.

I understand that you are dissatisfied with the professional conduct of a solicitor.

BERRY & BERRY, COCKER, SMITH & COMPANY
SOLICITORS AND COMMISSIONERS FOR OATHS

P.T. SMITH, LL.B.
J.A. HYTNER, LL.B.
K. BULLEN, LL.B.
S. MORTIMER, LL.B.
L.J. GROOCOCK
J.A. TOMLINSON, LL.B.
A.P. MOUNTAIN, LL.B.
J.P. TELFORD, LL.B.

J.E. THOMPSON, M.A. (Oxon)
Consultant

1-5 LONGLEY ROAD
WALKDEN, WORSLEY
MANCHESTER, M28 6AA

TEL: 061-790 1411/8
Fax No: 061-790-1971

When calling please ask for
Mr Mortimer

Also at Whitefield
061-790 7820 & 061-766 3997

OUR REF   SM.RP.ELS

Bolton
0204-382011/4

YOUR REF.   RC.TC.423

Wigan
0942-322820

We shall notify you of the new date in due course and perhaps you would be good enough to confirm to us just as soon as agreement has been reached with the local authority.

Yours faithfully,

The vehicle which became impossible to drive past the padlocked gate then repossessed. Plus, the registration from the address of Mr Trafford's solicitors' practice car park referred to below

The matter is at long last under investigation by the Lord Chancellor Robert Buckland QCMP with his independent review led by Sir Christopher Bellamy Q.C, a former high court judge.

I then went to the company that supplied the car to me and I got the details of the finance company I had arranged the finance with. They kindly gave me the details of Rover finance. I contacted them explaining who I was and that I was cancelling the agreement of 217-593681-19 and wanted the car to be repossessed. I explained the seriousness of the situation where my company was now in deadlock. Therefore, further payments for the car would not be met. I went on to explain that the police had been to my home and that my solicitor, without my consent, was driving my car to his place of work. I went on to explain that my solicitor was in an adulterous relationship with my wife, and he was unlawfully driving the car to work at his solicitors' practice in Manchester then back to our home. This without my permission makes him not insured to drive this vehicle. I gave Rover finance the full details of his address at his workplace to arrange repossession and I would be on the day at the address of that firm of solicitors; 'Berry & Berry Cocker Smith & Co' in Walkden, Manchester. I would be bringing the spare keys to the car and specifically asked for the repossession to take place without warning Mr Trafford of the intentions of collecting the Rover car, parked on the solicitor's car park. If they had done so it would not be there on their arrival to repossess.

On the day in question, we met up and they went into the solicitors' car park and saw the car was there. They went into the offices and asked at reception for Mr Trafford, explaining who they were and the reasons for their visit. Mr Trafford rushed down to the reception, I was told in absolute panic, after all it must have been so embarrassing for him. They asked him to provide them with his keys for the car and the reasons why it was being repossessed. At this point Mr Trafford told them he needed some time to remove his belongings. They escorted Mr Trafford to the car, when to his dismay he could see the door to the boot and the doors were already open and who should be standing there, me. He removed all of his belongings and reluctantly handed over his set of keys. At this point Mr Trafford started to become most unwell seeing the Rover finance man starting the car up and driving out of the car park and I stood watching him. Mr Trafford just managed to go back into the reception, and I was later informed that an ambulance was called to take him to hospital with shock and anxiety. He was not long after sent on his way and he returned back with my wife to our home, Hindclough Farm.

After the sale of this vehicle, Rover finance contacted me saying that there was no outstanding debt as the registration number on the car more than covered the cost of the recovery and any shortfall thereafter. So, my wife could hardly say it had been undersold or complain as the private number plate more than covered the short fall. They were also obviously aware I was now in an impossible financial situation but happy to have found out Mr Trafford could not take any legal action against me for my actions. I was mindful at this time that he was in receipt of legal aid funding at the same time whilst he was working, so he could not challenge the removal of the Rover car. This would have involved the police, of which I had all the details, and he would have been exposed as unlawfully driving my company car without insurance. Mr Trafford's wife when she became aware of this did indeed report this to the legal aid authority along with my complaint. Legal Aid did nothing but kept funding him and his solicitors, whose offices are at Church House in Manchester. This Church House property becomes relevant in the following chapters 41 & 50.

I was aware on my journeys out that they were entering the barn and taking further things for their needs, whatever they decided they were wanting. I didn't mind the children coming and going when I wasn't there. So, one day when they went out, I felt I had every right to enter my Farmhouse to have a look around. I saw his things; it was obvious he had not only his feet but his legs under the table also. The wardrobe was full of his clothes, his shoes, and slippers by the bed. On coming downstairs, passing the telephone fax machine, I noticed a printout of what she had last sent to her solicitors. I very quickly got a copy printed out then got out as quickly as I could; she wouldn't know I had got a copy of it. It was all done in her handwriting, and I knew from the content of the fax on the next page that she was giving reasons for her desire for a divorce. My world had fallen apart. It was abundantly clear what their intentions were. Shortly after this I received correspondence from their solicitors, in an application for an injunction now restricting my access to the Farmhouse, prohibiting my entering within 50 yards of the farm area. This was ordered on 13th of May 1991. I had to appeal it because 50 yards meant I couldn't go into my own barn home 25 yards from the farmhouse. This was what they wanted so they could take over the barn. Thankfully, my solicitors got it changed in time to 30 yards so I could enter my home with no breach of the court order.

But then my company accountants required information that was impossible for me to give about tax which had to be paid on all of her spending, all of which I had no idea about. Her leaving in December 1990 was obviously to remove herself from the unbelievable tax position she caused and put me in, which led to the tax. This led to the tax statutory demand upon me and not her and then my bankruptcy.

She was obviously sending notes to her solicitor Mr Robinson, trying to make me look like a heartless father and husband.

Met when 17 yrs old he was 25
Moved in with him at 18.
We saw his children infrequently
I looked after them more than him.
Built a house moved in .. had a baby. he would
consider marriage.
Bought an electrical shop I ran shop while
he did house rewires etc.
Bought me a car; employed a contracts manager.

Angela started school age 3.
Always blaming his father, childrens home,
for everything that happened.

Never discussed anything private only business
Acquaintince of his was murdered he
went off at deep end crying etc.
Aunty off mine died ended up having vans he
went off for the evening.
His brother died he went to London to
see his neice for days.
He never wanted to share any of his private
sorrows with me
Had Caroline 1980 July. 1980 October
My mum died on a Sunday

Caroline was bit 1983 by a dog Peter blamed me
Caroline was trapped in an escalator blamed Debbie
I stayed in hospital he wasn't happy with the
He pursued insurance claim with a total
disregard to the hurt Caroline was going
through. Money more important

This was regardless of the many years of working, giving and
devoting my time in chapter 22 with Tommy, my best and most
loyal friend, and his wife Nancy to try and get the escalator shut

down to protect others and go to solicitors in London to get compensation for Caroline. I did succeed and monies went in trust for Caroline. Whilst it was in my control it was kept in trust building up interest; that is until it was taken away from my control and spent on things other than Caroline, I was told. I did blame the nanny that day, who was inappropriately dressed and more interested in who was looking at her than giving all her attention to my children. Taking a push chair on an escalator with Caroline pushed too near to the side that then trapped her boot pulling her in then trapping her. I reflected on this when I read what she said in her handwritten note, sent by fax to her and his solicitor Guy R.J. Robinson, who would, for over 10 years, obtain all his legal costs from legal aid public funds. Absolutely unbelievable, but all will be revealed within the final chapter of this autobiography.

CHAPTER 33: Meeting Anita and her children

My working days up and down the country had come to an end and I was taking my girls to school each and every morning and collecting them at the end of the school day. I got to see all the parents. I first noticed Anita because of a long black cardigan she was wearing (seen in photo). It had a rather large colourful clown on the back which took me back to Coco the clown in my childhood; it looked rather nice and so did she. As Jennifer was going into her classroom, I noticed one of Anita's daughters was in the same class, we started with a smile and a nod. Then weeks went by when we were waiting outside school, we would have a chat as all the parents were doing. Some days though Anita seemed strained and distant, not seeming as friendly. One day I was walking up the steps to pick Jennifer up and Anita was rushing down holding her daughter Adele. Blood was pouring out of Adele's mouth, and she was crying. I stopped and asked if I could be of help. Anita asked me if I could quickly go and find Clair. She told me Adele had fallen and her teeth had gone through her tongue. I went to help get Clair out of class and escorted her to where her mother was parked. Anita also asked me if I would ring her husband to tell him she was going straight to the hospital. After that day I would stand and chat to Anita on days she was feeling happy too. Later in the year Anita was having Caroline stay for a sleepover with Clair at her house, then Clair would come and stay with us. Caroline told me how strange Clair's father was, and she went on to tell me he was hurting Anita at times. The children shared secrets together.

One weekend evening whilst I was living at the barn on my own, I had been out and, on my return, I found Anita bringing two of my daughters back home. Anita had been looking after them for my wife. I knew nothing of this. Before I got there, she met Angela whom Anita was led to believe was also going to a show with her mother. Anita was surprised to see Angela.

Angela refused to take Caroline and Jennifer from Anita. Anita, now confused, was desperate to leave my children as she said she wasn't feeling well. Her husband was in the car with her, and when she saw me, she called over telling me she was leaving the children with Angela and myself. I wondered why there had been some confusion. They drove away quickly; a few weeks went by, and the Christmas break was over. The children were going back to school, and I was no longer taking the children to school. My phone rang and it was Anita, she was asking if she could stay in one of our cottages. Apparently, someone had told her about them. I was very surprised, and I told her I had a problem in that me and my wife had parted, if I was to allow her to move in it could bring more problems for me. Anita accepted this and we said our goodbyes. I couldn't sleep at all that night thinking of what Caroline had told me. If Anita and her children were suffering at home I would help, now with my wife living next door having left me on Christmas eve. I thought to hell with it, so I redialled the number Anita had rung in on. I told her to meet me so we could arrange something; if that was what she was still needing to do. We met near school and Anita told me she wanted to get away from her husband, but no longer could go to her parents as they were frightened by the whole situation Anita was in. She made it clear that her husband could not know where she was, and that he had obsessive and possessive behaviour towards her, to the point of physical and mental abuse. I told Anita to leave it with me. I was so moved and saddened for her, it now made sense to me why Adele wouldn't speak to anyone at school. She just stood in a corner watching everyone a lot of the time; I got to think she couldn't talk at all, and she was introverted and timid. We arranged a move one afternoon whilst the kids were at school. I went up to Anita's farm where she was living and took all she asked for into one of my vans and moved her into the cottage and made it their home. It was still chilly outside, so I got some coal and built them a coal fire, filled the fridge for them, cleaned it and it was nice and ready for them to come home from school.

Anita moved into 91 Redlumb. It was a most difficult and unsure, scary time for Anita and her girls. She was worried about the children and how they would find living in the Village, but more so about her husband finding her. They seemed fine and I got out of the way telling Anita not to worry for now about the running costs and living in my cottage. Throughout this time, I would call on her whilst she was living in the cottage. I would see her and her two girls Clair and Adele.

It helped me manage my time of grief after losing my wife and children and now not being able to see my girls at all. Sometimes I would stay longer, and we would have a cup of tea together. Clair being the same age as Caroline, they were friends at school, so we would have a nice chat and Clair would tell me about her and Caroline at school. Adele was very shy and did not take to me at first. They would both stay upstairs sometimes when I called round, sneaking part way down to listen to me and their mum talking. This eventually led them to accept me, but Adele still kept her distance and hid behind the couch in the lounge. This went on for quite some time. Clair would take sweets for me to give to my girls at school and I would send little messages for them through her. Anita was getting worried. She told me her husband had left some money, but she had only taken half of it, leaving the other for him. On a visit to her bank, she wasn't able to take out any money because her husband had closed the account on her. She was told by one of the staff, whom she got to know in the bank, that he was very upset and disturbed whilst he was closing all ways of Anita getting any money for her and the children. Anita was fretting over not being able to give me rent or pay bills, but I told her not to worry and that I would help her as much as I could. She was a lovely girl inside and out; she didn't deserve all she had been suffering and all she was now going through. It had been going on for years, but she had been too scared to leave; he threatened to kill her if she did, and she believed him.

The evening came when I got a call from one of the villagers telling me there was a guy shouting outside 91; he had come in a big flashy Jaguar. I knew straight away it was her husband, he had found her. I rang 999 and told them about the situation and I rushed round. When I got there Anita had let him in. The children were sitting huddled up together at one end of the sofa and Anita was shaking and her colour had gone from her lips and her face was white. I faced him and told him to leave my property, it was only for Anita and the children to stay in.

We could hear the police sirens approaching and he left. I asked Anita why she had let him in, she told me she didn't want him kicking my door in and damaging it. I told her next time let him try, he would be sorry for any damage he caused. The police had a chat with Anita, and they left, going after him because he smelled of alcohol. We later found he had his license taken from him and this would slow him down calling on her and upsetting her. Sadly, we found out from Clair after Caroline had told her at school that it was my wife who had rung him and told her husband where Anita was. They knew of his history, but still caused upset for the children and Anita.

I told Anita I would put her a landline in so she wouldn't feel cut off and it may help to make her feel safer. Anita made a few friends in the village and so did Clair and Adele. There were donkeys and horses in the fields, and they started to feel more at home in between her husband and now father-in-law calling up. I helped Anita sort things out through the solicitors. Anita was very insecure and timid; it was all too much for her at times and she was a bundle of nerves.

A restraining order was set in place as far as the school; the school was also on standby. So, we were both going through difficult times. We helped one another greatly. Anita's children and family gained comfort in knowing I was around for them. Anita was being squeezed financially and so was I, but we managed together. Our friendship was growing. I would call and go home to the barn at 9.30 some nights.

One day Anita was crying, and she told me her husband and his family wanted the car back from her. She didn't want to send the children to school on the bus all the way up to Halifax, but her parents helped by being guarantors and she managed to get a new car on finance. She was also getting some maintenance at that point. It was obviously a ploy to try and force Anita to go back to her husband.

One teatime I visited Anita and the girls. We were sitting at the table having some tea when there was a knock at the door. Anita went to the door to find a policeman standing there. They asked if Peter Ross was there. She called me, they asked me to accompany them back to my barn. This I did, telling Anita I would ring her shortly and not to worry. My wife had reported to the police I was unstable and was going to burn the barn down. The police said to me that they had been told and had seen large open containers with petrol sitting on the floor inside the stable. I explained to the police that in my state I had inadvertently put petrol in my diesel van and the only containers I could get, I used to put the petrol in. Then I was able to put diesel into the van and, understanding the workings of a diesel engine (as I also had a JCB) I was able to purge the diesel by removing all the petrol before it got to the fuel injectors, and I got the van back up and running. I did all this at the petrol station then drove home slowly, with the petrol in the unsealed drums. The police accepted I was telling the truth but still with an air of caution and the fire brigade was also there, standing by for me to remove the petrol from the barn. I contacted Tony, who at that time was my friend, and I explained that the fire brigade couldn't leave until the petrol had been removed and stored safely. So, he drove down in his tractor with a 45-gallon steel drum and poured the petrol into it. I thanked Tony and I told him he could have it for his trouble. Then the fire brigade and police left, and Tony drove off more than happy. All the time this was taking place I had noticed at the upstairs window, which looked down onto the barn, that John Trafford and Elaine were watching all that was taking place. It was obviously all recorded at the police and fire department to try and support their case that I was deranged and would set fire to the barn, and this was because they had failed in their court order to prohibit me from going within 50 yards of the farmhouse. I was later told that they didn't like seeing me walking across to Anita in the village. Months went by and I was feeling a little bit happier with my friendship with Anita and her children. Then one afternoon I noticed my wife moving all the contents of the farm and leaving, to go away to their newly acquired home at Somerford Hall in Congleton.

Things went from bad to worse. A letter came my way, and I got a phone call later to tell me my middle daughter Caroline was in hospital. It was through terrible unforeseen circumstances and lies I couldn't believe, the worst a father could go through by an attack from the mother and solicitor. Anita was clearly upset for me, and I told her I wouldn't be around as much, and I have to leave. I eventually go and call on Anita and fill her in on what is happening. She was deeply saddened for me and told me she wasn't going to let it spoil our friendship after what she had learned from me and what my wife and solicitor had accused me of: the deadliest weapon through divorce, sexual abuse. A double prong attack, one to stop me from seeing my children and the other to break the relationship up I had with Anita. They even got the neighbour on the hill to try and put Anita against me.

I was afraid Anita might leave the cottage, taking her girls somewhere where she felt safer, away from all that was now going on, after all she hadn't known me that long. She told me not for one minute did she think I had done what I was being accused of doing. We had tears together and it brought us closer still; even Clair and Adele knew there was something going on and seeing me upset brought them closer. They began to build a safer and happier relationship with me. One night, Clair was dancing around all over the place with me and Anita sat watching the tv with the coal fire burning and I felt something touching my ankle. I moved my foot and felt something touching it again. I knew it was Adele, but I told her mum something is touching my foot. Then I look behind the couch and find Adele; I then pull her out. Then from that moment she spoke to me. She had been so quiet for so long but now all of a sudden, she had a voice and lots of laughter. I would pretend to be Mr Tickles and tickle her, Mr Pincher crab and gently pinch her, Mr crocodile even, this amused them both and brought Adele out of herself all the more. From then on, we got on so well it encouraged my visits, as now I am feeling love again and becoming much closer. Anita stopped flinching as much every time I went near her, and Adele was becoming a happier child as was Clair. It helped greatly all our time together with me having lost my wife and children who had later moved away to a very nice home in Crewe. The only contact with my children was on passing at Alder Hey children's hospital.

I now had Anita taking me in my car to hospital where she waited outside, sometimes for hours on end and in the early hours of the morning, so I could go out from time to time to sit with Caroline and get some fresh air and leave her bedside for a short time. She would leave Clair and Adele with her mother and father, their grandparents, on one of my journeys home to get fresh clothes etc. I told Anita that the cottage had to be sold because of the court order, ordering that it needed to be sold because of the divorce, so both my cottages were later sold. Anita now knew her, and her children were going to become homeless. I asked if she wanted to move from the cottage into my barn, which had six large bedrooms and plenty of play areas outside with an ATV to have fun with. We had helped one another so much during many difficult times and Anita would say 'you watch my back and I'll watch yours'. I rescued her and she me, I had a feeling in me that I never wanted to lose Anita's friendship or the girls. At first Anita was very unsure, anxious and insecure and was uncomfortable about this move; she didn't feel warm and relaxed around the barn. She had only visited a few times to post something for me and the times she visited when she looked after Jennifer and Caroline for Elaine. Now my wife had left I told her she could get used to it gradually; eventually make it her home in ways she wanted to. One morning Anita had taken her girls to school, and I rang her and asked her to call over to see me for a change. I had a surprise waiting for her; she didn't know this. It was cold outside, and she wasn't feeling well, and she told me she didn't want to leave the comfort of the fire in the cottage. I begged her and she got in her car and came over. When she got into the kitchen, I sat her at the table, putting a hot water bottle under her feet and a blanket around her shoulders. I placed a cooked breakfast in front of her. I had made it myself for her and as she was eating, I was filling her head with things about the barn and her girls would love it and they would be safer there. It took some time after she went home but later, she agreed.

So, it was agreed. I took my JCB over to Redlumb and put all Anita and her children's belongings into the JCB and drove them over to the barn. When the children came home from school Clair and Adele were told they are living at the barn. Anita and I were still both going through a lot of insecurities and so much upset in more ways than one. We got ourselves through, being together made it much easier and being there for one another each day and night. For a time, I stayed back in Liverpool in a parent's room so I could stay with Caroline. Anita looked after the barn for me whilst I was away.

During the time I spent at Alder Hey hospital I get to know Anita a lot more. I borrowed her car and had an accident in it. I explained to her my financial circumstances and that I am going through a very bad and difficult time. I was not insured so she could not recover from her insurance to claim another car. I told her to use my Mercedes. I contacted my insurers and taxed the car to enable her to take her children to school. In the meantime, she had to keep up with the monthly payments on the crashed car, which was on a thirty-six-month re-payment plan. She continued the remaining monthly instalments until the finance had been paid off whilst continuing to drive the Merc.

Throughout all this time Caroline was still at Alder Hey Hospital and I was still having great difficulty in understanding what was happening. The only way of having any contact with my children was by going back to the court, which was very complicated and costly, but I had no choice because Caroline was disabled and clearly at risk of losing her life. I made many applications through the family court only to be refused permission to obtain any information relating to the causation of my daughter's hospitalisation or all the medication that was being given intravenously. I had no choice but to disclose I had known of the investigation on my daughter which took place under anaesthetic without my permission, I had fifty percent parental guidance. There had been nothing said to me.

I had obtained information from my daughter's bedside files. I had to tell this to the court for the judge to understand the seriousness of her condition and why I was making the application. This did not go well for me. The high court judge found that through my honesty to the court I had removed information about the treatment of my daughter unlawfully so all the information I provided to the court was struck out. Therefore, my application was unsuccessful and in court when one is unsuccessful automatically all costs go against the applicant, me.

So, regardless of the costs, I had managed to put all the medical evidence before a high court family judge and for this at least he made an order that I should receive a full transcript of the hearing before him, but I must pay for it in full. For this I was able to thank the honourable judge. All the time I was at court, Anita or Tommy would always be waiting for me outside. She was always there now for me, asking how things had gone when she could see from my face that things had not gone my way. Had they done so it would never, in any event, reverse what had happened to Caroline, and I believe this was in the thoughts of the judge because the court had previously ordered a report to be obtained from the official solicitor, to act on behalf of my daughter who clearly was unable in any way shape or form to talk for herself. I knew her mother and my solicitor would only provide information that would not implicate them in what they had done to Caroline. Anita through all this said if she could help in any way she would do, because by this time she now was fully aware of what had actually happened as the official solicitor made her aware with plans to call and interview her and her two children Clair and Adele. Anita was very much disturbed by this in case her husband and his family would discover all that was going on with Caroline in hospital and the serious false allegations they had made against me. Plus, the social services were about to interview Clair and Adele and Anita, obviously finding out from my wife all that was going on, and then they might have tried to take Clair and Adele away from her. I assured her this would not happen. She still felt very worried about it.

At this point I thought Anita, who was going through her own divorce, would not want to have anything further to do with me and stay back at 91 Redlumb, until it sold. But she said no, she didn't believe what had been said. She had got to know my wife through her children and mine and did not feel comfortable in her presence even then. It was then obvious to me that my wife was using my children's friendship with Anita's children to be able to be with solicitor John Trafford. Anita discovered from her daughter Clair that my wife had gone to a Christmas party in 1990 with the solicitor J Trafford when she looked after my two girls, whilst I was on my own in the barn. This again was the same on New Year's Eve. Things started to make a bit more sense in that department.

Now, Anita was my only saviour when she agreed to move into the barn and was taking me to the hospital at

Liverpool. She cooked and did my washing and cleaning by this time. I had not wanted to be away from her or her from me. Through all my sadness and all my tears, she would be there for me as well as for her girls.

The time came when all emotions were poured out. We started a much closer relationship and from that time and night we started to sleep in the same room. This continued, then she found out that she was expecting a child. Instantly I told her this was meant to be, and from that time day and night I could not be separated from her. I became so in love with her that I would every night and morning put my hands on her stomach and feel our baby growing inside her. We went to see Dr Edward Tierney by special appointment, who was the only one local who did scans to tell which sex the child is. When I saw the scan, I could see clearly it was a boy. This brought so much joy to me but still throughout I continued to fight for justice, not now for me but for my daughter. Now I have Anita's unwavering support in many nights talking and leading into the very early hours of the morning whilst her children were asleep, with Darren who is constantly wriggling and kicking her, so we named him Kicks. We got milk coupons to get milk that goes around for all of us. I have to admit I also had a sample of what Darren was having when he was born and could well understand how and why he has grown up such a healthy son of mine.

During this time, I am still fighting in the courts but this time it is for maintenance and a brand-new car to be provided for Caroline's transport. She required full-time care and a wheelchair. This I certainly did not oppose, so an order was not required by the court. I simply consented for the court to make an order for my children's needs that were fully met from the rental income each month from the various tenants paying substantial rents on our industrial units in Rochdale. I, in the interim, received nothing from the rents until such time the court made its final orders. Thinking that justice would prevail, and the court would see that my wife had formed an adulterous relationship with our family and company solicitor, and that she would receive half of the value of all assets and rents from whatever is left, I assumed I would have to continue to pay maintenance for my three daughters. But no, this was not to be. The only thing that is ordered is a divorce on the grounds of adultery between my wife and the party cited, my solicitor John Peter Trafford, with the sale of all the assets to take place whilst continuing for maintenance payments to be made until further order.

I still had no contact with my three children, not for the want of trying. I am involved with all matters relating to my daughter's treatment and the cause of her then disabilities and brain injury. All because of my wife's and solicitor's actions, and there was nothing I could do about it except hand a document to the doctors that were treating Caroline, Dr Sills and Dr Jane Radcliff. I fully explained to them the police involvement, which they were obviously aware of, but I had to let them know that I was aware of all the treatments that were given to my daughter.

Weeks and months pass, and because of what was happening and had happened to Caroline, Anita felt it took the pleasure in being pregnant away from her. She felt quite alone and denied attention from me, she was also still worried about her ex-husband causing her upset with his idle threats, but she understood and was deeply sad and concerned for Caroline and me.

We had agreed if it was a boy, I would name him, if a girl she would. When my son was born on the 22nd of May 1992, Anita asked what his name was to be. I told her I wanted to call him Darren and when she asked why Darren, I told her on the day our son was born I had read whilst waiting and reading the Times newspaper that on Thursday 21st May 1992, a drunken lorry driver had run over someone's son with a 30-ton tipper truck and simply drove away. This little boy, Darren, was simply riding his little bike when the lorry driver drove over him. The little boy's father had seen the driver who was drunk and seemed not bothered, even smiling at the boy's father. He took a shotgun, went to him and shot him dead. I felt just like Darren's father; wanting to get hold of a gun or somehow kill my solicitor for all the pain and suffering he had caused, with both of them using my daughter as their most deadly weapon. A bit different, yes, to the drunken driver Kevin Taylor, driving over the little boy Darren, killing him, and now my daughter is an invalid for the rest of her life. It was agreed we would call our son Darren with his middle name Patrick after my good Irish friend Tommy.

When Anita had given birth, I was holding with such pride, my few minutes old little boy who gave me the greatest moments of my life; holding him as soon as he was born, leaving my little boy with a plastic peg on his little tummy, Anita took a few moments of recovery. From that moment on I could not leave my son or his mother. Thankfully my good friend Tommy and his wife would be waiting for us to appear with Darren and take us back home to the Barn, then collect Clair and Adele from their grandparents to meet their brand-new brother.

Her children Clair and Adele were happy being with their new brother at the barn which was now full of happiness until I received in my post a maintenance assessment from the Child Support Agency. With Anita's help I wrote back saying this had all been dealt with by the court and that a court order had been made for my children's maintenance to be paid from rental income each week that was in excess of that the C.S.A was telling me to pay. So, I wanted the strength of my son to submerge from the pains and suffering I was going through. At my time of writing this autobiography the death of Darren has submerged in my son, which keeps him alive in my mind along with thoughts for his father's love and the rightful action he took in killing the drunken lorry driver. Just go to chapters 38, 39, 44, 46, 47 & 55 to see how Darren had submerged in my son.

329

CHAPTER 34: Old Bailey Mapperton Case

I received a letter from the Metropolitan Police which was sent to my home at Hindclough Barn. On reading its content I went into complete shock, had a panic attack, a complete sense of shame and feeling of helplessness in how to respond. My two elder sisters, who had not spent as many years as I at the Orphanage were aware of only some of the abuse I had been subjected to. The orphanage was the subject of police inquiries about the 14/11/1957 incident when I was in 'Old Church' Hospital. The house father had beaten the hell out of me and said that no one would believe me and that I was just low-life scum. Another beating can still be seen to this day on the bridge of my nose, when my face was black and blue with a broken nose, and he told me he would show me who the boss was around here and that I was a little, low-life bastard. Then later on the 16/2/1960 whilst 13 years of age, I was placed in 'Rushgreen' Hospital with more injuries that were most painful.

Having reached the age that I am at the time of writing this, I reflect upon all those that had their bare bottoms smacked by Sir Cyril Smith, just as was my own experience in the 50s and 60s. Here I am now, living in Rochdale and very well-established in business but knowing of the exact same most disgusting behaviour. The local authorities simply put these matters out of their sight and turned a blind eye saying, it's just tittle-tattle. This most appalling dereliction of duty was in their knowledge in 1979 when Cyril Smith had confessed that he had abused boys at Cambridge House Hospital, of which he was a trustee in the 1960s, then 'Knowle View'. This tittle-tattle has led to no action whatsoever by R.M.B.C., save for removing the honorary plaque placed above the entrance of the Town Hall building in Rochdale.

At the time of my writing this true story it is being investigated and proven conclusively that Sir David Steel MP could have put a stop to his good friend Cyril Smith's paedophile actions against the children and saved so many of them just as myself from such humiliation, and in some cases referred to at the Old Bailey, their deaths. For anyone wishing to look into these cases then reflect this upon Sir Cyril Smith: please look into the 'Braintree and Witham Times' edition on the 23/1/2001. Then the 'Recorder' newspaper 12/10/2001 where the Metropolitan Police suggest the offences only came to light in 1995/6, and exactly the same reference as they refer to in the case of Sir Cyril Smith (and others) in the current 'posthumous' enquiry into their paedophilia. And now I read in the Daily Telegraph (April 2019) Pope Benedict refers to sex abuse crises in the 60s, saying in his words just before his Easter message, they are most abhorrent and 'Nudity in advertising helps to loosen moral bearings to exonerate the collapse in morality'. He said this in his view to shift his knowledge of such abuse away from the church. No wonder the 91-year-old Pope resigned in 2013. I leave readers to make what they will of these comments by the former Pope Benedict and take this into account in the 'Mapperton Case'.

Then I recovered from the London County Council Authorities my psychological report dated 26/2/1956 saying 'I am very slow and get confused, was timid and withdrawn and did not seem to develop at school', also saying on the 4/5/1960 'I had never actually misbehaved but showed no real ability, rather lackadaisical, ponderous and slow, does not seem to be very sociable'.

Throughout my years of incarceration, my best friend and his memories have stayed with me to this day, and I always talk to all my Grandchildren in the form of two mice that travel with me in my car wherever we go. They have written on them 'Peter & Harris'. Harris sadly after leaving the orphanage, I am told, was sent to prison for very many years. On reflection of all this in 1988, my home seen in the attached brochure was recently sold for £1.8 million in the same year 1988. Then I had invested on the sterling money market over £800.000, with his and hers brand-new top of the range Mercedes cars with their personal private number plates, and this is only a very small sample of the success I achieved whilst travelling all over the UK, with the past ugly memories haunting me as they do to this very time.

I urge those reading this most truthful account and evidence to do so very carefully, and then go to chapter 14 to see my experiences of Cyril Smith in the 'Turners Asbestos' Business.

Despite all the years gone by since the 1991 discovery of my wife and solicitors' actions, along with the sexual abuse case brought against me, they remain most dreadful. It was a distasteful and painstaking ordeal we all had to go through because of the lies. It just destroyed life and day to day living. The whole family suffered, but thankfully Anita and Tommy never left my side from start to finish. I don't know what I would have done without them.

Eventually, I was informed by Rochdale police child protection officers, Sergeant Sterndale and Janet Taylor that I was totally exonerated, but not thanks to the unlawful examination that took place on Caroline under general anaesthetic that most sadly led to my daughters, now permanent, disabilities. I was also doing all I could to avoid the Inland Revenue demands after continuously explaining to them my wife's deception but they were soon to make me bankrupt. Then in my post I received in 1998 the 'Mapperton Case', many, many years too late, where, to my utter dismay, the letter from the Metropolitan Police brought back memories of all I'd gone through and whilst on the green Dennis bus as a child, with many other bad memories.

I now at this time have a relationship that brings into the world my son Darren who is only 6 years old. His mother Anita who has done everything possible to help me has two girls Clair, 13 and Adele, 8 who had been interviewed in 1993 by child protection officers resulting from claims made against me from my wife and solicitor. So, here I am sat looking at this letter from the police with the heading 'Children's Home Hornchurch' and immediately I make the connection. How the child protection team at police HQ London would have discovered my address (Perhaps I am wrong?). I kept this letter to myself being too ashamed to show it to Anita and I wrote back to the police saying to them at the end of my poorly handwritten message "I have survived. Others have not and never will. Metropolitan Police, you are 35 years too late, why?" See chapter 36 and my questions why. I could not properly respond to this letter in the true way I should have. I just couldn't. This was because of all we were going through: with the prospect of losing our home and being made bankrupt, with the years of hell made by the C.S.A. bailiffs seen in chapter 35 in this matter coming to my home. This finally came to an end in 2002 after their admission of wrongful prosecution, then their making payment of my legal costs. But this

was

a year after I had been made bankrupt by H.M.R.C.

Little was I to know four years up the road I would be shot by my neighbour.

Those neighbours had throughout been keeping good contact with my former wife and solicitor and my three daughters. I believe the events taking place around my barn were warnings from my neighbours. At my time of life with all I was going through. I could not face the painful and difficult guilt and the suffering of my past in the orphanage, as now I have the responsibility of Anita and her two girls and of course my son, Darren. Anita had noticed at times I had been crying uncontrollably especially when she would play, unknowingly, 'Smile though your heart is aching' by Nat King Cole. Unknown to Anita I had spent my life working hard trying to forget my past and I did not want her to know. I could never erase the memories of my abusers, some of which were exposed at the Old Bailey on the next page. But as time went on and after being shot, I attended hospital and had psychiatric therapy that continued for many years. I was twice kept locked up in hospital with many others that were clearly far worse than myself, which made me go back years in my thoughts of the orphanage and see others in the hospital going around like zombies.

Thankfully I had visitors like Anita and Tommy and his wife and my son, Darren and particularly Derek and his wife and this gave me the will to show the hospital I was fit enough to be released from their care then visit weekly, monthly and so on. I now regularly take very strong medication for depression and anxiety disorder, and for the pressure build-up and damage in my head, every day as soon as I wake up, having previously attempted to take my life on more than one occasion because of Anita and Darren rescuing me it wasn't to be and I had been hospitalised. This is still constantly in my thoughts Anita doesn't like to leave me for long periods of time to date.

To try and explain this to those reading, I have lived my life as best I can with the discovery of my mother and then her brother's suicide, and I can understand their actions, but I wish they could have stayed to have enjoyed my success. When I am gone, I will have left behind the homes that I have built for others to enjoy with my thoughts going to those at Hindclough Barn and Anne & John and the family at the Hindclough Farm, and most importantly Anita and my son and all those giving me my proud name Gaga. I have certainly left my mark on this earth in more ways than most. So now I want to put my thoughts into words in this book and try against all odds to obtain justice when my past hope is gone, along with the massive financial costs spent on past, untrustworthy lawyers and barristers, acting on behalf of my former wife and former solicitor, all paid for by public funds.

Former councillor jailed for sex abuse
Sarah Hall

Tue 8 Oct 2001 03.12 BST

A former assistant director of social services, magistrate and Labour councillor has been jailed for abusing boys in a children's home scandal which may have had as many as 70 victims over 30 years, it emerged yesterday.

Alan Prescott, 62, who was described at the Old Bailey as a "pillar of his local community", was sentenced to two years in prison after admitting indecently assaulting four boys in his care between 1970 and 1980 while he was superintendent of a Tower Hamlets children's home.

After being in charge of the home, he became assistant director of social services at the borough, before moving on to become chief executive of Toynbee Hall, a charitable organisation, until his arrest in August last year.

The court heard that the former Havering councillor, fondled boys aged 15 to 19 as they lay in bed, confessed after the trial of William Starling, a colleague and "house parent" at St Leonard's, the home in Hornchurch, Essex, over which Prescott presided from 1968 until it closed in 1984. In April, Starling was jailed for 14 years for 19 offences including two rapes, buggery and indecent assault, on 10 girls and one boy as young as five over a 20 year period at St Leonard's and The Greensteads, a home in Basildon, Essex.

The men's sentences - handed down in April and, for Prescott, last Thursday - can only now be reported after the judge yesterday halted proceedings against Haydn Davies, 62, from Plymouth, a third alleged paedophile who was facing offences of assault involving boys at St Leonard's in the 1970s and 1980s.

The case against him was dropped after police lost video evidence from alleged victims, taken during an earlier, aborted, investigation - and the defence successfully argued that without this he could not be guaranteed a fair trial.

Speaking after yesterday's hearing, Detective Inspector Daniel O'Malley, said Operation Mapperton had unveiled a "harrowing" tale of systematic child abuse at the homes, and that the investigation was continuing. With 3,000 children having passed through the homes while Prescott, Starling and Davies were working there, he believed as many as 70 may have been abused.

I was told of a case where a young girl, being one of my long-term associated orphans from Hornchurch, had been sent to court on grounds of shoplifting. When she was sitting in court and the magistrates entered the room, she was confronted with no other than Alan Prescot. He sat with the other magistrates to sentence her. She certainly recognised him, and he recognised her. (See previous page) She was released without charge; it wasn't too long, and alarm bells rang.

It was said at the Old Bailey that, nestling in the Essex countryside, the St Leonard's Children's Home should by rights have been a mini-Utopia for the hundreds of youngsters in its care. With its 13 cottages, each housing up to 30 children, its own hospital, church, school, swimming pool and gymnasium, and generous avenues set amid 86 acres, the late Victorian village appeared a world away from the squalid council blocks where many of its residents had previously lived in the east London borough of Tower Hamlets. "It was potentially idyllic", said Carroll, who lived there with his brothers from the age of four, in the mid-1960s, until age 17. "We always said, when we were growing up, it would be a wonderful place to be – if it weren't for the staff".

For St Leonard's, which saw 3,000 children pass through its doors between 1965 and its closure in 1984 when I visited with my daughter Angela, was a haven not for children, but for paedophiles who meted out abuse while purportedly providing the children's care. I was taken into the orphanage in 1950. On the lifting of reporting restrictions at the Old Bailey, it emerged that one former house parent, Bill Starling, had indecently assaulted, raped or buggered 11 victims – aged from just five to 14 – over a 20-year period. Another defendant, the home's superintendent, Alan Prescott, a former JP, Labour councillor, assistant director of social services in Tower Hamlets and, later, chief executive of East End charity Toynbee Hall, had indecently assaulted four teenage boys at various points. Revealed was the sense of shame, the guilt, and the feeling of helplessness of the victims, and that the staff who weren't involved turned a blind eye and pretended not to notice. The few children who tried to challenge them were threatened. Life could be far worse at

Hornchurch. When we did finally tell someone, they did nothing about it, because Prescott was involved with teenage girls.

One of the original charges against Prescott – again dropped because of the loss of video evidence – also alleged that he indecently assaulted a boy who went to him for help against another abuser.

For Carroll – now a builder, with a partner and two young children – the abuse began almost from the moment he entered Myrtle Cottage, in 1965, with his three brothers. This followed the suspected suicide of their mother – a death he was not to be told about until he was 16, unlike myself who never got told. I then had to spend the years later finding out, only to be placed in this autobiography of mine.

At first, the abuse came from a perhaps unexpected quarter – his house mother, who died before police began investigating in 1995 and so evaded prosecution:

"It was almost instantaneous. It started with her fondling us, and she was very persistent – waking us in the night and touching our genitals under the ruse of putting us on the potty".

"The lights went out – we were plunged into darkness some were subjected to every kind of sex by alleged abusers. They were nurtured to want sex. He used to groom people; that was his way of securing his position with you. After he'd raped you, he partially lost interest – hence having so many victims".

And all the time the abuse was being secretly meted out elsewhere. Starling would bribe his female victims with money and cigarettes for sex and brutally rape the boys, while telling them no one would believe the tales of such problem children. Prescott, as head of St Leonard's, had the power to root out the abuse but instead did nothing. In fact, he encouraged it with others within the L.C.C. employment.

We were all suffering but suffering alone because each house was a world unto itself. We lived in an atmosphere in which we were just like meat. When I searched for my files, I kept seeing notes like "he's a pretty child" or "he's an ugly child".

Judge Martin Roberts, who presided at the Old Bailey case, said that although the defendants did not act together, each must have known what the other was doing.

Such an upbringing has devastated him, and this has overflowed into my family when they read all in this book. In the Mapperton case one person said:

"One brother flung himself in front of a high-speed train two years ago after being haunted for five years by rape flashbacks".

"I've one dead brother, one very ill brother, and one brother who's always struggled," he says.

"Our family paid an incalculable price. We were just four boys with the world at our feet – but sometimes I can't believe I'm alive."

He goes on to say, "He is pleased with the trial's outcome – despite Prescott's guilty plea meaning he could not testify against him – and suggests that the case has been cathartic." "The most important thing is that we've been acknowledged," he smiles sadly.

"We've claimed back a little bit of our humanity from these demons. Finally, we've gained the recognition that we were innocent, all of us, and the guilt and the shame isn't ours – it's theirs" and they were all the time well-paid in their employment with free living accommodation and food.

The Guardian 24/10/01

It is said a man who was sexually abused as a child by a worker in a care home has been told he will not be allowed full compensation because of his criminal record. Thomas served four months, 10 years ago, for handling stolen goods. That followed a string of probation orders and community service orders for breach of the peace. He will now receive only £3,000

– £10,000 less than expected – after being abused over an eight-year period at St Leonard's home in Hornchurch, Essex.

Last year William Starling was sentenced to 14 years in prison after being found guilty of 19 counts of indecent abuse at the home, which was run by the London Borough of Tower Hamlets. His boss Alan Prescott, a senior magistrate and Labour councillor, was also convicted of abuse at the home and served two years. Mr Worrall applied for compensation to the Criminal Injuries Compensation Authority (CICA) after last October's trial.

He was told by letter that he would receive £13,000 but that it was being reduced by 75% because of his criminal conviction. (My only hope is that when the authorities for criminal injuries like the C.I.C.A. and all those authorities like the now Croydon Shirley Oakes authorities, the L.C.C will read all the contents of this and other relevant chapters of mine, reflecting upon their total failures into their past employees and failed investigations into such criminality and posthumously order the proper criminal injuries. Compensation to Mr Worrall or his siblings if he is no longer with us with the top rate of punitive interest from the arrival date at Hornchurch Cottage Homes. I do not ask for any compensation save but to pay others that I know will never get over their memories until they pass away like myself). "I am stunned," he told BBC London. "I don't understand why they should punish you twice for a crime you've done many years ago."

Detective Inspector Daniel O'Malley, whose signature is upon my letter in 1988, said Operation Mapperton had unveiled a 'harrowing' tale of systematic child abuse at the homes, and that the investigation was continuing. With 3,000 children having passed through the homes while Prescott, Starling and Davies were working there, he believed as many as 70 may have been abused. There were clearly more than 70.

WHAT A WRONG STATEMENT! But he was not to know. I had my reasons not to join in the Mapperton Case; there will be many more for different sad reasons.

My heartfelt thanks to all those (cottage brothers and sisters of mine) who did find the courage to face this head on and bring justice and punishment to just a few from Hornchurch. Sadly, this kind of abuse will never go away. We are all different and we all deal with abuse of all kinds differently. This, we all know, it either makes you or breaks you. Time tells but time can heal, I just hope there can be more of the time of healing. The orphanage is now a beautiful place to live at for lots of different families. Some I am in touch with to this day, those living in Milton cottage. Gary and Dee kindly allowed me and my partner to have a look around and meet one young lady next door who actually grew up in the orphanage and now lives there to this very day.

A gruesome part of Essex that is now transformed into a brighter splendid place. A happy ending for Hornchurch and its new residents.

Haydn Davies, 62, from Plymouth, was a third alleged paedophile who was facing offences of assault involving boys at St Leonard's in the 1970s and 1980s. The case against him was dropped after police lost video evidence from alleged victims, taken during an earlier, aborted, investigation – and the defence successfully argued that without this he could not be guaranteed a fair trial.

Mr Percival (at Milton) who used to make us stand naked in a row and he would inspect our bodies and fondle us, plus using his stick he'd flick our willies and cane our bums. One of his punishments would be to make us stand on the landing in the nude. He would not face trial in the Mapperton case and Operation Harmon case.

Mr Cooper & family (Milton) were sent on their way eventually after the terrible beating I had sustained in 1959. I was 13. He and his wife were as bad as each other. They also escaped trial in the Mapperton and Operation Harmon case.

Mr & Mrs Jones (Milton). He was German, replacing Mr Cooper. When one thought things couldn't get worse, they did. The Jones were no better. They also had a very large Alsatian dog. We were all scared stiff of that as well. In 1961 I ran away from the orphanage and refused to go back. I was ill every day. I was 15 going on 16. I was so adamant I was not going back, and my brother had to make arrangements for me to live with him. Then eventually I met the Penhearows, Reg, Betty & children.

Miss Spooner (Milton) she was another who slipped the net. She was a nasty piece of work; she could make you feel bad just by her glaring at you. You could feel her eyes burning into you. One had to try hard and keep out of her way.

Mr. Perring, who drove the big green bus. If he wanted you in his clutches, he would trick you into having a so-called special ride on his bus and then horror. You couldn't leave his bus until he had his way with you, as I so remember, on the back of the L.C.C bus. He would fondle many whilst we were trying to get on and off the bus, he was always trying to kiss us, he always had cold sores, it was disgusting I have since suffered with cold sores it's also recorded on my medical records. He also escaped in the Mapperton and Harmon case.

On the brighter side Miss Surrage at Forbes and Miss Anne and Miss Dorothy at Milton, were the nicest Misses. I don't think anyone tried to keep away from them. So sad that they could not receive the commendation they so deserved when the other, not so nice staff, had been forced, or were willing to keep quiet for fear of losing their jobs.

I show some up-to-date messages from the internet on Hornchurch: -

One person said "It seems I avoided the cottages where sexual abuse was a regular occurrence. In Milton I did not see any – but we all know that abusers are cunning. In later life I knew many that had formed part of the police Mapperton Investigation.

Some I knew committed suicide – Carol, I Believe – others died of drug addiction. The fact is abuse happened in a lot of children's homes.

I was adopted by my extended family and went on to enjoy a good working life. One can't change the cards you are given in early life. But can – with effort, hard work and determination – change the later part.

I thank you I don't know Francis. Tommy unfortunately passed away age 46, he died on Blackpool beach on Christmas day of hypothermia, he chose to be homeless, he couldn't live in a house, he had quite a few problems, Billy spent 30 years in prison. He got out a couple of years ago, I'm ok, got a little business and have a wonderful family, love to all of us cottage kids, x

Valerie"

"Thanks for your reply, when I was in Milton Cottage the couple running it were strict – they had a son & daughter - all took the pommy £10 package to Australia, after being reported and it was taken seriously. Looking back the whole place was a pervert's paradise. Most single men with no childcare qualifications at all – some were themselves from children's homes.

The most caring staff I found were the casual staff like the cleaners. We were fed and clothed; more than can be said about my parents who were both severely mentally ill, both died many years ago. I own my own house in Cockfosters and am part retired now. Kind regards, Martin."

The final chapter in this book will show and demonstrate how I unlock that which the professional authorities are paid from the tax paying, working population of this country. In particular, those sex beasts and paedophiles who top up their employment earnings with the various local authorities. I am mindful of my involvement with Rochdale Council and Cyril Smith who did nothing but encourage unbelievable systemic sexual and physical abuse, and why would he when he was such a monster sexual, Lord Mayor, abuser of children himself. Then Sir Cyril, like Jimmy Saville and others, died with such wonderful praises for all their services.

Then in my case and so many others, our evidence was so called lost by the police enquiry team called operation Harmon and others. They said vital and important evidence could no longer be found and without the evidence, those rightfully accused could never be given a fair trial. So, they walked away from the court and their files of evidence were sent for destruction or hidden away in their archives.

Only those still living like myself have to live with the memories of those put into positions of trust with the care of us children whose paedophile carers were never detected or dealt with because the police lost the evidence. But after all, who would listen to us backward, lying children, who were just an inconvenience and, so called, not to be trusted? We were all just classed as dirty troublemakers. One example; how does a child explain a paedophile that used Brylcreem - 'a little dab will do you'- but it was not only used on your hair? It should have been called paedophilia cream for those like Jeremy Thorp, Cyril Smith, under the pillow and so many others in just this autobiography.

Should those reading this book be interested in the reason for the street signs being changed at Hornchurch, see Old Bailey about this Mapperton case and Operation Harmon investigation.

CHAPTER 35: C.S.A. and cheating solicitor

Throughout all these disputes my children's needs always came first. I had a joint bank account with my wife, along with company accounts where she had the cheque books in her possession. My children's needs did not require any child support and certainly no involvement from the C.S.A! However, this was not the case for Mr Trafford and his wife in regard to his children's needs. Throughout all of this Mr Trafford was living with free rent, food and poll tax at my Farm whilst making no contribution to his own wife or children. He failed to disclose his income, which was £74,000, to the C.S.A. which can be seen within the news article, 'Cheating Solicitor Left Kids Homeless'.

These actions brought on the C.S.A. assessment of his means to nil and incredibly, he and my wife failed to disclose the provisions I was making to my children's care. As a result, the C.S.A. started to communicate with me for child support for my three daughters. This was on the back of their nondisclosure of the payments that were being made regularly for my children.

No matter how much information I provided to the C.S.A. it was never accepted, and this went on for years. I even received bailiffs calling at my home with threats that I would be sent to prison if I continued to obstruct them. To say the least this made me suicidal, and I was eventually taken into a psychological ward at Birch Hill Hospital as I simply could not cope with, not only the loss of my children, but also all of the events surrounding it.

Throughout the years from 1992 and whilst staying at the bedside of my daughter Caroline at Alder Hey in intensive care, the child support agency was making demands for substantial payments that they claimed I was not paying for my children's care. This action went on for years and eventually arrived at the courts where it was demonstrated and confirmed through all my payments that throughout I had indeed met all my child support payments that were previously ordered by the courts.

The reason for the C.S.A.'s wrongful actions against me was because both my wife and solicitor were claiming various state benefits (it is to be noted that throughout this time he was a practicing solicitor). But over those many years they were claiming legal aid funding without disclosing their joint incomes or my weekly payments to my children's support. Therefore, the C.S.A. had not taken into account my payments and their wrongful actions referred. The C.S.A. nightmare came to an end with them making payment of my privately paid legal costs along with an ex gratia payment for the distress they had caused me. Meanwhile, I still had no contact whatsoever with my three daughters.

Because of the serious legal issues referred to in this chapter, it is shocking that the involved solicitor was still to this day practising law and a member of the Law Society and also being the main principle and owner of a Law Cost Consultancy business, advising solicitors on their invoices between the Legal Aid Authority. I exhibit a few supporting documents below to remove all doubt into the existence of these unlawful actions.

I then received a further letter from the C.S.A. Again, I reminded them with a copy I had sent previously that payments were being paid each week, and I sent a bank statement to prove it. Still, this made no difference and I kept receiving demands which were increasing each time. Then, to my horror, a letter came to tell me that bailiffs would be calling at my home. I could not believe this. I had no choice but to instruct solicitors. The torment and upset Anita and I had to keep going through. I was unable to obtain legal aid, so I had to pay upfront for the solicitor's cost and each time I was receiving invoices until the matter went to court. I made those payments to Taylor's solicitors, in Blackburn. Not long after that the doorbell rang and there were Equity certified bailiffs from Birmingham and Mr Paul Sharples standing at the barn door with the door open and a foot into the door. They gained entry into my home. Those reading this story will no doubt ask how Anita was coping with all this. She explained she has my son and the C.S.A. had not taken him into account; at this point I went to the door holding my son and I told the bailiffs to look. This is my son you have no right to call at my property, my solicitors have made contact to the C.S.A. on this matter. I gave them a copy of the letter asking them to please leave my property, and thankfully they agreed and went. All I could say to Anita was not to worry. I contacted my solicitors to let them know, which I knew was going to cost me more money. Then I continued to receive demanding letters from the C.S.A. so I ignored them. This went on for years until the matter got to court, this time I was the petitioner and I won. It took until 10/6/2002, to receive an apology and a special payment of compensation from the Crewe C.S.A. special payment section from the manager, Helen Shakespeare.

Whilst eventually the C.S.A. accepted their misgivings, all this had only ever been possible due to the dishonest actions of my wife and solicitor. A payment received by us from the C.S.A., supposedly for all the stress they had caused us was simply paid out to the solicitors, proving they were wrong.

My son Darren by this time was now 10 years old. We had been hounded for ten years with a lot of other things going on in our lives, but it did not break us.

The tragedy of all this is for Christine (see her copy letter at the back of this book) who had lost her home and had no child support for her four children. Christine did not know that I was making payments for my children's maintenance on top of the rental income, on a 50/50 basis to my wife whilst her husband, John Trafford (seen below in his C.S.A. assessment) did not declare what his total household income was to be taken into assessment of child support for his four children. The C.S.A. simply accepted that he was on benefits, therefore assessed him £1.

GLAD it's all over ... Peter Ross with his partner Anita and son Darren

At last - an end to years of torment

Michael Byrne
20/ 8/2002

A FATHER hounded for five years over child maintenance payments has been offered compensation by the Child Support Agency.

But Peter Ross believes he faces a bigger battle than the one fought with the government agency - that of rebuilding a relationship with his estranged daughters.

Three times Mr Ross was taken to court by the CSA - as well as being threatened with bailiffs and a prison sentence - who claimed he hadn't paid maintenance to his former wife Elaine and their three daughters.

From his first contact with the CSA in January 1997 Mr Ross protested that he had paid the maintenance. This May an independent tribunal finally ended his nightmare and the CSA has offered to repay all the money he has wrongly been forced to pay over the years, compensation and cash towards his legal costs.

Mr Ross said: "I'm challenging the compensation figure because the attitude of the CSA, even though they've been found to be in the wrong, is that they are above the law. No amount of money will ever truly compensate me for the loss I've suffered, the stress and emotional affect this has had on me. This has had a devastating effect on my life. I love my daughters. One day they may knock on my door, but I don't know if I will ever be able to rebuild my relationships with them."

Peter says his marriage began to break up in 1990 and his wife later remarried. He says Elaine was a director of his businesses, PLB Ross Electrical Contracting Company Ltd and Linkside Development Company Ltd, which folded after the marriage break-up.

Peter started a relationship with his current partner, Anita, and they have a son, Darren. Their nightmare with the CSA started when they received the first maintenance inquiry form in January 1997. Peter says the man his former wife married was claiming income support as their only income was child benefit. But Mr Ross says, in addition to the maintenance from him, they were receiving approximately £19,000 income from rent on commercial units owned by PLB Ross under a court agreement dating from October 1995.

Despite his protests Mr Ross was taken to court in April 1998 and again in April and May 2000. Bailiffs visited

All this time he was the owner of a Law Cost Consultancy firm. But he did not show this when filing information at Companies House, hiding that he was the main principal of the company. Instead, he put my wife and daughter down to avoid being assessed on the income derived from the law company he was involved with whilst he was in full receipt of benefits so he could obtain full legal aid at the same time as my wife.

CHAPTER 36: My three daughters and doctor from hell

Throughout this time, I was without any contact with my three daughters. They were all now living at Somerford Hall Congleton, right next to the Jodrell bank observatory radio telescope, as seen within the newspaper article above. My wife's solicitor, Mr. Guy R. J. Robinson has contacted my solicitor Mr. Hayman to tell Mr Ross that his daughter was in a very serious state in Macclesfield General Hospital. He did not give any further details or reasons behind her ill health. My solicitor contacted me to let me know I needed to go to the hospital.

I contacted my best friend, Tommy. On my arrival, the hospital would not tell me any details as to why my daughter was there or what treatments they were giving. I was kept completely in the dark and was treated like a leper. I went to see my daughter with Tommy and when I left, I hoped that she would recover from whatever was wrong. I left the hospital confused. I went home with my friend, keeping in touch with the hospital but they still told me nothing. After a few days I received a phone call from my solicitor saying that my daughter was on life support and I was told that she is being taken, by ambulance in a coma to Alder Hey in Liverpool.

I went to Macclesfield Hospital where my five-year-old daughter Jennifer had been left behind and was being taken care of by the hospital staff as she could not go in the ambulance with her mother. I was on the way when their mother left word with the hospital nurse saying her Dad will call and take Jennifer to Alder Hey, so this I did. Jennifer was hungry on the way to Alder Hey, so I stopped at McDonalds on the East Lancs Road A580 then continued on to Alder Hey where I found out the real seriousness of my daughter's situation. My wife took Jennifer's hand and told me only that Caroline was in a coma and that is all she told me. I am at a complete loss to understand why.

Eventually, I was allowed to go to her bedside, and I could see that she was in such a dreadful state that she could die. I sat with her, holding her hand and only two people were allowed at her bedside. I am sitting opposite my wife who is holding her other hand. Not a word is said. Eventually I left to go to the loo, and I noticed in the waiting room Mr. Trafford with my other two daughters.

Whilst I am away from Caroline's bedside, I make a phone call and then rush to be back with my daughter, only to discover that Mr Trafford has taken my place. As such I would not be permitted to be with my daughter as now there would be three at her bedside and this would not be allowed. I was not going to accept him in my place, so I went into the ward and up to my daughter's bed and thankfully my wife had noticed me approaching and she told him. He got up, passed me and blew me kisses on the way. He was trying to provoke me. Then he left the ward, as did my wife. What a pile of shit he was, by the side of my daughter's bed trying to cause upset.

I was now sitting on my own with Caroline and I stayed with her all night. Her mother briefly came to see Caroline and noticed I was still there. Throughout, the nurses were doing the necessary changes of transfusions of drugs and so on. I was without any understanding of such events taking place. It was clear to me I was going to lose my daughter. I knew that my wife and solicitor also knew this as my wife herself had been in nursing at Bury General Hospital. So, what my wife saw would not be as big of a shock as it was to me. After sitting with Caroline all night and into the day, the nurses finished their various changing of drugs then put their comments on Caroline's notes which were kept at the end of her bed. I decided to have a very sneaky look at the notes when the nurses had gone. It was there that I discovered the seriousness of what was going on. I was now in absolute horror. I discovered Caroline had been subjected to an investigation for an alleged sexual assault that it claimed I had committed. The investigation had been resisted by Caroline and her new Asian GP Doctor Thomson, but she had no choice because her mother was by her side. Then the GP managed to give, without any diagnosis, a drug from his surgery called Diflucan! On my discovery into the seriousness of this I became aware that Doctor Thomson had prescribed another dose. Now she has 500mg in her system of a drug, and the drug data clearly states not to be prescribed to a child. Caroline was only 11 years old and as a result Caroline became very unwell and came up with a rash and a very high temperature. The hospital gynaecologist, Dr Scott, agreed to a further investigation at Macclesfield Hospital and at the time, she was forced to be investigated under general anaesthetic and the combination of these events caused her to go into convulsion. I sit in disbelief.

On my discovery of this I drove to Macclesfield police constabulary to report that a crime had taken place under their jurisdiction. At that time, I had no idea that Dr. N. O Thomson himself was already under investigation by the police and G.M.C. and the police did not make me aware of this fact either. Then I left, driving as fast as I could to be back with Caroline at Alder Hey. Because I was driving so fast on the motorway to get back to Liverpool Alder Hey, I crashed the car. I managed to get out of the car with my leg bleeding and blood pouring from my face and nose. A passing taxi stopped and asked me if I was ok. I told him I had to get to the hospital, Alder Hey, which was a short distance from the crash site. He must have thought I needed to receive treatment. He contacted the police reporting the accident and the police soon arrived. I told the police that I needed to be with my daughter who is on life support at Alder Hay, using my shirt and handkerchief I clean the blood from my face, the police made frantic calls and directed cars away from where I had crashed. To my amazement the police then helped me, telling me to get into the police vehicle, leaving behind a police officer to deal with the crash site.

The police officer drove me at speed with the lights flashing and told me he is taking me to my daughter. On my arrival at Alder Hey Hospital the police officer stays with me until I reach the intensive care ward. He spoke to the hospital staff, and I go and try and clean myself up the best I can. I then got to the closed door at the ward and rang the bell. The nurse opened the door, and she said nothing just looking at me and asking if I would like a cup of tea. I said yes and asked for some Aspirin and a damp towel.

The time was approximately 2 am and the ward was in darkness, other than the lights that swung from the walls over the beds for the nurses to see each patient. I walked over to my daughter's bed, and I heard the air blowing into a special air bed that was designed to lift the weight of my daughter directly from the mattress. Caroline was still in the same state as when I left to go to Macclesfield. I was now covered in blood, with my head thumping inside. The very kind nurse arrived with a cup of tea that had sugar in it (I never drink tea with sugar in), but this cup of tea was so wonderful and refreshing. The nurse gave me some tablets that were only allowed after they had been given permission and they also gave me a damp surgical cloth to clean my face, nose, arm and leg.

I stayed at my daughter's bedside throughout the night and only moved to allow the nurses to change her drip or for my visit to the bathroom. Nothing was said to me in regard to my state. On the morning visit from the clinicians/consultants, Dr Sills and Dr Jane Radcliff, there was no suggestion that I should be removed from my daughter's bedside which I thought they would because of cross contamination of blood and plasma and other things that were being dripped into my daughter.

At approximately 9.30 am, I was asked by the nurse to go into the waiting room. On walking away from my daughter's bed and looking up towards the waiting room I noticed a police officer waiting for me. We went into the waiting room immediately and I said to the police that the car I had crashed was not mine, and that I had borrowed it from Anita, who was living in my rented property in Redlumb, Norden. When I said this the officer explained that they knew who the registered owner of the vehicle was and that they were now happy I had confirmed this so did not need to contact her. After the police were satisfied, I had driven her car with her permission, I never heard from the police again. Because I had driven the car through a school wall and fencing the police had made arrangements for the car to be recovered. I was not given any paperwork or a ticket of any kind from the police or even asked to see my driver's licence or insurance.

It turned out that Anita's brand-new car, a Mitsubishi Galant, that I was driving was a total write-off. Anita, the owner of the car, still had no idea that her car had been in an accident. Now I had to let her know so when the police had left, I went back to the bedside of my daughter and thought about how I was going to tell her. It was then approx. 10.30am and everyone had seen me covered in blood. I didn't have any change of clothes, and everyone was looking at me as though I was a leper. What made matters worse was that my wife arrived and saw my state and I knew inside that she was wondering how I could have got into such a state.

I walked past the waiting room, and I noticed my solicitor sat reading his newspaper and I got the sudden urge to kill him. I went in to get a drink; there was a kettle in there for people staying. We were one-on-one now, and he was feeling very uncomfortable when he noticed me entering the room. He lifted the newspaper up higher so he couldn't see me, hiding behind the paper and I could see it shaking a little. I was much larger and stronger than him and I could have picked him up. I wanted to do so very much and throw him through the window. Whilst I was boiling the water, I wanted to pour it all over him. He wouldn't have noticed if I had approached him because he was hiding behind the paper. Instead, I said to him "You are a pile of shit"; the newspaper moved closer to his face. I knew if I had done anything I would have had to leave the hospital in handcuffs and that wasn't the answer. My daughter needed me, I needed to be with my daughter at her bedside. My wife would have been delighted if I had done anything. I made myself a drink and went into the corridor to drink it. I noticed he never moved an inch; he was a frozen, dirty excuse of a man. The newspaper just shook, then eventually my wife came in and rescued him. Boy, must he have been glad to see her. She probably came wondering if I was doing something untoward to him. I had the sense and decency not to. It was totally the wrong place and the wrong time.

I continued to go to the public telephone, and I phoned Anita. When she answered the phone, she asked how I was. Little did she know I was covered in blood and her car had been written off. So, I told her and for a moment I thought the phone was going to go down on me; instead, she asked with a very concerned voice if I was okay. I told her I was, but her car was not. She said the main thing was that I was alright and then we talked. As I was in Liverpool and could not get home to change my clothes and could hardly go on the train looking as I did, I asked Anita to contact my best friend Tommy and explain what had happened. He knew more about these things. I told Anita I would simply stay with Caroline and phone her in the evening. I was mindful that she had two children to look after and now she has no transport.

That afternoon at approximately 4pm Tommy turned up at Caroline's bedside. He saw Caroline still in a coma and told me that Anita was outside. I was surprised and he told me she was in the car park. We left and I gave Caroline a kiss and passed the nurses who were all looking at me. We got to the car park where I noticed Tommy's Mercedes car, but Anita was not in it. Then I noticed his other car with Anita at the driving seat. She was looking at all the blood on my shirt and face and all in my hair. She got out of the car and asked if I was okay and then tells me she has been with Tommy to the barn to collect clean clothes and food. She had a lovingly, big smile on her face. I think she was more shocked at seeing me but nevertheless gave me a hug and a kiss and to my great surprise said she was going home with my friend Tommy.

Tommy then told me that I could have the keys to his car and his phone to use whenever I wanted and to bring it back when I could. We said our goodbyes and I quickly went back to Caroline. I had something to eat, and the hospital authorities then told me that I could have a room to stay and sleep in overnight in the hospital. Now I have another key for a bed sit and a key for Tommy's car. The night after I went through Caroline's files again, but this time writing down as much detail as I could understand for me to pass on to my good friends who would understand, Dr Ivan Blumenthal and Dr Edward Tierney. They were both involved with my daughter in relation to the escalator injuries. At the same time, I was having to deal with my solicitors, Heyman & Co, who were dealing with my divorce. I told Mr. Heyman that my family solicitor Mr J Trafford was at my daughter's bedside whilst his own wife and children were to become homeless and that this had been reported in the newspapers. I also told him that my daughter had twice been given her last rights and blessings by the hospital chaplain. Caroline was seen clearly with toxic shock and blistering all over her body from all the medication she had been given and had suffered a brain insult from the effects of all the treatments to resuscitate her after her heart had stopped on more than one occasion.

This treatment for Caroline continued for many, many months and if by miracle she recovers from the dreadful ordeal she will clearly be disabled for the rest of her life.

Then I told the doctor that my wife and solicitor had taken my daughter to Dr Ninian Omond Thomson, who gave her incorrect medication. Throughout the time my daughter had been in hospital, he had been under investigation himself by the same police force that I had reported my matter to at Macclesfield. He had been charged with serious professional misconduct on the 26th of January 1990 and the general medical council were also investigating him separately and against this background. On the 6th of May 1992, Cheshire Constabulary Macclesfield Division's Detective Sergeant Pickford wrote to me and said that the matters I reported did not constitute offences for which the police have a duty to investigate. The newspaper article on this matter is included: "Doctor from hell & Solicitor from hell".

Now I have to go and obtain another specialist solicitor to assist me with the unbelievable events that I witnessed being with my daughter through such an ordeal. It required a specialist to act on behalf of my daughter. My daughter clearly did not want to have the doctor she had not trusted to do an investigation. Or would she have understood her mother and solicitor were using her as their most deadly weapon? They would say anything untruthful to support their false and malicious allegations. Caroline was only 11 years of age.

'Note the cheque was paid from by my best friend Tommy's wife's bank account. Sadly, she is now deceased, but she will always be very much in my thoughts'.

First of all, I made payment and instructed a firm of solicitors and consultant Mr Halton. He acted on payments for his firm's services until he moved to become the senior partner of his own solicitors practice under the name of Halton Scates & Horton. Mr. Halton received all the information I provided him. With counsel's opinion he then made an application in Caroline's name for legal aid in her own right with me as her parent/guardian. I was aware from the legal costs I had paid in the escalator matter that this was going to be vastly in excess of what I had experienced at that time. This was especially so knowing what I had discovered from the hospital notes and the help that I had received from my good friends and consultants in my daughter's case previously. A great deal of work on my part had to be done to convince the legal aid authority to give full legal costs, unlimited in these circumstances. I had to convince them that not only had my daughter suffered catastrophic injuries but that I was fully aware that the people responsible for my daughter's state were her mother and my solicitor Mr John Peter Trafford and also the doctor that they took her to, Dr Ninion Omond Thomson.

At the time I instructed my solicitor, Mr Halton, this was also the time when he was at his previous firm. I had no idea at that time that doctor Ninion Omond Thomson was already under investigation and cautioned for misconduct, or that he had been under arrest and bailed out at the time he carried out his investigation on my daughter. I had thought that Mr Halton was not taking my matter seriously and giving the care that was required of the first solicitors, and then his own solicitors Halton Scates & Horton. More time was clearly being taken up obtaining legal aid certificates to slowly obtain as much cost as possible and less time was spent listening to me. Then I discovered the delays on my daughter's matter were because Mr Halton had in fact also been arrested by the police for theft of clients funds. So, now Mr Halton was no longer acting on behalf of my daughter or myself.

Then I discovered on the 27th of January 1995 that Doctor Ninian O Thomson made a payment into court of £5,000 plus interest at punitive/top court rate agreed to be backdated to the 26th of January 1990, the date on which he committed his crime of sexual assault before he carried out his investigation upon my daughter plus he was ordered to pay all the court costs. Then on Wednesday 19th of March 1997, the general medical council professional committee in the investigations of Doctor Ninian Omond Thomson found him GUILTY of indecent assault. This was broadcasted in the Sunday Times on the 6th of February 2000, naming and shaming this doctor and also the General Medical Council proceedings in the wake of the 'Doctor Shipman Scandal', quoting Dr Ninian Ormand Thomson who admitted he did a 'Profundo' by moving from Cheshire to Ayrshire in Scotland. Now with all the information that I have I made an application to the court in the family division and was constrained from putting all the evidence into an affidavit. The reason for this was that Alder Hey Children's Hospital would be affected most seriously. I referred specifically to Doctor Sills and Doctor Radcliff, and the best efforts that they had made to treat my daughter and keep her alive when she arrived at Alder Hey from Macclesfield Hospital where she sustained all the injuries that she received at the hands of those she trusted most: her mother, stepfather, solicitor and her GP Doctor Ninion Omond Thomson.

I exhibit one single page of twenty that was transcribed with the full consent of H/H Judge Smith in his Crown Court. I had to agree not to share the information that I had consented not to. To do so could cause serious harm to my daughter. I looked directly into the eyes of the Judge and said that I understood. I had no legal representation, but I knew that the Judge was himself in a very difficult and dangerous position and therefore I had left matters; one could say I let sleeping dogs lie, as my daughter did indeed live after this ordeal but has lifelong medical treatments that she will receive till the day she dies.

PRESTON COURTS
Verbatim Reporter

(D-01772 832 478)   P.0

Before His Honour on Monday 9th December 1996

JUDGE SMITH: Any reason why---

MR. ROSS: I would agree, with respect, until she attains 18.

JUDGE SMITH: What do you want to say about that?

MR. ROSS: Your Honour, I understand everything that you have said. I have done the best that a father could possibly do for his daughter. You are not with the benefit of all the facts relating to the matters surrounding Caroline but I understand that until Caroline reaches the age of majority, when any claim that she may have for those who have caused her the suffering and damages that she has suffered, will be lost---

JUDGE SMITH: As it happens, she has a period of time after her majority in which she herself can sue for anything that happened to her as a child. You understand that, do you not?

MR. ROSS: I was not aware of that but regardless I will not pursue matters any further than this Court and the reason I won't pursue matters any further than this Court on behalf of Caroline is because of what you have said which is right and proper because I would not wish to harm Caroline in any way whatsoever.

Having said that, I have made certain points to this Court and in affidavit form since 1991 which are true, which have taken place while these matters have been dealt with by this Court, that has unfortunately seen the events that have taken place with a solicitor to the Supreme Court and the mother of a child that has

Page 19 (6) Father shall have leave to have transcribed at his own expense a transcript of this Judgment

16 OF 20

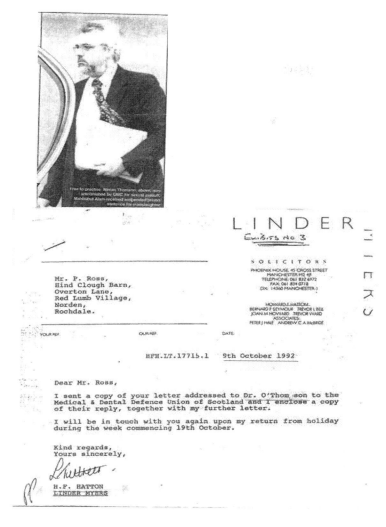

LINDER

 Em.B.TS No 3

SOLICITORS

PHOENIX HOUSE, 45 CROSS STREET
MANCHESTER M2 4JF
TELEPHONE: 061 832 6972
FAX: 061 834 0718
DX: 14360 MANCHESTER 1

HOWARD J. HAZICAL
BERNARD F SEYMOUR   TREVOR L BELL
JOAN M HOWARD   TREVOR WARD
ASSOCIATES:
PETER J HALE   ANDREW C A McBRIDE

Mr. P. Ross,
Hind Clough Barn,
Overton Lane,
Red Lumb Village,
Norden,
Rochdale.

YOUR REF.   OUR REF.   DATE.

HFH.LT.17715.1   9th October 1992

Dear Mr. Ross,

I sent a copy of your letter addressed to Dr. O'Thomson to the
Medical & Dental Defence Union of Scotland and I enclose a copy
of their reply, together with my further letter.

I will be in touch with you again upon my return from holiday
during the week commencing 19th October.

Kind regards,
Yours sincerely,

H.F. HATTON
LINDER MYERS

From Sunday Times 6th February 2000 also in the Cook Report 'Doctor from hell' 24th August 1999. Doctor Clair M. Thomson divorces him in 1993 when they are no longer in a joint husband and wife practice in Congleton.

Note the date above in 1992, then later see that the matters were previously reported to the police and the trusted solicitor I had put all my faith in had been struck off for theft of his client's funds, mine included.

CHAPTER 37: Court order in sale of matrimonial assets, Hindclough Farm & 2nd Neighbour from Hell

Near the end of 1991 Anita and her two children were now living in the barn with me. My wife and solicitor had moved to 'Somerford Hall' in Crewe. No doubt I had paid for most of the deposit for that from monies she had stashed away that I didn't know about. Our assets hadn't yet been sold; all the animals had gone, and they did a good job of taking everything, even down to hooks on the walls and all my company computers and filing cabinets, everything. There were still many things I was dealing with through the solicitors. Anita was going through the battle in her divorce. It was a sad and painstaking time for both of us. We were travelling to try and see my daughters but being denied access when we got there. A very upsetting time for me but it was nice seeing where my children were now living, and they did seem happy. They had some of the dogs and cats there and Caroline was looking as well as could be expected.

One morning I went out and noticed Mr & Mrs Sinclair were next door at the empty Farmhouse with their tractor and trailer, loading the internal contents: carpets, snooker table, fridge freezer, and many other items, placing them on their trailer and taking them back to their home. They even had a police escort. To do this they obviously had to obtain the key which my wife would have provided to them. I didn't bother going anywhere near, there was no point. I did take some photographs for evidence if needed. Maybe they hoped I would, then when we were next in court, I would look like a troublemaker. My friendship was totally over at this point with the Sinclairs. I had a battle on my hands knowing I was up against solicitors and now disloyal friends, living next door and acting like vultures.

One morning in my post we received correspondence from Rochdale Council enquiring about the conversion of the barn into residential property. I refused to answer their questions at that point, I was still going through my ugly divorce. On the 1st of March 1993, another document came my way and I saw that Elaine and John Trafford's solicitor, Guy Robinson, president of the Manchester Law Society, was being paid for his legal work from public funds. It was he, through my wife, that had reported the barn being used as a private dwelling. R.M.B.C. wanted to know if this was the case. I did not think my wife would do this; she had already had all the rental income from our units and had taken so much, selling all the livestock and much more. I knew this could turn out to be very ugly.

I warned Anita to be careful of anyone knocking at the door, wanting to come in for any reason. I didn't tell her about the situation at this point, I didn't want to worry her. Not long after there was a knock on the door and Anita went to the door. She spoke to the man on the doorstep through an intercom. He was Mr R Butler from R.M.B.C. He gave her a story that he needed to use a phone and would we kindly allow him to use ours. She told him she was sorry but no. We later found out from a letter that he was from the planning enforcement department. We were now being watched and under threat.

On Tuesday the 10th of January at 10.30 in 1995, I had to go before the master at the Royal Courts of Justice in London in regard to my daughter's fund which I had put into trust. It was the funds I had obtained from the escalator injuries on her behalf. I was the trustee as father and next friend over her fund. I immediately knew what it would be about. I went all the way down to London before the court, trying to protect my daughter's fund for her, leaving Anita very nervously in charge of looking after the barn and whilst in court another court date was set. I now had to make my way back home. There was so much going on in my life I was feeling broken on the inside, but I knew I had to be strong and carry on.

Also, in 1995 the court order has managed to obtain a sale of Hindclough Farm at, sadly, a substantial reduction from the price as it had been emptied by the neighbours and left for quite a while after my wife and solicitor had left the property, and I also learnt the cottages were being forced to be sold. I knew the cottages would have to be sold and that was why I had asked Anita to move into the barn. We noticed the arrival of a removal vehicle, bringing items into the farmhouse, then the day after work took place, decorating and so on. We now have new neighbours move into the property. It wasn't long before the doorbell rang. There were two females standing at my door. I looked through the peephole and to my horror I recognise them as friends of my wife and the next-door neighbours, the Sinclairs. I quickly told Anita she had to be careful of them and what is said to them because it would get back to my wife and solicitor. Plus, I had the R.M.B.C biting at my heels. We were now trying to live together but being forced to tread on eggshells, being suspicious of them and not comfortable at all having them living next door.

A clever move really. Joan obviously wanted Jane Edwards living next door to her because we were told her sister was part of the Bridleways Association and they were massively into horses as was Mrs Sinclair. They certainly had their thoughts and wanted to go into our arena. Anita had told me she had been asked if this was possible by Jane. I was not going to agree to that request. I don't think they knew I was getting wise to their hidden intentions. I just wanted to keep my distance from all of them. We were now living in the middle of a terrible, terrible situation.

After some time, we noticed many cars coming and going and over the following months there were many, many more cars parked up all over the place. We were wondering what was going on. Jane, who had rung our doorbell, was having discussions with Mrs Sinclair. Then we noticed a horse grazing on the garden belonging to the farmhouse. Now we had Mrs Sinclair as a regular visitor, only 30 yards away from my doorstep. Things couldn't be worse. It wasn't long and our new neighbours knew I had realised what they were trying to do. Anita had thought I was mad when, yet again, I told her not to trust them or get too close to them. They were in cahoots with my wife and solicitor. My wife and John Trafford couldn't have a better way of containing and controlling our lives.

So, putting two and two together, it was obvious that the Sinclairs had made the purchasers aware that the barn next door was also ordered to be sold and they knew that the barn would be part of the assets ordered to be sold. They were clearly determined to purchase the barn by flooding Hindclough Farm and the surrounding areas with cars. All this whilst I am still going through the most ugly and painful divorce. I had little or no contact with my children, save for Caroline whilst in and out of hospital, and to compound matters even further, cars were driving down to our property, people ringing our doorbell and on answering they ask for Jason or Jane, stating they have come for a test run.

It turned out that Jason and Jane had registered their car business and the limited company under the address of Hindclough Farm. It was a nightmare; people were sitting on our bridge waiting for test drives and obviously loving the position in the countryside where the business was located.

Jason and Jane; either they were both stupid or they hadn't been told by their solicitors, or they were convinced that they were going to obtain the barn at a knockdown price. What they wouldn't have known is that the council were taking legal action against me in relation to the breach of planning.

It was another very stressful time; and now Anita knowing all of what was happening and her trying to be helpful and taking strides forward with me even though she was so affected by her life before meeting me. It was a lot for her to have to handle but handle she did. My solicitors were eventually successful in dealing with and getting a variation in the court order that the barn be removed from the forced sale of the joint assets. This was because I was the previous owner of the farm and before I gifted it to my wife, I put a covenant in place, a legal restriction, that upon any ongoing sale of Hindclough Farm, it would be for the sole purpose of a family living within the property and strictly for no business use whatsoever.

So, Jason and Jane were in clear breach of the covenants upon which they should have been aware. It was going to cost them very dearly. I had told them to cease their car business and remove the cars and I told them to study their deeds, but instead they made matters even worse. A car salesman was now in the office that was built at the side of Hindclough Farm and on nice days he was outside with a clip board in his hand, doing his sales pitch to customers constantly coming and going. Then a huge trailer truck full of cars tried but could not reach Hindclough farm from the main road and had no choice but to park up on the water board's land on the opposite side of the main road and drive off all the second-hand cars. When they were all offloaded, they drove them down to the farmhouse, blocking off the only access into and out of Hindclough farm and the barn. Now we were trapped in, with cars surrounding our property and we had to ask them to move them so that we could get out to do school runs. With all this activity that could be seen in the pictures in this chapter, the intentions of Jason and Jane was to put off any possible sale of the barn other than to them.

Unknown to them my solicitors were drawing up all the necessary legal documentation and couldn't believe all the evidence I am able to provide. We were doing this work whilst completing the unbelievable tasks in dealing with my divorce and my former solicitor in his adulterous relationship with my wife. They also had to deal with the matters that caused me to lock the gate to prevent, my then solicitor, getting out to work and now, the same solicitor is drawing up an injunction in an emergency application to the court, as clearly our life has become unbearable. We had neighbours from hell that would not stop and persisted in carrying out their second-hand car sales with their workmen steam cleaning all the engines and under sides of the cars, valeting them and carrying out repairs to take photographs of them in the beautiful countryside surroundings of the green belt. The application to court is to prohibit unlawful commercial business. Also, the most serious pollution into the stream running between the two properties. The barns drinking water came from a bore hole by the side of the house where there was a well that was now contaminated with the detergent/acids used in cleaning all the oil and grease into the ground which percolates down into our drinking water.

A court hearing date was given and Jason and Jane are clearly not happy with us as their barrister has advised them to settle this matter without it proceeding to court as it was impossible for the barrister to defend the most defenceless case.

At this point our new neighbours approached Anita several times and want to try and talk to us and they came down, ringing our doorbell to see if we can discuss matters with them to bring about an amicable agreement to stop the matters going any further, but this was not possible. The matter proceeds in the high court. Without going into in this chapter all the ugly details that took place as well as the car business, one example is that Anita planted quite a few cherry blossom trees in a row coming up the drive. Jane was caught on camera pulling them back out, causing damage. Things got very tense between us all. They managed to take a section of fencing out, allowing the farmers' cows to tread all over the garden that Anita had carefully made nice. Her lawn was ruined, and her plants and shrubs were eaten; the place looked like a mess. We also had our quad stolen one night from our stable. Our post and parcels were going missing Anita and her girls had abuse herald at them.

Then, unbelievably, we get a knock on the door and there are the police with a member of the R.S.P.C.A. who wanted to interview me about an alleged incident that had taken place where I had injured their pet dog. I was cautioned by the R.S.P.C.A. Anything I said would be taken down etc. When they told me what I had allegedly done, I explained to the police that it was untrue and malicious. I am totally unaware at this point that Jane's former husband was a police officer, Sergeant Carlton. Jane had given a sworn statement of truth as a witness.

After listening to all I had been accused of, claiming I had got hold of their dog and thrown it out of the stable door from the barn, I explain it was impossible for me to have done this because the stable door hadn't been opened. I asked what time of day it was when they alleged, I had done this to their dog. They gave me an approximate time and that they had a witness to the event. So, I said to the police and the R.S.P.C.A man, "come outside and look at the door they are referring to, and right opposite that door on the stables is a CCTV camera. It records everything including recording your two vehicles driving down and parking up outside my barn and walking to my front door". We rewind the recording on the day in question

and prove conclusively that the stable door never opened once. Therefore, there was no dog thrown by me from the barn as they had alleged to have caused any injury to their dog. On seeing the evidence, they decided to take no further action, but I had retained the statement they had made and provided to the R.S.P.C.A and I still have it to this day.

These matters indeed proceeded to court when they were ordered to cease trading in the second-hand car business and to pay all costs and damages and not to cause any further nuisance or disturbance or pollution into the stream running between the two properties. Not very long after this case was concluded with payment of all they were ordered to pay, Jason and Jane's relationship ends. They removed all cars, closing down the business and they put the house up for sale. At this point Jason came down to see me and he gave me his most sincere apology; I accepted it. He told us that he genuinely had no idea of the full relationship with Jane, his partner and the Sinclairs. Had he known, he said, he would never have gone to the expense of setting his business up in the way he did and all the unlawful events that took place. Jason brought me a letter which gave me permission to obtain all his legal documents from his solicitor, which I did, to assist me in anything I may need them for. He was genuinely full of remorse about what we had been through with Jane. All these matters he heard through the court. Jane had joined forces with Guy Robinson, my wife's solicitor, and allowed private detectives to park a van in their garden and spy on us and gain recorded evidence of us living there. Jane was seen by Anita taking pictures of our washing on the clothesline. She even took in parcels from the delivery men that were Anita's and kept them.

Jason gave me permission to obtain all his files to help me in the enforcement action against the barn. Jane was using her former husband, Sergeant Carlton at Oldham police HQ, and he obtained information through the use of the police national computer. He was able to obtain all the details relating to the cars that they were taking in part exchange deals. They had instant and full details making it possible to understand the history of all the cars they were purchasing, and it was costing them nothing. Or could it be that Jane was making secret payments to her former police officer husband? To do what would have been lawful but costly in doing H.P.I checks, which would have taken much longer. The national police computer made it possible that cars could be bought and sold with no fear of outstanding finance or MOTs; and this was what made such a success of this car trading business, advertised with all the cars in its glory in the car trade magazines in the surrounding countryside, attracting the purchasers to visit our home and cause unbelievable disturbance 7 days a week.

Sergeant Carlton was admonished by the police for the wrongful use of the police national computer. Jason closed down his business of which Jane Edwards was a co-director. Jason was happy to be free of Jane Edwards after hearing the awful abuse and other things that she did to Anita and her girls, myself and to Jason's business. In a lot of ways, he went on to say that it was a blessing for him to find out all that had gone on through the court, but he was saddened by all the suffering that had taken place, especially the near trampling of my young son. Jane made her horse bolt one day, from her land, whilst Anita and my son Darren, a toddler, were in our garden sitting playing.

Enforcement Notice. Then on the 12th of July 1996 the ENFORCEMENT ACTION starts. We are all very distressed as a notice is placed on the lane for everyone to see that Hindclough Barn is now to be demolished. Give in, we did not! Another battle commenced, we stood together, and we took on Rochdale Council and the government planning inspector. When this day came it was freezing cold and took place in thick snow at Rochdale Town Hall. It was a very nerve-wracking and sad time for us, wondering if we were going to lose our home. I had told Anita that if the barn was to be demolished I would do it myself with my JCB. Anita was shivering and very quiet, feeling sick to her stomach. Everyone had difficulty in getting to the public enquiry but getting there many did. Then came the inspector who wanted to visit the site, but we had to explain that when we left our home it was in deep thick snow and if the council couldn't provide a vehicle that was safe for him to travel to carry out his visit, we were prepared to transport him safely there. The planning inspector gladly agreed with this, and he had to be accompanied by a member of Rochdale Council. So, we all travelled to our home in our 4x4 vehicle and entered the entrance gate which was fortunately left wide open. Throughout the journey we were not allowed to say anything to the inspector, but we heard him say as we reached the gate, "What a delightful place". We continued along to the barn feeling, to say the least, comforted by what he had said. He didn't even go into the barn; he looked around from where we parked up and his words were "What am I here for?" He came back to our car, got back in with R.M.B.C., and Anita drove them back to the Town Hall where the public enquiry was concluded. I gave thanks to the blistering cold snowy day and the deep snow that winter because we were able to see and hear the inspector's approval of all we had done.

On the 29th of July 1996 I received confirmation from the borough solicitor, confirming that on 12th February 1993 they received letters from his solicitors, my wife and my solicitor's solicitor, giving the grounds in and bringing about the enforcement action upon the barn. All the involvement of his solicitors was directly the responsibility of Mr Guy Robinson, the then president of the law society referred to in the letter of complaint. Thankfully, through legal disclosure, the council were forced to provide documentary evidence upon those responsible for taking the enforcement action to follow.

This letter on the next pages gives only a snapshot of what shows conclusively that the council had acted unreasonably in serving the enforcement notice. It goes on to say that they had caused his client, me, to be put through unnecessary expense. This unnecessary expense continued for over two years which all resulted from a complaint as above, brought about by the then president of the Manchester law society, G R Robinson, again with full payments of his costs throughout, with public funds. See throughout this chapter and other chapters of the massive legal aid fraud.

SOLICITORS

3-11 Drake Street, Rochdale, Lancashire. OL16 1RH. Telephone 0706 356666.

John F. Kay
Peter Rhodes B.A.
David Morrell LL.B.
Joanne Shaw LL.B.

Kitsa Efthymiadis LL.B.
Paul F. Dixon B.A.
Ian Lettall LL.B.
Alan Berry LL.B.

The Planning Inspectorate,
Room 11/11 (7),
Tollgate House,
Houlton Street,
Bristol,
BS2 9DJ

Your ref:

Our ref: APP.C.94
Contact: P4225.633389
Date: RSC.BT.30228
           Mr. Corran
           23rd August 1994

Attn. Mr. Trevor Harrison

Dear Sirs,

Town and Country Planning act, 1990 (As Amended)
Section 174 - Appeal by Mr. Peter Leslie Bernard Ross
Land at Hind Clough Barn, Overtown Lane, Red Lumb, Norden

We refer to our letter dated 18th August, 1994, when we informed
you that we wished to make an application for costs against the
Council.

We are making this application for costs, because we consider
that the Council have acted unreasonably in serving the
Enforcement Notice and that as a direct result, our client has
been put to unnecessary expense.

Details of the expense will be put to the Inspector on the day,
when this matter will be more fully explained.

We consider that the conduct of the Council has been unreasonable
for the following reasons:-

1.   The Council made insufficient attempts to make proper
       contact with the Appellant, so that the matters in the
       Enforcement Notice could be considered prior to issue
       of the Notice. It is accepted that the Council did
       attempt to contact the Appellant, but the Appellant
       will adduce evidence that such attempts were
       insufficient in the light of the Appellant's personal
       circumstances.

2.   The Council were able to inspect the items referred to
       in the Enforcement Notice from Overtown Lane. In
       particular, the Appellant will show that the paddock
       and concrete blockwork structure were easily viewable
       from the said Lane, which would have allowed
       inspection.

MOLESWORTHS
— SOLICITORS —

-11 Drake Street, Rochdale, Lancashire. OL16 1RH Telephone: (01706) 356666

Mr. P. Ross,
Hind Clough Barn,
Overtown Lane,
Norden,
ROCHDALE.

Partners

John F. Kay	Kitsa Efthymiadis LL.B.
Peter Rhodes B.A.	Paul F. Dixon B.A.
David Morrell LL.B.	Ian Lettall LL.B.
Joanne Shaw LL.B.	Alan Berry LL.B.
Associate Solicitor:	Sue McCardell LL.B.

Your ref:

Our ref:

Contact: HSC/SM/ 30238

Date Shazia
16/10/95

Dear Mr. Ross

Account Number 55279
Re: PLANNING DISPUTE - HIND CLOUGH
Amount outstanding: 235.00

We note with regret that payment of the above account is now overdue.

In accordance with our standard terms and conditions of trading
interest is now being charged on the amount due. To avoid further
action we should be obliged to receive your remittance by return. In
the event of payment being made within 14 days from the date hereof
the claim for interest will be waived but not otherwise.

If you have paid the account within the last three days or already
agreed a formal arrangement to pay with our Credit Control Department
please ignore this letter.

Yours Faithfully

Shazia.

MOLESWORTHS

P. 24.10.95

This Molesworths' letter and the Town Planning Consultants Michael Courcier & partners are just two of the mass of correspondence, involving the planning inspector and a public enquiry at the Town Hall in Rochdale.

All these events resulted from the unlawful access to public funding by the president of the Manchester Law Society. Their planning matters were all taking place simultaneously with my divorce referred to in the chapters above, and the only justice there was in this matter was that the inspector did not accept the complaint and enforcement action of Rochdale council upon the barn, leaving me to continue to reside in my home. I had suffered the massive costs in this unwarranted and unlawful action on top of all the other events in regard to the unlawful car sales business taking place at the same time.

1997. After the near loss of the barn, we were still licking our wounds. We still had many legal actions on the go. My divorce had not been made absolute and I still had the Inland Revenue on my back. I was dealing with complaints to the solicitor's complaints authority in regard to John Trafford and Guy Robinson and their wrongful doings, also the legal aid board and child support agency. At the same time Christine Trafford is visiting us and seeking some help, she gives me all her divorce papers plus all her complaints papers to the legal aid board and the solicitors complaints authority and her MP.

The Office of the Legal Service Ombudsman in Manchester Case Ref: 7640. I am dealing with Leonard Charles Gordon QC's association with Guy R J Robinson, president of the law society.

A letter of five pages was sent in December 1996. It illustrates that the matters of Charles Gordon were referred to the ombudsman who did nothing to intervene in the fraudulent access of vast sums from public funds.

This letter and complaint continued to the 18th of September 2019, to the Director General Dr Vanessa Davies the head of the Bar Standards Board under Ref: PCPA-2019-0282. Due to the fact that Charles Gordon is now H.H.J. Leonard Charles Gordon QC, there is no further action, and the Bar Standards Board are unable to take their investigations into the criminal actions at the time he was an advocate barrister for Guy Robinson president of the law society for his fraudulent claims and his legally aided clients Mrs Ross and Mr Trafford.

I am also involved with the police in complaints relating to solicitor Howard Halton, who was struck off and Dr. Thomson who got divorced from his wife and lost his G.P. practice. Also Guy Robinson, and John Trafford, who is being prosecuted by the crown prosecution for fraud and deception. I still had correspondence from the child support agency. I was with my MP communicating with Mr Taylor, MP Lord Chancellor's department to deal with legal aid fraud and I am having to deal with my companies and the bar standards board in a complaint against Leonard Charles Gordon QC. He was the barrister acting for John Trafford in his crown prosecution case.

Throughout all of this ordeal I have had no contact with my children and Anita wishes she was still living in the cottage. The barn is so big, the gardens are huge and there is only Anita doing the gardening and housework, plus looking after us all. Then she starts doing all the typing for me, so I don't have to pay others to type for me. We have had no holidays, we couldn't afford to leave the place because of all the legal work, and we still had a stalker coming round some days and nights causing havoc. I still have masses of mail that was posted to me in different languages. I had death threats with dates of when it was to be. Anita and her girls were all on tenterhooks. Anita was having to take me to hospital for psychiatric treatment, I began to start to want to take my own life.

Mass of some of the post & magazines March 1992

CHAPTER 38: The round table charity

During the early 90s, with my many long years of friendship with Steve Barton, the main principal of estate agents 'Barton Kendal' in Rochdale, Andrew Crossley and Chris Bell of H. Bell & Sons collected plenty of provisions for those in need at Christmas. This was for charitable work which were for the Round Table organisation where Darren and I were fortunate enough to give a helping hand each year. It gave us great pleasure doing so as well as taking my mind off all my problems. I would also help by looking after the float, year on year. This was a large trailer with reindeers on each side and all lit up, being pulled by one of the H. Bell & Sons vans. We would all join forces and travel from different areas, parking up, then running from house to house collecting bags of food donations. Other members of the Round Table would take and deliver to designated housing estates, leaflets were placed through each letter box giving details, dates and times when Santa and his helpers would be calling.

This would happen with Santa giving out sweets to all the children then collecting any food can donations for those on their own, the elderly and the struggling. At the end of these, after many collections of food cans, the Round Table would then set to work placing different cans into parcels ready for making deliveries to the addresses given by social services. I would bring the float back to my home, knowing it would be safely stored until the following Christmas.

During these years of keeping the trailer I would make many alterations and re-painting with others. Steve Barton had the large Round Table logo resurfaced and painted. This was a large circular Round Table emblem, fixed at the rear of the float. One year I installed a petrol generator and also fixed it into the rear of the float, fitting it out with Christmas lighting so when it was driven around the roads into all the housing estates it would be operating each year, a music PA system loaned by 10cc. This famous rock band owned a home on the same road, Norford Way, as my very good friend Dr I Blumenthall and his good wife Liz, making it fully illuminated all over.

During these yearly events my son very happily grew up and took part in them. He could see all the parents and children waiting for Santa. One year he wore a Santa outfit himself and went around, giving out sweets and collecting food parcels; rushing back and passing them to those loading the vans up. This happened for many Christmases with heavy snow, but this did not stop Santa's workers. These were fantastic, memorable, times seeing so many children's smiling faces with their parents giving them their bags of food & tins. Even the houses without children would leave bags with tins of food on their doorsteps.

Monetary donations were never asked for, but some would insist on giving money which would be given to Steve, Chris or Andrew, to deal with appropriately. Since the last year of being part of these Christmas activities, my son had grown up. Spending Christmases with his own 8-year-old son, we would hear the same music that we played whilst doing the Round Table collections, and this brings and will always bring back the most wonderful memories. Memories of those past fun and fantastic Christmases.

Since these events when I was driving around and saw Chris Bell or Steve Barton or Andrew Crossley, we noticed each other instantly and these wonderful memories came flooding back, with fantastic, reciprocal smiles all over our faces.

See the news article of my son and the float referred to above, remembering everything we did. This was given without question and completely free and voluntarily. If I could do this all again I would do so in an instant, but sadly time has taken its toll. Thankfully it cannot take the most wonderful memories that I wish to share with those taking the trouble in reading this particular chapter.

This is what the parents and children would see in the dark, all-around Rochdale. Can collecting with Christmas carols blaring out. It was absolutely fantastic; it was a tonic for us all.

Darren giving his mum a hug before leaving to do the can collecting.

CHAPTER 39: Dog attack and having a sandwich

Over the decades, as reflected on in past chapters, I had built up a very strong friendship with an Irish man called Tommy/Pat which is short for Patrick. Patrick is the middle name I have given to my son. As mentioned, he came over to England with a ten-shilling note and a suitcase, with all his worldly belongings in it. We both started off with more or less a few shillings and the clothes we were standing in.

On a Sunday morning in June 1998, my good friend Tommy asked me if I would drive behind him as an escort so he could get the JCB to Manchester, ready for an early start for work on Monday morning. The security guard was informed that we were visiting the site. Of course, I would take a bullet for my friend Tommy and his wife (I took much more than a bullet), so I immediately agreed, and took my son and Tommy's grandson Kieran, both around 6 years old, in my van. Tommy driving the JCB without an escort behind on a public highway would not be safe as normally a JCB would be delivered on a low loader. With the roads on a Sunday being quiet and very little traffic, my son and Kieran had no seat belts on, standing most of the journey and looking out of the windows of my van at the JCB in front. Every now and then Tommy looked behind at us and waved.

We reached the Manchester central building site nice and early to open up the gates, allowing the JCB safe access onto the site. I then parked up my van, leaving my son and Kieran safely watching, thank goodness. Tommy pulls in with the JCB and as soon as the JCB is off the road and inside the site it's my job to then close the gates, which I do. Tommy then drives the JCB to a position to safely leave it with me, walking in front, looking for any timbers with nails or anything sharp which would puncture the very large JCB tyres. What I did not notice, to be sure, was that there was a guard dog roaming around. I heard my friend Tommy shouting and piping his horn on the JCB, but it's too late. Like a bullet from of a gun, I saw a German

Shepherd guard dog coming straight into me with its teeth into my groin area. It went with such force to my groin but luckily, I managed to stay on my feet. I stood with blood pouring down my legs holding my private parts, thinking it had bit them off. I was screaming with pain. The dog came at me again and again, then the dog came at me from behind, sinking its teeth into the back of my leg, then my behind and then my other leg. I was in shock and pain, and I heard my friend shout "Run to the JCB Peter," so, still managing to keep on my feet I start staggering to the JCB and the dog still managed to get more bites into me. It was terrible. Throughout this time, I can just about hear my friend shouting "Hail Mary Mother of God," over and over. I managed to stay on my feet and grabbed the handrail of the JCB and pulled myself up whilst the dog was still attacking my ankle. At last, I was out of the line of attack from the dog.

With the dog having the taste of my blood it had gone into a real attack against me. I had blood pouring from all my wounds, the worst pain was from my groin. I had both hands free to hold on to what was left of what I had, and Tommy was still shouting "Hail Mary Mother of God". Then a girl comes running over and gets hold of the dog and puts a lead on it whilst it's still barking and wanting to have another go at me. Then a security man comes over, by which time my friend Tommy has parked up the JCB and turned off the engine. I tried to climb out of the JCB still holding on to my bits. I cannot hold on to the handrail. I stumbled out of the JCB then I twisted my back during my fall off the high step, so agony was everywhere. Next thing I am on a stretcher passing my van with my son and Kieran watching. My trousers, well, what was left of them, were full of blood. I can only imagine what the boys must have felt, especially Darren, my son, when they saw me.

The Ambulance took me to North Manchester Hospital with the emergency sirens blasting out. In horror, my best Irish friend, Pat instantly telephones Anita to try and explain some of the situation but with great difficulty. He just said that I had been bitten by a dog and had to go to the hospital. She instantly thought it was just for a jab. He explained I was taken on a stretcher by ambulance and that he will travel with her to the hospital after he takes Darren and Kieran to his daughters, then come to me but for Anita to drive over to pick me up with him and take me home, and that he can explain more on the way to hospital whilst she drove. He told a few bits on and off on their journey. I believe he told her where the first bite was as she was parking up in the hospital car park. I was told she took it fairly well. She noticed how everyone made a point of looking at her when she walked into A&E department and when she walked to the cubical where I was, which made her more nervous about how she was going to find me.

When the hospital nurses cut away at all the lower half of my clothes, which were full of blood, the nurses saw the state of my injuries; thankfully they were male nurses. I know it was difficult, after hearing what had caused the injuries, for the hospital staff not to laugh. I had to accept the need for my wounds to be treated with the utter most care. Whilst I am getting cleaned up, the hospital can now deal with all the areas requiring stitches and I noticed the police were now asking questions from the hospital staff to assess the extent of my injuries. It seemed like hours, with me still waiting to be stitched up and I was told I had visitors and if I was happy to see them. I asked who it was, and I was told it was Tommy and Anita. I said yes to Tommy and no to Anita at first, then after talking with Tommy to find out what he had told Anita I was happy for him to go and fetch her. I asked where Darren was and if he was okay. She told me don't worry about him, he is ok, he is still with Kieran and his mother. She told me to just get sorted out and get back home in one piece, and I laugh and say I will try with what is left of me.

Anita and Tommy leave to go and sit in the waiting area as it is now time to have all the stitching done. The pain relief of morphine kicked in and I had been given two cups of tea. Even today, I cannot remember how I got home. I then discovered that the security guard, who was meant to be watching over the building site, was instead watching over his girlfriend in his car and the dog was left roaming around the site. We managed to have a few laughs with the nurses, having a few jokes about my attack, particularly when my friend Tommy told them what the security man was up to in his car. Tommy had noticed from his advantage point, high up in the driving seat of the JCB, that neither the girl or the security guard had any clothes on, so before she could get to the dog and get it under control, she had to put her clothes on, leaving the security guard getting dressed in his car. Tommy and I had to tell the whole story to the police and again there were jokes being made, and Anita heard the laughter so was getting a bit impatient. She wanted to see me again. A nurse came to ask when she could see me, then I walked over to her, bent over like an old man. The hospital gave me a gown to wear, and they put my clothes in a bag. She said she could see how much pain I was in as soon as she set eyes on me. My eyes were bloodshot, my face was flushed, and I had difficulty walking. They brought me some dressings, and with a cheeky smile gave them to Anita with instructions on what they wanted her to do.

The police were very interested in getting as much information in this case as it was a most unusual, a sad and bad attack, but fortunate with me being the only victim.

A week went by, and I had parts that went septic. Apparently, all dog bites are prone to go septic, so I had to go to the doctors to get antibiotics. The police came to see me and then I discovered that this case was going to court and the security man was being prosecuted for his failures and putting me in danger. My good friend, whilst working on the site on day one, found a diary of who and when people were on site. Also, an incident book which at first looked like the whole thing hadn't been logged and there were no security cameras on site. The security man was giving a different story to ours. Tommy brought home a page that had been ripped out of the diary and the guard had stupidly thrown in the bin, so we were able to give this to the police proving his made-up version was a lie. In the interim period, whilst waiting for this dreadful incident to go to court, the court was told that he had sold the dog. This was to avoid having it put to sleep. Sadly, the new owner of the dog had a child, and we were told the dog had attacked the child and then was ordered to be put to sleep. It could have been much worse had it not been for me falling to the floor during the attack, and my good friend Tommy shouting as much as he did, whilst I managed to reach the JCB and pull myself away from the dog's grip and with him helping to drag to safety. It would have been much worse if it had gone for my face, and I was too good looking for those sorts of injuries. For many nights after the attack, I would get flashbacks and my thoughts went to the two children, thinking about what would have happened if they had followed me onto the site; I dread to think. Then the case went to court, and you could hear a pin drop. Anita came with me, and we were amazed at how many came into the courtroom when my case was called. It had already been in the newspapers, so there was a lot of interest for a good story of man who lost his manhood after a dog attack. As you will see from the news article the owner of the dog was called Shitul Desai. He was the member of security, guarding the site at this point. In court all the jury and members of the court were looking at me, sat opposite in the witness stand and the jury was told that he had been caught undressed in his security van with his girlfriend (having a sandwich). He panicked on hearing the JCB and let the dog off its lead. This was a lie; the dog was left to roam the site. He didn't want to get into deep trouble. He knew his job was at risk because he had let the dog roam. A security dog has to be on its lead and kept under control at all times under the Dangerous Dog Act. The truth eventually came out in court. He was found guilty, and he had to tell the court he no longer had the dog at home which didn't go down well, at all, with the judge.

I went to give my evidence and obviously I had Anita with me, and it was rather obvious what most of the jury and court staff were thinking whilst looking at us both. My thoughts were of the poor child who had been another victim of Shitul's untrained, unleashed, German Shepherd dog which had simply been trained for one thing only: to do the job that Shitul could not be trusted to do. The first issue was him having sex with his girlfriend on the building site he was meant to be looking after; and the second was leaving his dog to roam around the site. Thankfully I did not take my son or Kieran with me and left them safely in my van. Had I not done so then the events would have undoubtably been more tragic for my son and my good friend Tommy's grandson.

Groin agony of guard dog bite victim

A BUSINESSMAN savagely mauled by a German Shepherd guard dog said: "I'm lucky my manhood is still intact."

Peter Ross, 51, was speaking after a Manchester court slapped a £500 fine on security guard Shitul Desai, the dog's owner.

Mr Ross added: "I'm still in pain after eight months."

Desai, aged 29, of Birch Avenue, Haslingden, admitted failing to keep the dog under control. The attack happened as Mr Ross and a colleague delivered a JCB to a city centre building site.

The court heard Mr Ross, from Rochdale, was pursuing a claim for compensation.

£500 fine for mauled 'manhood'

A BUSINESSMAN savagely mauled by a German shepherd guard dog said: "I'm lucky my manhood is still intact".

Peter Ross, aged 51, spoke after a Manchester court had slapped a £500 fine on security guard Shitul Desai, the dog's owner.

The Rochdale-based businessman said: "I'm still in pain after eight months and I don't think I'll ever be right."

Desai, aged 29, of Birch Avenue, Haslingden, admitted failing to keep the dog under control and was also ordered to pay £200 costs.

The attack took place on a Sunday morning last June, as Mr Ross and a colleague were delivering a JCB to a city-centre building site.

Prosecutor Kevin Rogers said the dog went for Mr Ross injuring his groin and legs. The animal was eventually brought under control by Desai's girlfriend.

Mr Andrew Brooks, defending, said Desai had not been told about the JCB being brought to the site.

When the attack happened, Desai had been in his girlfriend's car eating a sandwich.

The court was told Mr Ross, who lives in Rochdale where he runs a building firm, was pursuing a claim for compensation through the civil court.

Rochdale Observer 21-1-98

It was many years later with Tommy my Irish best friend at the passing of his wonderful and loving wife, and Anita and I were with his children and grandchildren at her final resting place on the 13th of February 2014. Since that time, we have regularly met him during our visits to her grave. Both of us are still holding on to life and having more time to just sit in the quiet, talking and reminiscing. I learnt he was much like myself, but he didn't go into an orphanage. He was a grafter, even as a child he worked on a farm, and he would dig on the peat bogs. It was hard work for a child to fetch and carry and he worked hard for his keep. He also had a poor education like me. He became a boxer for a short time and then a heavy weightlifting champion. He came from Ireland to Manchester at 15 years old with nothing but a few shillings in his pocket. He found a job and started work the day after he came, digging trenches and drainage work. He had grown up and achieved so much success in his life without his parents from a very young age. We met up at each other's homes and we exchanged stories and remembered times when we worked together in our past.

To this day I thank God I was the only victim as I would have found it impossible to live with the sight and memory of two such young children in the jaws of a savage, German Shepherd, Alsatian dog. Just imagine Anita finding that our son had been mauled and hospitalised or both, and all three of us. How would my good friend Tommy have coped, being sat in the JCB and watching all of this happen being unable to help.

CHAPTER 40: Barnardo's charity

Never was I under the care of Barnardo's charity. My only connection with Barnardo's charity was with my background as an orphan and on our camping holidays I noticed that Barnardo's children were camping in what I can only describe as upper-class accommodation in comparison with the Hornchurch L.C.C orphans.

However, whilst working all over the UK and seeing the Barnardo's charity, and walking through town centres, we would be approached by those collecting for Barnardo's. I would always make a contribution as well as go into the stores and purchase items for my grandchildren to get some happiness from.

I decided to become involved many years ago, making monetary donations to shops springing up in the places I travelled to. I went in my company vans that could be used to transport items that were of value to the Barnardo's shops. For example, each time any of my friends like Ivan and Liz Blumenthall had surplus items, or I would move home and not require items such as good quality beds, wardrobe, furniture, curtains and many others. I would drive to the Blackpool large furniture store with children's toys and clothes to St Anne's and Lytham and many other shops.

Then, word went around to my friends and business acquaintances. They would contact me saying that they had items they no longer required, so I would drive to their home and collect the items, storing them up at my home where I had plenty of space to make up arranged deliveries to the various Barnardo's stores, always over weekends when I could enjoy the journeys with my little helpers in the loading and unloading at each end.

At the seaside in St Anne's, we would park on double yellow lines to get us as close as possible to the shop. The parking attendant would pass on, not bothering us. There were times when unloading items that were being sold by the members of staff before they even got into the shop. After unloading was completed, we would spend what time we had left visiting the sea front or the Blackpool lights and returning empty and ready to do the same again until all the items had gone. The vans I had, although large, would need to make many journeys with the number of items we had stored.

In between all this, whenever I would do an event or birthday or a charity event, there would be a promotion of Barnardo's, see photo. Over the years these activities this gave me such satisfaction that it has all been done for a cause for such unfortunate children like me, even though I did not receive in my childhood such charity. Now in my late years, with all my large vans gone, I still regularly pack as much as will fit in my car, many times each year and take them to my local Bernard's shops.

The copy above shows just a few of the many thank you cards I received, and still receive, from Barnardo's, with a cake made for a children's birthday party.

CHAPTER 41: My bankruptcy by the Inland Revenue/Tax man

Throughout the passing years, having not been able to make any sense of all that is happening, the Inland Revenue held back in proceedings for the recovery in tax they said I owed, after I explained my situation and that any tax, I was assessed in their statutory demand was not correct. This was because I had discovered many payments that my wife had received and not declared by the forgery of my signatures upon company cheques and my private pension policies.

Regardless of all that I had explained, including being at the bedside of my very sick daughter; that my family solicitor had made it impossible for me to continue with my business affairs; and that one of my companies had been struck off because I was unable to sign off the 1989-90 accounts until I was satisfied with them, H.M.R.C. would not wait any longer. So, they carried out their bankruptcy proceedings at the same time that my industrial units, which were bringing in rental income, were to be sold. Still, the Inland Revenue would not grant any further time for the sale proceeds to be paid to H.M.R.C. Instead, they made me bankrupt on the 19th of July 2001, one day before my birthday. I do not believe this was a coincidence.

As seen from the court order, I had to appear in the London court, but it was not possible to travel from Manchester on the first early train, making it impossible for me to be at court on time for the hearing. So, I packed an overnight bag the day before and reached London in the afternoon. The hotels I stayed in previously at Euston were fully booked up, and now I was unable to afford luxury hotels as I did in my past. Knowing London as I did, I decided to wait until it went dark and made my way to Trafalgar square, thinking I would be able to sleep on one of the wooden benches close to the fountain. I got there and for a short while there were very few people passing. I sat in readiness to lie down to try and get some sleep. It would be around 10.30pm when a security guard came over to ask me to move on, as after 10pm I was not allowed to be around the area where I was intending to sleep. He could see I was dressed well, and I explained the situation, that I had only come down to London to be at the bankruptcy court and I couldn't do this on the day, so I had to come down the day before and wasn't able to find a hotel for the night. So, my only option was to sleep here to be up early the following morning, then I'd walk the distance to the Royal Courts of Justice.

I could see he took pity on me but said it was not allowed for anyone, regardless of the circumstances, to sleep or be inside the area where the benches were. But he told me he would get me a cup of tea and I would then have to move on. He went away and arrived back with a cup of tea. Then my basic phone in my pocket rang and it was Anita, checking to find if I was okay. She wanted to accompany me, but she had to look after her sick mother and her daughters and Darren. She was obviously very worried about my well-being. I explained to her that the security man has told me I can't stay where I am, but he is just walking back with a nice cup of tea for me. I asked Anita to explain to the security man and reaffirm my story in the hope that he would let me sleep on the bench as, clearly, I was no threat to anyone, and I passed him my phone. He talked at length to Anita then gave me back my phone, by which time I had drunk most of my tea in the mug and he told me to follow him, which I do whilst continuing my conversation with Anita. Then I told Anita to phone me again later.

Following the security man, we reached Nelson's Column where there was a very nice car parked up. The lights started flashing on the car and he opened the passenger door and told me to get in. He went round to the driver's seat and because it was rather cold and damp outside, he started the engine, turning the heating on to full. Then he said you can spend the night in my car, just turn off the engine when you're warm and comfy and I will keep a watch over you throughout the night until I go off duty at 6am. I thanked him so much for his kindness and he left, closing the door and I eventually got to sleep after I turned the engine off.

I woke up occasionally and wiped the front window which got all steamed up just to have a look outside, then went back to sleep. I later fell asleep properly until I heard a knock on the window. I opened the door to find him standing there with a mug of tea for me. He told me to take my time and get ready to go on my way to court. All the windows were still fully covered with condensation. He returned with a cloth to clean all the windows by which time I had got out of the car. He shook my hand and wished me good luck in court. I offered him the two London embossed mugs that I had had my nice tea from, and he told me to keep them as a memory of our meeting. He then got into his driving seat, driving away from me and waving goodbye. I only wish I could have obtained his address or phone number so I could contact him and tell him how I had got on. Now it would be wonderful if I could contact him to let him know I am putting this story into my autobiography. Perhaps with God's help he will get to read this.

I walked the distance from Nelson's Column to Holborn, then down to the law courts. I went through security, passing the bear garden and going up in the lift. Then I got to the very nice clean toilets to get undressed and have a wash and brush up to put my nice clean shirt, tie and suit on with my nice black brogue shoes. Unfortunately, I had to wear the same socks I had spent the night in; I had forgotten a new pair of socks. I bagged up all my belongings then went to the cafeteria for another drink and sat before it was time to walk over to the Thomas Moore building. I had found it most difficult to find the Thomas Moore building on my previous attendances, but I became an expert in finding it on this occasion, and I was even able to help others find the court who got lost as I have done in the past and I put them right.

It was the worst experience; I was without any legal assistance, and I was made bankrupt. It was like the world had ended. The only thing I wanted to do was to climb over the balcony looking down on to the main court marble floor and jump off. This would have left the court to have to clear up my dead body and blood that would have clearly splattered all over. The height of the balcony would have been approx. 20 feet above the ground floor concourse. But as I stood waiting simply to fall over, many thoughts were going through my mind, mostly of Anita and Darren. Then of my mother's actions and my uncle's. I decided instead to make the lonely journey back home to then tell Anita that I was bankrupt. I wanted Anita to think my phone had died just as I wanted to as it rang out.

I was on the train going back home and had many hours to think how to explain all this to Anita. I got back home to her, and she gave me her usual hugs and kisses with the kindest words, saying she loved me and would stay with me whatever. At the time I knew they came with the warmth from her heart and soul, as she held me and hugged me.

My next mission was to, at all costs, have the bankruptcy annulled, otherwise our home would have the bailiffs call again and this time we would have to leave and become homeless; time was against us. It took only so long to make an application to the high court to have the bankruptcy annulled. Thankfully my very good friends Eric and Kath stepped in and became our saviours. Both Eric and Kath told us to start an appeal and he and his wife would help save us from the loss of our home.

I will say no more on this issue, except to mention Eric and Kath, giving my thanks and love and continuous thoughts for them both. There is so much more I could write in regard to Eric and Kath, but this will stay in my thoughts for the rest of my life.

On the first of November 2000, I discovered my eldest daughter and her mother had resigned their positions from their law firm. I also discovered in the year of my bankruptcy that she divorced him because he had made my daughter's carer, Paula, pregnant. Now, he had to leave my former wife and my children along with the matrimonial home, which was also the company registered offices of his firm, taking with him Paula and his child to another address. Typical, after the mass of devastation and destruction he had caused; tearing down my life's hard work and being the cause of such damage to my children, especially Caroline; and not forgetting his ex-wife Christine and their four children, he walked away from. He is able to build a new life and to continue in his law cost business at his new address, leaving my daughter Angela and her mother resigning from the company.

During this time my industrial properties were sold to the church. They were the landlords of the solicitors who were acting for them both. I am now with the loss of all rental income and service charges. All my shares from the sale proceeds were paid directly to H.M.R.C. and only with the kind help of my friends and Anita, the substantial balance outstanding was paid from a loan secured upon my home. This help enabled me to have solicitors annul my bankruptcy, otherwise I would have lost our home, The Barn, with H.M.R.C being successful in their bankruptcy application. Having now managed to pay off all the amount H.M.R.C. demanded with interest, plus all my legal costs, I was left with no income whatsoever and I could only rely upon what was left of my private pension to which I have paid another most substantial sum of tax to cover part of the costs I had incurred over the years. Those costs amounted to well in excess of £500,000, plus the repossession of my home of 30 years. At further expense my solicitors communicated with the pensions ombudsman to unlock the pension fraud and my substantial loss resulting from the criminal actions of my former wife and my pension adviser, Kevin Booth, after he was made bankrupt following the serious fraud office's actions. In this again, I was unsuccessful. The argument of the ombudsman was that he didn't deal with the criminal matter as he had no jurisdiction relating to fraud, and he questioned why a wife would steal her husband's private pension and how the husband would not notice this. This was regardless of all the evidence I had provided my solicitors with, to put before the ombudsman. The judge simply dismissed the case and again I suffered all the costs including my former wife's costs. The court decided that I was obsessed and that it was a husband's vendetta because his wife had formed a relationship with his company and family solicitor. He went on to say that it may be immoral, but it was not criminal. I had no choice but to accept a loss to my pension and go home.

At that time Anita had come down to London with me because I was not in the best of health. I have to say, with a heavy heart, that if it wasn't for Anita pulling me quickly back, I would have been run over by a lorry. I deliberately walked out hoping to be no longer here. It was a very near miss and everything on the lorry, because of its sudden braking, all shifted to the front. The driver was obviously not very happy. Anita apologised and explained we had just come away from the court and were unsuccessful in my attempts. He went on in his journey. Anita kept hold of my arm until we were back at the hotel. All this happened on Anita's birthday.

So, here I am now no longer bankrupt with my former solicitor no longer married to my former wife. I have no contact whatsoever with my three children. I am aware that throughout all the years, since 1991, up until my former solicitor's divorce from my former wife, they were both in full receipt of legal aid, funding all their legal costs. Mr Trafford's first wife and children were made homeless and were in receipt of charity handouts, but not from Mr Trafford's vicar father, Cyril Trafford's church contributions.

Throughout the whole of this time when public funds were being granted to my former solicitor and former wife, they were the directors of a most successful law cost business.

I discovered that Mr Trafford had been claiming income support of £144.25p each week with a Giro payment for £783.07p whilst he was on 'sick leave', whilst he was in fact, attending courts in relation to his legal work, with my former wife for solicitor's taxation of their costs in legal aid matters before the court. I obviously reported this to the various authorities but under data protection laws and strict confidentiality it was not a matter for those various authorities to take sufficiently seriously for them to investigate. Again, it was said by Mr & Mrs Trafford that this was my obsessiveness and vexatious vendetta against them, therefore it was not reliable as evidence of fraud. Also, being a solicitor with his skills, he would be able to convince those authorities of his entitlement. That is, only until they are exposed in fullness in this true autobiography. If it is thought that I was obsessed, what loving father wouldn't be, especially having been at the bedside of my daughter, seeing her suffering first-hand, which I put down to their greed, and I find no forgiveness after all my daughter had gone through. I thank God she pulled through, but a very sad she lives with the after-effects to this day. So, now I am left with having to live out the rest of my life with my state pension. I am told not to make any further complaints as I already had during early 1991. I had included his wife Christine and reported this rogue solicitor and his criminal conduct to the Solicitor's Complaint Authority. They investigated, and the solicitor rebutted the suggestion that he had done anything untoward. The solicitor's complaint's authority concluded that morals were not matters that they could investigate even though there had clearly been a most serious conflict of interest, in that Mr Trafford had continued to act as a solicitor in his partnership with solicitors in Manchester until 1993, when in 1991, throughout the years, he was in full receipt of legal aid, but again this was not a matter for the solicitor regulation authority to regulate as they were criminal matters. They wrote to confirm that their files on this matter were now closed.

CHAPTER 42: My meeting with George Carman QC and Imran Khan

Imran Khan the famous cricketer, now the prime minister of Pakistan, and his wife were at the High Court on July the 30th of July 1996. Whilst I was going through the nightmare of all my court appearances, when I stood waiting to appear before the judge, I met George Carman and got to talk with him. I told him I had come down from Manchester to attend court. I had been a regular visitor to the court and represented myself, and he took great interest in all I was telling him I was there for. He was having a cigarette outside the court with his black gown and small bobbed wig on. Then along came Imran Khan and his wife. They went into court, so with some spare time on my hands I decided to go and have a look from the public gallery overlooking the process.

I noticed the England cricketers on the front bench with George Carman QC doing his legal work. Then after leaving to attend my hearing that lasted a very short time, I went back to watch George Carman. There was an adjournment and George Carman QC was talking with Imran and his wife, then they went to the hall, with me following. George saw me and asked how I got on in court. I told him I wished I had him representing me and I handed him one of my court orders to see and asked George to sign it. He said he couldn't, but he did take his pen and signed it, then passed my high court order to Imran who also wanted to sign it. This was July the 30th 1996, 10 days after my birthday, and then they wished me good luck. With this I decided to stay in London at my foster parents' home, in Morden in Surrey, then went back the following day to watch George Carman QC win his case in spectacular fashion. Imran and his wife were delighted with their success. I watched George Carman take off his wig and shake hands with all the advocates in their gowns and wigs, then I left to make my way back home to Manchester. I was in disbelief that I had met and conversed with such an eminent expert barrister QC, and who much later on in years I discovered had represented Mr Jeremy Thorpe in 1979. This led to the BBC drama, the real history, called A Very English Scandal about the Jeremy Thorpe affair. He got Thorpe off all the charges against him. Never in my wildest dreams would I have thought all this would become so relevant and important to this autobiography of my life.

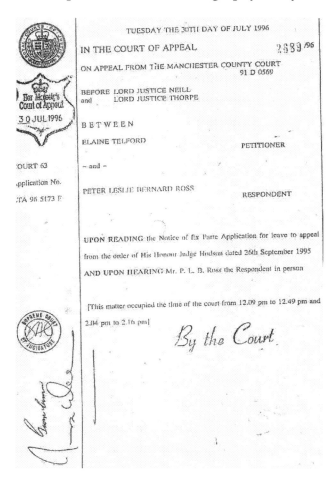

CHAPTER 43: My attempted murder & lifelong injuries

On the 29th of May 2006, it was a wonderful time to go outside and carry out some repairs as since Christmas 1990 nothing had been done in the upkeep of fencing. There was a gate that was impossible to open to allow children to gain access on to my ménage. So, I obtained the necessary materials in readiness for the bank holiday to carry out the necessary repairs such as to replace the gate and pull-out overgrown weeds and cut back branches from the trees. I took my JCB over with all my tools and materials to start my work.

Then on this lovely sunny bank holiday, my neighbour Thomas Anthony Sinclair, referred to in chapter 31, who was one of two directors of his Wasteline Skip Ltd company business, his wife Joan was the other, drove down to where I was busy working on my land. He stopped his vehicle, got out and came over to me and asked me what I was doing. I told him that I was replacing my gate, incidentally this was the gate I had paid him to fix in 1988/9. He then walked back to his skip wagon. I carried on thinking he was going, then he approached me a second time then I heard him say loudly, "Cop for this". I looked up and was then looking through the barrel of his shotgun. I had not noticed him stopping and getting out of his vehicle with a shotgun, all I remembered was looking through the gun sight and because he was so near to me, I was able to see the colour of his eyes, which were Blue. I didn't have time to feel fear or stand there trembling, as I can imagine anyone would do, or think that he was larking around and there was no cartridge in it. I just remember a massive bang and flash and what felt like a massive ball of fire in my head, and I was virtually blind whilst being thrown up off the ground. I was sent flying backwards and was completely deafened. I was thrown to the floor. I managed to get up limping, and part running for cover from the JCB. My head was on fire and blood was gushing from my head, neck and shoulders.

I accidentally ran into the JCB I had parked up near me, I was blinded by the impact, then I felt pain in my chest because of running into the JCB. I remarkably began to stagger away from him, my balance had gone, my head was ringing, and I was in a lot of pain. Unknown to me and thankfully Anita had seen all of this. She was in the kitchen and was able to look directly over to where I was. She was feeding her mother and was looking out as she was waiting for her mother to finish her late breakfast. She noticed Tony driving down the hill towards me which made her look out constantly, knowing that after my divorce our friendship with the Sinclairs had come to an end. She knew there would be harsh words shouted out at me. She couldn't believe what she was seeing. She saw our neighbour Tony approach me standing a couple of meters away pointing a shot gun at my head. She ran to the door then heard the gun shot in disbelief she ran back to the window and couldn't see me at all. Frantically she said, "I kept looking for you in disbelief". I then managed to stagger to my feet and hobble staggering with blood pouring from my head in the direction of my barn. When I nearly managed to reach the barn, I noticed my son Darren, who was off school after breaking his tibia and his leg was in a plaster cast. Darren and his friend Toby came and helped me; I was approximately 30 yards away from the old barn.

In disbelief I was told they heard the bang and came running to my assistance. I am told that this neighbour from hell was re-cocking the gun but didn't seem to be able to find another cartridge in his pocket whilst I was staggering back to the barn he then simply got back into his vehicle and drove to his home. I was helped into the barn, and I fell on the kitchen floor. In time with my heartbeat blood squirted out of the back of my head. The shot had made a large open wound. I was pushing myself round and round in a circle, because my head was spinning, and I was sliding in my blood which was going everywhere. My son, who had his mobile phone immediately alerted the police and the emergency services; the ambulance got to the front of the barn before the police. The police could not allow the ambulance or their staff to enter what was now a dangerous zone as the gunman was still at large. My son was so panicked that he ran and pulled one of the paramedics into the barn. He was scared I was going to die. Anita had been trying to help me by putting dishcloths or whatever she could find over the wounds until the paramedics took over. At this point the police helicopter was very loud and circling around above, and full-scale, armed police with guns and dogs and shields had circled around my home and the home of the skip business. They were shouting down through a loudspeaker when they brought down the gunman, seen within only a very small sample, taken from the helicopter camera.

After the gunman, Mr. Sinclair had been taken down by the armed police, it was only then considered safe enough to place me in the ambulance and transfer me to hospital, with blue flashing lights and sirens going all the way. The helicopter was hovering and a full squad of police with shields and guns and dogs were surrounding the whole area. Obviously, I didn't see any of this until I watched it played out at court in the trial of my attempted murder. The honourable judge ordered that I would be provided with the full police helicopter recording to do with it as I saw fit, his words.

I learnt through the court papers that the police and their dogs eventually found the shot gun and spent cartridge which were hidden in separate places which can be seen in the next chapter. The gunman, Tony, had changed all his clothing in the hope that no gun residue would be found on them, then he was arrested and ordered not to return to his home. The police sniffer dog had found all his clothing which had gun residue on it. He was bailed to live at a relative's home. I also discovered that the gunman, Tony, had no license for his gun or a license for his ammunition. He managed to return back home after a few weeks because he claimed he was ill and sorry. He said he would travel up to his home from the back of his farm so he wouldn't pass our property or cause us more tension and upset. It became clear to me he was allowed back home because of the influence from his daughter and ex-son-in-law who were serving as police officers and helped in all the ways they could think. His daughter was still a senior and long-term serving police officer. She had obviously wanted to avoid her father going to prison for his attempted murder and they actually managed to get it reduced under section 18 to Actual bodily harm. It was also said that they couldn't prove his intent to murder me. I then asked why he drove down to me then got back in his vehicle and came back to me with a gun and placed cartridge in it, aimed and fired at my head, re-cocked it and tried to place another shot in it.

Since this attempted murder I have been extremely hard of hearing, the only blessing is that this could have made me completely blind and deaf.

Small sample of the shot gun wound 29/05/2006

Bruising from running into the JCB due to being deafened and blinded by the gunshot

Chapter 44

Now living next to the 2nd neighbour from hell

When I returned home from hospital, I looked out at the gate I had been trying to replace. I could see blue and white police tape, saying 'Do not cross,' all over the area. I stood for a while, pondering and seeing that my son, stepdaughters and Anita were frightened and worried of what next was to come to our doorstep. I had not long ago built a large, lovely log cabin and one night someone had set fire to it whilst we were in our beds. Now there was an attempt on my life and Anita had seen the whole event unfold.

Before all this everything was difficult but manageable. Our neighbouring farm owners for years were always in our pay for their services in much of my work, and I allowed them the use of my facilities to build a good, neighbourly, relationship. After eight years of neighbourly friendship, then my wife leaving me, things changed dramatically and so did our life with such dreadful impact. These nice neighbours had, without a license, started up a skip and waste transfer business from their farm. Each day, seven days a week their skip vehicles 'Wasteline Skip Ltd', would pass our home over a public footpath called 'Overtown Lane'. This was also a bridleway and the safety and upkeep of it was the responsibility of the Rochdale local authority. I had purchased, as referred to in chapter 31, then completely demolished and redeveloped this farmhouse and barn in the green belt after I had battled with the council over the green belt issue for the conversion of this derelict 16th century old barn for residential use, at vast legal costs. Now here are these neighbours tipping, burning and turning the green belt into a scrap yard mess, right on my doorstep and Rochdale council did nothing.

In the winter months and dark nights, we would constantly hear Thomas Anthony Sinclair and his wife in their

JCB and Hymac, digging up large holes in the surrounding lands of their farm, then tipping their rubbish in and covering it over. This would always be after constant fires, burning off as much as would burn, with the fall out of all the pollution coming down all over our home, over our cars and children's toys that were left out; for example, in the summer the children's plastic swimming pool would be covered in particles from their fires. This went on for years. I noticed the skip vehicles clearly displayed the name of the company and its logo with a phone number and the address of Wasteline Skips Ltd. So, it was taken to be by me and obviously others in 'Redlumb', where the local councillor, Anne Metcalf lived, that compliance of this business with the local authority must, we all thought, have been accepted. In fact, because these activities had gone on for over four years without any complaints, that would make it a permitted development. However, though no complaint had been made to the council, an unpalatable animosity had set in. Then one weekend our very large, luxurious, log cabin was set on fire, with the fire brigade staying all night putting the fire out and damping it down. They wouldn't leave until it was completely safe so to do so. Considering all the legal battles I had gone through earlier, with the council enabling my proper development and conversion of my farm and barn, I still felt it not possible or safe to make a complaint for fear of further reprisals. So, this Wasteline skip business continued uninterrupted until I got shot.

These nuisance neighbours banged and clanged, up and down, passing my home with skips empty then full, numerous times each day with cash in hand. Enough was enough, now I was going to put a stop to it. After all, here's me trying to make the area beautiful, with Anita working so hard landscaping the gardens, with them on top of the hill for all to see, making the place look like a scrap yard. And they came down and tried to kill me. I then decided to contact the local authority before the matter went into the newspapers, to simply ask if my neighbours had their planning permission for this Wasteline skips business and tipping all around the surrounding areas of my home. I was simply told that they would get back to me; they didn't.

It wasn't long after he was allowed back home that Anita had to ring the police because Tony, the gunman, was now in breach of his bail conditions. Anita was out doing the gardens and he was standing exactly where he shot me, intimidating her. This happened a few times, even with witnesses. Each time the police went up and came back down, unsurprisingly they made the decision to do nothing, after all they have family in the police force. Some days he sat in the field and had what looked like a gun, and he would aim it at us, trying to scare us and make us think he was going to shoot us. We still carried on with our day-to-day living, but it was made unpleasant with these carry-ons, and he was getting away with it. It gave us more determination really; we stopped calling the police as there simply seemed no point at all.

Then one day my son got in the JCB which I had taught him to drive and on trying to stop the brakes, which failed and we found that the pipes had been deliberately cut. Thankfully my son was not injured and with his quick thinking he managed to bring the JCB to a stop by using the front bucket and back legs. We were lucky he didn't crash into the well or the barn. I then contacted the Environmental agency HQ in Warrington to ask them to visit my home to see what was so obvious. I was informed, as I expected, that they had no license to run their skip business, or fly-tip, or burn at night in the green belt. The whole exercise was unlawful, yet Rochdale council had let this activity continue for years unchecked and unregulated with criminal negligence for years continuing after he had shot me. The councillor, another neighbour close to us, simply turned a blind eye to this because she had a friendly relationship with these neighbours from hell and she lived close by. She also had a horse and used to go up to their farm, taking her horse trekking with others. Even after all these activities, local authority still did not put a stop notice against these unlawful activities, unlike that which they did on my barn conversion, this was another story.

Then it took approximately three years before the case went to trial, and Tony was continuously on bail. Then Tony, the man behind the trigger on the shotgun, walked away from the court, not having to serve a single day in jail for attempting to kill me with an unlicensed gun and unlicensed ammunition plus all his other crimes. Instead, he went back home to continue his unlawful skip waste business. The police and the crown prosecution presented the section 18 case to the Crown Court in Bolton and put a lot of pressure and strain on us. We did start to wonder if he was going to simply walk away after shooting me. Because of all my injuries I was put out of work, our lives changed. I was a good electrician, builder and now I can't even climb a small step ladder, let alone change a light bulb in the ceiling. It took years for him to be placed before the court and a jury to find him guilty, to which he simply pleaded insanity at that time. So, with no punishment or going to any mental hospital/home, he walked away and continued to live next door to us and harass me and my family. Anita broke down in court. One of the barristers commented how he was surprised she had taken it so badly and asked her why. She replied saying that she had worked with me, making the barn our dream home and, now I could no longer work beside her, she felt as though she had lost her left arm, her best work mate, and now her dreams were shattered plus she saw me nearly taken away from her yet again.

It was unfortunate, for Anita, having still to visit the hospital with me for all my treatments but also now I had the added stress of having to instruct solicitors to act on my behalf in these civil matters, that the council had a duty to put a stop too. Only after being found guilty of his crime did the authorities later bring an end to his unlicensed skip waste business, which has scarred the surrounding lands around our beautiful home, all in the green belt. His wife now drives the skip wagons and has been blatantly tipping Japanese Knotweed in the field adjacent to my land, which became another nightmare for us. The wildlife ensured we had a growth of the dreadful weed, giving us more expenses. All this is in the so-called protected, green belt areas of Rochdale and under the nose of our local counsellor who did nothing to help us or herself, and not long after these events, she died. At the time of my writing, the buried waste is continuing to cause pollution within the water courses, running into the very large reservoir below, referred in the following.

Three weeks after I had been shot, as if that hadn't been enough, Anita was going out to the shops and she noticed the gunman Tony's wife now in her tractor with a big spike on the front, driving down to the gate where I was shot. She was placing big, half-ton, black bails in front of our gate. The gate I had just replaced so the neighbouring farm's children could go through to enter our arena. Anita and our son and his friend went over to her, and Anita asked why and what she was doing blocking our access onto the bridleway. She would not communicate and carried on driving up the hill to come back down with another bail. Anita decided to stand in the way to put a stop to all this, but she carried on driving towards Anita with the big spike with a bail on it. Darren was videoing this on his phone. Then at the very last-minute Anita jumped out of the way, seeing there was no stopping her and hearing Darren shouting, telling his mum to get out of the way because she would crush her. Then we all see Sarah, their police officer daughter, standing there watching and videoing and encouraging her mother to carry out this act. We got her on video. In total there were 13 bales of hay that she had placed along our boundary and in front of our gate to stop us accessing the lane from our arena and stopping the children coming in with their horses. We were confused as to why she was doing this at this time. We then complained to the police, and they did nothing. We complained to the council, stating it was on the bridleway and they did nothing. No-one would do anything, especially where the gunman was near because of health & safety regulations making it not possible to visit without police presence.

Darren and Anita went out to push one of the bails away from the gate so we could get through, whilst taking the dog for a walk. Police officers came hours after and told us not to touch or damage their property. We were in disbelief. Another day police officers came to tell us to walk down the pathway with our dog always on a lead. No-one had their dogs on leads, the neighbours from hell especially; it was ridiculous. We had abuse hurled at us by her and her family. She managed to get police on our doorstep for anything in minutes. It became barmy. It made us all feel even more on edge. We felt not only did we have all sorts of crazy things happening to us but now we had the police against us for no reason at all.

One Sunday afternoon the family were in the kitchen, and I was in the sauna relaxing. I heard Anita shouting there was a man at the window looking in. Anita told the kids to get down behind the cabinets. The man had a balaclava on with just two holes where the eyes were. Anita was very shocked and fearful and came running to me. We quickly went outside, and we tried to catch him through the fields with me just having a bath towel around my waist, but he was quicker than us and he outran us. In the early hours of the morning our phone would be ringing; we counted 13 times in one night. The police told us to contact BT, which we did. We had to press a number when we knew it was the nuisance caller for the police to hopefully detect where the call was coming from, but they always rang from a phone box. Our doorbell rang at silly times, things were being moved, we had death threats and life after death magazines left on the doorstep, it went on and on. The children were all terrified at night.

These neighbours then interfered with the lane that ran by the side of our arena. They got their Hymac digger and started to raise the level of the lane making the rainwater flood our arena. Sometimes half of it looked like a swimming pool, it was heart-breaking. Anita's hard work in the garden was ruined and became a bog, trees were falling over in the wintertime, all flowering shrubs died through too much water collecting. Then the lighting and fencing were beginning to come loose, the surface on the arena was being washed away during heavy rain fall. It was a very costly surface.

We went to the council, after all it was an offence to interfere with a highway, public footpath and bridleways. Unsurprisingly we had no joy from the council. The inspector from walkways and paths came out but it turned out she was friendly with the neighbours and our cries fell on deaf ears. We eventually had to go to solicitors, bringing about more costs. We even took on the council through the courts. It took time and determination, but we got there, and the council had to pay us money for our contactors to bring the public footpath back to the legal condition required for a public footpath. This work was extensive and very expensive and which the council had to pay for in full, with all my legal costs.

Then we received a letter, six days to the year after being shot at point blank range, from the Environmental Agency and saw in disbelief, its content! They wouldn't come near the place without police protection. The Environmental Agency HQ in Warrington told us to video three months of these wagons coming and going, only then they would be able to do something. So, we took it in turns to set to work to try and capture every single time these wagons came and went. It was a stressful exercise, but we were adamant we wouldn't be defeated by these neighbours from hell. It did help because of the noise they made 6 sometimes 7 days a week. It wasn't hard to get to the window in time to do this videoing. We even managed to get them at night, burning and digging and burying.

Eventually the business came to a stop. It didn't make us feel any better, but the countryside was much quieter, and we were showing that we wouldn't be intimidated or back down from whatever was thrown at us.

Then we became successful with civil actions that had taken place against the council for damage to the public footpath in these unlawful skip activities. I managed to have the business shut down, and all the skip and scrap vehicles were taken away for metal recycling. Work was forced on them to completely tidy up and deal with the Japanese Knotweed in the green belt. It took days for them to clear the place, bringing rats and mice running in and out all over the place. In addition, the rubbish buried in the surrounding ground, after being buried for so many years, is now rotting and leaching out into the water course called Royds Brook. This runs through and downhill into a brand new, very expensive Russell Homes housing development called, 'Green Booth Village' (formerly Rainshaw Cotton Mill). The contaminated polluted water runs into a very large 'Green Booth' reservoir, providing drinking water by the water authorities. The saddest reality in all this is that my son and his mother and sisters have had to live with these dreadful memories! Then there was a substantial loss in the value of our home for the reasons mentioned, such as having a maniac, nightmare neighbour from hell, living next door bringing various disputes.

WELLBEING PLAN — Pennine Care NHS

Full Name:	Peter L B Rowe		Date of Birth:		NHS Number:	402 734 1579
Address:	Hirst Clough Barn, Chew Town Lane, Red Lamb, Rochdale				Post Code:	OL12 7TG
Care Coordinator/Key Worker: Heather Wilson / Sean Campbell				Contact Number: 01706 475400		

| On CPA: | | Not on CPA | ✓ | Section 117: | Yes | | No | ✓ | SCT: | Yes | | No | ✓ |

EIT service only: Has the Service User been offered access to Psychological Therapies — Yes / No

Now I have to live daily with the trauma and injuries for the rest of my life. Then thankfully, I was told the gunman Tony was dead in March 2017, see and read chapter 53, making it now possible for me to start making arrangements to sell up and leave. This was meant to be my final home, shared with my family and I wanted to leave this to them and their families. Now being disabled and not having the ability or funding, our beautiful home had to be left and we were forced to downsize. One of the best memories I have is the continuing friendship with my good neighbours Doctor Anne and her husband John, who had been living at the farmhouse, a very short distance from the barn and also now those who have recently moved into the barn. This takes me back to the public enquiry and our last battle to help the green belt around the beautiful countryside, before leaving our beautiful barn after many other long battles, and very stressful and emotional times. Now I offer my thanks to the many who attended and gave evidence at the public enquiry on the 11th of October 2016. After 8 days the owners of the surrounding lands, Peel, were at last refused permission on appeal to extend their existing wind turbines on Scout Moor. This refusal brought about a massive multi-million-pound loss, in legal costs and future exportation of electricity to the national grid network for the future 25 years and longer. Those revenues were shared with the various local authorities, and they have lost those incomes that would have been derived from the multi megawatt generation of electricity and, had they been successful, provide electrical energy much greater than the demand, for those living and working within the North of England. It was for these reasons of my near loss of life, and Rochdale Council's negligence in their refusal to protect their green belt land under their jurisdiction, that I attended, giving extensive, detailed and irrefutable evidence bringing about their failed appeal at that public enquiry resulting in the rightful justice and conclusion by the government inspector.

This is how R.M.B.C protects it's 'green belt' from rogue traders such as 'Wasteline Skip Co Ltd', despite various complaints and evidence of wrongdoing being provided. Illegal landfill, tyre burning, etc.

These were a few snapshots from the GMP's helicopter video evidence. Footage which was provided to me via court from HH Judge Everett who stated the footage may be used as I deemed fit.

After Tony the gunman's arrest, as seen in the pictures, the police with their dogs sniffed out the gun from the residue scent off the gunman. They found the gun and the cartridges, supporting what Anita said that he was trying to find and load another cartridge into his gun. After three long years of waiting for justice, this was the evidence that found him guilty of his crimes against me.

Here proves another of the injustices of him not spending a single day in prison. He was well and able to think of also hiding the gun and ammunition and changing all his clothes and boots.

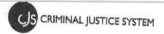 CRIMINAL JUSTICE SYSTEM

The Prosecution Team

Mr Peter Ross
Hinde Clough Barn
Edenfield Road
Rochdale
OL12 7TU

Witness Care Unit
4th Floor
Newgate House
Newgate
Rochdale
OL16 1XD

01706 515 689
mahmoona.bashir@gmp.police.uk
08:30 -19:00 Monday to Thursday
08:30 - 16:30 Friday

1st May 2008

Dear Mr Ross

Case Against Thomas Anthony Snowdon
Unique Reference Number 06P1000230306

Notice to attend Bolton Crown Court

I am writing to confirm that **you are required** to attend court to give your evidence.

At the hearing on 6th March, 2008 at Bolton Crown Court, Thomas Anthony Snowdon pleaded "not guilty" to the following offences:

1 WOUNDING/CAUSING GRIEVOUS BODILY HARM WITH INTENT
2 POSSESSING/PURCHASING OR ACQUIRING A SHOTGUN WITHOUT A CERTIFICATE
3 POSSESSING/PURCHASING OR ACQUIRING AMMUNITION WITHOUT A FIREARM CERTIFICATE//AUTHORITY
4 POSSESSING A FIREARM//AMMUNITION WITH INTENT TO ENDANGER LIFE
5 Wounding with intent to do grievous bodily harm
6 Possessing shotgun without certificate
7 Possessing ammunition without certificate

What happens next

The trial is set to begin on 29th September, 2008 at the Bolton Crown Court.

There are a large number of witnesses for the prosecution and we are awaiting details of the order in which they must give their evidence. However, it is likely to be early on in the trial

The attempted murder case in 2006, conviction in 2008 / important at the trial. An

After this verdict and being in hospital with my good friends coming to see me, through the following nine years I am receiving psychological therapies with various medication which will be required for the rest of my life. These include

HOME INTERVENTION SUPPORT to consider whether admission to hospital would be required to monitor response to medication, in terms of therapeutic effects and side effects and also to receive regular reviews by consultant psychiatrist as I am constantly wanting to end my life. I have to be honest as this is a true story and this continues to this time of writing, but less now that I have good reason to write these true stories which have been most difficult as I am disabled. But no-one notices this from my outward appearance. Inside I am in constant pain and hate having to keep on top of the pain with medication, then further medication to get me to sleep at night. There are many times during the day when I'd fall asleep for three or four hours when I awake. I always try to hide the fact that I am going through so much depression, and I can understand how many people have their happy times socialising, with their props of alcohol and cigarettes or food, none of which interest me at all and never have, except for food.

My efforts below are discussed on the next page in bringing the R.M.B.C. multi-million-pound loss from the wind farm at 'Scout Moor' Future electricity generation.

in', Knowl Hill, which

nes on land between
by the Friends of Kr
the proposals were g
inquiry. The campaig
ghts to stop the

ury on Bagslate
here Rochdale Go
Tavern as a reminde

Man charged over alleged gun incident

A 67-YEAR-OLD man from Rawtenstall has been charged with assault and firearms offences after an alleged shooting incident in Norden.

Police were called to Over Town Lane on Monday afternoon following reports that a 59-year-old man had been shot in the head. The victim, who has not been named, was treated at Rochdale Infirmary and later released.

The accused, Thomas Snowdon of Bury Road, Rawtenstall, appeared at Rochdale Magistrates Court on Wednesday.

Arrest follows shooting

A MAN has been arrested on suspicion of attempted murder after a 59-year-old man was shot in the head in Norden.

Police were called to the scene, close to Over Town Lane, at 2.15pm on Monday.

The victim, who has not been named, was taken to Rochdale Infirmary where he was treated for non life-threatening injuries to his head and later discharged. His injuries are thought to have been caused by pellets. The suspect, who is 67, remains in police custody and officers leading the investigation say inquiries are continuing.

ORST KIDE SKIS

Norden's Parish Church of St Paul, built in the mid-19th Century, overlooks the heart of the village and stands next to Norden Chimney, one of the few memorials to the textile industry's part in the village's history.

Nutter's Restaurant complex, run by chef Andrew Nutter and his family, is housed in the former Manor House of the Wolstenholme family at the western end of the village.

ilness. Her request to be buried in the bird reserve was granted.

The previously mentioned monkey-puzzle trees are to be found near Three Owls - at the Millcroft Tea Gardens on Roods Lane. The tea gardens, which have a Victorian atmosphere, serve refreshments on Sundays. Many customers at Millcroft are walkers or cyclists, but visits there were considerably reduced last summer because the wooden footbridge at nearby Cheesden Brook was destroyed by high waters earlier in

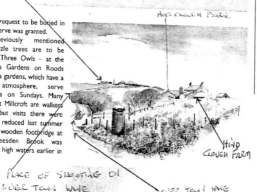

HIND CLOUGH BARN.

HIND CLOUGH FARM

PLACE OF SHOOTING ON
OVER TOWN LANE

OVER TOWN LANE

The Planning Inspectorate

Report to the Secretary of State for Communities and Local Government

by John Woolcock BNatRes(Hons) MURP DipLaw MRTPI

an Inspector appointed by the Secretary of State for Communities and Local Government

Date: 3 April 2017

3. A local resident, Mr Ross, requested at the Inquiry that I hear his evidence under oath, and that I issue a witness summons to require the author of a witness statement, which was submitted to the Inquiry by the applicant, to attend the Inquiry. My rulings about these matters, concerning a private dispute between adjoining land owners, are set out in Annex B to this report. This issue was foreshadowed at the PIM, where I advised that private legal matters would be unlikely to be relevant to the Secretary of State's consideration of the planning merits of the proposal in the public interest.[25] At the end of the Inquiry Mr Ross requested that I make a recommendation about costs against the applicant in

See chapter 43, 44, 45.

PAGE 8

Town and Country Planning Act 1990

Section 77

Applications by

Scout Moor Wind Farm Expansion Limited

Rossendale Borough Council and Rochdale Metropolitan Borough Council

187. Peter Ross is a local resident who is concerned about the maintenance of Overtown Lane, which in the past has been the subject of flooding, and of the management of other land that has been in the ownership of the operators of SMWF1.[138] Inadequate maintenance of land and drainage ditches on the A680 has in the past resulted in flooding and road traffic accidents. Overtown Lane provides PRoW access to Scout Moor.[139] Mr Ross is in dispute with the adjoining owner about the maintenance of the lane and nearby land.

188. Mr Ross also noted that construction of SMWF1 at 0700 was in breach of a condition stating that no construction works should occur before 0800 hours. If the proposed development was permitted stringent conditions should be imposed. There was an error made in consenting SMWF1 without a bond to cover decommissioning costs, and the turbines have now been sold on with no bond. If the scheme is permitted a minimum of £500,000 per turbine should be deposited before any construction work is started. This bond would be divided between RBC and RMBC to be used at the point of decommissioning over the various years, to restore the site and its hydrology.[140]

Scout Moor Wind Farm, Rochdale, Lancashire

File Refs: APP/B2355/V/15/3139740 and APP/P4225/V/15/3139737

265. At the Inquiry stage 22 written representations were submitted to the Planning Inspectorate.[188] These are summarised as follows.

PAGE 63

(1) Peter Ross raised similar concerns to those that he spoke about at the Inquiry and are reported above. His written submission includes a stateme from Darren Ross concerning the lack of a detailed decommissioning and restoration plan, given the very significant costs likely to be incurred in

444. The long-running dispute between Mr Ross and the adjoining owner is a private matter for the respective landowners. This is not a consideration that should influence the Secretary of State's determination of the applications. However, the relevant planning considerations raised by Mr Ross are addressed elsewhere in my conclusions. [13,88,187]

PAGE 106

Report APP/B2355/V/15/3139740 and APP/P4225/V/15/3139737

PAGE 121

ANNEX B – RULINGS BY INSPECTOR

Ruling day 1 of the Inquiry

In response to Mr Ross's request that I hear his evidence on oath I ruled that it would not be necessary to do so, particularly as if his evidence was given on oath it would be necessary to hear all other witnesses on oath, and given the relevant planning matters at issue in these applications this would not be appropriate for these proceedings. I added that the standard of proof at this Inquiry was not the same as that which would apply to a court of law.

Ruling day 3 of the Inquiry

In response to written submissions to the Inquiry by Mr Ross the applicant submitted a witness statement by Mr Harvey. Mr Ross requested that Mr Harvey be required to attend the Inquiry to answer questions about his statement. I heard submissions about this request at the Inquiry and, having regard to the written submissions along with the oral arguments for and against calling Mr Harvey, ruled as follows.

It is evident that there is a dispute about drainage between adjoining landowners and that the documents submitted make reference to a nuisance action. It seems to me that the matters addressed in the witness statement concern a private dispute between the respective landowners, and that I have not seen or heard anything to indicate that this is also likely to be a matter of public interest with which the planning system should be concerned. Therefore I do not consider that the matters at issue in the witness statement are likely to assist the Secretary of State in determining these applications on their planning merit. That does not mean that the matters raised in Mr Ross's submissions regarding management and restoration of the application site are not material to the Inquiry, particularly as site restoration is a matter referred to in Government guidance. Evidence about this would be relevant and this would be discussed in the without-prejudice Inquiry session about suggested planning conditions.

Document 9

PAGE 194

Written statement and bundle of documents submitted by Mr Ross objecting to the applications.
Including Final statement on decommissioning and restoration of the proposed Scout Moor Wind Farm Extension, dated 26 October 2016.

CHAPTER 45: My very good Doctor – Dr Schroeder

In 1994 Dr Schroeder met his demise on Edenfield Road. He had been travelling down Edenfield Road and lost control, sliding into and through the same stone wall where other incidents had occurred. One day I decided to take a walk along Edenfield Road to count how many drains I had noticed, that like others, were in desperate need of cleansing. Sadly R.M.B.C. had failed to cleanse the drains along this road or the ditches either side of Edenfield Road, such that the road was like a flowing river. In winter it was like an ice rink causing drivers to lose control of their cars, even when there was just slight rain because there was nowhere for the water to drain into. This was the cause of my doctor's demise and brought about some basic roadwork at the entrance of the now famous Nutters restaurant, but not uphill on the ditches on Edenfield Road that had been so neglected.

The drainage grids in the road outpoured into the ditches and were so overgrown with grass and rubble that water simply ran down the tarmac road, causing further accidents on the road, which was a 60-mph road at the time of the inquest. Mr Gorodkin the Coroner relied upon evidence of those involved in the crash saying that the doctor was believed to be travelling at 80 mph and that, when his car started to slide, the wheels locked and his Mazda went off the road, lifting into the air. However, the coroner was not provided with the true picture of the event that took place. I was one of the doctor's patients and I got to know him well. He was timid, most careful and considerate of others. He was not a maniac, speeding driver like many I have seen coming down Edenfield Road. He was a very good GP who sadly lost his life due to the negligence of others, proof being in the work carried out on the road since his death. These were my reasons in my referring to the massive evidence partly seen at the end of chapter 44 where, along with my son and my very close friend Anne we had successfully provided to R.M.B.C. and is held at their HQ. More importantly it was provided at the government inspector Mr John Woolcock's enquiry of over one week starting on the 11th of October 2016, where I gave evidence throughout the enquiry with exhibits and sworn statements and photographs on the state of the road and drainage. The photos showed grass growing out of the grids. They were so that full horses wanted to stop and graze. Throughout the work that were carried out by Bethell & Co Ltd in 2013, drainage did not form part of the new stone wall. There wasn't one drain put in place along the full stretch of the new wall which looked delightful, even with NORDEN placed in stone in the middle of it. Instead, it caused further flooding from Peel's land. At the end of the enquiry Peel thankfully lost their appeal, amounting to a financial loss of tens of millions up to the public enquiry and over the following years.

I repeatedly reported the dreadful, dangerous state of this road and its drainage. I had spent a lot of my time doing it, even though I had many problems myself. I didn't want there to be any more accidents on this part of Edenfield Road. I made a call and one from the Highways department came out to meet me at long last. This then brought about further drainage work and cleansing of the ditches. This is all recorded at R.M.B.C. with my constant complaints into their failures in keeping this fast road safe for horses and their riders, pedestrians and motor vehicles. When the freeholders of the land, Peel, required planning consent for wind turbines that received approval from both authorities Rochdale and Rossendale (In 'Peel's' hundreds of millions of pounds investment) I made my objections, placing all my evidence and attending an eight-day public enquiry. I visited the ditches and assisted the government inspector on one of the days of his public enquiries. The applicants in their appeal LOST, amounting to a massive and worthwhile success for those attending the full appeal, including the fantastic submissions from my Hindclough Farm close neighbours. Then I noticed whilst driving along Edenfield Rd in May 2019 that Rochdale

Council has employed the service of F.W. Sherratt Ltd Engineering Contractors to carry out the essential work on drainage, with a new retaining wall to deal with the flooding that I had brought to the attention of the inspector at the public enquiry over the years. I had repeatedly notified Rochdale council of these problems and had they taken heed of my concerns, Dr Shroeder in my opinion would not have suffered the most serious injuries and death that was caused by his car aquaplaning out of control across Edenfield Rd and through the stone wall, which sadly killed him.

There was another time before the drainage problems were solved, when I was going to collect my son after his night out. He'd phoned to tell me he was at Rochdale railway station to go and get him. It was early in the morning, and I was in the sauna relaxing and listening to music. I put a towel around me to simply drive to Rochdale and back to get back in the sauna, possibly with Darren. Anita did comment about my leaving with only a towel and shoes on, but I jumped into my van with just a towel round me on a very cold morning. I drove a short distance from my home to the main road and noticed a car had driven into the dry-stone wall and the driver was still in the car, slumped over the steering wheel. The air bag had clearly gone off and the engine was still running. I slammed the brakes on my van and ran over to check if the driver was dead.

I was first on the scene to see that a car, yet again, had driven into the stone wall on Edenfield Road. I thought the driver was dead as I went to his car. There were clothes everywhere from a suitcase. I looked to see if there was anyone else in the car with him. The first thing I thought of after the immediate shock was to avoid a fire. I forced open the bonnet ripping off the cable connected to the battery and pushed the shut off to stop the fuel. There was glass all over. By this time a passer-by had come over to me and with their mobile phone called the emergency services, then tended to the man in the car.

There were two ladies in the car, one of them told me she was a nurse and got on with doing the best she could for him.

By this time others arrived, and I left, as throughout all this I was holding on to my towel. As I was driving away, I passed the ambulance and fire engine and got to my son who was anxiously waiting and wondering why I had taken so long. He complained because I never had a mobile phone, I can't do with them. I told him to phone his mother to tell her we were ok, but we would be delayed. I explained to him all I did and the two girls that came. On approaching home, sure enough, the road was closed whilst the services got him out of the car and removed it and cleaned up, so we were late getting back home. It was later discovered when my son came home from school one day that the driver had made a full recovery. His car was a right-off, his son was the same age as my son and attended the same school, 'Oulder Hill School'.

There had been many accidents at that same point over the years I was there. My fond memory was managing throughout this ordeal to keep my dignity with only a towel, but I did have my shoes and socks on.

CHAPTER 46: Helping hand

Throughout my life I have always gone to help anyone, whether it be in passing and seeing anyone in need or when they have called me asking me for help. If I was able to help them in their difficulties, I would.

One of my favourite stories is about my sister, Sally. She is now deceased, God bless her. One morning my phone rang, and it was Sally asking me if I would call and have a look at her cooker as it was giving her electric shocks. On this occasion I went specially for her. She lived in Litchfield, Staffordshire, a fair distance from me but I thought nothing of it. Little did she know, on my way I called and bought her a brand-new cooker at my usual discounted price from a wholesaler on my company account. When I got there, she was very worried and hoped I could solve her problem before her husband arrived home. Whilst I was looking at her cooker, I pretended it gave me such a shock that I hit it repeatedly with my hammer. She stood there in complete horror and shock. She became a little frantic and I walked off to my van. She stood watching me asking how she would cook David's dinner. Then I pulled out the new one and her face lit up with a huge smile. I left her so happy, and I put the old one outside the garage so when her husband came home, he would see the cooker and wouldn't be happy at all, until she took him into the kitchen and explained what had happened and then he was very happy as well. She of course contacted Eileen to tell her what I had done. A story that lives on in her two children to this day as they were there and thought it was hilarious.

Around the year 2018, an old man was stuck on a fairly busy road with a totally flat tyre on the front driver's side. I could see he was struggling to jack up his car. On passing him I asked Anita to turn the car around and go back. She said no because of my disabilities as my head and neck were constantly giving me pain. I told her to go back, and she turned the car round and then parked our car behind his, putting on our hazard lights. I got out and went to the old man and told him I would help him. The relief on his face was so worth it, his wheel was so flat it wasn't possible to get his car jack to lift his car. I got my jack out of my car, which managed to fit under the small gap between the road and the underside of his car and lifted it safely as my jack was for a much heavier car. This enabled me to undo the nuts and put his spare on. All the time the traffic was passing close to me, and the car was on a fairly steep hill. I wasn't bothered, I just got on with it telling myself if I come unstuck what the hell. I have escaped so many life-risking events why bother about another. In this case it was just nice to see the old man getting back in his car and driving off happy. I went back to Anita after putting my jack back and she told me I was mad to do the things I do when I know I shouldn't. Perhaps she is right, but I would rather be the person who stops than the person who just passes. Anita then took me on my journey to my mission I was on before, whilst passing the old guy, and that was to go to the graveyard to tidy and water plants, flowers and speak to Stefan and Charlotte and most of all Nancy and others. I was so proud of my son on an occasion when we were in Manchester on an escalator, he stopped me, and many others being seriously injured. Whilst slowly traveling down from the top of the escalator, we saw a pile of bodies. People were stumbling over and on top of each other. It was becoming very dangerous. My son quick on his feet, jumped over the moving handrail; that was a task in itself. He ran down the steps and pushed the panic button, then proceeded to help everyone to get back on their feet. Thank God there were no serious injuries like my daughter sadly suffered. I went to the owners of the C.C.T.V. at Manchester Piccadilly railway station, giving them the date and the time of the incident. They provided me with a copy of all that had happened and sent me an invoice for ninety pounds for the copy. This was later refunded to me but only after I was able to show what my son had done which ensured no one got hurt.

My son Darren age 12

Me descending towards the truck below

My son Darren as he vaults the escalator handrail to activate the emergency stop button.

Thankfully

Me adding to the increasingly large dog pile at the bottom of the escalator. Each addition rendering it more and more difficult for the elderly lady to breath below.

Darren was successful in stopping the conveyor of human bodies being piled on the ground below. I recall how amazed I was at the masses, engaging the freeze response and just toppling over at the bottom. I also recalled my pride for my 12-year-old son, the only one who had the vision to stop the mass of bodies in its steps. Fortunately, the only injuries he incurred were a grazed shin, a torn 'Nike Shock' trainer and a broken case.

Northern**Spirit**

Peter Ross
Hind Clough Barn
Overtown Lane
Red Lumb Village
Norden
ROCHDALE
OL12 7TX

Media Office
Northern Spirit
M7
Main Headquarters
Station Rise
YORK
YO1 6HT

Tel: 01904 522196
Fax: 01904 522583

31st January 01

Dear Peter

Please find enclosed a ticket for you and the family to travel to York and back this weekend. You need to sign the reverse.

Also enclosed is a 'First Stop York' booklet giving you some great discounts on all the major attractions in York.

We have booked you two rooms at the Queen's Hotel in Skeldergate, which is right next to the river. Northern Spirit will cover the cost of accommodation

I trust that you will be on the 09.03 train from Rochdale which is due into York at 11.00. I plan to meet the train and look forward to meeting you on Saturday.

Yours sincerely

Simon Godfrey

CHAPTER 47: The very lucky escape on the train and the silver lining to this rainbow

It is the year 2000, I was on regular journeys to London by train, having to attend the courts, The Old Bailey and also the High Court leading up to my bankruptcy. On occasions I would stay over with my foster parents Reg and Betty in Morden, Surrey. Sometimes I would stay in local hotels that were near to the courts to ensure I was at court on time. On one occasion I slept on a seat in a church, right next to the Ritz hotel. When my son Darren reached 8 years of age, I took him on his first train journey to London then on the Underground (thank God there were no mobiles phones then) for the first time. Father and son stayed at the Swiss Cottage Holiday Inn, which had a basement swimming pool and a sauna and all the things that we could do at the Holiday Inn together without mum, it was fantastic.

Then we went on the Underground to Morden, which Darren thought was brilliant because of the hustle and bustle and the speed that the underground trains travel. When reaching Morden, we then got on bus number 93 to my foster parents' home in Morden, Surrey. There we stayed for three days and four nights with my foster parents taking us to see their two now well-grown-up children whom I had grown up with and they were now able to meet my son. Then my foster parents decided to take us in their car to Brighton. For the first time my son is seeing sights from all over London and Brighton in my foster father and mother's car with Reg driving and stopping at the sea front and going on the Brighton pier. Darren went on all the rides and slot machines with my foster father and mother insisting on paying for everything, Darren had a great time.

Throughout our stays I would then take my son to see the orphanage at Hornchurch, getting on the Underground at Morden on the Northern Line, then changing to the District line and getting off at Hornchurch. Darren by this time was very well adapted to the Underground madness. We were like Peter and Harris all over again, but this time with money in our pockets.

We got to our stop, and we then walked the distance along Hornchurch Road. On our journey to the orphanage we passed the pub on the right side of the road 'The Harrow Lodge' (see photo) where I tell him, "This was the pub and off license that I took the empty beer bottles back with Harris for the return monies back on the bottles". This was on a regular basis until we would be caught then taken back to the orphanage in the Black Maria police Van. It was a strange and sad walk, but I was enjoying taking my 8-year-old son on a walk through my past and I was happy my son wasn't going through anything like Harris, and I had.

Now on the left we came to the orphanage, which looked very nice but splendidly different. There we were, able to talk with some of the new residents in their new apartments. One couple nicely invited us in and showed us around what used to be Milton cottage. They were called Gary and Dee Lock. She even gave me their phone number if I ever wanted to contact them, which I did, sending them Christmas cards and telling them of my writing this autobiography, sending them some partly finished chapters. They told me they are thrilled with this and asked if I would let them know if and when it gets published. Milton had been converted into luxury apartments. They very kindly allowed my son to have a look around the place where his father had spent all his childhood but at his tender age of only eight, I could not tell him the truth about my experiences whilst we were walking round there and some of the awful things that had happened to me. The memories were all coming back, thank goodness walls can't speak. It was nice of the couple to have invited us in and on leaving their apartment, formerly Milton cottage, I couldn't help but hear in my thoughts the usual sounds of the voices of children from every direction, which at this time was silent. We said our goodbyes, me with a sad and heavy heart and my son leaving, thinking what a nice place it was. The lovely young couple insisted on taking us back to Hornchurch Underground station which was really nice of them. They enjoyed being with one of the young orphans, long before their time living at Milton cottage. I was able to tell them some of the routines we had to go through and where everything was. I even showed them where the air raid shelter was, and I told them how we would play there and hide our special belongings in the hole we would dig out in the ground to keep them safe. Sad and happy feelings were going through my mind and body. We then said our goodbyes one last time and took our journey back on the Underground and returned to my foster parent's home. I took plenty of pictures whilst I was there so I could show my foster parents at a later date and now I place only a few of them in my autobiography.

The next day it was time to take my eight-year-old son in a stretched Limo which was taking us to Her Majesty's Theatre, in Leicester Square to watch Michael Crawford and Sarah Brightman. They were playing in the Phantom of the Opera. He had no idea we were going to travel in style. He was so made up and couldn't wait to get into the large Limo. The stretch White Limo was full of drinks, with the chauffeur telling us to help ourselves, but I did not take up the offer. Darren had a Coke, and we just enjoyed the journey in the comfort and luxury of the Limo. On arriving at the theatre, we thanked the chauffeur and entered the theatre. I had already seen the play twice, so I knew the large chandelier would be falling, but my son being only 8 he had no idea and as it fell towards the stage he was in such surprise and shock and was totally amazed by all of this. At the end of the show, we went to KFC and then we made our way back to Swiss Cottage on the underground. It was a great experience for an eight-year-old boy. Having had a great time, we went back in the swimming pool and sauna then back to our room where there were machines nearby with drinks and snacks that Darren found cool. He had what he wanted out of it then phoned home to speak to his mum before we both went to bed.

The following day after breakfast we decided to stop at the 'Trocadero' back in Leicester Square, where at a great expense we went to a fancy-dress place and got all dressed up with my son choosing a gangster outfit for us both.

We looked the part wearing a gangster hat each and we got to hold a gun each. Then the photo was taken and framed which was well worth it and we carefully carried it with all our things back home to show mum our fun. All this for my son was the most fantastic learning experience, seeing so much of London and the River Thames, and going on the war ship the Belfast, with all its guns; Darren would dream he was at war firing them all the way. We went to Big Ben, Buckingham Palace and Trafalgar Square and many others. He had entered into my past life when I was always accompanied by my best friend Harris. My son was not aware of the horrors Harris suffered as orphans. I felt myself, at times, actually missing my best pal Harris, but to be able to reach out and touch my young son and see his face full of wonder and surprise and me knowing he has the feeling I never had: the safety of having his father with him, a feeling I can only imagine. But I had the experience of travelling by my young son's side, sharing his experiences of London and the Underground and that was a perfect gift in itself for me.

I enjoyed myself very much with my son, memories we both will never forget, but there were many times behind my smiles that I felt deeply saddened and heavy in my heart. Being with my son soon shook these feelings off me and I enjoyed the freedom and the feeling of being a kid again but through happier times. The time passed by so quickly and it was soon to be time to return back home to his mother so he could tell her of all his experiences. We made our way back to my foster parents to say our goodbyes to them with plenty of hugs and kisses given to Betty. They were kind enough to drive us in their car to the railway station and we shook hands and I hugged Reg and then they left us outside Euston station with all our bags.

We caught our train home and on reaching Manchester Piccadilly we got the tram to Manchester Victoria then got the Leeds/York train, first stopping at Rochdale at approx. 10pm and the train was full. Our bags were safely in the hold, and we sat at the rear of the train talking of our good time and keeping watch on our bags with all the items my son had collected whilst visiting the places he had been to. Then not long after the train guard had checked our tickets, the train was jam packed with football supporters and my son felt very uneasy. When the guard reached the top end of the train all hell broke out. We heard chanting by a crowd as if there had been a goal scored at a football match, then we heard the singing of a nursery rhyme and it goes 'This old man he played one, he played nik nak on my bum, with a nik nak paddiwack give the w-g a bone, my old man said Fuck off home'.

The train was still moving fast, and I sat with my son wondering what was happening, when the guard ran past being chased from behind and two thugs grabbed at him. The guard just managed to reach the door at the very rear of the train but could not get in so at this juncture not thinking of mine or my son's safety, I just jump up and throw myself fully at the two thugs, one going over on the floor to the left and the other going over to the right against the door. I grabbed the nearest one to me around his throat and pushed him back, the guard then managed to get through the door with his leg and foot stuck but manages to grab his phone to alert the train driver who stops the train. By that time, I had the thug in a strangle hold and the other thug I managed to use my foot to take his feet from underneath him then another passenger managed to hold him with me. The door on the train was eventually opened by the conductor and I threw the thug off the train. Then I grabbed the other thug and pushed him off the train to join his friend.

The conductor immediately closed the doors, then I went back to my son who was shaking nervously from the event and saw that the thugs were banging on the train windows as it pulled away. I then heard the passengers shouting their thanks and clapping. No-one seemed to come and confront me, and the train carried on in its way. I was just glad Darren had the sense to stay put on his seat. He was a brave; young boy and I was super proud of him.

The train then arrived at Rochdale where we grabbed hold of all our belongings and got off the train, when all the remaining passengers stood watching us get off and loudly screaming thank you. The guard came over to me with his hand out to shake my hand and I put my bags down and he thanked me and said the police are dealing with it. He asked if he could have my details to pass to the authorities. I gave him my name and address and he shook my hand and got back onto the train and closed the door. When the train pulled away people were waving to me and my son through the windows. On the way back to my home from Rochdale station in a taxi, I told my son not to say anything to his mother about what happened on the train, or she would not forgive me.

We arrived home with mum happy to see us all in one piece with greetings and hugs and kisses having missed us all of the week. We put our bags down and went into the kitchen to have a cup of tea and rest up with mum asking if we had a good time and I told her we had a fantastic time. Then I made the tragic mistake of asking Darren what the best thing we did in London was, thinking his answer would be the drive to the theatre in the stretched limo, but instead he said it was what happened on the train. His mum asked what happened on the train and I said, "nothing much", but she would not let go of it and found out from Darren what happened on the train. She asked what I would have done if they had a knife, and what if this and what if that. She asked what if something happened to Darren when I left him alone, and if I could've lived with it, so now there is a full enquiry into what happened before I got my cup of tea with Darren loving it all. I looked at him with a grin on his face saying to him, "thanks for that Darren".

Then days later the newspapers wanted to talk to us and arranged to meet us. We met up at Rochdale station where they wanted to take a picture of me and my son. Then I received a letter from the owners of the train. They wanted to send us on a short family break. We took up the kind offer for all my family to stay in York for the weekend and Darren's mum is now very happy. We are staying in the brand new, just opened, Queens Hotel with first classrooms looking over the river. The day and night with the hotel's complimentary food was perfect, with the staff giving us a full run of the hotel, even letting Darren ride his micro scooter up and down and all over the place. The following day after breakfast we went on to visit the Train Museum which was all complimentary. We had a fantastic time, and then we went along the river. We went on to look around York Castle and the York dungeons. We go back to the hotel and get washed and changed, then in the evening we go to the theatre to see Gerry and his Pacemakers and at the end of the show we go and wait with others to get Gerry's autograph. Anita is invited by

Gerry to sit on his lap to have a picture taken of her with him, they both had big smiles on their faces. see photo attached.

The following day we went back home leaving me questioning why I got such a telling off when my son put his little big foot in it and spilled the beans. This memory of our stay with mum sat

Businessman calls for cameras after tackling train thugs

on Gerry's lap will stay in the lives of Anita, Darren, Clair, Adele, with the story passed on to their children, for the rest of their lives, but in my case sadly not much longer. I have the framed picture of Gerry and Anita proudly on our wall ever since and see it every day.

The silver lining to this rainbow was to show my son the journey of my life that readers read in this book and the smile seen on the face of Darren's mother and Gerry's and the smiles on her three children's faces watching whilst I took this photograph of their mother's happiness. It has been clearly captured in this true story.

So, so sad I heard the news on the 3/02/2021 that Gerry has passed away from a heart attack and sadly was on his own because of Covid 19.

The best discount was being with Gerry and the Pacemakers. He will forever be in my thoughts, and I sing his song, "You'll never walk alone," on every occasion that celebrates the N.H.S and its staff

In addition to Darren having many adventures with his dad, notably the one on the train back from London, here he is in his real world with his friends becoming the members of his 'Bad Boys club'. This continued for many years, bringing lots of fun and fond memories for all and still remembering now they're in their 30's and keeping in touch with Darren and mum and dad. Each little person had to abide by the club rules with each little finger having to swear their allegiance to the club members in their blood. The club retains their D.N.A. forever. Each member also had to do an electric shock test to see how brave they were. All but one passed.

Each member got a 'Bad boy club' sticker to stick on mum and dad's taxis. Every time driving to school, they all knew who the members were. We organised swimming outings and trips to Blackpool with them all draping their clothes out of the windows on the journey home to try and get them dry before mums picked them up.

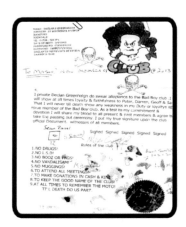

NAME: DECLAN J GREENHALGH
ADDRESS: 25 MACKREATS AVENUE
BAMFORD
ROCHDALE
ID: 1.57.08 - 12477?
DATE OF BIRTH: 3/4/2002
PASSPORD NO: 77000551?
PASSWORD: IMPROVOKING
DECLARES MEMBERS BE EXTRA
DANNY'S CLUB

To MASON NEW MEMBER of **CLUB** ® 2013

4.

I private Declan Greenhalgh do swear allegiance to the Bad Boy club. I
will show at all times loyalty & faithfulness to Peter, Darren, Geoff & Sam.
That I will never till death show any weakness in my Duty or loyaltye as
a true member of the Bad Boy club. As a test to my commitment &
devotion I will share my blood to all present & past members & agree to
take the passing out ceremony. I put my true signiture upon the club
official Document. witnesses of all members.

Sean Ross!   Signed Signed Signed Signed Signed

Rules of the club

1. NO DRUGS!
2. NO L.S.D!
3. NO BOOZ OR FAGS!
4. NO VANDALISAM!
5. NO MUGGINGS!
6. TO ATTEND ALL MEETINGS!
7. TO MAKE DONATIONS IN CASH & KIND
8. TO KEEP THE GOOD NAME OF THE CLUB!
9. AT ALL TIMES TO REMEMBER THE MOTO!
    TT'L DEATH DO US PART.

Driving lessons were had for those brave enough. Fantastic times and brilliant memories. My life has been turned upside down, but the one thing no one can take away from me is the pleasures I get making others happy with what little I have left to offer. If I can bring happiness to those around me, especially children, it's an achievement in itself for me and it gives me more to live for. Inventing the 'bad boys club' took me back to a few of the good times I had with Harris, making dens etc. Darren became very popular. The fun I brought to all his friends brought others flocking and queuing up to complete the initiation. They played football in the very late hours of the evening under flood lights. I used to take them all on days out to Blackpool, Southport. We would go on Birthdays events i.e., swimming parties cinemas. I bought an enormous swimming pool, so they all had a swim and got warmed by a 'bomb' fire with BBQ's. I only wish sometimes that Harris was still around to share it with us. One good thing about being in the orphanage is the bitter and awful experiences us cottage homers had to endure that spill into me, bringing some light and happiness to children where possible. At 74 I am still a big kid at heart and everyone who knows me knows it.

Many late nights were spent with bonfires and music, firework on bonfire nights. Anita would cook black peas and treacle toffee. It had built in electric for a tv, a kettle for warm drinks, but often others snuck in. Another facility turned into a large bed with inflatable mattress for two but always had four at a push. There were tents around the bottom for other bad boy members. The bottom of the tree house was the second room for storing or changing. At the side was a cold water, homemade shower.

The above picture is Darren's school work describing his visits to London on the underground and how he sees it with a child's eye. He doesn't manage to show how I jumped off the train whilst he was still on it and sitting looking at me through the window. He shows me waving at him, bye, bye Darren. I knew he would know to get off at the next stop and wait for me to join him. This was a regular trick bringing fun after the first shock of it.

Darren in 2017 with my 4-year-old grandson, Mason.

CHAPTER 48: Psychic

Anita was very much into psychics and on hearing about some of the experiences she had I thought I would go with her. I went with Anita, not feeling very enthusiastic about it but I kept telling myself all the many remarkable and unusual experiences I had had and felt along my journeys. It was my partner Anita that wanted to go to see the psychic she had watched on TV. I was the sceptic in our barn, but I went because of all the strange experiences I had.

I set off to Manchester Theatre but found the tickets were all sold out. I went to the telephone box down the street to tell Anita what was happening. She was waiting to hear from me and was wanting to see this psychic to hopefully get a connection with her father whom she had not long lost through cancer. Whilst I was on the phone to her, and she was feeling disappointed at me not being able to obtain the tickets, a busker came near to the telephone box where I was making the call. He started to play the trumpet and a tune that Anita immediately recognised and said, "Oh my lord my dad played that in his days of playing the trumpet". Her dad played with the Whitworth Band in Lancashire. She got a bit emotional, and I told her not to despair. There is another booth I can go to and try and get tickets. She wished me good luck and told me that was a sign. I go on my walk to where I knew I may be able to buy tickets and I was successful. I just made my way back to the station to head home.

Anita was overjoyed and couldn't wait to go. The evening came and we made our journey down to Manchester in the car. When we had found our seats, we sat, and we were a bit disappointed because we were not far from being totally at the back in the top of the theatre. We got to speak with some other psychics because we were a bit early. One of them asked me if I had had a head injury at some point in my life. I told her yes and she told me there was a spirit around me touching my head.

Well, this I was amazed with. Then some people came and said that we were in the wrong seats. On checking, now with glasses on, it was the case and we had to move. Anita was getting more upset because it was yet further up at the back, and she said that we would never get a connection now. We sat, not expecting anything and just thought we would enjoy the show.

The place was filling up quickly now and it was heaving. On came the lady and I was very impressed with her communications and connections with others. There were lots of emotions and it was a great atmosphere. Half an hour before the end of the show came a connection for us both. The full audience was looking at us with the glare of a very strong spotlight on me. I was in complete shock. The psychic told me my mother was standing by my side and she was holding and fussing around my head. Amazingly, with a full audience she was making contact with me through my mother's spirit. She told me that I had suffered head injuries and I nodded. Unknown to her, whom I had never met in my life before and not long before she identified my mother holding my head, I had been shot in the head in an attempted murder which was on 29/5/2006. The injuries I received had caused lifelong head and shoulder injuries with brain damage that I will suffer from for the rest of my life. I just could not believe what was happening to me. She also went on to tell me that my mother was so terribly sorry for what she had done. She went on and told me there had been plenty of tears in the spirit world, as well as the living and said she is always around me, and she is very proud of me. She told me she had my brother with her and my other brother whom she named correctly. My brother Bill, whom I loved dearly told me off and told me to go and see my sisters because I hadn't seen them for some time. Other things were said and so to this time I am lost in understanding how she could have seen my mother who was clearly not alive or known that I had a serious head injury. There is absolutely no doubt that she saw my mother holding my head and she even mentioned my mother's name.

Never had I heard anyone speak my mother's name before. I felt all the hairs standing up all over my body and felt very emotional. She went on to say that my mother wanted to say, "She is sorry". She then told me that the things my mother was saying to her were not things she could discuss in this theatre as it was not the right place to discuss the matters, and she would have to leave them with my mother for now. The whole audience were glued to me. Anita then got some contact with her father and the daughter she had lost, Sally, getting names and things right that were just mindblowing.

Later my partner Anita decided to visit another local psychic, again the same thing happened: what she said was that my mother was with me in spirit, but this was not the place to go any further in front of this audience. I obviously knew the reasons for not carrying on; it was awkward and very upsetting. I had not gone back to have any further contact with my mother in the spirit world as I truly feel my mother's presence with me in her letters and giving me support and willing me on in these memoirs. I can say I do believe now there is definitely something in the spirit world and for me it is the presence of my mother and brother. It was my mother's force behind me that took me on the journeys I was meant to take.

I must say that this experience gave me so much happiness and has brought my journey with my mother to an end. I do believe my mother is around me in spirit and it comforts me knowing she will be waiting for me with my brother when it's my turn to leave this world.

I leave all you readers to understand all in chapter 27 and all that I have gone through to understand if this has been a journey with my mother and her brother. Whilst we were with the local psychic, Anita also got some contact with her father which was also an unbelievable experience. She still has occasionally visits to this day.

CHAPTER 49: Farewell to Reg

All the earlier described comings and goings with Reg, to work and back home to his wife Betty and two children, Steven and Sally, became my understanding of family life. At the age of nearly 16 they saved me when I was at the point of losing control in myself, in despair, desperate, even wanting my life to end rather than go back into the orphanage with the now German house master & mother and their dog. My brother Bill realised this and contacted Reg, then Reg & Betty took me in and saved me. I loved them dearly and I have kept in touch ever since.

The most painful heart-breaking day came when my foster father passed away. On the 27th of February 2011, I with only Anita, attended my foster father's funeral along with Betty, her son and daughter, and their families with their children, and a mass of others and many of Reg's former work mates from Gratt Brothers Ltd. The priest allowed me to give my speech whilst holding on to Reg's coffin. The final song of the service, the closing music which I had no idea was to be sung, was the music of the Beatles called 'In my life', a song I know and remember each and every word too. Holding on to the coffin, singing the words "There are places I remember all my life", with a massive lump in my throat and tears falling from my eyes looking at Anita, Betty, Sally and Steven seeing me with my tears falling like rain. What was so lovely was that Betty had made specific arrangements to put me and Anita in the first car behind the hearse, carrying Reg to his final resting place, and before this she took me and Anita to see him, resting at the chapel.

I was so proud to be given a place to hold his coffin and give a speech to all that had attended the funeral, which was packed out. I stood at the front with his wife and family all grown up, with everybody watching me and I managed to keep myself together. I did what everyone said was a brilliant speech. It was a lovely service and send off for Reg. A heart-breaking time and the end of a most wonderful person in our lives. His spirit lives on with us all and many fantastic memories are sketched in a lot of people's hearts. He is terribly missed by all, a most dearly loved man Reg.

I shall always be forever in my foster father's shadow, and I am forever grateful. I thank God that I met such a lovely, kind and wonderfully gifted and talented man, who set me out in my life in a way I never dreamed of or expected. My foster father's son Steven to this time is a most senior person working for the same company 'Gratte Brothers'. His father (Reg) had brought him into the company when Reg had gone off the tools and started working in the office as a senior member in the design of electrical drawings and pricing and supervision of all the contracts all over the country. He was in control of the contracts for all Marks & Spencer's stores throughout the UK. My foster father's family continued to the time of writing this book to stay in contact with me, and still are. My foster mother Betty is still with us; she will receive a copy of this book when it is completed with lots of love and kisses when I hand it to her.

CHAPTER 50: My loss, but my gain of a friendship with the Travelling people

After all the pain and suffering through the separation from my wife and my solicitor which brought about more suffering for my children, especially Caroline, I ended up with no income from all my hard work. I thought I was building a great future and an income for the rest of my life and for my family. My greatest and biggest mistake, with much regret, was making my trusted wife a fifty percent director, and opening my home to my business solicitor and making him a friend and family solicitor.

Never in a million years did I think my solicitor would betray me in his position of trust and as he had a lovely wife and four children and was a son of a most prominent priest in the priesthood of Greater Manchester, so I was surprised. He saw my success and he made sure he was going to take it. He and his solicitor Robinson, along with my wife, were all in cahoots with one another. Like vultures on a dead carcass, the solicitor, who I paid most generously, used his skills to advance his finances. They were all fighting over my hard-earned money and assets. They used their positions to strip me and used the public legal aid funding unlawfully and wilfully, to pay for it all.

With a backhanded thanks for the errors of the solicitors involved, it brought about the mistaken belief by my former solicitor in all the information provided to the court by him along with my wife's solicitor Mr Guy R Robinson, the then president of the Manchester Law Society. My defence and fight were no match for these greedy, legal sharks. They, along with my wife's support and all the pillow talk given to Mr Trafford, then provided his mistaken information to the Dean & Cannons of the Cathedral, College Gate Church in Manchester. They, by coincidence are the owners and landlords! of the premises from which Mr G Robinson's solicitors firm operates.

Mr Robinson, my wife and my former solicitor managed to convince the judge that Mr Robinson would be best ordered to have the conduct of the sale of my industrial units. Of course, Mr Robinson's full commitment in this sale is to his landlords. This would all be charged and paid for and more from the proceeds of the industrial units' sale! I had built called 'Heritage Park' Rochdale. Can be seen in chapter 50.

The court, against my objections to Mr. Robinson having the conduct of sale, still made an order that Mr. Robinson would have the conduct in this sale, even after I had made it abundantly clear to the judge why I could not consent. I had discovered that Mr. Robinson's landlords, the church, was waiting in the wings to make the purchase at bargain basement price in this forced sale. The church successfully and instantly on their acquisition carried out retrospective rent reviews along with back payments of all past service charges, which I could not apply because these matters were all with the court over the years it took to bring this to court. During these years my hands were tied, and my money and assets were frozen by the court, via my wife's solicitor that is. I was having to maintain the upkeep for all our tenants of the work that I had done over the passing years in line with my obligations as the landlord. But I couldn't make any charges for any of those work whilst she and my solicitor were living in their lavish property, Summer Ford Hall, in Crewe without a care in the world. In my contract provisions in the leases, there were three-yearly rent reviews. These had not been implemented upon my tenants. So, upon the successful purchase, with the help of these greedy sharks and my former wife, whose father-in-law was associated with the Deans & cannons of the church and a regular source of information between the now successful purchasers. 'The Dean & Cannons for the Cathedral Church's offices are situated at Church house, 90 Deansgate, Manchester, the same address as Mr Robinson solicitors' firm. This terrible injustice caused me a total loss of my units and what should have been an income for life. I was robbed.

I solemnly believed that the eminent judge knew what was going on. I was pushed aside by the judiciary system in favour of the president of the Law Society and the rest of the sharks and I am sure those reading this story will take the same view. Having to suffer the indignity, I have to somehow pick up the pieces and get on with my new life with Anita and Darren, Clair and Adele, plus deal with the tax man, leaving me with nothing but monies still outstanding. The tax man was chasing me still for the money my wife had taken in the hundreds of thousands, for her and my former solicitor, all from the company and our private joint account. Because of working hard all the over the country, I didn't know about all of this and much more that was going on.

Anita and I were in contact with Christine Trafford, and we managed to help her. We gave her a few clothes for the children, and she helped us by giving me documentation with permission to use it as I saw fit. She suffered with her children terribly and was made homeless whilst her solicitor husband J. Trafford, was living in luxury with my wife. They gave Christine next to nothing, and she was forced to look for charity handouts. Even the vicar's former father-in-law wasn't helping her. One day I thought I would let the congregation know of what a lovely man the vicar Trafford was. Early Sunday morning I went to the service of Mr Trafford, intent on standing in front of the whole church on behalf of Christine.

Mr Trafford was the one and only vicar Reverend Cyril Trafford seen on the above official church document. Vicar Cyril

Trafford and his wife would give sermons at his church with my children in the front pew; about this I had no idea until I arrived.

I went along to the church, standing in the front pew, looking directly at him whilst he was giving his sermon. He certainly knew who I was, as my children were looking and glancing over at me and because of this I couldn't proceed. After the service was over, I walked over to the vicar and asked him if I could have a word with him and I followed him into the side room of the church where the collection dishes were being brought to him nicely full of money his grandchildren were in desperate need of. Whilst he was taking his tunic off and over his head, I said to him "I have come to the church to talk to you about your son's activities and matters that your daughter-in-law has confided in me". The outburst that came for the Reverend Cyril Trafford was, and I quote specifically his words, overheard by one of the ushers with the collection plate.

He said, "I am sick to the fucking belly of my son and daughter-in-law's fucking activities". I could not believe that this was the reaction I would get from such a church-going vicar. There was no point in any further exchange of words as I was aware my children were sitting with the vicar's wife in the front pew and so I decided to leave the church and my children saw me walking away.

After the church had now made their successful purchase of my industrial units, making it no longer possible to operate my business from it, they carried out the three yearly rent reviews along with the service charges backdated over 10 years. This effectively ensured that their purchase of the whole development had cost them next to nothing. As far as I am aware there was no stamp duty because the church is a charitable organisation. But the church then discovered that the grassed area I had marked out on the picture, I exhibit shaded in green, was not in fact included in the sale as they had expected! The area shaded green was at all times in my own name and had nothing whatsoever to do with my divorce or my former wife.

In all my development plans, the green shaded area was for future development, where planning consent had been granted at the time. I was carrying out the necessary work as the landlord for my tenants. One example was in the winter, gritting all areas of tarmac to make the site safe, painting and carrying out repairs as necessary over those years. The future development marked in green incorporated all the services and drainage which went

through and under my land. This was not understood by the solicitors involved at the time of the sale to the church, they didn't care in any event. When I discovered that the church agents had taken this land to be part of their purchase, I then made them aware the land was in my ownership, but they permitted their tenants to have use of this land. They placed a skip on it and installed a substantial amount of fencing upon which they were later to discover was not their land. I was now forced to take legal action against the Deans & Cannons of the Church on the 27th of March 2009, for trespassing upon my land. I had large metal containers on the site with lots of different contents of tools, electrical equipment, drains etc. The contents in each were of some value. One day I visited my site to find all my containers were gone, taken. Again, I eventually went to court, only to find nothing could be done. I came away with nothing. My total loss now seemed to be my way of living from one extreme to another. I was being forced to live with so much suffering.

Seven years they prevented me from developing my land. They knew that I had been shot in 2006 and I was in great difficulty. Throughout these years they were asked to remove the fencing by my solicitors but to no avail. My situation, life was becoming weaker in more ways than one. The more I needed solicitors the more money it cost. I no longer had deep pockets thanks to the pillow talk between my former wife and solicitor. The Deans & Cannons knew this from my former wife and solicitor. After being shot in 2006, in 2007 I experienced another terrible relapse that took me back into intensive care fighting for my life. I made a remarkable recovery, leaving me with brain damage and now I am disabled for the rest of my life. I managed, with help, to take matters to court and force the removal of my land being landlocked. The church, rather than allowing this matter to proceed to court, removed all their unlawfully constructed fencing after putting us through years of misery. They then agreed on the amount paid for my legal costs and damages for their trespassing on the 22nd of March 2010. The many, very draining, stressful years it took to obtain these costs and damages.

My now small but important plot of land, thanks to the kind work of my friend Tommy, had all the preparation work carried out, architectural approval and groundwork done, ready for the final industrial unit of mine to be built. I would now have to carry out this work and build these industrial units and live alongside the church Deans & Cannons as my neighbours. This now would never work. Obviously, this was never ever anticipated in my plans or many other misfortunes that I had experienced with my wife and solicitor, those who I had placed my unwavering trust in.

The full development was always to be under control of one owner and now there are two, me and the church, After giving great thought about how to go forward in this matter, my only option was to sell, but I knew the only purchaser would be the church and this is what they were waiting for. I just did not want this. They were part of my downfall. I needed to find a way to sell my small plot to someone other than the Deans & Cannons. I put it up for sale and waited patiently. The church thought they were sitting pretty; they wanted it given to them knowing I hadn't much choice. I spoke to the Travellers and then I got an offer from them. I immediately thought this was the sting in the tail I needed.

Indeed, the church agents contacted my sales agent, Steve Barton, having discovered that it was up for sale and sold, subject to planning, having an offer to purchase. They wanted to know what the purchasers were prepared to pay, if indeed there was a buyer for the site. Obviously, my agent, Steve Barton, was on strict instructions not to give out this information. What a brilliant move, thanks to my good friend Steve & Terry Moore at R.M.B.C. legal.

So, in the passing of time, the authorities and the solicitor involved in these matters were fully aware of all that was taking place and decided that granting the change of use from its existing commercial use to residential was acceptable because it assisted the local authority with their legal requirements to provide living accommodation for Travelers. So, the planning authorities agreed to change the use to conclude this most ugly matter. Having managed to obtain this change of use, I then gave my full and undivided attention and help to the new owners. The Deans & Cannons were in disbelief. What a fantastic move on my part. The Gypsies, see newspaper article on next page, were to me a Pyrrhic victory but a most important conclusion/victory. It had been a long and outstanding victory against those that had committed their trespasses against me.

Having a legal and binding agreement, I insisted on registering upon the land that no onward sale of this land can ever be sold on to the Deans & Cannons of the church. See land registry covenant attached. Then the Dean & Cannons for the church decided they didn't like having Travellers as neighbours. Enough is enough, and the Deans & Cannon's sold up at their loss with a clause in their sale for the purchasers to identify the Deans & Cannons of the church against all future liabilities for any breach of their covenants or declarations to comply with section 53 (1) (B) of the law. The area shaded green has legal access over the entrance and exit gates and all areas marked A, B&C are where all services and drains run under the land shaded green. The Deans & Cannons didn't like this one bit. Even though the land had been sold, all my monies went to the Inland Revenue to cover the bill I was forced to pay for my wife's dishonesty within the company.

Here the restricted covenant can be seen

Even though I am suffering in every way possible, I make it my wish to help the Travellers. They came to my home asking me for help. They didn't understand the documents relating to the land as they couldn't read or write, just as I couldn't when I left the orphanage. My new mission was to help the Travellers pay the church back for their bad deeds. Very sad, but happy time after the suffering we had to go through (in this, my thoughts will always turn to Steve Barton through our can collecting years also Terry Moor in legal at R.M.B.C.).

CHAPTER 51: The last chapters and such a difficult search for justice for Peter

Those reading this truthful autobiography of mine will or may ask, where is the justice Peter is hoping and looking for? Could it be those who were sent to prison in the Mapperton Case? No, is the answer, as there were so many others that did not receive any punishment at all for all the pain and suffering, they had caused (so there is no justice here).

Was it justice when I received £20,000 from the legal aid board in an ex-gratia payment for the maladministration in August 1999 or special payment compensation from the Child Support Agency in June 2002? No is the answer, because I was wrongly made bankrupt on the 18th of July 2001 (so, no Justice here).

Was it the guilty verdict in my attempted murder? The person pulling the trigger on the shotgun did not spend a single day in prison nor was he ordered to pay a fine or any financial punishment (so, no justice here).

Was it that the police did not prosecute me for the damage I caused to the school wall and lamp post when I crashed the car, when there was still outstanding finance on the car which had to be paid (So, no justice here)?

Was it the I.P.C.C. on the 14th of April 2016, who wrote to confirm I had not received an acceptable standard of service from the Cheshire & Greater Manchester police for over 25 years (so, no justice here)?

The only justice for me was to be in this position to write about the injustices in this most truthful, autobiography in the hope that those who read it will be happy in their lives not having to suffer such injustices as I have in the judicial system. Where those who implement the laws fail to abide by them themselves, taking from those less fortunate like myself. Writing this story has been most difficult and very time consuming, taking me up to now nearing five years and reliant upon others to give up their precious time and using their abilities which I do not possess. It has made me ashamed that I cannot do the things my son takes for granted. My grandchildren do the things I cannot do that are normal things to them, but far from normal in my childhood days when mobile phones did not exist or computers or the computer games that people and children are addicted to today. These games that the children play wouldn't have even been invented but for the first ever computer made by the hands of Alan Turing at 'Bletchley Park', and just look at the price Alan Turing paid, with sadly losing his life in his suicide.

We have inventions such as simply saying 'Hey Google what is the name of the man who broke the German code at Bletchley Park', and it will give you the full details of 'Alan Turing' and his three Polish workers that broke the enigma machine code, shortening the war and saving many lives. Alan Turing, like me, never got justice except when he received a posthumous medal for his bravery and suffering for his way of life. He was a brilliant mathematician. Thankfully Alan's letter from the king, amongst other stolen items, will soon be repatriated to his private school. So, from his most sad grave has come some little justice. Now in 2021, Alan Turing is seen honoured in all the high value currency notes that we will be using for all cash purchases in the future. The currency was issued on the 23rd of June 2021, celebrating the anniversary of his birthday on the new £50 notes.

CHAPTER 52: My justice

My Justice has been after 28 years of reporting the fraudsters and the mass of claims upon public funds and how the various complaints authorities over the legal profession do everything and anything to protect those within their eminent positions. No different to those in the Mapperton case at the Old Bailey and the many other authorities that simply turn away from their moral responsibilities. It is now for those that have taken the time to read and understand these most dreadful injustices, that are now fully exposed within this book.

Here is my justice. I am a survivor, as seen from all the chapters in my autobiography. Without any fear, I make this quotation from the most honourable QC's letter to the 'Professional Conduct Committee' signed with the ink from his most precious fountain pen: Charles Gordon. In between yours sincerely and Charles Gordon Q.C. and his signature.

I quote his words: - "I was, of course, aware that the defendant, solicitor Mr Trafford LLB, was legally aided and had no reason to doubt that he was entitled to legal aid". End of quote. He failed to abide by his code of ethics where he blatantly disregarded the children's act in regard to the eight children, he was fully aware were affected since in the newspaper article in chapter 35.

In fact, Mr. Gordon concealed this from the judge in his court. He was also aware at the trial he had been conducting that the crown prosecution witness, Mr. Haughton, was his good solicitor friend and again I quote his words Quote: - "Mr J.A. Haughton LLB, he has known professionally for many years playing an annual bridge match with him between the Northern circuit and the Manchester Law Society". End of quote.

What he also failed to reveal to H.H.J. David Clarke QC in the trial, was that he had been involved in the C.S.A.'s false declarations on behalf of his same client solicitor J.P. Trafford LLB. He was still a major shareholder and solicitor partner of the crown prosecution witness Mr J.A. Haughton LLB at the 1993 date of Mr Gordons advocacies in the C.S.A. assessment for solicitor Mr J.P. Trafford LLB with Guy Robert Jean Robinson, president of the Manchester Law Society, who was throughout. Mr Gordon was under a duty to apply the children's act 1989 when the legal aid was his paymaster. This continued for many years with payments from the legal aid board for both of his clients, Mr Trafford and my former wife.

For these reasons I will not cash the cheque that has remained in my possession for the past five years, payable to me from the legal aid board, because one reason alone makes these matters abundantly clear. The fraudulent conduct that has taken place in the above chapters.

Mr Gordon was at all times of his advocacies, fully aware of his client's insured items, of my wife's gold, gemstones, diamonds and specifically a 'Piaget' watch which was itemised on the papers in Mr Gordon's possession and of course Mr. Robinson's to the value of £25,000. This alone should have and would have prevented Mr Gordon acting on behalf of the legal aid board, let alone the fact that my wife and former solicitor's joint income was far in excess of a legally aided litigant, as referred to in the national newspapers.

I am not going to become a victim, as Stefan Kiszko, with his mother. Also, Alan Turing who went to his grave without justice. I worked hard from leaving the orphanage. Never would I have imagined all my gains being torn apart by vultures, fighting, wanting a piece of what I had built and made. This includes the item valued at £25,000 to which I still retain all my old, very detailed insurance policies, including their insured items in Summerford Hall property at the time they were both in receipt of legal aid, and for my former wife's diamonds, gold and other jewellery.

Some will ask what has driven me to write such a detailed autobiography as this. It is because I am aware of those with far greater advocacies skills than mine, would look to find grounds to sue me. I have no fear of such legal action.

I recall very well a friend of mine saying "Peter, stop, don't burn all your bridges, there will only ever be two winners, your wife and solicitor". I went against this advice. I just could not stop as I continue to do now. Even, I suppose, had I known in 1991 that it would cost me over half a million in legal costs, my bankruptcy, the loss of my home, and against all the good advice given to me by my friends. But they had not seen the dreadful state of my daughter Caroline in Alder Hey children's hospital's intensive care ward and why she was there, except my most loyal and best friend Tommy with doctor Ivan Blumenthal and also doctor Edward Tierney. They never wavered in their support and gave me strength at my lowest ebb. And, of course, at all times, day and night, Anita did. Tommy said he would stay with me forever, and when I was at my lowest, having been at my hospital bedside recovering from my attempted suicide, Tommy said that our help is worth far more than the tons of pity, and that we are here for you with that little help. His help was there at all times, as that of Anita who helped me through, and she now helps write this autobiography for me, which I would not swap for one hundred million pounds.

I could not fail to travel this dreadful journey after I had discovered what they, my wife and solicitor and others in their legal profession, had done to my daughter Caroline. No amount of money, no matter how much, will ever put my daughter back together again, fit and healthy as she was before she visited her GP from hell, holding on to her mother's hand and Mr Trafford's, after her mother giving her signed consent to the investigation under general anaesthetic.

So, to those that will ask why I did not stop when I could have, and most would have, saving me from all the costs from the solicitors I have instructed in all these matters, I explain I would do it all again. To expose the most serious corruption and fraud within this British legal profession and here with God's grace, is my justice. To expose the unbelievable systemic corruption within our judiciary that I have suffered since my many childhood years of incarceration at the L.C.C orphanage at Hornchurch.

It is said that the courts and its judges and our judicial system were for fairness. That the children's act 1989 was to give protection to our children. It is abundantly clear from all that you have read of our judicial system, it just simply does not work or is not fit for purpose.

Whilst I did not receive an education, I provided for my three daughters private schooling at Rishworth in Yorkshire, as then I could well afford this. My son now goes on to Brighton and Bolton University and receives his Honorary Degree in Engineering and now is halfway through his Masters. Here I am, so proud, with his mother and his son standing watching him receive his Honorary degree, me with tears flowing down my face. Here I am going back in my years without such education. I first became recognised by Reg's firm with a five-year apprenticeship and most proudly worked and lived with him. After five years of my apprenticeship, I became an electrician. Then I became an approved electrician with a J.I.B. No 10653 (Joint Industrial Board). Then I become an approved member of the E.C.A No.9922 (Electrical Contracting Authority). And then I became a member of the N.I.C.E.I.C No.10563 '(National Inspection Council for Electrical Insulation Contracting), where every year an inspection of my electrical work was carried out by an inspector for the N.I.C.E.I.C. So, I was very successful; but there came an end to my success in the divorce courts, all of which went before the civil courts through my wife and solicitor's actions, with the civil court not interested one bit in the fact that all my company transactions and work have come to a complete standstill and a deadlock as a result of my solicitor's activities. Nor is the court taking any notice of all the matters that I have dealt with in person as it was impossible to instruct solicitors on my behalf in such complexities. Also, with my daughter having been used as their deadly weapon. This was in clear breach of the courts' code of practice along with the child protection act. Instead, the courts' judges are only interested in their friendly solicitors and barristers who play bridge together between the northern circuit of the Manchester Law Society. All this moved on through the court system in Manchester till 2001, after I was made bankrupt as referred to.

I have Mr Gordons signature upon his letter giving false information relating to his client's financial situation. His pay master was the law society's president, paying him from legal aid funds. Mr Gordon would never have thought this evidence of his fraudulent conduct would be revealed, 30 years. later. Will this 2021, independent review of legal aid, led by ex-judge Sir Christopher Bellamy QC, take into account these fraudulent claims upon public funds by the above QC and his associates in these past many years of injustice? (No). The review will simply be another whitewash and total waste of time at further costs to public funding. So, for these reasons I put them into this unbelievable autobiography of mine.

Mr Trafford LLB solicitor was living in Crewe with his new wife, but they are now divorced because he is the father of another child, conceived under the roof of his new wife but not the child of his wife, (my former wife) but that of another. One can only imagine the damage all this has inflicted upon my three daughters.

So, the only justice I can obtain now in all these miscarriages of justice is to put them into this unbelievable autobiography of mine.

CHAPTER 53: Now 74 plus years & the injustice of Stefan Ew'an Kiszko and his loving mother

I have mentioned Alan Turing's unbelievable strength and determination to break the Enigma code which helped end the Second World War and the subsequent injustices he suffered. I now look at how justice failed Stefan Kiszko and the young, 11-year-old, Lesley Molseed as another example of the injustices that have taken place in my lifetime. The most horrendous injustices that never should have taken place. I have been drawn to become involved in Stefan's unbelievable injustice. I remember so well, all the police involvement that condemned an utterly and completely innocent young man. A gentle giant of a man along with his most loving mother up to their early deaths, Charlotte and Stefan Ew'an Kiszko. In some ways Stefan's mother Charlotte was much like me. She never gave up on her case in obtaining justice to free her most beloved and only son from prison, just as I will never give up in my search for justice for my daughter Caroline, not just for myself. In many ways I will keep on fighting just as Stefan's mother did, sadly until it killed her. With this my true and unbelievable story lives on for others to understand the sheer greed of all those in their very well-paid legal professions, including judges that were there to protect our children but instead abuse them. I, being a survivor of this abuse. What happened to me in my childhood gave me strength rather than the opposite, but sadly not for poor Stefan. He was brought up by his loving and caring mother and father, unlike me, only to suffer a most unbelievable miscarriage of justice. This injustice was well known by the police, who forced Stefan to confess to a crime that was impossible for him to have committed, all the time whilst Stefan was in prison. Stefan had worked in his prestige employment with Rochdale Inland Revenue, (H.M.R.C), bringing much pride and happiness to his family and friends.

When I first became aware of the poor little girl, Lesley Molseed, the police were looking for her in the area where I lived in Rochdale. This was the place where I had proudly built my first, beautiful, detached house. I knew Deeplish area very well and visited the shopping area frequently. I remember the police were searching for Lesley. I had only just finished building my detached home in 1975, number 11 Hastings Street, Deeplish, Rochdale. My shop and warehouse were a stone throw away from my home, all at the time poor Stefan had been wrongly arrested and accused and set up for a crime it was impossible for him to have committed. I have no doubt, working in Deeplish, I would have crossed paths with Stefan's mother or possibly Stefan himself, along with Lesley Molseed, playing as she had done in the Deeplish area. I had done so much electrical house re-wiring and pre-war prefab homes in the areas of Stefan and his family.

I got to meet and know so many families there, I even had young Asian children bringing food to my electrical shop with their mums or dads as a token of their appreciation of my work in their homes. I was a trusted electrician and invited to remove all the old wiring with the old round pins and convert to the recommended and safe fused plug tops. I would spend a lot of my time meeting many families of my now fellow good friends to this very time. I still meet up with many of them. One example of many is Arien, an Asian refrigeration man and his extended family at their place of work or, for a long time now, at the cemetery, where with complete surprise I would hear my name being called out. I would join up with my very good Asian friends. I have even proudly taken the shovel with them at the grave side of their lost ones, and every single week I visit the cemetery. All the staff working there know me. I visit Stefan and his mother and father's grave; I keep it clean and decorated. I have also placed a permanent sign for all those passing to notice, and it automatically lights up when its dark for all to see and read of Stefan's dreadful injustice and the loss of his life as a direct result of those highly respected and well-paid, detectives. And the most disgraceful law and judiciary. They simply sat back to enjoy each Christmas up until February 1992 when he was released. Stefan and his mother endured sixteen long very painful and lonely years, whilst all the time the police knew Stefan was innocent. But still, they had him incarcerated as a result of the police conspiracy leading him into his most appalling, very cold and ugly prisons. There he was subjected to the most serious, appalling assaults, with the inmates calling him a nonce, taunting him and treating him as if he had been a child murderer, whilst it was clearly known by those authorities that he was completely innocent of such a horrendous crime. They all continued to sit, enjoying their Christmases and celebrating their new years with their families after successfully engineering their knowingly wrongful conviction. On the 23rd of November 1992, two days before Christmas, Stefan died. Enjoying their alcohol, cigarettes and good food, they knew they had been ultimately responsible for killing Stefan and his mother Charlotte who died not long after his passing. All this at the same time the person who had indeed committed the most heinous crime against the little girl Lesley was known to the police and authorities as he was serving time for other, unrelated crimes.

In 1991, the Birmingham six were released from prison for crimes they were clearly never guilty of committing, whilst Stefan continued to remain in prison for a crime impossible for him to have committed. In 1993 we just happened to be fortunate to be in the place where Stefan was visiting his bank, the Halifax Building Society, where he saw Anita and gave her a very big, nice smile which Anita will always have the picture of in her memory forever. She remembers him standing with his mother, Charlotte; she could see he was just like a little boy, happy with his mum. He had his mother's shopping basket in his hand whilst smiling over at her.

Whilst on one of my visits to work on Stefan's grave I noticed a tractor and trailer driving into the cemetery. On the trailer there was a coffin; I noticed a sign on the back of the trailer 'T.A. Sinclair'. This was the man who shot me! Then I noticed the wife of the gunman who had taken his shotgun loaded it and shot me at the time his wife was with him except when he pulled the trigger. Now I am looking at his wife, having got out of the hearse and she is so upset, placing her hand on her husband's coffin. At this time, I move to get into a position where I cannot be seen by her or any other mourners. His coffin stayed on the trailer whilst the service was taking place inside. After the service the coffin went directly into the furnace to be cremated, and all the visitors left along with the tractor and trailer through the side entrance.

When all had gone, I looked around and noticed on the ground next to a tree near a stone wall, a very nice lady's handbag with all the belongings scattered around it. I very 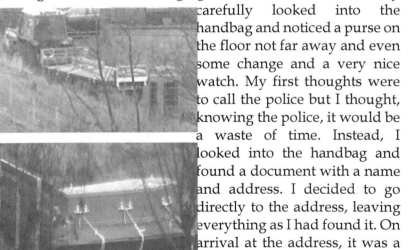 carefully looked into the handbag and noticed a purse on the floor not far away and even some change and a very nice watch. My first thoughts were to call the police but I thought, knowing the police, it would be a waste of time. Instead, I looked into the handbag and found a document with a name and address. I decided to go directly to the address, leaving everything as I had found it. On arrival at the address, it was a brand-new build, and very nice house. There was no one at home so I went to the house next door where a very nice, well-spoken, Asian man answered and confirmed the name of the person I was looking for. I explained to him the reasons why I had called and asked him to let his neighbour know when she got home to contact me. I gave him my phone number then I left to go back home. Not long after arriving home my phone rang, and it was the person who had lost her precious belongings and her handbag. I explained to her that I had found them and told her I would meet her at the cemetery to show her where I had found her handbag along with its contents.

We agreed to meet up at the cemetery junction explaining our vehicles registrations. On our arrival at the road junction, she had her headlights on. We stopped and told her to follow us into the cemetery. We parked up at the nearest position and walked across to the wall where her bag was. At this time, we became aware that we knew this lady; she was Sheila, the manager of all the work and up-keep of the cemetery and crematorium work. We took her to the place where we looked over the wall and she saw all her belongings all over the ground as we had told her. Rather than climbing over the wall to retrieve her handbag and belongings, she immediately contacted on her mobile phone one of the grounds men. As soon as he arrived, he noticed me and also knew Anita. So, we are like one big happy family, and the grounds man climbed over the wall. Thankfully it hadn't rained since her bag was stolen on the morning of that same day. It was taken from her vehicle which she had not locked; because of the workload she had forgotten to do this. The grounds man collected all her belongings, coins and other bits and handed them back to Sheila. She clearly was so happy to have recovered everything, including her lovely wristwatch which she had feared she had lost for good, except her credit cards as she had already contacted her bank to cancel them. It was all thanks to my being with Stefan on that day, which turned out to be a bad day for Sheila, that she managed to get everything back. We then told Sheila how I came to find them in such a place that no one would ever normally have seen or found them. I explained that I went over the wall to watch the cremation of the coffin on the tractor and trailer explaining that he was the man who had shot me with his shotgun causing me lifelong injuries. I will not go any further into what was said. I leave that to all those who read this story, as I believe they will know my thoughts on what was said to Sheila and her grounds man. Since the recovery of her handbag, I would say I see Sheila at least once or twice a week on my visits to the cemetery and she shows me a very nice warm and friendly smile. I leave this for you readers, who I think by now will also have a very nice warm smile on your faces.

A part of my tree decorated for Stephan's & Charlottes grave along with a section to Lesley. God rest their souls.

"INNOCENT" & HOW OUR FAILED JUSTICE SYSTEM "KILLED" STEFAN IWAN KISZKO & HIS BELOVED MOTHER CHARLOTTE.

FOR ALL OF THOSE TAKING THEIR TIME LOOKING INTO STEFAN AND HIS MOTHER & FATHER'S GRAVE.

PLEASE GIVE YOUR THOUGHTS ALSO TO THE 11 YEAR OLD BEAUTIFUL GIRL LESLEY :

THEN REFLECT UPON THOSE HIGHLY PAID LEGAL EXPERTS AND POLICE OFFICERS WHO TODAY STILL RECEIVE THEIR GENEROUS PENSIONS FOR THEIR SKILFUL & THOUGHTFUL KINDLY SERVICES TO OUR QUEEN AND COUNTRY!

THEN ASKING "WHY DID THEY ALL LET THIS INJUSTICE HAPPEN TO THE MOST GENTLE GIANT OF A MAN" WHO'S ONLY WISH WAS TO BE SPENDING CHRISTMAS IN 1979 WITH HIS MOST LOVING , CARING DEVOTEE, MOTHER CHARLOTTE KISZKO.

INSTEAD THEY SENT THIS MOST INNOCENT GENTLE GIANT OF A MAN TO 16 YEARS IN PRISON LEADING TO HIS MOST PUNISHING DEATH.

PLEASE PAUSE FOR THOUGHTS AND SAY :-

"GRACE BUT FOR THE LOVE OF GOD DO I"

COVID Christmas 2022. 16 Christmas Trees for 16 Christmases of wrongful imprisonment.

CHAPTER 54: Did I receive my justice against NatWest Bank? (No, being the answer)

In 1996 my case was lost and struck out on grounds that any action against the bank would require the consent of both directors of the limited company; my wife being the other director would not agree to this action. I was then left to pay all the costs associated with this case. Throughout the years following the various governmental departments, police and legal aid authorities were contacted by my solicitors and myself to investigate these fraudulent actions by granting public funding to a Manchester practicing solicitor, Mr J.P. Trafford along with my wife, whilst he was still on the court record acting for my companies.

It will be observed from the public records at Companies House in the years up to my wrongful bankruptcy that my companies had ceased trading with 'Linkside Development Co Ltd' No 1561226 struck off.

With loans from my friends, I obtained help to pay my legal costs with new solicitors and accountants to have the company restored for the soul purpose of taking various actions against my wife and solicitor, in particular the substantial loss suffered in my pension where many documents were found with forgeries of my signatures and conducted from the accommodation address referred above. Over the trading and accounting years of 1988-89-90, the accounts for those years I discovered had masses of monies removed without my knowledge. The accounts in 1991 -1993 at court which I refused to sign, were provided to me in court and signed only by Mrs E Ross (I still retain those original accounts) where there have been vast amounts of fraudulent transactions covered up.

These were later admitted by Mrs Ross throughout those years where this fraudulent conduct was taking place. Mr Trafford was my family and company solicitor and would travel with me in my car to various sites around the UK in planning disputes. I had been totally unaware that between him and her in 1988, Mrs Ross took and paid in cash a payment for a brand-new house, plot No 41 (No 18 Henwich Hale Avenue, Ramsbottom. BLO 9YJ) where all transactions and correspondence between her and her solicitor were to and from the accommodation address referred above, (6 Southbrook Ave) including the substantial fraud against my pension where communications were again to that accommodation address from 'Target Life Insurance'. Mr Kevin Booth, as a result of police action, was closed down and made bankrupt. I have a court order that was made available with all the documentation into his bankruptcy. At the High Court (see attached law Report) in London. 'Linkside Development Co Ltd- Ross-v-Mrs Elaine Trafford and another, Mr Trafford being the other. The court ordered, as seen in the attached report, that it could not break the dead lock between the directors, again leaving me to pay all the associated costs, including Trafford's in 1991.

Mr Trafford had, as referred above, taken £10,000 on valentine's day without my knowledge or consent. This was paid into his solicitor's practice whilst at the same time he was in receipt of legal aid. Just one example of many was in the case of (see attached) the C.P.S document. In this matter he did not disclose £25,000 of gold and gemstones to the legal aid authority for assessment into his legal aid eligibility. I have provided most of his many legal aid references. Mr Trafford continued in his ownership of his law consulting company. His tax reference is WL/01/42/82/D seen on his benefit cheque; his employer reference was 187/00/P1371. I have provided only some of his legal aid reference numbers (Not all) with much other documentation to Karen Douglas at H.M.R.C. with her reference in this matter that has been ongoing for the last 3 years - 1/1641138639.

Despite all the evidence that I have provided, I have explained why it has not been possible for me to bank the cheque that I received from the Legal Aid Authority in November 2017.

Also, it can be clearly seen that the 'Statutory Charge Order' by H.M.R.C made against me was wrong. My bankruptcy along with all the associated costs was also wrong. This had a catastrophic effect upon me, having discovered that my wife and solicitor had put me in this predicament by their joint actions, in taking advantage of the trust and loyalties that I had placed in them both.

Since my discovery of their actions along with her admissions of forgeries of my signatures, I took matters to court in my pension loss, where, again having to pay massive costs in the court proceedings in London with all the evidence I had provided to the pension's ombudsman. As I was the trustee of the pension it was deemed that I ought to have known what was taking place and indeed I must have accepted this practice of my wife placing forgeries of my signatures upon all the documentation whilst I was away from home and office working.

Accordingly, the full chapter 41 has been received by H.M.R.C., Director General with a direct request to Angela McDonald CBE, the director general at H.M.R.C to claw back. A full assessment of my loss was most significant, but impossible to fully quantify along with all the tax on payments I have wrongly paid before and after the actions leading to my bankruptcy. Also, the most significant deductions from my pension having received no income whatsoever from my companies since 1991. At that time the court ordered all rental incomes received to be held to cover child support, medical costs and transport for my 11-year-old invalid daughter. This was caused by the joint actions of my solicitor.

In my bankruptcy, the loans to cover all legal costs were secured against my home then repossession proceedings took place of my home in 2016. Furthermore, it will be noticed from the public records held at Companies House, the legal costs involved in having new solicitors and accountants dealing with the restoration of Linkside Development Company No 1561228.

Part of my undertakings were ordered in the restoration of the company. These legal actions were unsuccessful and left me responsible for all the associated costs whilst throughout, both my former wife and solicitor were still in receipt of legal aid. Under the terms of the consented court orders upon myself to the treasury solicitor in the restoration of my company 'Linkside Development Co Ltd, the sole purpose was to take these legal actions against those referred, with a full explanation of the company's affairs up to 2018 as required in my undertakings and court orders.

THE TIMES FRIDAY JULY 4 1997

There has been no accounting required for those companies to the present time as undertaken in the consented order as there has been no trading whatsoever. Save for otherwise the vast amount of legal work that I had undertaken in line with the treasury solicitor's agreement in the restoration of the company.

It is under these circumstances that I have asked consideration under claw back for these vast amounts that include the most substantial amounts of VAT on all the solicitors' invoices (this is where I still live in hope that some justice will come).

There are those that will question why I have gone to such lengths and costs in these matters. The answer to this is a very difficult question to answer. Remember that throughout 1992 whilst staying at Alder Hey children's hospital I was watching my 11-year-old daughter in intensive care and she had been used as the Trafford's deadly weapon to stop all at any costs; then my discovery into their past fraudulent actions that are laid out in these papers lodged now at H.M.R.C. and Companies House; then over twenty five years on after the I.P.C.C. confirmed in writing on the 14/4/2016 their failures in investigating these matters that were reported to them throughout the 1990's.

So now my putting this evidence in this book is my only option. I am left to bring my reader's attention to the most difficult journey through life when one wrongly puts trust in marriage. There is a saying in life that is so appropriate Quote: "If you cannot trust your wife or your solicitor or the church, - vicar Trafford- then who can you put your trust in" other than oneself any other is a most difficult judgement call, "that we must all face up to in life". On reflection upon all my childhood, I can say that I see such trust in the eyes of the children in my life, today with their mothers who have grown up around me to hear first-hand from me some of the true stories you read in this book which I hope will give good guidance to those that read this unbelievable true story.

So, Mr & Mrs Trafford (or Barbara Windsor and Sid James in 'Carry on Camping' mindful of Barbara Windsor's relationship with the Kray twins) are like the scorpions saying and begging, "You don't sting me, and I won't sting you," making their divorce on my former wife's terms. So, taking into account the Law Society's rule, chapter 11 'Conflict of interests' 11/02 principle 'there can be no better claim appropriated upon each of them other than that in this case'. Sadly, in my case I was never able to afford solicitors costs to apply this principle in my divorce, (except now this book).

CHAPTER 55: My best memory: going to Brighton with my son

At the end of all my chapters I feel it fitting to tell a tale about my son and I. When Darren thankfully came along, he filled a large, empty sorrowful hole in my life. After losing my three daughters and near enough everything I had worked hard for, and last but not least the near loss of Caroline, his arrival brought a lot of comfort and some more happiness back in my life, as well as his mother and of course, Clair and Adele. When he was only 11 months old, I put him in a sling, facing outwards so he could see things front on. I took him on my Big Red quad for a drive around and when I brought him back to his mum, he was crying his eyes out. Whilst growing up he went on it with me many times until someone came and stole it one night. That's all I ever got to know at that time, people stealing from me wanting what I had.

From 4 years old I had Darren riding quads. His first was a battery-operated batman quad. Then when he was 6 years old, I got him a petrol three-wheeler quad; it was fast for a kid that age, but he soon got the hang of speed and his skills soon set in. We had lots of fun together, especially in winter months. It wasn't long before I decided to get him his first car. It was an old Capri from an auction. He was going to be 8 years old. I did some adjustments and made it so he could reach the pedals. I was re-living my childhood with him. After school he had lessons to learn how to drive. He mastered it well and people thought I was bonkers, we thought it was cool.

As well as having a car we got him a bigger red quad so now he was speeding all over the place around the Barn, into the village up the fields, to a friend's house who also had a quad. I then got him into mechanics as I did with my brother, history repeating itself. Darren soon grew into a fine young man who has many talents and was able to drive everything from scooters motor bikes, quads, cars, vans and a JCB. He started camping outside our old barn; then we decided to go off camping all over Britain when the school holidays started. We had many great adventures though as Darren grew up.

Years quickly passed and then he rode his 500cc motorbike, just for pleasure and he had a brand-new Mercedes CDI. After carrying out his studies at Oulder Hill School, he decided he wanted to go to university, and he got a placement at Brighton University. So first I tell him that I know Brighton very well, remembering the time at Brighton when I am 65 still with all my faculties, saving all my pension to make all happy as can be (la de dar de dar as the song goes).

One weekend we filled up the van with fuel from our JCB, knowing the distance to Brighton would empty the fuel tank at least twice for the journey there and back, so we borrowed 2 five-gallon drums of red diesel from the JCB. Darren knew that his dad was doing something illegal but kept his gob shut, another thing I taught him well. We put them safely in the back of the van where we had made room for a double inflated mattress, gas stove, kettle and food. Then, first thing Saturday morning, mum waves us goodbye and we set off again on our long journey. After passing Birmingham with my son, and him having such good skills at driving my JCB and car, I let him take over, with me as his driving instructor, watching him at all times. This would be his first experience of driving at speed down a motorway and he loved it.

We got to Brighton where we swapped drivers and I drove past the Brighton Pavilion and on to the seafront. It would be late afternoon by this time, and we wanted to find a place to park up and sleep off the journey, so we parked up on a section of grass land opposite the marina with all the boats being there for us to go and see. Thinking this would be ok we park up, noticing a lot of Travellers' caravans and vehicles. I thought it was safe to fill up our van with diesel to continue our journey the next day, with Darren helping me.

Eventually, after having a cup of tea and a bite to eat we got onto our mattress and slept the night. Next morning, we got up and went down to the sea front. It was nice and sunny with lots of boating activities, and we spent a good deal of time there and went for a swim in the sea. All the time our van was safe, parked on the grass and not on a parking meter so it did not require a parking ticket, just as all the Travellers with caravans. I was happy to relax and have fun knowing we would not get a parking fine. After our swim in the sea, we got dried and dressed at the side of the road, then made our way back to the van and I was right, the parking attendants did not dare to approach the Travellers. I thought this was a brilliant move, having the Travellers as our minders, bragging to Darren about what a clever move his dad had made, saving us a tenner from parking up at a pay and display.

When driving away to get to the university I noticed my van was nearly empty of diesel at this point; Darren looked at me saying it was a brilliant move. I had realised that I had been a fool to park up next to the Travellers. Anyhow I had the fortune of another 5-gallon drum in the back, so we pulled over and filled up again. After an interesting visit to the university, it was time to return back home, and it was getting dark. I was confident in my son's driving, so again I let him take over when we passed Birmingham. By the time we reached Warrington my son told me the diesel was low and there were services not far ahead. I told him to just carry on and that we would make it home. Darren wasn't sure, but he did as I asked and kept on going. Then all of a sudden, the van came to a stop. There was no hard shoulder to stop on and we noticed a slip road for the police and emergency services so, I take the driver's side and we both push like mad.

We managed to get the van safely off the motorway onto the police slip road then it was time to decide who was going to go for the diesel. I could not leave the van and leave my son behind, so he had to be brave and go, taking a 5-gallon drum with him. I only had a £10 note left and no credit card. I gave it to him and stayed with the van. It would be approximately 3am and very dark. He told me he would be able to find a petrol station on his mobile phone. He was gone for ages. I was dying for the loo, thankfully I had loo roll, and gas to make tea and put my feet up whilst waiting and, luckily, not one police car passed in all this time. After what seemed a lifetime of waiting, I heard and saw my son in the dark, holding a different drum and told me that the garage would not let him put fuel into the drum that he had because it wasn't legal. So, he had to get a gallon container costing £5 then he put the other £5 of diesel into it. I asked him why he had been gone for so very long and he told me that when he was making his way back to me walking along the hard shoulder, he was stopped by the police who would not allow him to continue on foot, especially in such darkness with diesel fuel. My son explained the situation to the police and the very kind police officers drove my son safely all the way in the other direction back to where he came from telling him that he wasn't allowed to walk down the motorway. He knew it was his only way to get back to me. Luckily no charges were brought against him.

Thinking on his feet, he decided to jump over a fence into a farmer's field and walk through a few large fields. Whilst I was sat making tea with my feet up and trying not to worry too much and knowing I had brought him up to survive, I could only hope my thoughts were right and that he was safe. He was then spotted by the farmer's dog, so he had to leg it with the dog not far behind running after him. He told me he just managed to get over a gate and thank goodness he was safe to carry on. I was thinking to myself and thanked God the police did not come to me and dip my tank. In any event they would have found it was empty.

We were then on our way back home. This time my son was old enough not to tell his mother about running out of diesel on the motorway and pushing it as the story goes. But she did smell the stink of diesel and saw Darren's dirty clothes having gone to get the diesel and going through his ordeal. All that mattered was we were home safe regardless of the time it took to get home. It took a long time before she got to know the true story of our first visit to Brighton (the other visits were never the same....) or not worthy of putting into this true story of the boy with no hope.

CHAPTER 56: The Greater Manchester and Cheshire Police Along with many MP's to include Jeffry Archer.

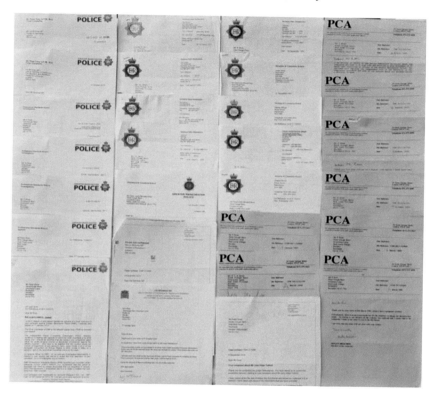

The various Cheshire, Lancashire and Merseyside police have been involved in these matters starting in 1991, continuously until 2016. Also, various MPs over the many passing years and most unfortunately my daughter's matter to include my Rochdale MP Sir Cyril Smith.

Just a small sample of MP's encrusted letter heads who I have turned to enlist their help: -
Cyril Smith   Jeffry Archer   Andrew Stunell   Allister Bert   Hon
Mrs. G Dunnwoody   Liz McInnes   with others including Police
Authorities Rochdale, Manchester, Cheshire & Merseyside.

On one of my visits to London, I visited the 'House of Commons' taking with me my papers headed to Jeffry Archer. I was permitted to go to the House of Lords where Jeffry Archer was called, and he collected my papers. He later sent me a letter which I show. At a later date I met him personally and had a photograph taken with him.

On another of my many visits to London working in the surrounding areas as seen at chapters 21 & 25

Over those passing 27 years, I have had no choice but to pay substantial sums of money in solicitors' costs. The starting date of my payment of costs in these matters was to my solicitors Heyman & Co in Leigh on October the 18th 1991. Then throughout the same years Mrs C.E. Trafford MSc BSc hons ARICS, also making contact with the police and the court and in particular the Law Society. Then on the 4th of July 1996 it was confirmed to her that her husband was admitted to the supreme court of England & Wales as a solicitor on the 1st of October 1982. He was also a partner with a solicitors firm from 1987 until the 30th of April 1993, and thereafter the owner and director of a law cost company.

What is amazing is that the Law Society will not become involved in his criminality as a solicitor. So, the fact that Mr Trafford was throughout all these years in receipt of legal aid, starting in 1991, was of no concern for them. So, I pay for my solicitor Hayman & Co to communicate with the police in these matters because, whilst Mr Trafford was in receipt of his fraudulent access to legal aid (Ref No: - 07/01/91/16545E, 07/01/91/01296N, 07/01/94/35269V, 07/01/96/3956B, 07/01/97/13379N 07/01/91/318342), he also received a payment at that crucial time in the sum of £10,000 on valentine's day the on 14th of February 1991. This payment was obviously unknown to me and was paid by one of my companies by placing a forgery of my signature upon my company cheque. This was all made possible whilst he was living with my wife and children in my home and driving my company car and throughout his employment as a senior partner. He was in full receipt of all the legal aid funds under the above references; therefore, his solicitors and barrister have all misappropriated public funds, see chapter 52.

It is for these reasons and many others that I have held on to a cheque paid to me by the legal aid authority, that I have not presented to my bank for payment.

The court orders which follow in the next document are only a small snapshot of hearings that I have attended over the years. There is a mass of others which I have paid for, where the solicitor and my wife were in receipt of public funding throughout. Then in 2001 he fathered a child in an adulterous relationship and became divorced from my former wife, all whilst being the owner and main principal of the law cost consultancy business, with his benefits paid to him at his company's registered office.

On the 28th of January 1993 Mr Trafford whilst on legal aid benefits signed his signature on his solicitor's correspondence confirming there is still £327.20 of my money remaining in their clients account. This has remained in their clients account until the time of writing this autobiography in July 2022. Go to chapter 57 noting the date the QC put his signature in pen on his letter 5th September 1995

495

F STANDS FOR FATHER
M " " MOTHER

19.7.94

Order DJ Fairclough:
F not to harass M or children.
F not to approach their home.

26.7.94

Order HHJ Caulfield:
1. F's application for SI dismissed.

ATTENDANCE NOTE

FILE: Peter Ross

DATE: 11/8/94

Peter Ross telephoned me with details of all the court orders which he has in his possession.

Schedule of Court Orders in Possession of Mr Ross

1.	13 May 1991	- Injunction from Miss Steel	order 12	*All paid*
2.	16 July 1991	- Order		*for by*
3.	17 September 1991	- Order Judge Owen		*Myself.*
4.	19 September 1991	- Order Judge Owen		
5.	26 September 1991	- Order Judge Owen	order 15	
6.	27 September 1991	- Order Judge Owen	order 16	
7.	7 October 1991	- Order Judge Owen	order 17	
8.	15 October 1991	- Amended Order 7 October 1991		
9.	16 October 1991	- Order Judge Lees		
10.	5 December 1991	- Order District Judge Fish	order 13	Circuit
11.	9 January 1992	- Order Judge Beattie		
12.	22 January 1992	- Order Judge Fish		ing in
13.	24 January 1992	- Order Judge Gee		
14.	3 February 1992	- Order Judge Beattie		
15.	10 February 1992	- Order Judge Fish		
16.	30 March 1992	- Order of Lee County Court to agree that the cost petition be dropped in favour of the Manchester Petition.		forma.
17.	9 April 1992	- Order Judge Fish		erious
18.	14 May 1992	- Order Judge Fish		
19.	13 July 1993	- Order Judge Fish		
20.	12 August 1992	- Order Judge Fish		
21.	7 September 1992	- Order Judge Fish		
22.	8 September 1992	- Order Judge Fish	order 10	
23.	5 November 1992	- Minutes of the Order		at F's
24.	12 November 1992	- Minutes of the Order		
25.	12 January 1993	- Minutes of the Order		ths.
26.	5 April 1994	- Order Judge Fawcus		
27.	24 May 1994	- Order Judge Fish		
28.	24 May 1994	- Order Judge Fish		
29.	23 June 1994	- Order Judge Griffiths		
30	19 July 1994	- Specific Order Judge Fairclough	order 9	: M to

S:\ORD\YARDNOTE

This is only a small sample of court hearings that has taken place with total disregard to the children's act 1989 and all paid from public funds. The starting date of solicitor John Peter Telford's legal aid certificate was in 1991 and all taking place at the same court at the same time with another judge District Judge E.R Jones. I have attended all of them even whilst Caroline was in hospital.

24.2.95	Order DJ Griffiths: Application for leave dismissed.
3.3.95	Order DJ Griffiths: Application for leave to vary order of 19.10.95 dismissed. Noted no impediment to hospital giving info to F.
16.3.95	F gives notice of appeal against order of 3.3.95.
16.4.95	Order HHJ Carter: F's appeal against order of DJ Griffiths 3.3.95. F to pay M's costs
11.5.95	F writes direct to the Court enclosing video and inviting Court to give leave to deal with children's matters.
11.9.95	F's application for leave to bring SI to order:- M to state date C admitted to hospital To remove order F to supply envelopes To repeat applications of 14.7.94 and 7.9.94
15.9.95	Order DJ Griffiths: F's application for leave dismissed. F to pay M's costs. F appeals.

All this above is only a small part of my application to the court in Manchester then to the High Court in London whilst my daughter was in a coma and intensive care at Alder Hey Children's Hospital. This was the most serious reason for my failed attempts to obtain justice, not just for myself but more importantly for my daughter, who had been through the worst ordeal a child could be put through whilst the children's act that was there to protect her, failed her. This is all regardless of the massive costs I have incurred in all these matters including a most substantial loan against my home thus leaving me with impossible financial tasks. I leave to the readers to interpret this unbelievable injustice and try to understand how, against all odds, I kept going.

In addition to this small sample of court hearings there was also: Dr Vanessa Davies, director general head of bar standards board, dealing into the complaint on the 13th of December 1994, against Leonard Charles Gordon QC; her response to the bar on the 14th of September 1995 which, along with all those associated with her, are referred in chapter 52, named 'My Justice'. These matters are things I had become aware of and should be in the criminal court, hence the above list of orders is only 47 of the mass of orders. Note, the High Court order where I had to pay the full costs for a transcript of H.H.J Smith's orders. I could not disclose to the judge all that I had discovered in the files at the bedside of my daughter, because these matters were in the civil realm with my many failed visits to the police.

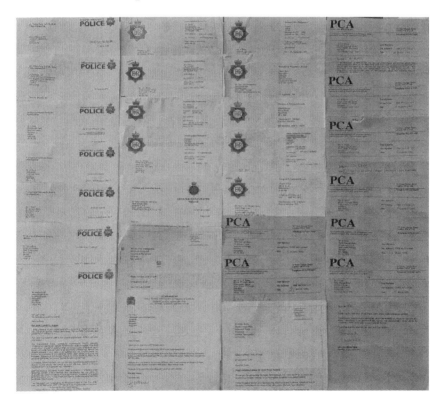

CHAPTER 57: Public funding fraud

There is no legal challenge and no liabilities or action for defamation that can prevent what I write. I can say what I want when all these matters are truthful. Much is already in the public domain, as seen in the newspaper paper articles throughout. Just because these lawyers have far greater access, with their legal skills, does not stop the truth about their unlawful actions being published. So, my last, but most important job left is to expose the most serious corruption within the legal system & its professionals.

The various chapters within this book do no more than explain the true-life story of an orphan boy's struggle through his life. For those who have taken the time and have hopefully been glued to each chapter, you will now get to understand this last and most difficult job that I must do. I remember the words that are always in the back of my mind, from an Honourable Judge: - "Mr Ross you have had to swallow the most bitter pill". The blatantly ignored children's act with the overwhelming evidence of the most serious dishonesty, will take place in another case at a three-week trial at Manchester Minshull Street High Court in October 2019, where there will be newspaper reporters in the case brought by the D.W.P against another solicitor Dr, Alan Blacker, Lord Harley living in Heywood. His successful claims to unlawful benefits were no different to the solicitor J.P. Trafford, with his legal executives I have referred to within the various chapters of this book, who were repeatedly reported to the various authorities including the police. The solicitor John Peter Trafford, along with his co-legal team were all paid from public funds, and all had the legal skills to simply outmanoeuvre those less skilled, including the police officers dealing with such fraud. See the short list of Judges with police involvement along with the many MPs.

Further examples are repeated complaints and reports made to the Law Society and the barrister's Bar Counsel into the conduct of those serving and paid within their legal professions, all from public funds. None of those authorities dealing with these complaints were prepared to take it on because it would bring into such serious disrepute those at the very top of the legal profession who were in control of those meant to, and paid to, investigate such crimes. This is the same as in the Stefan Kiszko case, which is no different to the case taking place in October of 2019 of which I shall be in attendance throughout.

Whilst the case in October 2019 is nowhere near as serious as mine or Stefan's, the solicitor in this case was a Rochdale solicitor who will undoubtedly be found guilty of his crimes, that are no worse by a million miles than the crimes committed by the solicitors within my case. For example, no crime can be worse than that of an 11-year-old's suffering that will continue for the rest of her life. These are the reasons why I have kept going in this most difficult decision, with both arms firmly held up my back from doing anything that would have been unlawful. This would have played right into the hands of those who had committed such heinous crimes, thus leaving me with the impossible tasks financially and in every other way imaginable.

Now I put to paper this true and unbelievable story of those who will face the courts on oath and otherwise in their legal professions and will commit perjury. They have sworn an allegiance to the Supreme Court, not to commit perjury before the various Honourable Judges. Yet we have seen Charles Gordon QC not being truthful in his letter signed by him to the Bar council on 5/09/95 exhibited above.

In my case alone against this Manchester solicitor over the past 28 years, I have attached only part of a small list of just some of my court attendances. Many are not on this list and have taken place in the London Courts. Returning to the Rochdale solicitor's acts of perjury and fraud and corruption that was fully exposed in October 2019, I have exposed most conclusive evidence of far greater fraud and deception orchestrated by those who were far more senior to this Rochdale solicitor on trial in October. This Rochdale solicitor, Lord Harley, had, without any fear, carried out such deception. He would undoubtedly have been confident of how easy it would have been to act as he had done, when he was acting in the various courts as an advocate and barrister, with all the various clients and judges along with the authorities accepting his services before them just as in the case of mine, leaving so many innocent, injured parties to live and pass away with such injustices. Just as I have lived the life of hell through my childhood to the grave, I shall not allow the life of my daughter's hell made by the legal profession to go unpunished.

The trial in October 2019 is long before this book will reach completion, or possible publication. An addendum to this chapter may be provided on the outcome of the trial in October along with the impact this will have upon the legal profession after I provide all the supporting 2019 evidence with my statement, bringing the legal professions most serious fraudulent actions to the public attention. In particular I also mention Dr N.O. Thomson who continues in his GP practice, but no longer with his GP wife; also, the very long list of all the MPs that over 25 years have given their support in bringing attention to the various authorities of these most unlawful actions but without any success. Each document had the 'House of Commons' logo at the top, signed by each of these serving MPs to include Sir Jeffery Archer MP. Finally, and most importantly, to understand all the mass, fraudulent claims to public funding/legal aid since 1991 that have been paid and greatly received at the solicitors shared offices with the 'Deans & Cannons' at Church House, Deansgate. This made way for the Deans and Cannons to become the successful purchasers of my industrial buildings with all rental income referred to in chapter 50, where only a small example of this fraud has been shown, and where all meetings with Charles Gordon QC along with his invoices took place at Church House. Deansgate, Manchester

These are just some of the reasons that I have not banked the cheque that I received from the Legal aid authority.

CHAPTER 58: Final chapter. The 2001 independent review of legal aid and Covid loan scandal

So, now at long last, after 31 years of my representations of fraud and maladministration of public funds, there is to be an independent review led by Sir Christopher Bellamy QC on behalf of the Ministry of Justice. Reflecting upon my Chapters 52, Chapter 54, Chapter 56, and Chapter 57, where I refer to a trial in October 2019 that will expose the fraud and corruption of solicitor Alan Blacker Lord Harley, he has now been found guilty. I was at court each day throughout his full two-week trial, all paid for from public funding/Legal Aid. Throughout his trial it was held back from the Jury under privilege law that Alan Blacker Lord Harley had already, prior to the hearing, been struck off by the Law Society. He had been made bankrupt by the Law Society until his fraudulently claiming disability (D.L.A.) benefits were discovered by the D.W.P. benefits agency. He was at the same time working and travelling for the Citizens Advice Bureau as a benefits appeal lawyer, including representing his clients in the high courts as a barrister in his usual, full court gown and wig. Then driving his model coal - operated steam railway train with end-of-life true noble children, sitting in his train carriages at the Welsh seaside location including Spring Field Park railway track in Rochdale and at the same time receiving D.L.A benefits

Alan Blacker, Lord Harley was in receipt of over £60,000 between 1997-2015 in incapacity benefits, whilst he was capable of driving his Rolls Royce to the various courts and other venues. This is no different from my own solicitor referred to in Chapter 56, where it will be noted that he was driving my car to work when I had it legally repossessed.

This January 2021, a long overdue independent review will be carried out to investigate Legal Aid spending. The review will be led by the retired Honourable Judge, Sir Christopher Bellamy QC, who has received my mass of irrefutable evidence at his chambers. They have been passed on to the M.O.J. The barrister representing the case of solicitor Blacker, with the benefit of full public funding, was the most eminent Dominic D'Souza. He travelled from his London chambers to be at Manchester Minshull Street Crown Court each day of the hearing, all paid for under Blacker's Legal Aid certificate, which was exactly the same situation as my former solicitor's legal aid certificates. In the following pages you will notice my ex-gratia payment. This has now been passed to the M.O.J legal aid review. Also see the 1996 letter from the legal services ombudsman where he says, 'No further action or recommendations will be made'. Note – The Lord Chancellor says, "He will not become involved in these matters because the legal profession is a self-regulatory body"?.

Now in 2021 we shall have the findings of the public enquiry, put to the Lord Chancellor Robert Buckland by Sir Christopher Bellamy QC, dealing with the most serious, fraudulent actions by the above solicitors and barrister QC upon public funds (From the boy with no hope to the men who stole from the world). Mr Greensill still goes to his doctor Mr Cameron saying, "I just cannot stop stealing millions of public funds, what can I do?".

Dr Cameron says, "Just try to resist the temptation but if you can't, what the hell, get a few million for me". How those kind words that came from Louie at chapter 19 have come true to Cameron. "Never bite the hand that feeds you".

So, now in December of 2022 there is at last a criminal investigation into Douglas Barrowman and MP Michael Gove along with Baroness Michelle Mone in her company P.P.E Med Pro. Supplying completely useless and worthless P.P.E between the health secretary who can be seen on the send in the clowns document on the next page and now he is in the jungle! "Get me out of here" will be answerable to the national crime agency, who at long last are carrying out criminal investigations into the unlawful contracts between baroness Michelle Georgina Mone and her husband Douglas Alan Barrowman gaining high priority lane in the provision of P.P.E to the N.H.S. leaving the past health secretary Matt Hancock now answerable for his involvement in these crimes.

506

SEND IN THE CLOWNS

P.M. David Cameron with
Lex Greensill C.B.E
missing £Billions of public
funds.

Sacked NHS Mat Hancock MP
with his special advisor
girlfriend Giva Coladangelo and
Lord Bethell NHS Health
minister in their £90 million
covid fraud contract deals.

21/01/2021   Independent Review of Criminal Legal Aid - GOV.UK

🏛 GOV.UK

1. Home (https://www.gov.uk/)

Independent Review of Criminal Legal Aid

The Independent Review of Criminal Legal Aid will look at ensuring the long-term sustainability of the criminal legal aid market. The review is chaired by Sir Christopher Bellamy QC, who will put forward his conclusions and proposals to the Lord Chancellor in 2021.

About the Review

Led by Sir Christopher Bellamy QC, the independent review into Criminal Legal Aid will look at the criminal legal aid market in its entirety, specifically it seeks to ensure that it:

- continues to provide high quality legal advice and representation *Sick Joke #1*
- is provided through a diverse set of practitioners *Sick Joke #2*
- is appropriately funded *Sick Joke #3*
- is responsive to defendant needs both now and in the future *Sick Joke #4*
- contributes to the efficiency and effectiveness of the Criminal Justice System *Sick Joke #5*
- is transparent *Sick Joke #6*
- is resilient *Sick Joke #7*
- is delivered in a way that provides value for money to the taxpayer *Sick Joke #8*

G Cox QC

The Secretary of State
& Lord Chancellor
the Rt Hon
Robert J V Buckland QC

Ex-Minister the disgraced
Matt Hancock

Takes up his 2021 October
appointment to the United
Nations.

This is the latest step in the Criminal Legal Aid Review, which has already led to up to £51m per year *Sick Joke #9* in new payments for the sector announced in August 2020. It forms part of wider work to ensure criminal defence remains an attractive career for practitioners now and into the future.

Chair and Advisory Panel

The review will be chaired by Sir Christopher Bellamy QC. Sir Christopher is a former judge with a wealth of legal experience. He has recently stepped down as Chairman of Linklaters global competition practice and joined Monckton Chambers to focus on mediation and arbitration. Sir Christopher will lead a dedicated review team within Government which will support him as he delivers the review's recommendations.

Sir Christopher will also be supported by an Expert Advisory Panel who will provide support to the review by testing and challenging the review's analysis and recommendations. The Panel will be composed of individuals with a range of backgrounds, skills and experience that will aid the review in its analysis of the Criminal Legal Aid System

Sacked by the Peppa PM on
16/09/21 making his yearly
involvement in the
Criminal Legal Aid Enquiry a
total waste of public funding.

Terms of Reference

Independent Review of Criminal Legal Aid - Terms of Reference
(https://assets.publishing.service.gov.uk/government/uploads/system/uploads/attachment_data/file/948615/term
s-of-reference.pdf) (PDF, 220KB, 9 pages)

For any enquiries or if you would like to get in contact with the Review Chair (Sir Christopher Bellamy), please contact iclar@justice.gov.uk.

DON'T BOTHER THEY'RE HERE

The most unbelievable jokes 1-8 are similar to the jokes Bernard Manning would tell. Instead, on his behalf I put in this autobiography which I know would have had approval but more so the eminent barrister QC in chapter 42 where you will see his signature upon my court order.

Bill Crowther's head of
Cameron government.

2018 late Sir Jeremy
Heywood cabinet
secretary Lex Greensill's

Advising Lex Greensill &
PM David Cameron

Sanjeev Gupter G.F.G Alliance Liberty Steel S.F.O Criminal
Investigations with Swiss Police raid on their bank.

Peppa business offices at
10 Downing Street

507

To the adjudicator Helen Megarry.
Adjudicators   Office
Mr P. Ross
    PO Box 10280   *This letter was received on 12/08/2021*
confirmed by
    Nottingham   *Mr Oliver Smith on 17/08/2021*
    NG2 9PF

Ref: - 21/88504
11   August 2021

Dear Adjudicator,

I have received a letter from your Mr Clive Salt dated 27th July 2021.

Firstly, his letters do not disclose that he has been dealing with my complaint with H.M.R.C under their reference number: Ross/Fraud GETO/25153/2020 nor does he confirm to understand that this fraud matter is possibly still under investigation.

He simply states he is unable to investigate this complaint as it falls outside of his remit to do so regardless of all my detailed evidence of more than 235 pages, he has received on the 7/5/2021. He states that future correspondence will be read and placed on file with any additional correspondence that I send will not receive any reply from his organisation, unless information I send is new and central to my complaint. This autobiography certainly confirms that.

Therefore, I take this opportunity to send directly to yourself as it will be understood from all my evidence received that my complaint by a small example set out on pages 59-63 along with many others were indeed made by my many MP's to the police the legal ombudsman, the solicitors regulation authority, The right HON Michael Gove MP and secretary of state also David Osborne Chancellor of the exchequer during the period of the David Cameron premiership.

Correspondence was sent throughout his premiership to the legal aid authority and its executives. It is now clearly proven evidence of criminality taking place at the offices of No 10 Downing Street SW1 2AA throughout the David Cameron premiership where billions of pounds of taxpayers funds were all fraudulent during the correspondence between my various MP's along with the P.H.S.O.

Accordingly, I am placing on record for you to consider or not uphold the suggestions by Mr Clive Salt not to respond to this latest correspondence of mine directly to your good self.

For the avoidance of any misunderstanding, it was and is the duty of H.M.R.C and not me to put these matters of criminality that have been repeatedly reported to H.M.R.C to the court. My complaint is that they have failed to do so, and I hope you will agree to up-hold now this complaint as I have also forwarded all my correspondence directly to the Director General Mrs Angela McDonald CBE quoting each time the above fraud reference number Ross/GETO/25153/2020 which has not as I have stated been referred to in Mr Clive Salts correspondence. Therefore, I ask now that you will do so. It is understood the adjudicator will deliver an impartial service for all that in my complaint, I have referred to having received a cheque made payable to myself from the legal aid authority since 2017 that I have not banked and for perfectly good legal reasons I will not do so.

I have provided the evidence sent to your office to the new independent review chaired by H.H.J Sir Christopher Bellamy

QC whose experts advisory panel's findings will be put before the Lord Chancellor Robert Buckland QC MP by the end of this year whilst the evidence of the criminal actions of the former prime minister Cameron with his associates will be revealed in the S.F.O. criminal investigations. (Now all the MP's referred above are gone along with the PM. All the criminal barristers are now on strike)

Accordingly, I ask your reply to confirm receipt of this letter confirming your Mr Clive Salt has investigated the grounds of my complaint under H.M.R.C's reference Ross/Fraud/GETO/ 25153/2020. As explained my MP has previously put these matters to the P.S.O by my then Liz Lynne MP.

I will await your response but finally I will not wait for the vast amount of evidence of criminality to be made available to the public showing the various politician's failures in the Cameron Government dealing with my such serious matters and now it would seem the same with your Mr Clive Salt, in dealing with this complaint.

I hope you will agree there will be little point in my re-visiting all the past correspondence sent to the P.H.S.O unless I hear from you in the alternative with your reasons so to do.

Yours Sincerely

As expected, there was no reply to this letter. So, I put this letter in this autobiography for all to see the unbelievable

So, now taking all you readers of this unbelievable autobiography back to the beginning of this dreadful story and the events that took place in 1992 with my daughter Caroline in the most dreadful state at Alder Hey Hospital (see the invoice showing the desperate state I was in) and pleading for the help of my good friend P. R. Alison and his good wife. Never was I pursued for his good work. I show you and now I reach the end of this most unbelievable nightmare of events that I have lived through.

Now having gone through my life without ever smoking or drinking, my only crime is being the fool that I have been in placing my trust in those closest to me.

Here I am 73 years old outside the front door of my 16th century barn, to end this story, reflecting upon the value of copper through my working life and how it brought such success. The little boy pulling his cart is the little boy I once was.

Legal Aid Agency

Jane Harbottle
Chief Executive, Legal Aid Agency

Legal Aid Agency
11th Floor
102 Petty France
London
SW1H 9AJ

DX 328 London

www.justice.gov.uk

Mr Peter Ross
14 Northolt Fold
Hopwood
OL10 2WH

Ref: 7265

16 August 2019

Dear Mr Ross,

Re: Your Recent Complaint

Thank you for your letter of 29 July in which you have outlined your concerns regarding possible legal aid fraud.

Having fully reviewed your correspondence and the supporting documentation you have provided I must inform you that the Legal Aid Agency (LAA) is unable to investigate or assist you any further.

As you are aware we have written to your MP on a number of occasions and this matter has been investigated by the Parliamentary and Health Services Ombudsman (PHSO). The PHSO completed and closed its investigation into this matter in September last year. As a referral to and an investigation by the PHSO is the last stage of our complaints procedure, the LAA must consider this matter concluded.

Any further correspondence received from you in relation to this complaint will be placed on filed without acknowledgement or response.

I trust this clarifies our position.

Yours sincerely

J Harbottle

Jane Harbottle
Chief Executive

Christmas 1989 unaware of all that was to follow in this autobiography.

Peter on his quadbike

Figure 1. For all to hear on arrival at the party

Figure 2 Michael and Barry referred to in the book

Figure 3. Michael and my daughter Angela

Figure 4. Party in the Marquee

This Letter is from my Foster-Brother:

17 ~~████~~ Road
Frimley
Camberley
Surrey
~~████ ████~~.
23rd December 2020.

Dear Peter, Anita and family

Thank you both for your letters.

It's good to see you have not lost your sense of humour Pete. I liked the decoration of the envelope. Did Anita see it!

Judging by Anita's letter she is well aware of your sense of fun. In fact I've heard, you make the neighbours smile with your practical jokes. Don't over do it though, putting up bunting, climbing up steps etc is dangerous now days. You should be supervising.

I am pleased you are getting on well with your autobiography, with Anita's help. Computers are a nightmare. I like the 2nd version of the front cover with your photo as a young boy. Don't know who those Tories are though collecting votes! You have lots of interesting paper work to sort out hope the wrist stands up to it. It was OK to push a motor bike three miles.

I remember when I visited you and worked for you that week. All your men thought highly of you. They told me the story of when you had a topping out party at Colindale and had a food fight in the restaurant, started by you, throwing a bread roll. They really enjoyed it. I also played you at table tennis for the bungalow. Did I win it ? SEE CHPTR 18 PAGE No 102 GO TO CHAPTER 29 PAGE NO 127 THE PARTY SEE CHPTR 18 PAGE No 102

What about the time you were going to replace the patio door in the games room. You said if you lost at pool you would throw the cue ball through the door. You lost and you did, joined by the others

The door was completely demolished which you wanted all along as you were replacing it. The neighbours called the police, thinking someone was vandalising the place.

What about the sauna. I sat on the side that got most of the steam, which I did not know at the time and you kept pouring water onto the coals. I only realised what you were up to when you kept laughing. We then jumped into the pool to cool down.

The TV room was good. We watched a documentary about the Falklands on the big TV. It made us both laugh, because the good old british Gurkha's were the first in to fight.

I was sorry to hear of Anita's brother's loss. I am sure he will manage to find some peace in time. It's good to have memories, but sometimes they can be a double edged sword. I wish I had seen your barn, but the home you have now is much easier to keep and lighter on the pocket.

Mum has been moved to a new home, because the home she was in closed; (She pulled one of those faces Anita) but it is very comfortable and they look after her well. It's free of Covid as they test all the staff (and visitors when permitted.)

Stay safe and have a good Christmas and new year.

Steven X

This is a key to the heart. When it is turned it will activate a musical box within and the song *Smile though your heart is aching, Smile even though its breaking* will be heard

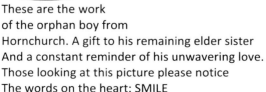

These are the work
of the orphan boy from
Hornchurch. A gift to his remaining elder sister
And a constant reminder of his unwavering love.
Those looking at this picture please notice
The words on the heart: SMILE

The following pages constitute just a few of the supplementary documents of evidence in this, the appalling story of the boy with no hope.

PRIVATE AND CONFIDENTIAL

Mr Peter Ross
Hind Chough Barn
Overtown Lane
Norden
Rochdale
OL12 7TQ

Our Ref: PC 95/295
4 October 1995

Dear Mr Ross

COMPLAINT BY YOU AGAINST MR
OF COUNSEL _____ ____ _ QC

Thank you for your letters and faxes of 26, 27 and 29 September 1995, the contents of which have been noted.

Although the Bar Council supplied you with Counsels' responses to your complaints as part of its investigation into your complaint, and the privacy marking seeks to preserve your privacy, it cannot prevent you using the material supplied to you in any way you see fit.

I will be in touch in due course.

Yours sincerely

JENNIFER MACLEAN
Executive Secretary - Professional Conduct

C:\OCT\LT3664.95 JM/lf

THE GENERAL COUNCIL OF THE BAR
3 Bedford Row London WC1R 4DB Telephone 0171 242 0082 Records Office 0171 242 0934 Fax 0171 831 9217 DX 240 LD
Chief Executive: Niall Morison

18 September 1995
PC 95/295

Mr Peter Ross
Hind Chough Barn
Overtown Lane
Norden
Rochdale
OL12 7TQ

Dear Mr Ross

Thank you for returning your copy of my letter to you dated 1
September 1995 highlighting the error in quoting Mr ~~XXXXXXXXXX~~'s
name. Please accept my apologies for this error. I confirm that
your complaint is registered against ~~XXXXXXXXXX XXXXXXXXXX~~ QC.

I will be in touch in due course.

Yours sincerely

Jennifer Maclean

JENNIFER MACLEAN
Executive Secretary – Professional Conduct Committee

cj c:\wp51\jm\2738.sept

THE GENERAL COUNCIL OF THE BAR
3 Bedford Row London WC1R 4DB Telephone 0171 242 0082 Records Office 0171 242 0934 Fax 0171 831 9217 DX 240 LDE
Chief Executive Niall Morison

Our Ref: PC 95/295

Mr Peter Ross
Hind Chough Barn
Overtown Lane
Norden
Rochdale
OL12 7TQ

16 January 1996

Dear Mr Ross

Re: Complaint by you against _____ and _____ of Counsel

Thank you for your letter of 16 December 1995. You will appreciate that the delay in replying was due to the Christmas holiday and, indeed, our move of office. I also acknowledge receipt of your letter of 28 December 1995.

Mr _____ was not asked to respond to your letter of 26 September 1995 as the matter was referred to the Professional Conduct Committee once your comments had been received. I confirm that all your correspondence was taken into consideration.

The reference in paragraph 3 of my letter of 14 December 1995 refers to a 'lay client'. A solicitor would have been referred to as a 'professional client'.

I should remind you of your right to refer the matter to the Legal Services Ombudsman and you should contact his office in writing by 14 March 1996 whether or not you have submitted further evidence for the Professional Conduct Committee to consider.

Yours sincerely

Jennifer Maclean

JENNIFER MACLEAN
Executive Secretary - Professional Conduct

f:\jenny17se.jan

THE GENERAL COUNCIL OF THE BAR
Main Offices: 3 Bedford Row, London WC1R 4DB Tel: 0171 242 0082 Records Office: 0171 242 0934 Fax: 0171 831 9217 DX: 240 LDE
Complaints, Education & Training Departments: 2/3 Cursitor Street, London EC4A 1NE Tel: 0171 440 4000 DX: 325 LDE
Fax: (Complaints) 0171 440 4001 Fax: (Education & Training) 0171 440 4002
Chief Executive: Niall Morison

No CO2669/96

Exbit No 2

IN THE HIGH COURT OF JUSTICE

FAMILY DIVISION

PRINCIPAL REGISTRY

BETWEEN

ELAINE ROSS

and

PETER ROSS
J T FORD

It is ordered that the above-named

PETER ROSS
J   FORD

do within fourteen days from the date of this Order pay to

ELAINE ROSS

(hereinafter called "the payee")

care of DAVIS BLANK FURNISS

of 90 DEANSGATE

MANCHESTER LANCASHIRE

M3 2QJ

the sum of £ 2,793.35 (including £ 365.99 V.A.T)

the amount of the taxed costs of the payee.

Senior District Judge
Dated the second day of December, 1999

Ref: 9903375

-2 DEC 1999

Cheshire Constabulary

Mr. P.L.E. Ross
Hind Clough Barn
Overton Lane
Red Lumb
Morden
Rochdale
Lancashire

The Superintendent
Macclesfield Division
Brunswick Street
Macclesfield
Cheshire SK10 1HQ

Tel. 0625 610000

Our reference	Extension	Your reference	Date
DNJ/smb	5199		6th May, 1992

Dear Mr. Ross,

I refer to the complaint you made to Macclesfield Police on the 22nd April, 1992 concerning the actions of certain members of the Medical profession involved in the treatment of your daughter Caroline.

Although I can understand your concern over the treatment of your daughter, I am satisfied having considered the papers supplied and read a detailed report from my Detective Sergeant Pickford, that the matters referred to by you do not constitute offences for which the Police have a duty to investigate. It may be that there are matters you should address through your Solicitor concerning the professional actions of the Medical profession.

I am sorry I am not able to be more helpful in this matter, but if I can be of any further assistance, please do not hesitate to contact me.

Yours sincerely,

Superintendent
Divisional Commander

LORD CHANCELLOR'S DEPARTMENT

Trevelyan House 30 Great Peter Street
London SW1P 2BY

DX 117000

Telephone Direct Line 0171 - 210
Enquiries 0171 - 210 8500
Fax 0171 - 210 8549

Mr Ross
Hind Clough Barn
Overtown Lane
Red Lumb Village
Norden
Rochdale
OL12 7TQ

Your reference

Our reference   C.93/1671/10

Date   8 November, 1995

Dear Mr Ross

Thank you for your copy letter dated 28th October 1995 addressed to Davis, Blank, Furniss, Solicitors.

The issues raised in your letter are ones for the Legal Aid Board to address and I have consequently sent a copy of your letter to the Chief Executive of the Legal Aid Board.

I refer you to Mrs K P Allen's letter of the 28th September 1995.

Yours sincerely

C Morter
LAD1

Exhibit C

P L B Ross Esq.,
Hind Clough Barn ' aid fraud
Overtown Lane
Red Lumb Village
Norden ROCHDALE

3 October 1995

Ref A·06 YMC.0332/95

Discipline and Complaints Branch
Boyer Street
Manchester

FAO CI Tetlow, DI Jackson

Dear Sirs

I list below the catalogue of failures of G M Police and correspondence between,

29.7.91	J Taylor
11.8.91	J Taylor
18.10.91	Rochdale Police CSDS Henderson
16.1.92	J Taylor and Sergeant Sterndale
6.5.92	Macclesfield Police
6.7.92	Y Department Superintendent Smillie Visit
15.9.92	Y Department Superintendent Smillie - Letter
4.2.92	Rochdale DS Henderson
21.3.93	Salford Police DI Kelly Mortgage application/Affidavit
23.3.93	Y Department My Statement
25.3.93	Rochdale HQ "No evidence of a criminal nature"
2.4.93	Rochdale HQ Ref to original documents!!
8.4.93	Rochdale HQ Re Nationwide Fraud
18.5.93	Rochdale HQ "cannot take matter further"
8.7.93	Y Dept CS Lomax
9.8.93	Rochdale HQ DS Henderson
11.8.93	DI Kelly Re my document and tele calls
13.8.93	DI Kelly letter re Nationwide files
12.8.93	PCA No further action
7.10.93	PCA Nothing further to add
14.10.93	DI Kelly letter re Legal aid and ref to DSS
8.3.94	Urgent FAX to DI Kelly Re Legal aid fraud ✳
	GRJ Robson J P Telford E Ross
8.3.94	DI Kelly Fax reply
8.6.94	DI Kelly Re fraud Mortimer Telford Robson ✳
15.6.94	Rochdale HQ Re my visit to DI Kelly
12.7.94	GMP CS Bootle Street Re legal aid fraud GRJ Robson solicitor copy to Legal Aid

Board

5.8.94	Confirmation from Bootle Street Re Legal aid fraud
7.9.94	Reply to Bootle Street
26.8.95	DI Kelly Ref Legal aid fraud
29.8.95	DI Kelly "No evidence to support LA Fraud"?
5.9.95	DI Kelly to pass on my complaint Re his conduct
14.9.95	Discipline and complaints branch PE Blewitt

Ref Aob YMC. 0352/95

To Peter. Copy of my letters to Mr Crook.

17 Davenport Ave,
Radcliffe,
Manchester,
M26 4HS.
4th February 1995

Mr Crook, Area Manager,
Legal Aid Board,
Cavern Walks, 8 Mathew Street,
Liverpool,
Merseyside, L2 6RE.

Re: PHRC : RCD: C5(4)
15 / 1/ 90/ 27556C

Dear Sir,

I refer to your recent letter, sent to my MP Mr Sumberg, in particular, your allegation that my certificate was revoked. My legal aid has not been revoked. My ex-husband, Mr ████, and possibly Mrs E. ████ have had their certificates revoked.

I take exception to your presentation of the issue, and in failing to address any of the points I have raised in my correspondence. Your letter was inaccurate in places. If I am to be presented as a unreasonable complainant I would suggest you account for all the money that was expended to make us homeless, while coincidentally Mr ████ (a solicitor) remains in a £243,0000 house.

You presented my position as one of someone unreasonable .It seems to have escaped your attention that your office has funded 7 or 8 solicitors, of whom , coincidentally, none were able to enforce any court orders to our benefit, and we have been made destitute despite having court orders seemingly in our favour. If I was you I would be asking why the solicitors were wasting public money on unenforceable Court Orders? If someone would have actually protected our interests instead of looking after their colleagues interests, we would not have been left homeless.

It seems that the honesty and integrity of solicitors are beyond question and yet we are being made to pay £20,000 + for the pleasure of protecting my ex- husband's lifestyle. I do not share your veneration and esteem for the solicitors, who, have over the course of the last few years "milked " my legal aid certificate for their own benefit. I do not propose to be in total awe of these "sharks" who have ruined my children's lives to protect their colleague. I note from your manner of address that you obviously echo the attitude of the solicitors in opinion of the people who are unfortunate to need legal aid.

I refer you back to the points in my letters which you have not answered and I ask again for a reply. I also raise the following points:

2

1/ *Why are Court Orders obtained with Legal Aid unenforceable?* Is it not a waste of public money ? What could the legal aid board do to make their finance effective in benefiting the client.

2/ *My ex - husband lives in a £243,000 house*, he breeds dogs and keeps a pony . I have photographs of the redecoration and re carpeting of Somerford Hall last year. He was supposed to be unemployed then.

3/ I was left in a house without any equity, I was told in divorce proceedings that I was responsible for the debt. I knew that this was wrong and in the final hearing Pannone's refused to present my case to that effect. Later when Mr ███████ refused to comply with the Order (and by this time 2 more firms had told me it was unenforceable and there was no point in appealing because Pannone's were such a big firm they never got things wrong) , I went to the Banking Ombudsman and the charge was released on the sale of the property. The last firm I was with did actually apply for legal aid on this issue and were refused!!! *How ironic that the money that you have taken is money that you said should pay Mr ███████ debts.*

4/ Despite my enclosure of the application forms you do not respond to why you see fit to overlook the lies on John ███████ application form. I say again that someone is helping him at the Legal Aid Board.
How is it you accept he was earning £74,000 in 1991 and he had £70, 000 in his capital account and he was still eligible for legal aid ?
By way of contrast , myself not being a solicitor , I had to pay almost £2,000 out of a compensation settlement for a neck injury, to the legal aid board.) It was not the sum stated in your letter.

5/ *The lack of disclosure in this matter is disgusting.* His professional colleagues insist he runs a large property with animals on seemingly no income, and he can afford to redecorate and re carpet the Hall and buy a new suite when he has no money? In her own proceedings his wife discloses that the dogs cost £10 per week each to feed, and yet Mr Telford's children get nothing. It seems you are in favour of this behaviour .

6/ Pannone's refused to let me have the answers the Rule 63 Questionnaires. There were 2 sets and they only let me have brief sight of the second set of replies. They were invoices for debts etc. I still maintain that I could have disproved many of his lies if I had been given the information. An Example of the solicitors covering up was a response to a questionnaire under the Matrimonial Proceedings Act in which Mr ███████ says he went to South Africa in 1991 in connection with a Company called Bayside Investments. It is in a reply dated 8/6/92 , however my enquiries reveal that Bayside Investments (Co. Incorp. No. 2847009) was not set up until 23 August 1993. This so characteristic of the solicitors refusal to doubt their colleague to our severe detriment.

7/ *The Legal Aid Board have overlooked the rules on Deprivation and Conversion of Resources.*

8/ Another little oversight to Mr ███████ advantage, was when *over £20,000 disappeared from his capital account in 1993.* The presence of this sum was given as

3

evidence in the County Court Proceedings and yet the disappearance went without comment despite my protestations.

9 I was refused legal aid to try and get spousal maintenance in the Magistrates Courts in April 1993, even though I was receiving nothing and he was formerly a Magistrates Court Solicitor. He lied and I lost . I was so disgusted I appealed to the High Court , once again having been refused Legal Aid to take any form of action against my ex-husband. Cyril ,Morris, Arkwright even got a Barristers nonsensical advice which said I had a hopeless case and I was not entitled to any maintenance despite Mr ▓▓▓▓ lifestyle. It was utter rubbish. I went to the High Court on my own and won on 2 counts against the remittal of maintenance and also on the level of maintenance payable. I have persistently been refused legal aid if my proposed action has been contrary to Mr ▓▓▓▓ interests.

Interestingly in 1991 the Legal Aid Board gave Mr ▓▓▓▓ finance to have a QC. fight his case at an Interim Maintenance Hearing (Mr ▓▓▓▓).

The removal of my matters away from Manchester has served well to block the lines of communication and the taking of the £20,000 that you refused. to acknowledge is totally unjust. Many of the financial issues of the divorce proceedings have been disregarded by you when they benefit Mr ▓▓▓▓ and yet once the Royal Bank of Scotland gave me the money you presume to take it because it was not released for Mr ▓▓▓▓ benefit.

The solicitors that you revere have taken over £20,000 to make 4 young children homeless to keep their father in luxury . I couldn't find the appropriate legal aid regulation appertaining to the destitution of 5 year olds. The rules I read referred to moneys being used to house children , not leave them homeless? Furthermore I have proved that he lied to obtain the liabilities that put him on legal aid.

May I please have a reply to my correspondence. I have sent a copy of this letter to my MP and the Lord Chancellor's Dept who will no doubt share my concerns about legally aiding the destitution of young children.

Yours faithfully,

Christine Elizabeth ▓▓▓▓ BSc Hons ARICS

Our ref: PR/CIDCONG/AJ

Your ref:

Date: 7 December 1999

Mr P Ross
Hind Clough Barn
Overton Lane
Red Lumb
Morden
ROCHDALE

In reply address correspondence to:
DC McDonnell/DC Broadhurst
Telephone: 01244 613535

Dear Mr Ross,

I write this letter to update you regarding the allegation of Indecent Assault that you made to the police concerning a Doctor Ninian Thomson.

Following your original complaint to the police, an investigation was undertaken into the given facts. After consideration of the case, you will be aware that a decision was made by the Crown Prosecution Service and the Police to take No Further Action in this matter.

As a result of recent events, in particular the Roger Cook programme televised on 24th August 1999, entitled 'Doctors from Hell', a decision has been made to review all available information with regards to your original complaint against Doctor Thomson.

The purpose of this letter is to advise you of this fact and inform you that the officers who have been detailed to carry out this review are DC 2721 Luke McDonnell and DC 2839 Paul Broadhurst from Congleton C.I.D. Tel. No. 01244 613535. These officers will contact you in due course to discuss the matter further. In the meantime please do not hesitate to contact them if you have any queries regarding this matter.

Yours sincerely

pp P Rigby
Detective Chief Inspector

NOTE ALL AT CHAPTER 36 THAT
DOCTOR N O THOMSON WAS FOUND
GUILTY OF HIS CRIMES

Professional Standards Branch
Investigations

Liz McInnes MP
House of Commons
London
SW1A 0AA

Our Ref: Y,1455/15

Your Ref:

16 November, 2015

Mr Peter Ross

I am writing in connection with your complaint against police, on behalf of your above named client, which was received in this branch on 21 October, 2015. Your complaint has now been formally recorded under complaint reference number Y.1455/15. Thank you for raising your concerns with us.

After a careful review of the circumstances, your complaint has been allocated to Detective Sergeant Tuer to resolve your complaint.

You will be contacted in due course in order that we can fully investigate your complaint.

Yours faithfully,

NOTE AIL @ CHAPTERS 26 35 36 44 56

David Hull
Chief Superintendent

Professional Standards Branch Investigations
Greater Manchester Police, Openshaw Complex, Lawton Street, Openshaw, Manchester, M11 2NS
Telephone: «tO_TEL_NO», Fax: 0161 856 2906, Minicom: 0161 872 6633

L9c

Professional Standards Branch
Investigations

GREATER MANCHESTER
POLICE

Liz McInnes MP
House of Commons
London
SW1A 0AA

Our Ref: Y1455/15

15 January, 2016

Dear Ms McInnes

Ref: Y1455/15

I write further to the recent correspondence sent to the Professional Standards Branch at Greater Manchester Police dated the 13th January 2016.

I can confirm that Mr Ross has submitted an appeal to Greater Manchester Police. Mr Ross was sent an acknowledgment letter on the 4th January 2016. Mr Ross has specified that his solicitors and yourself be contacted following the outcome of his appeal.

Yours faithfully

John Brennan
Appeals Officer
Greater Manchester Police, Professional Standards Branch

NOTE, MY FIRST COMPLAINT STARTED IN 1992 SEE CHAPTER 56 PART ONLY LIST OF POLICE DOCUMENTS

Professional Standards Branch Investigations
Greater Manchester Police, Openshaw Complex, Lawton Street, Openshaw, Manchester, M11 2NS

L10

You can contact me on: 03000611539
james.brannan@ombudsman.org.uk

Our Reference: C2042648

SENSITIVE

**Parliamentary
and Health Service
Ombudsman**

In Confidence
Ms Liz McInnes MP
House of Commons
London
SW1A 0AA

21 September 2018

Dear Ms McInnes

Mr Peter Ross' complaint about the Legal Aid Agency (LAA).

We have completed our consideration of Mr Peter Ross' complaint about the LAA and I am writing to tell you the outcome.

In order to reach our decision we reviewed the information Mr Ross provided. After doing this, we have decided not to take any further action on his complaint. This is because we have found his complaint is partially out of remit, and the remaining complaint part held no indications of maladministration on the part of LAA. This means we cannot look at Mr Ross' complaint, and will not be taking any further action.

I will explain the reasons for this and the factors we have considered in our assessment of Mr Ross' complaint.

Mr Ross' complaint

Mr Ross complains the Legal Aid Agency (LAA) fraudulently granted legal aid to his former-solicitor who represented his ex-wife in their divorce 1991, which led to Mr Ross accruing legal fees of over £500,000 to expose this. Mr Ross also complains the LAA ignored his solicitors and did not appropriately communicate with them when deciding he should pay off the legal fees he owed in full rather than in instalments, which left him with no choice but to have his house repossessed in July 2017 for much less than its value.

Mr Ross states he has faced unnecessary stress, distress, and financial hardship.

As a result of an investigation Mr Ross is seeking an acknowledgement of failings by the LAA, an apology for them, and a financial remedy.

 **INVESTORS
IN PEOPLE**

Millbank Tower
Millbank
London SW1P 4QP

Enquiries: 0345 015 4033
Fax: 0300 061 4000

Email: phso.enquiries@
ombudsman.org.uk

www.ombudsman.org.uk

SENSITIVE

COOPER & JACKSON
P a r t n e r s h i p

CHARTERED ARCHITECTS

109 DRAKE STREET,
ROCHDALE,
LANCASHIRE, OL16 1PZ.
TEL: (0706) 31347
FAX: (0706) 342902

VAT No. 306 7673 48

Date: 1/12/92

Ref.: PRD/DEB

FEES ACCOUNT

Account No.: A 1825

Linkside Development Company Ltd.
c/oMr. P.L.B. Ross,
Hind Clough Barn,
Overtown Lane,
Red Lumb Village,
Norden, ROCHDALE.

To confidential secretarial services executed during
1991 & 1992, including correspondence, taking & making
many telephone calls to Alder Hey Hospital & various
Solicitors, Doctors & Medical Authorities.
Faxing documents & recorded post to Police at Liverpool,
Macclesfield & Rochdale, Law Society & Ombudsman.

1991

Typing 125hrs x £5.24p per hr.	655.00
Postage	13.39
Telephone/facsimilies	10.50
Photo-copies	20.50

1992

Typing 166hrs x £5.58p per hr.	926.28
Postage	26.78
Telephone/facsimilies	21.00
Photo-copies & Copier paper	32.00

1,705.45

+ VAT @ 1   298.45

£ 2,003.90p

Dear readers.
If you have taken the time to read this far - thank you.
The invoice I have included in this book is a small reflection of all you have just read. After
the issues of this invoice, in 1996, you will see in the court transcript shown in Chapter 36,
H.H.J Smith said to me, "Mr Ross you have had to swallow a most bitter pill." A pill which
contains all that you have read in this autobiography. 32 years later and I am still unable to
swallow it!

P. R. DAWSON
R. F. WHITELEGG
P. R. ALLISON
N. M. WOOD B.A.(Hons.) Dip. Arch.(Manc.) RIBA

It was one of these judges who said to me, "Mr Ross, you have had to swallow a most bitter pill."
(This was at the time when I met George Carman QC who signed my court order.)

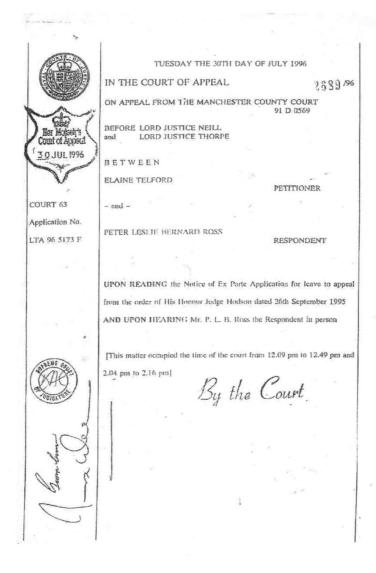

TUESDAY THE 30TH DAY OF JULY 1996

IN THE COURT OF APPEAL   2689 /96

ON APPEAL FROM THE MANCHESTER COUNTY COURT
91 D 0569

BEFORE LORD JUSTICE NEILL
and   LORD JUSTICE THORPE

B E T W E E N

ELAINE TELFORD   PETITIONER

– and –

PETER LESLIE BERNARD ROSS

                              RESPONDENT

UPON READING the Notice of Ex Parte Application for leave to appeal

from the order of His Honour Judge Hodson dated 26th September 1995

AND UPON HEARING Mr. P. L. B. Ross the Respondent in person

[This matter occupied the time of the court from 12.09 pm to 12.49 pm and

2.04 pm to 2.16 pm]

By the Court

Her Majesty's
Court of Appeal
30 JUL 1996

COURT 63

Application No.

LTA 96 5173 F

To all those who have taken the time in reading this unbelievable story. This very final picture is showing the author and his young son Darren at a hospice special fund-raising event at the Norton Grange Hotel. This was organised by Liz and her husband Dr Ivan Blumenthal where all those in attendance were all medical professionals having their meal and dancing the night away entertained by G.M.R Radio broadcaster Mr. Michael Kieran Tommy's Irish best friend.

The Autobiography of Orphan Peter.

The End